TEACHING: Vantage Points for Study

$14-130-699$

THE LIPPINCOTT CURRICULUM AND INSTRUCTION SERIES
Under the Editorship of
Alexander Frazier, Ohio State University

TEACHING:

Vantage Points for Study

Edited by Ronald T. Hyman

Rutgers University

J. B. LIPPINCOTT COMPANY   *Philadelphia & New York*

Dedicated to P.C., J.F.B., R.C., and R.R.C.

Preface

This collection of readings is based on the conviction that teaching deserves—and needs—serious study. It asserts that teaching is a complex activity, that it demands a plurality of approaches, that we must continually expand our knowledge of teaching, and that an anthology needs a framework and a focus which will invite the reader to explore in some depth the several themes presented. No attempt has been made to cover the subject comprehensively. Rather I have focused on several selected vantage points. The present collection is also based on the conviction that teachers need primary source material in their study of teaching and that an anthology which makes such material readily available serves a definite purpose.

It is hoped that this book will serve to initiate some into the study of teaching and encourage others to continue their study. One objective has been to broaden the reader's scope by presenting several vantage points on the same topic. Some readers may be interested by one of the more unfamiliar viewpoints presented in this collection; others may profit by discovering new material on a viewpoint already familiar to them.

The selections presented here reflect the recent emphasis on description, rather than evaluation, in the analysis of the teaching process. This approach, together with the study of psychology and philosophy, may provide clues to what constitutes effectiveness in teaching, lead to a serviceable theory of teaching, and help classroom teachers teach skills, knowledge, and values more effectively.

The book is divided into seven sections, each of which discusses teaching from a different vantage point. The seven vantage points are cognitive and intellectual behavior, communications, social climate, emotional climate, aesthetics, games, and strategy. These viewpoints spotlight work already done in this field, as well as illustrate the various approaches used. An overview to each section introduces the articles, shows connections between them, and suggests directions for further study.

It is a pleasure to express my thanks to my students and teachers who encouraged me to explore various points of view, to the authors and publishers who permitted their works to be included in this book, and to the Lippincott editors who made this venture a rewarding one, especially Alex Fraser, Bob Richards, Tom Abrams, and Alex Frazier.

New Brunswick, N.J.   RONALD T. HYMAN
February 13, 1968

Contents

Introduction

Changes in the field of education within the last decade have opened up a new area of study that focuses on the process of teaching. This area is to be distinguished from other efforts focusing on teacher personality traits, on teacher effectiveness, and on how people learn. It has been primarily descriptive rather than evaluative. This expression of interest in understanding the nature of teaching has taken many forms because of the diversity of the people who constitute the corps of investigators. The result has been the publication of articles, research reports, and conference papers in scattered places. The purpose of this book is to make available significant and representative material from this growing body of literature on the analysis of teaching.

REASONS FOR STUDYING TEACHING

It is reasonable to ask about the need and motivation behind this interest in teaching. Obviously, there is no single set of answers; several factors are salient and deserve attention. First, men engage in some activities for their own sake, activities that offer their own intrinsic satisfaction. The study of teaching is one of these, and if there were no further justification, this motive would suffice.

Second, educators and psychologists have openly acknowledged that the focus on teacher effectiveness for the past fifty years has yielded very little helpful knowledge. Philip Jackson, an educational psychologist, has put it this way:

1

First is the lamentable, but undeniable, fact that our search for the good just doesn't seem to have paid off. Almost all of the noble crusades that have set out in search of the best teacher and the best method—or even the better teacher and the better method—have returned empty-handed. The few discoveries to date (it would be unfair—and, . . . imprudent as well—to deny that there have been any) are pitifully small in proportion to their cost in time and energy. For example, the few drops of knowledge that can be squeezed out of a half century of research on the personality characteristics of good teachers are so low in intellectual food value that it is almost embarrassing to discuss them (10:8-9).

The shift, as noted, has been from studying teaching effectiveness and teacher personality to analyzing the teaching process itself, with the hope that this approach will yield clues to what constitutes effectiveness. The ultimate aim is still the improvement of teaching.

Third, educators have finally taken to heart the exhortations of the psychologists not to rely on learning psychology as the sole means of understanding teaching. The psychologist Jerome S. Bruner stated in his 1963 speech to the National Association for Supervision and Curriculum Development that its members should investigate teaching in their search for clues for improving the curriculum of our schools. He said, "I find that the dependence upon learning theory among educators is as touching as it is shocking" (4:524). Bruner went on to explore four possible aspects of a theory of instruction.

A similar statement was made seventy-one years earlier, in 1892, by William James, the father of modern psychology. In his *Talks With Teachers,* James pointed out that psychology by itself will not enable teachers to teach well.

I say moreover that you make a great, a very great mistake, if you think that psychology, being the science of the mind's laws, is something from which you can deduce definite programmes and schemes and methods of instruction for immediate schoolroom use. . . . To know psychology, therefore, is absolutely no guarantee that we shall be good teachers. To advance to that result, we must have an additional endowment altogether, a happy tact and ingenuity to tell us what definite things to say and do when the pupil is before us. That ingenuity in meeting and pursuing the pupil, that tact for the concrete situation, though they are the alpha and omega of the teacher's art, are things to which psychology cannot help us in the least (11:23-24).

It has taken many years for James's insight to have its effect on teachers.

Fourth, it is hoped that a study of teaching will eventually lead us to a theory of teaching that will serve as a guide for teachers; it will direct them in their teaching of skills, knowledge, and values. B. O. Smith and his associates did not formulate a theory of teaching from their investigations, but they did come up with some concepts which "might become elements of a teaching theory" (17:1).

Fifth, educators recognize that teaching is a common phenomenon in our society and an integral part of our efforts to sustain our cultural heritage and democracy. As an activity in which close to two million citizens in this country engage, and which serves or influences in turn about a quarter of our population, it deserves study. It follows that we should know as much about teaching as we can.

Studying teaching because it is vital to us provides a particular motivation. It asks us to look for the significant in the interaction between teacher and pupil. What we learn about teaching has definite implications for our future. Vital self-interest is what Bettelheim says was his reason for studying the activity around him in a German concentration camp. What he learned helped him to keep his freedom for making decisions, which, he says, is the essence of humanity. In a sense, he was able to become the master of his condition. Bettelheim's experience can be applied to teaching, though admittedly his situation was extreme.

Inside the camps I did not study my behavior, nor did I study my fellow prisoners or question them because I intended to make a disinterested survey of a problem that had roused my scientific interest. Quite the contrary; not detached curiosity, but vital self interest induced me to study my own behavior and the behavior I noticed around me. To observe and try to make sense out of what I saw was a device that spontaneously suggested itself to me as a way of convincing myself that my own life was still of some value, that I had not yet lost all the interests that had once given me self respect (2:111).

Observational Frameworks: Need and Types

The question thus becomes "How do we observe the activity around us in order to make sense out of it?" We know that observation is selective. People simply cannot observe everything, for "what goes on in the world at large at any time or the human phase of it is too vast in extent and too complicated in intension to be fully described or understood in any finite time. . . . Each observer or recorder is restricted to some fragment of what is going on. The best we can attain is some indication of what is outwardly visible from a single point of view for a limited time" (5:24). Since we cannot observe everything, we select what we will observe and do so from a particular orientation. Newspaper accounts and legal eye-witnesses are constant reminders of this basic fact in communications—that different people select different things to see. Historians, for example, are aware of this relativism, and it has become a part of their professional preparation to examine the various frameworks employed by different historians writing on a common topic or period.

In this light, it is clear that if we are to understand a person's description, explanation, or evaluation of teaching, we need first to understand the nature of his vantage point. As Belth has stated, frameworks are "windows through which we see the world and our own transaction with the world, and they make that world meaningful to us in their own terms. No man ever sees the world other than through some conceptual system, whether he is aware of this or not" (1:61).

When we observe a teacher at work, we need to know the framework he is employing if we are to understand his actions. "Consider now an observer, O, of N's behavior. If O wants to predict how N is going to act, he must familiarize himself in terms of which N is viewing the situation. . ." (19:91). By way of illustration, let us examine two types of frameworks commonly utilized when people observe others.

Max Black in his book *Models and Metaphors* (3) identifies four kinds of models: scale, analogue, mathematical, and theoretical. Of these four, the most frequently used in the field of education today is the analogue. Let us turn to this type of framework first. Here, we look at teaching *as if* it were, for example, psychotherapy, gardening, or an athletic game. Then what we can say about psychotherapy, athletics, or gardening we will also be able to say about teaching, once we have shown that they have common features. This type of *as if* thinking can be very fruitful.

Analogies are a means of transferring to a new situation the "structure or web of relationships" of the original one (3:222). They are a means of explaining how the various parts of something fit together. We form relationships between events, objects, people, and abstractions by considering them as similar to others we already know. Analogies provide a means of organizing the incoming raw data in some meaningful way, particularly when we encounter novel and/or complex situations. In order to make sense of what he sees on his trip, the tourist will often say, "That looks like _____ back home."

But in spite of the help they offer, analogies also yield problems. The very path that leads to easy and quick understanding can also lead to error and confusion if we are not careful. To avoid trouble, we must be judicious in the use of analogies. "An adequate analogue model will manifest a point-by-point correspondence between the relations *it* embodies and those embodied in the original: every incidence of a relation in the original must be echoed by a corresponding incidence of a correlated relation in the analogue model" (3:222). By this criterion, surely few analogies, if any, are adequate. Most analogues have only partial correspondence with the original situation. Trouble arises when we accept and act upon complete correspondence when, in fact, it cannot be demonstrated. The analogy that does not hold completely is potentially misleading. We must drop it before we stretch it beyond its helpful limits. If not, we come to believe that certain relationships exist when they do not.

A good analogy can also narrow our scope. When we find an adequate analogy that seems fruitful to us, it is easy to forget that it is only one way of looking at teaching. The use of a single analogy to view teaching is obviously inadequate since teaching is very complex. By their nature, complex situations require us to consider them along several avenues of approach.

Many people, recognizing the pitfalls present in the use of analogies, choose not to employ them when discussing teaching. Instead, they frequently use implicit analogies or what Stephen Pepper calls "root metaphors" (13:91) and Max Black calls "archetypes" (3:241). In this second type of framework, a person takes the key words, expressions, concepts, and categories from an area he knows and "in terms of these categories he proceeds to study all other areas of fact whether uncriticized or previously criticized" (13:91). In this way, someone may even unwittingly speak of "planting" the "seed" of knowledge to watch it "grow" in the "sunshine" of the "green" classroom. Indeed, the word "kindergarten" is a result of this root metaphor.

Why we must identify and understand the model, whether analogy or root metaphor, from which a person views teaching is clear. The framework leads us to focus on certain aspects of teaching. It suggests that we ask certain questions about teaching. It is the guide to enquiry, the guide for collecting data about teaching (15:25). And, most importantly, it "can even, in particular situations, imply action to be taken" (1:91). Surely, we wish to understand why teachers and observers ask certain questions. Surely, we wish to understand the actions they take. As Susanne K. Langer says:

> The formulation of experience which is contained within the intellectual horizon of an age and a society is determined, I believe, not so much by events and desires, as by the *basic concepts* at people's disposal for analyzing and describing their adventures to their own understanding. Of course, such concepts arise as they are needed to deal with political or domestic experience; but the same experiences could be seen in many different lights, so the light in which they do appear depends on the genius of a people as well as on the demands of the external occasion. Different minds will take the same events in very different ways (12:3).

It is appropriate to mention that the recognition of the need of a framework is not restricted to the philosophers. Several educational psychologists and curriculum specialists, as well as numerous social and natural scientists, have written on this matter. Reference to one who writes about his observations of the classroom will suffice. Ralph Tyler, a curriculum researcher of considerable experience, stated in his paper to the First Annual Phi Delta Kappa Symposium on Educational Research:

> If when one entered a classroom he had no prior conceptualization of teaching and learning, he would see children and an adult, he would hear several

children and the adult speaking, he would note physical items in the room, movements of people and the like. What gives it meaning for the investigator of classroom instruction is a "model" which he conceives, a simplified picture of the structure and process of classroom instruction. This model usually includes such elements as a teacher, pupils, objectives of instruction, methods of teaching, materials of instruction, learning outcomes. If he holds such a model in mind, he has a basis for focusing his observations and for arranging and analyzing his data. This development of a formal model provides a way of viewing the complex phenomenon in a fashion which permits scientific study (18:57).

The Concept of Teaching

To this point, we have discussed teaching without defining the term. To proceed beyond this point, we will have to consider definitions. The literature on teaching contains various uses of the word; and if we are to understand that literature, we need to be aware of the issues involved in defining it. An effort has been made by some analytic educational philosophers to clarify the concept of teaching since such a clarification is obviously necessary for effective communication among educators. It is also needed by the empirical researcher since the notion of teaching that he accepts guides his endeavor. Marie Hughes, in a paper on the assessment of teaching, writes, "There are many ways to analyze the records of actions in the classroom situation. The manner of analysis is controlled to a large degree by the definition accepted for teaching" (9:26). Questions, then, about the definition of teaching are not trivial but central to our concern.

An analysis of many definitions of teaching reveals two main questions: one, what is the scope of teaching; and two, what is the relation of teaching to learning. Let us look briefly at each.

Three typical definitions will suffice to illustrate the scope of teaching.

1. Smith: Teaching is a system of actions intended to induce learning (16:88).

2. Gage: By teaching, we mean, for the present purpose of defining research on teaching, any interpersonal influence aimed at changing the ways in which other persons can or will behave (7:96).

3. Scheffler: Teaching may be characterized as an activity aimed at the achievement of learning and practiced in such manner as to respect the student's intellectual integrity and capacity for independent judgment (14:131).

The definitions by Smith and Gage are clearly broader than Scheffler's. They allow for such actions as indoctrinating, lying, propagandizing, advising, and mothering to be counted as teaching. Even "brainwashing," with all its negative connotations, can fit these two definitions, for it does induce learning and change the ways people behave.

Scheffler's definition is obviously narrower. It does attempt to separate "teaching" from "indoctrinating" and other synonyms; yet this very narrowness raises many questions by answering one. What constitutes intellectual integrity? How shall we measure and know the student's capacity for independent judgment? By what criteria shall we know when the teacher's actions respect the student's intellectual integrity and capacity for independent judgment? If we so restrict teaching to such narrow behavior, what shall we call the multitude of other actions which a teacher performs? Is there an implication that indoctrinating and training are not desirable in the classroom? For example, in light of Scheffler's definition shall we say that the following four statements by a teacher constitute teaching?

1. Robbing and murdering are bad.
2. The United States was justified in revolting against England in 1776.
3. The way to read and write English is to go from left to right.
4. The United Nations is an effective agency for maintaining world peace. It is a step towards world government.

The second issue involves the relation of teaching to learning. The question here is whether learning must result if we are to call the teacher's actions "teaching." The three definitions cited earlier all keep teaching and learning apart. That is, teaching is seen as aiming at or intending to bring about learning. Other definitions make "teaching" dependent on the successful outcome called "learning." That is, if there is no learning, there is no teaching. This notion stems from the comparison of teaching with selling i.e., selling is to teaching as buying is to learning. If no one buys, no one sells. Similarly, if no one learns, no one teaches.

Currently, most educators accept the intentional rather than the successful end of teaching. Nevertheless, the research and writing of some reflect the opposite view. Indeed, the relation between teaching and learning remains unsettled. We do not know exactly how and to what extent teaching contributes to or causes learning. Part of the problem is that we are not certain *which* learning we are talking about (can there be no learning at all when a teacher acts?) and just what constitutes learning.

From this brief discussion of only two issues involved in defining "teaching," it is clear that the wider issue is tangled and complex. Sev-

eral writers, especially Green (8), have attempted to resolve the problems by using different terms for discussing teaching. Yet in spite of the
further analysis we still have no precise way of deciding what we will and
will not call teaching.

In the selections that follow, the reader will find various explicit and
implicit meanings of "teaching." The author's concept of teaching becomes a part of his frame of reference and along with the analogies and
root metaphors he uses we must seek it out. His concept of teaching
serves as a criterion for what he deems appropriate in the classroom. If a
teacher holds one concept, he will behave one way; if he holds another
concept, he will behave differently. The concept guides his behavior.
Winch's statement regarding war in his chapter on concepts and actions
is also appropriate to the concept of teaching.

The idea of war, for instance . . . was not simply invented by people who
wanted to *explain* what happens when societies come into armed conflict. It is
an idea which provides the criteria of what is appropriate in the behavior of
members of the conflicting societies. Because my country is at war there are
certain things which I must and certain things which I must not do. My behavior is governed, one could say, by my concept of myself as a member of a
belligerent country. The concept of war belongs *essentially* to my behavior
(19:127-128).

To understand, then, what is written about teaching, we must know the
writer's vantage point and his concept of teaching.

OVERVIEW OF THE SELECTIONS

The selections that follow have been chosen and grouped according
to selected vantage points on teaching: cognitive and intellectual behavior, communications, social climate, emotional climate, aesthetics,
games, and strategy. These vantage points reflect the editor's way of
viewing and comprehending the growing literature on teaching. These
seem to him the major vantage points on teaching. They do overlap in
some ways; they do have elements in common. The intention has not
been to create a definitive instrument for classifying all studies on teaching but to provide a means of organization that will reveal the points of
view and concepts underlying each selection. Other vantage points are
not included here because of limited space and because of their relative
lack of development. These seven major vantage points illustrate the
work already done on teaching and suggest the potential of future work.

Within each chapter, the articles may differ from one another in several respects, and this possibility should be kept in mind when reading. Some authors employ an empirical approach to studying teaching. They have developed instruments to measure selected aspects of teaching and present the data that was collected with them. Others have concentrated on an analytic and/or speculative study of teaching. Some of these have a fully developed framework but lack the field work for collecting data.

Some selections focus on the teacher, and others on the pupils. Still others record and analyze the behavior of both the teacher and the pupils. Most focus on verbal behavior in the classroom as the prime means of communication, considering it to be a representative sample of the total classroom behavior. Others include or focus on the nonverbal behavior, considering it too significant to omit in spite of the many limitations inherent in dealing with it.

Some have chosen to go to the classroom to study teaching. Few, if any, of the recent empirical studies have been conducted under laboratory conditions. Some who work directly in the classroom rely on audio tape recordings to catch the ephemeral talk of the teacher and pupils. They then categorize the discourse when listening and/or reading a typescript of the recording. Others categorize the discourse as it occurs "live" without using any means of preserving it. Some study elementary school students, while others work with students in secondary school. Some study teachers in one subject area, while others focus on teachers from several academic fields. Some study gifted students, while others use heterogeneously grouped pupils.

In this way, these selections represent a wide range of approaches to the study of teaching. The decision about which path to take reflects the judgment of the author. Obviously, the study of teaching welcomes a multitude of approaches. Certain studies seem more fruitful than others, but each offers some insight into the nature of teaching not otherwise available.

CHAPTER OVERVIEWS

The introductions to the seven chapters are intended to place each vantage point in context, introduce the separate articles, show connections between them, and suggest some possible directions for further study. The purpose of these "overviews" is not to point out the main ideas of the various selections or to summarize them. To do so would be to usurp the main task of each reader. The reader is urged to read the articles carefully, for each was chosen for the insights it contributes toward the understanding of teaching.

EXAMINING CATEGORY SYSTEM INSTRUMENTS

Virtually all of the recent empirical work on teaching conducted directly in the classroom has been done by trained observers using category systems to gather data. This is one salient characteristic of the recent surge of interest in teaching. Therefore, the reader should be aware of six central questions asked about category systems used for gathering data on teaching.

1. Are the categories all-inclusive? That is, do all instances of the observed behavior fit into one of the categories. If it is not possible to categorize a specific instance of behavior, then the set of categories is incomplete and requires further expansion.
2. Are the categories mutually exclusive? That is, are the categories so precisely defined that each is distinct from the other? If so, then each instance of behavior fits into one and only one category. This is necessary if we are to answer the next questions affirmatively.
3. Are measurements with this set of categories reliable? That is, can trained observers agree as to which category to use in a given instance? Reliability is necessary if objectivity is to be attained. And objectivity is desirable. What degree of agreement is to be considered acceptable is a matter of judgment, however. What is acceptable depends, too, on the method for statistically arriving at a percentage of agreement.
4. Are the categories useful? Reliability obviously must not be achieved at the expense of having so few categories or such obvious ones ("teacher talks," "pupil talks") that the usefulness of the data would be limited (6:197). On the other hand, if there are too many categories, reliability is likely to decrease along with a decrease in the utility of the instrument. A large set of categories would require so much skill on the part of the observers that its usefulness in the future would be severely limited. As Flanders says, "somewhere between too many and too few categories is an optimum number" (6:197). This optimum number depends on many factors, including the vantage point, the purpose of the observation, and the skill of the observers.
5. What is the unit of analysis? That is, how often do the observers categorize? Do they do so according to a time unit? For example, do they decide after every three seconds, or after every five seconds, or after alternating two minute periods? Do they categorize not according to time but according to each complete verbal thought unit? Obviously, the various investigators use different units of anal-

ysis, and their choice of unit depends upon several factors including those mentioned in question four above.

6. Are the categories fruitful? That is, do they fit teaching in such a way as to give us new insights and valuable data about this complex act called teaching.

Outcome of Studying Teaching

From this collection, the reader should gain new insights into teaching. These should help him to clarify and define his ideas about teaching and to review these ideas from a new and broader perspective. This gain in precision and breadth should lead to new questions, and these, in turn, to new answers; thus the reader may be encouraged to modify his own views about teaching.

In any case, he should be better able to understand, assess, and compare the teaching that he reads about and sees; and he should be in a better position to explore the possibilities of devising and using instruments of research based on the various selections.

Summary

This book has many purposes. It provides an anthology of articles on teaching grouped according to the authors' frames of reference. It breaks new ground by presenting in readily available form material to be used by pre-service and in-service teachers as they study the multiple vantage points from which educators view teaching. It offers the reader the prospect of new insights into teaching. It suggests the acknowledgment of a new field in education for which no name presently exists. (Perhaps the term *pedagography* would be appropriate.) This book is the result of a new effort to shed light on teaching and is presented in the hope that it will help some improve their own teaching, enlist some as "pedagographers," and encourage others to join the growing corps of investigators of teaching. It is offered as a seed rather than as a harvest.

References

1. BELTH, MARC., *Education as a Discipline: A Study of Models in Thinking*. Boston: Allyn and Bacon, 1965. 317 p.
2. BETTELHEIM, BRUNO. *The Informed Heart*. New York: The Free Press of Glencoe, 1960.

3. BLACK, MAX. *Models and Metaphors.* Ithaca: Cornell University Press, 1962. Chapter 13.
4. BRUNER, JEROME S., "Needed: A Theory of Instruction." *Educational Leadership,* 20:523-532, May, 1963.
5. COHEN, MORRIS R., *The Meaning of Human History.* LaSalle, Illinois: Open Court Publishing Company, 1947. 304 p.
6. FLANDERS, NED., "Some Relationships among Teacher Influence, Pupil Attitudes, and Achievement." *Contemporary Research on Teacher Effectiveness.* Ed. by Bruce J. Biddle and William J. Ellana. New York: Holt, Rinehart and Winston. 1964. pp. 196-231.
7. GAGE, N. L., "Paradigms for Research on Teaching." *Handbook of Research on Teaching.* Ed. by N. L. Gage. Chicago, Rand McNally and Company, 1963. p. 94-141.
8. GREEN, THOMAS F., "A Topology of the Teaching Concept." *Studies in Philosophy and Education,* 3:284-319, Winter, 1964-65.
9. HUGHES, MARIE M., "Utah Study of the Assessment of Teaching." *Theory and Research in Teaching.* Ed. by Arno A. Bellack. New York: Bureau of Publications, Teachers College, Columbia University, 1963. pp. 25-36.
10. JACKSON, PHILIP W., "The Way Teaching Is." *The Way Teaching Is.* Washington, D.C.: National Education Association, 1966. pp. 7-27.
11. JAMES, WILLIAM. *Talks to Teachers on Psychology and To Students on Some of Life's Ideals.* New York: W. W. Norton, 1958.
12. LANGER, SUSANNE K., *Philosophy in a New Key.* New York: Mentor Book, 1942.
13. PEPPER, STEPHEN C., *World Hypotheses.* Berkeley: University of California Press, 1942.
14. SCHEFFLER, ISREAL. "Philosophical Models of Teaching." *Harvard Educational Review,* 35:131-143, Spring, 1965.
15. SCHWAB, JOSEPH J., "Structure of the Disciplines: Meanings and Significances." *The Structure of Knowledge and the Curriculum.* Ed. by G. W. Ford and Lawrence Pugno. Chicago: Rand McNally, 1964. pp. 6-30.
16. SMITH, B. OTHANEL. "A Concept of Teaching." *Language and Concepts in Education.* Ed. by B. Othanel Smith and Robert H. Ennis. Chicago: Rand McNally and Co., 1961. pp. 86-101.
17. SMITH, B. OTHANEL. "Toward A Theory of Teaching." *Theory and Research in Teaching.* Ed. by Arno A. Bellack, New York: Bureau of Publications, Teachers College, Columbia University, 1963. pp. 1-10.
18. TYLER, RALPH W., "The Contribution of the Behavioral Sciences to Educational Research." *First Annual Phi Delta Kappa Symposium on Education Research.* Edited by Frank W. Banghart. Bloomington, Indiana: Phi Delta Kappa, 1960. pp. 55-70.
19. WINCH, PETER. *The Idea of a Social Science.* New York: Humanities Press, 1958. 143 p.

SECTION ONE

Communications

OVERVIEW

T HAT teaching involves communication is a truism which nobody challenges, whatever his concept of teaching. Yet only recently have educators begun to analyze teaching with the help of concepts from communications theory. This lag is partly due to the relative newness of communications, cybernetics, and information theory as fields of study in themselves. These areas have developed only within the last quarter of a century.

The six selections that view teaching from the vantage point of communications represent a wide range of attacks and purposes. Lewis, Newell, and Withall employ communications concepts as a means of studying the classroom from the standpoint of mental health. Gerbner sees communications as the process which humanizes man; he presents a model of this process and considers its implications for teaching. The Packers view communication in the teaching-learning process with the aid of concepts drawn from cybernetics, making particular use of information bits, uncertainty, entropy, and feedback. Ryans bases his approach on the idea of general systems, an idea derived mainly from the biologies and Von Bertalanffy. As in other sections, these articles supplement one another so as to yield the broadest possible application to the study of teaching from this perspective.

It is important to note that these selections do not present teaching *as if* it were communications. They describe teaching as one instance of human behavior that involves communications. That is, teaching is a specific case of a more general abstraction called communication. This procedure is in contrast to other selections in this book, which, for example, say that teaching may be likened to short-story writing or psychotherapy or a game or a computer. Hence, the selections in this chapter cannot be criticized as using inadequate analogies for teaching. Teaching involves communications in a special way and it is the task of educators to identify it. Indeed, this is precisely the task of the current surge of investigations on teaching.

All the complex models of communication have as their base a quite simple model that may be diagrammed as follows:

This diagram may be slightly embellished by the addition of three more concepts:

This simple model applies to verbal communication that, we are reminded by our authors, concerns cognitive, affective, and skill behavior as well as nonverbal behavior such as physical actions, facial expressions, written symbols, and, according to Galloway, a speaker's tone qualities. This simple scheme serves as the foundation of the models by Gerbner, the Packers, and Ryans. Galloway also uses this model when he claims that the culturally disadvantaged child can more easily decode nonverbal behavior than verbal behavior and that teachers must be more sensitive to the nonverbal messages which they transmit.

It is necessary to remember that, though all the articles but Galloway's emphasize verbal communication, their ideas apply to nonverbal behavior as well. Their emphasis in no way implies that

verbal communication is more important than nonverbal communication. Rather, verbal behavior is the prime means of human
communication. This notion is advanced by Flanders in the section
on classroom social climate as justification for coding only verbal
behavior in teaching.

The concept of mobility introduced by Lewis is similar to the
concept of lifting the cognitive level as presented by Taba in her
article on teaching strategies. Similarly, Lewis' concept of responsiveness connects with the Packers' and Ryans' articles in this section
as well as with all those articles in other sections that view teaching
as *interaction* between the teacher and the pupil, e.g., the articles by
Hughes, Bellack, and Rogers. Hughes herself, in an article[1] not included here, uses the word *responsiveness* to describe the notion of
interaction, which, with the idea of teacher power, is one of the two
key concepts underlying her research. Ryans' definition of information as a set of symbols that convey meaning resembles Bellack's
idea that the "function of language is the communication of meaning." This notion led Bellack and his associates to concentrate on
three types of meaning in the classroom. Lewis' concept of accuracy
overlaps with Gerbner's notions of correspondence, coherence, adequacy, and validity between the event and the statement about
the event. The concept of accuracy also reminds one of evaluation
in the sense that the teacher checks the pupil to see if he has correctly received and learned the transmitted message. This form of
evaluation appears in several articles.

The concept of a communications system described by Ryans and
the Packers and implied by Lewis, calls to mind the four pedagogical moves by Bellack and his associates, for these moves also constitute a system; two of Bellack's pedagogical moves (structuring
and soliciting) are initiatory, while two (responding and reacting)
are reflexive. Indeed, Bellack has combined these moves into various
teaching cycles. Smith's[2] model of the teaching cycle of classroom

[1] Marie Hughes. "Utah Study of the Assessment of Teaching." *Theory and Research in Teaching.* Ed. by Arno A. Bellack. New York, Bureau of Publications,
Teachers College, Columbia University, 1963. p. 27.

[2] B. Othanel Smith. "A Concept of Teaching." *Language and Concepts in Education.* Ed. by B. Othanel Smith and Robert H. Ennis. Chicago, Rand McNally and
Co., 1961.

discourse also resembles the systems idea. According to Smith classroom discourse may be considered as:

$$\mid \mid P_t{\rightarrow}D_t{\rightarrow}R_t \mid \rightarrow P_p{\rightarrow}D_p{\rightarrow}R_p \mid \mid$$

In this formula, P_t is "the teacher's perception of the pupil's behavior." D_t is "the teacher's diagnosis of the pupil's state of interest, readiness, knowledge, and the like made by inference from the behavior of the pupil." R_t is "the action taken by the teacher in light of his diagnosis," P_p is "the pupil's perception of the teacher's behavior," and so forth. Thus, the ideas from this vantage point tie in with other systems.

Galloway's material is significant in several respects. First, as Flanders notes, it is more difficult to get agreement on the meaning ascribed to nonverbal behavior than it is to reach agreement on the meaning ascribed to verbal behavior. Yet Galloway has successfully created an instrument for categorizing nonverbal behavior and that instrument is presented here. Second, Galloway's instrument for focusing on nonverbal communication overlaps with certain ideas in the sections on classroom climate. Galloway states in his field study that he built the sub-categories for encouraging and inhibiting communication upon the work of Flanders, Hughes, and Withall, to name but three. A careful comparison of this instrument with the articles by the authors mentioned will reveal the points in common. The instrument is important in that it uniquely offers us a structured framework for observing and categorizing nonverbal behavior of teachers. It further directs us to keep in mind three elements in nonverbal communication affecting classroom climate—facial expressions, actions, and vocal quality. Furthermore, Galloway gives examples of each element for each category so as to assure understanding of the category.

Similarly, Lewis, Newell, and Withall present a study based on an instrument for classifying the dominant intention of classroom communication (primarily verbal communication). They, too, give examples for each category to assure observer agreement. The reader is alerted to the fact that the unit of analysis in this study is a ten second time interval, as opposed to the "communicative act" employed by Galloway. Furthermore, the results of this study conducted with graduate students are consistent with a parallel study with undergraduates also conducted at the University of Wisconsin.[3]

This section, more than any other, illustrates a major point of this book. Perception of events is selective, and meaning varies according to the receiver's point of view. This is particularly evident in the articles by Lewis and Gerbner. It is also stressed by Galloway and the Packers when they ask the teacher to consider which messages they are transmitting to the pupils are in reality being received. For the Packers, this act of determining which message is received distinguishes the teacher from the scholar. This idea of selectivity applies as well to what the teacher receives in feedback from the pupils.

Gerbner makes the strong point that if we do not provide for free selection, a representative context, and equitable availability in communication we manipulate rather than educate. He asks us to challenge cherished assumptions so as to lead the pupil to self direction. In his study with undergraduates cited earlier, Withall reports "many of the hard core educational values and procedures by which student teachers are guided seem to have been derived in part from their elementary and high school teachers and from the cooperating or master teacher in whose classroom they teach during their student teaching experience."[4] This, too, is a call for research on ways to change teachers' communicating skills and values in order to improve their teaching.

Further research on teaching from this communications perspective is clearly needed, as Lewis aptly points out. Many questions for research are raised. For example, what are the effects of various kinds of "noise" on classroom communication? (*Noise* is used here in its technical sense to mean any additional information transmitted to the receiver not sent by the sender. That is, more information is in the output than in the input.) Are there different effects for the various subject-matter fields, age levels of pupils, and ability levels of pupils? How much "redundance" does the teacher need to provide in order to eliminate the lack of communication due to

[3] John Withall. "Mental Health-Teacher Education Research Project." *Journal of Teacher Education*, 14:318-325, September, 1963.

[4] *Ibid.* p. 323.

"equivocation," which refers to the situation where there is more information transmitted than received? That is, where there is more information in the output than in the input. Does the amount of redundacy needed change according to subject-matter area, age level of pupils, and ability level of pupils? Is it different for communication of cognitive matters, affective concerns, and motor skills? Will learning increase if formal feedback procedures are instituted that go beyond the usual written examination? Will learning increase if students are taught to assess communication, as suggested by Gerbner? These are but several of the questions that need answers. Obviously, it is fruitful to talk about teaching in these communications terms.

1. A Theory of Communication and Its Implications for Teaching

George Gerbner

Is there a "communication approach" to human problems? If the answer is yes, what is it? What are reasons for taking such an approach? What are reasons for the development of it? What can such an approach contribute to understanding and judgment? And what implications can be derived for teaching and for the curriculum?

These are the questions I would like to reflect upon with you.

Let me define communication as social interaction performed through messages. Messages may be defined as formally coded or symbolic or representational events which are of some shared significance in a culture, and which are produced for the purpose of evoking significance.

My distinction between the "communication approach" and other approaches to human behavior rests, therefore, on the extent to which (1) messages are germane to the process studied, and (2) concern with the production, nature, and uses of messages is central to the approach employed. If there is a "communication approach" or theory or discipline, it can be distinguished from others in that *it makes the nature and role of messages in life and society its central organizing concern.*

Reprinted with permission from *The Nature of Teaching*, edited by Louise M. Berman. Copyright © 1963 by the University of Wisconsin-Milwaukee. (Numbering has been retained as in original article.)

There are many reasons for studying the nature and role of messages in life and society. Some are traditional. Certain familiar reasons include the acquisition or improvement of communication skills, appreciations, tactics, and the knowledge itself which messages and message systems signify and convey. The same reasons underlie our studies of language, composition, rhetoric, literature, art, and various other modes of verbal and non-verbal expression.

Another and less familiar reason exists for studying the nature and role of messages in life and society. Although applicable to all ages, this new reason is the outgrowth of the historical and cultural circumstances of the twentieth century. As the industrial revolution has transformed man's relation to society, the communication revolution—an extension of the industrial revolution to the mass-production of messages—has transformed man's relation to culture. This transformation has brought about the need to re-examine basic assumptions about the nature and role of messages in life and society, to inquire into the humanizing potentials of communications and of communication systems. That need is, in my view, the basic reason and historical rationale for the emergence of a "communication approach" to human problems.

This approach is primarily analytical and critical. It does not necessarily take the objectives of communicators or existing institutional goals as its point of departure or standard of value. Rather, it attempts to raise questions about all these components as parts of total communication situations to be assessed in order to arrive at a fuller understanding of the humanizing potentials of messages in communication, and of communications in culture. A by-product of this effort might be the improvement of skills, appreciations, and tactics. But the end result should be an improvement of standards.

It is in this way that I would like to approach a theory of communication and its implications for teaching. First, we shall consider, in a very brief outline, a view of communication as a humanizing process. Then I will sketch the development of a theory and model of communication not inconsistent with the demands placed upon theory in our view of the humanizing functions of communication. Our model will help illustrate some operational elements and relationships in communication on the process level; it will help answer the question: What happens when we interact through messages?

Next we shall ask: What *should* happen when we interact through messages? What are the desirable qualities of our operational elements and relationships in the light of our view of communication as a humanizing process? What communication and teaching functions serve these values?

After discussing communication and its implications for teaching on the value level, we shall conclude with some suggestions on the institutional level. The question there is: What happens when industrial institutions mass-produce message systems making up much of the popular culture in which all educational enterprises operate? What are some roles and responsibilities of formal education in the new cultural situation?

Communication, a Humanizing Process

How did *Homo sapiens* become human?

A hundred million years of evolution is compressed in the word "comprehend." It stems from the expression "to grasp with the forehand." The ability to grasp with the hand and with the mind literally developed hand-in-hand.

Life in damp tropical forests freed the forearms of a certain group of primates from the burden of carrying the body, and made them into hands—strong, sure, and delicate instruments. Exceptionally deft manipulation required an exceptionally large and complex control system—the human brain. The needs of hand-brain coordination made it possible to develop the brain capacity necessary for holding an image long enough to reflect on it, store it, and retrieve it. This capacity is the prerequisite for the production and use of messages, and thus for human communication.

The invasion of glaciers robbed hominoids of their arboreal paradise and forced them to taste the fruits of a new type of knowledge. Huddled in cold valleys, flooded even during the warm spells, hard-pressed to develop resources of collaboration, community, and communication, *Homo sapiens* transformed himself into what we would recognize as human. He emerged from the Ice Ages a pretty accomplished artist, scientist, and organizer.

Communication played, and plays, a unique part in the human transformation. The original "wisdom" of *Homo* the *"sapiens"* stems from his symboling ability which arose, along with his tool-making talents, from marvelous hand-brain coordination and development put to communal uses. This symboling ability is the capacity to produce messages; to record, represent, and re-create aspects of the human condition; to encode, share, and decode significance; and thus, to extend the scope of consciousness beyond the reach of the senses, and to create a vision of human potentialities and requirements beyond that of any living species.

Communication infuses the other humanizing processes of collaboration and community with our most uniquely human characteristics. It does that by performing certain specialized functions in society and culture. I call these the humanizing functions of communication.

HUMANIZING FUNCTIONS OF COMMUNICATIONS

The shaping of sounds, forms, images, and stories into language, magic, legend and ritual arose from the needs of survival through living and working together. One function of these communication activities was to make work easier, life meaningful, ways of looking at life and the world convincing to those born into a culture. Let me call this the *art* function of communication as a social enterprise. Man the communicator as artist informed and inspired, frightened and entertained as he helped all to bear the hardships, share the joys, avoid the dangers, and celebrate the accomplishments of communal life. He made the truths of the tribe—or of the culture—believable and compelling.

From the taming of fire to the sowing of seeds man learned not only the arts of making truths believable, but also the importance of making beliefs truer. Man reached out, got burned, and fled in panic. But not always. For he could also reflect and so he could contemplate an abstract proposition: Which end of a burning stick could be seized with impunity? Let me call this the *science* function of communication as a social enterprise. Man the communicator, as scientist, undertakes to assess the validity of propositions. His function is, therefore, to make beliefs truer.

The art of moving men and the science of moving mountains confer the power to move men to move mountains. The distribution and use of this power is the third social function in communication. It is the *organizing* or administrative, or governmental function. Man the communicator as organizer is responsible for the structure of conscious reflective choices. He deals with the production, availability, and selection of messages. He decides the balance of representations available; he stacks the decks of any message system; he controls the purpose, nature and extent of freedoms built into those systems. As the humanizing role of the communicator as scientist is to make beliefs truer, and as artist to make truths more believable, his responsibility as administrator is to organize the energy and power of message systems to promote liberating ends and to make knowledge freer.

This is my view of communication as a humanizing process. I submit that theories and models of communication become useful in a general way if they have some relevance to problems of conceptual organization, judgment, and action in the humanizing process.

A COMMUNICATION MODEL: THE PROCESS LEVEL

If communication is interaction through messages, we must be able to *produce* messages, and we must be able to *perceive* messages. In other words, we must be able to perceive events in a special way, and produce events in equally unique ways reflecting that special type of perception.

If we draw circles for elements and bars for interactions between the elements, a diagram can be made of a communication act.

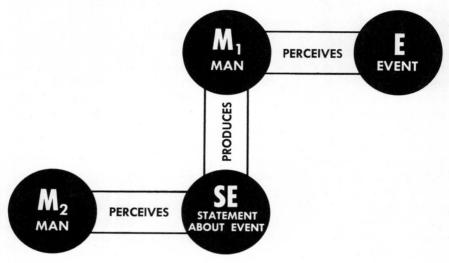

FIGURE 1

Figure 1 is the skeleton of a basic communication act. A man perceives an event (horizontal dimension) and produces a statement about it (vertical dimension); another man perceives the statement (horizontal dimension).

Let us now look more deeply into this process, first along the perceptual (horizontal) dimension. Events (including statements) must be *available* to be perceived; you can't play the game without cards. (But the kind of cards available will, of course, determine the kind of game played.)

Secondly, the event (or statement) must be *selected* for perception. We cannot attend to all things; attention is selective. Choices depend upon availability of items. But choices also depend upon a third element of the perceptual field: context.

Context describes the method in which parts of a whole are woven together in time and space. It is the way the deck is shuffled. It affects chances of selecting any one event in a series or field of events. In addition, the context of presentation (structure of the outside field) and the context of interpretation (structure of the inside field) affect the meaning we attribute to perceptions.

Availability, context, and selection lead us from the world outside to the world inside. Let us draw a smaller circle inside "man" (M) standing for the event (or statement) "as perceived" (E' or SE'). If we also write in some of the terms of perception, the horizontal dimension of our model takes on certain changes.

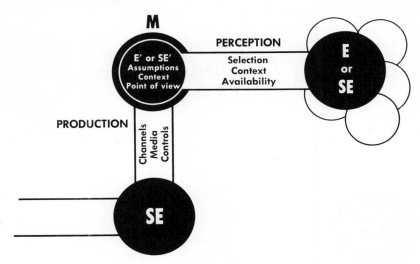

FIGURE 2

As Figure 2 shows, I am suggesting that we perceive in terms of prior *assumptions*, that we fit our perceptions into a *context* of our own, and that we can only perceive (or conceive of) something from where we are —from a *point of view*. Let me illustrate.

If I ask you the shape of Figure 3, chances are you will say it is a trapezoid. If I ask you the shape of a window, chances are you will say it is rectangular, even if you see it from a side view. Yet, if you see the window from a side view, its shape might look something like Figure 4. And the shape of Figure 4 is the same as the shape of Figure 3.

Why does that happen? We live in a world of rectangular shapes (some would say squares); but trapezoids are rare. So when we see a trapezoid in a familiar *context*, we *assume* that "really" it is a rectangular object seen from a *point of view* which makes rectangles appear trapezoidal.

We learn to perceive things in this way. We learn this unconsciously; but we learn this way of perceiving so well that sometimes we see a rectangle in perspective, even when looking at a shape we *know* is really trapezoidal. The assumptions, contexts, and points of view which have formed the terms of our perceptions make it difficult to see some things as they "really" are. Figure 5 shows that our "window" is not, in fact, rectangular. But it is easier to assume that the yardsticks are cheating, or even that the hands holding the "window" in Figure 6 are of different

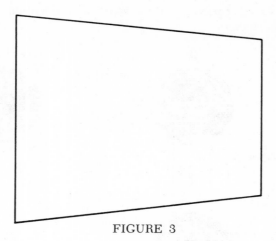

FIGURE 3

size, than to see a trapezoidal window. Every perception, therefore, is a judgment based on past experience and present expectation.

The significance of these statements for communication is two-fold. First, the messages we produce reflect the terms upon which we perceive. (The history of perspective drawing, for example, shows a growing awareness of these terms.) Secondly, the way we perceive messages will be determined both by the terms of perception *built into* messages, and the assumptions, contexts, and points of view *brought to* the perception of messages.

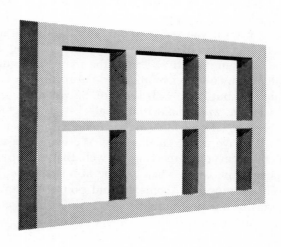

FIGURE 4

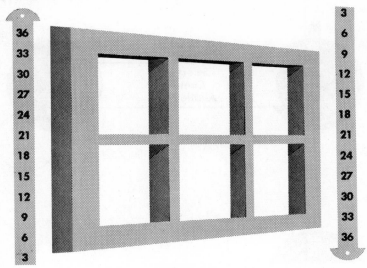

FIGURE 5

We can now complete our basic diagram of a communication act.

Figure 7 shows that an event (or statement) available in a certain context is selected for perception in terms of the perceiver's assumptions, context, and point of view. The perceiver is also a communicator; he uses some means and controls (channels, media, *etc.*, as I am using language and print on this paper) to produce a statement about the event. In this way the process continues.

FIGURE 6

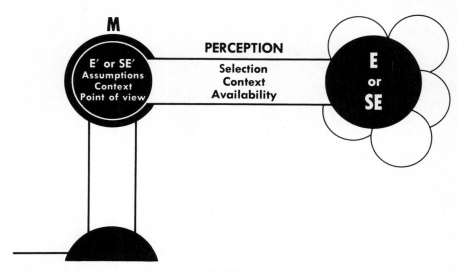

FIGURE 7

Failure to understand terms implicit in our messages may leave us in the dark about what happens, and why, as the exchange goes on. . . .

THE JOB OF THE TEACHER

What is the job of the teacher? Is it to cultivate existing assumptions, whatever they might be, in order to put across the desired "message"? This is, in effect, what some lists of "helpful hints" on "effective communication" tell us. This is what much narrowly conceived and superficially interpreted research on communication "effects" tells us. But cultivating existing assumptions in order to put across the desired "message" is manipulation, not education.

Often the teacher cannot honestly convey his message without challenging cherished assumptions. And, at times, unexamined assumptions implicitly reflected in messages counter and negate the explicit "lessons." Therefore, the analysis of messages in teaching first leads to self-analysis: What am I communicating besides what I think I am teaching? Am I talking about "a government of laws and not of men"—but from a Lone Ranger point of view? Do I need monsters to make a unit on space travel or on life on other planets more believable? If so, I may be an "effective" communicator, but I should not be in the classroom. I should not be in the classroom for the simple reason that successfully manipulating people, even into the "right" conclusions, only impoverishes the bases of self-direction and, therefore, negates the aims of education.

People learn best not what their teachers think they teach or what

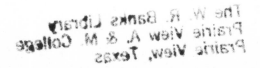

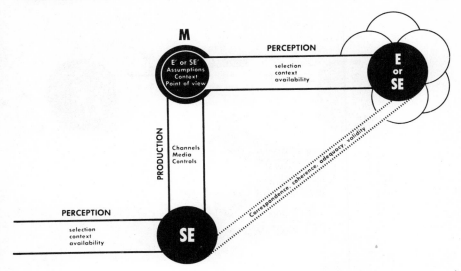

FIGURE 11

their preachers think they preach, but what their cultures in fact cultivate. We "teach" many things, most of them short-lived. But we cultivate
the assumptions, contexts, and points of view in terms of which we
communicate all things. These terms are likely to be the most lasting
and least examined parts of our lessons. So the questions I ask as I reflect
on teaching as a communication process are these: What approach to the
subject and to learning itself did I cultivate when I only meant to transmit a few "facts"? What perspectives on man, life, and the world did I
present when I only meant to teach English or geography or math or
physics?

THE VALUE LEVEL

These questions bring us to the level of values. That teaching has
elements of art, science, and organization is no news to anyone. It should
not be surprising, then, that teaching has the values of these activities as
humanizing functions in communication.

Let us develop a value-oriented version of our communication model.
First, we shall supply a dimension missing from the operational version of
the model, but present in every real communication situation: the relationship between the statement (now conceived as a single specific
proposition) and what the statement is "about." This is the hypotenuse of
our model, shown in Figure 11. This relationship may be characterized by
the presence or absence of qualities of correspondence, coherence, adequacy, or validity attributed to the message.

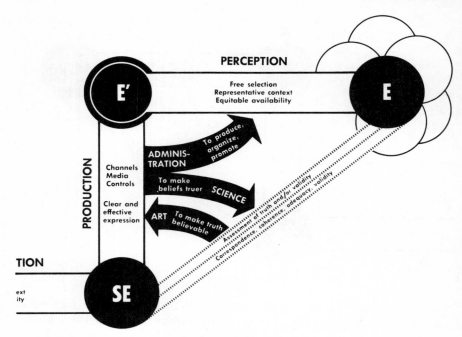

FIGURE 12

Now let us ask the question: What *should* happen as we interact through messages? What are the desirable, the *humanizing* qualities of each of the three dimensions of our communication model? And how do the functions of organization, science, and art serve these qualities?

Along the perceptual dimension we have selection, context, and availability as operational elements. What do we ask of these? We ask that selection be as *free* as possible, that context be as *representative* as possible, and that availability be as *equitable* as possible. So the ideal (even if troublesome) criterion of value along this dimension is *free selection in a representative context of pertinent evidence.*

The hypotenuse of our model is the relationship between statements and what statements are "about." Here we consider it desirable to *assess* qualities of *truth and validity* built into our messages.

The production dimension relates the terms of our perception and cognition—our "beliefs"—to the statements we make. Here we want skillful use of channels, media, controls, *etc. to* reflect these "beliefs" in effective forms. We want to produce *clear and believable messages.*

Figure 12 shows these qualities of the three dimensions. It also indicates how the functions of administration, science, and art serve these qualities.

The teacher as administrator and organizer of communication activities uses means, facilities, and controls to promote free selection in a representative context of pertinent evidence. The teacher as scientist assesses the truth qualities of information and the validity of assumptions, contexts, and points of view implicit in statements. The teacher as artist uses his skills and materials to express true and valid beliefs in clear and convincing forms.

Combining the humanizing functions of administration, science, and art in communication, the teacher thus strives to make choices freer, beliefs truer, and truths more believable.

Scrutiny of communication in the classroom is analysis of messages and processes. It leads, on one hand, to self-analysis, and, on the other, to a concern with the full range of consequences implicit in communication as a humanizing process.

THE INSTITUTIONAL LEVEL

Finally, we come to the institutional level. Concrete historical developments give our concern with communication processes and values its urgency and relevance. If it is true that most people learn best what their cultures cultivate, a revolution in culture has brought about a transformation in learning and altered the position of the teacher and the school in society.

The industrial revolution has shifted into the communications phase. Message-systems which provide many of the raw materials of our consciousness (and of the terms of our perceptions) have become mass-produced, institutionalized commodities. Bigness, fewness, and costliness in cultural, as in any other, mass production brought centralization of control, standardization of product, streamlined efficiency of technique. These changes meant increasing penetration of influence into many spheres of life and across many previous boundaries of place, time, and social status. We can safely say that never before could so many people in so many places know and talk so much about the same things at the same time.

The shape of human affairs has changed. Instead of the slow filtering-down process, we have the almost simultaneous introduction of information, ideas, and products at all levels of society. Mass production and distribution of communications to scattered, heterogeneous audiences means potential enrichment of cultural horizons incredible by all previous standards. But it also means that the assumptions, contexts, and points of view which cultivate our perceptions of what is real, what is important, and what is right, now roll off the assembly line bearing a brand name, a corporate image, a marketing approach.

The words of Andrew Fletcher, uttered in 1704, reverberate in the halls of the Academy and, at times, of Congress. "I believe," he said, "that if a man were permitted to write all the ballads, he need not care who should make the laws of the nation." For ours is a revolution in the writing of all the ballads.

The mass media have increasingly taken over democratic national responsibilities for transmitting the cultural heritage, for illuminating the realities of today, and for setting the agenda of tomorrow.

How did the mass media fulfill that responsibility? As well as could be expected, perhaps even better. Being free from public control but lacking guarantees of public support in using that freedom, the mass media must, on the whole, merchandise such gratifications as can be profitably cultivated under the circumstances.

How does formal education find its place and its responsibilities in the new cultural situation? I think we have only begun to diagnose the situation. There is little doubt that we can and should find ways of using the riches available to all for the first time in the history of cultures. It has often been pointed out that we should also help make some order out of the distortions, confusions, and general cultural chaos characterizing the new situation. But all these worthy activities do not go to the heart of the problem.

The new situation is a radical transformation of the ways members of our species became human. Seen in that light, the problem is not only that of tastes, appreciations, discriminating consumership. The problem is also the organization of culture, with all its humanizing functions, both as a public and a private matter. The task is one of citizens' building and molding social institutions for democratic human purposes. We have opportunities to exercise policy choices in the field of popular culture, or to let these choices go by default. The difference is likely to affect our survival as a nation; and, if we survive, it is certain to determine the outcome of our experiment with self-government.

A role education can play in communication on the institutional level is to prepare itself, and the new generation of citizens, to exercise such choices. It makes little difference whether we think about such studies under the heading of Social Science or Citizenship or English or Mass Media. It is more important that they be conceived as part of general education on all levels rather than only as training in the specific applied skills of communication or of consumership.

Such studies should develop ways of observing modern cultural institutions mass-producing images of man, life, and the world, and of the uses we make of them. They should examine circumstances of cultural production and consumption, and consider what kinds of humanizing aims can be fulfilled under what kinds of conditions. These considerations should result in the development of standards for the citizen as well as for the consumer.

I might now summarize my attempt to present a theory of communication and its implications for teaching as follows: The reasons for the emergence of a "communication approach" rest, I believe, in the trends and developments of the last century. Such an approach or theory or discipline makes the nature and role of messages in life and society its central organizing concern. It attempts to analyze what happens in communication as a teaching process, and to assess the values of what happens. Then the approach turns to the institutional developments from which it sprang. It uses the insights of process and of value to find the place of the school, the role of education, and the responsibilities of the teacher in the new culture in which both we and our students live and grow and learn.

References

Certain aspects and topics in this paper have been developed in greater detail (although in earlier formulations) in the following articles:

Gerbner, George. "The Individual in a Mass Culture," *Saturday Review,* XLIII (June 18, 1960), 11-13, 36-37. Also (abridged) in *The Executive,* IV (1960), 14-16, and *The National Elementary Principal,* XL (February, 1961), 49-54.

———. "Education and the Challenge of Mass Culture," *Audio-Visual Communication Review,* VII (Fall, 1959), 264-278.

———. "Content Analysis and Critical Research in Mass Communication," *Audio-Visual Communication Review,* VI (Spring, 1958), 85-108.

———. "Toward a General Model of Communication," *Audio-Visual Communication Review,* IV (Summer, 1956), 171-199.

The following sources may be useful to those interested in further exploration of the perceptual aspects, especially the "window" and other similar demonstrations.

Cantril, Hadley. *The "Why" of Man's Experience.* New York: Macmillan, 1950.

Kilpatrick, Franklin P. (ed.). *Explorations in Transactional Psychology.* New York: New York University Press, 1961.

2. Teacher Behavior Theory and Research: Implications for Teacher Education

David G. Ryans

TEACHER BEHAVIOR AS INFORMATION PROCESSING AND THE TEACHER AS AN INFORMATION SYSTEM

The point of view from which this discussion proceeds is that the teacher may be considered an information-processing system that functions for the purpose of aiding the pupil in acquiring an appropriate behavior repertoire.

Teacher behavior is defined genotypically by reference to a set of hypothetical constructs which have their focus in teacher decision making. These constructs are assumed to characterize the teacher-system. They are postulated to interact with and mediate between (a) the conditions (i.e., inputs) influencing the teacher and (b) the observable teaching response in a particular situation. The functioning of the teacher-system we describe as "teacher information processing."

This theoretical model proposes that information processing on the part of the teacher-system culminates, in a given teaching situation, in certain overt and directly observable "information-forwarding" responses which are directed at the teacher's pupil or pupils.

The *ultimate* objective of teacher information processing is the acquisition of information (i.e., the learning of facts, concepts, and rules relating to cognitive, affective, and psychomotor behaviors) by pupils in order that it subsequently may be retrieved (i.e., subsequently recovered from the individual's "memory" or information storage) for use in some life situation. The information transmitted by teacher to student, when duly processed by the student and incorporated into his "association hierarchy" by the process we commonly refer to as "learning," may be retrieved by the individual either in essentially the same form in which it was originally received and acquired, or in some adapted form which represents alteration of the information to permit application of the earlier learned facts, concepts, and rules to new situations; or even to the "discovery" of previously unrecognized information, or through recombination to the "creation" of new concepts or products.

Teacher information processing, resulting in teacher behavior, is ac-

Reprinted with permission from *The Journal of Teacher Education*, 14: 274-293, September, 1963.

complished, then, for the purpose of facilitating the attainment by a teacher's pupils of specified behavioral goals which include the acquisition and development of skills, procedures, knowledge, understanding, "sets," work habits and other behaving styles, attitudes and value judgments, and personal adaptation-adjustment patterns acceptable to the culture or community in which the teaching is accomplished. And, in addition, to promote this pupil acquisition-development "in optimum time, with optimum retention and transfer, and with no harmful personal effects."[1]

The observable information-providing responses of the teacher are postulated by this theoretical viewpoint to be instrumental and telestic in nature, directed at influencing the acquisition of certain information-behavior on the part of the individuals who are being taught.

Without going into details of the hypothesized general classes of teacher behavior, it may be noted that this information system theory of teacher behavior assumes five major categories into which teacher behaviors fall:

1. *Motivating-reinforcing* teacher behavior;
2. *Presenting-explaining-demonstrating* teacher behavior;
3. *Organizing-planning-managing* teacher behavior;
4. *Evaluating* teacher behavior;
5. *Counseling-advising* teacher behavior.

Were space available it would be appropriate to describe the background and salient aspects of the information system theory of instruction in some detail. Here we will attempt only to indicate the general influencing conditions which led to the conceptualization, to define superficially some of the terms, and to present a diagram which schematically indicates the nature of the hypothesized teacher information processing system which leads to decision making and the programming of the teacher's thinking and action to suit best the needs of the pupils in attaining certain learning objectives.

The theoretical position presented has been influenced largely by four conditions:

1. The thinking preceding the Teacher Characteristics Study and the research resulting from this study; (also relevant research on teacher behavior reported by other investigators and earlier experience with

---

[1] This quoted phrase, "in optimum time, with optimum retention and transfer, and with no harmful personal effects," was once employed by B. O. Smith in an unpublished paper on "Educational Psychology and Philosophy: Values and Science," presented at the 1957 meeting of the American Psychological Association.

data accumulated in connection with the National Teacher Examinations);[2]

2. The introduction of certain concepts of "general system theory";[3]
3. Sears' formulation of the "dyadic sequence" as an explanation of social behavior;[4]
4. The growing interest in concepts associated with information theory and communication theory.[5]

THE TEACHER CHARACTERISTICS STUDY

Since it was largely the Teacher Characteristics Study which provided the motivation and stimulated the writer in formulating the information system theory of teacher behavior, somewhat disproportionate attention will be given this particular influencing condition as compared with the others noted in the preceding paragraph.

The Teacher Characteristics Study was an eight-year investigation, consisting of over one hundred separate but integrated research efforts. It was directed at the determination of teacher behavior patterns observable in the classroom, the development of inventory estimates of certain teacher characteristics, study of background and environmental variables related to teacher behavior, and analyses of relationships between teacher characteristics and observed pupil behaviors.

More specifically, and in terms of the major objectives of the Teacher

[2] Ryans, D. G. "Psychology as Learning." *Education* 60: 55-59; September 1939.
Ryans, D. G. "Theory Development and the Study of Teacher Behavior." *Journal of Educational Psychology* 47: 462-475; December 1956.
Ryans, D. G. *Characteristics of Teachers.* Washington: American Council on Education, 1960.
Ryans, D. G. "Appraising Teacher Personnel." *Journal of Experimental Education* 16: 1-30; September 1947.
[3] von Bertalanffy, L. "An Outline of General System Theory." *British Journal of the Philosophy of Science* 1: 134-165; 1950.
Miller, J. G. "Toward a General Theory for the Behavioral Sciences." *American Psychologist* 10: 513-531; 1955.
[4] Sears, R. R. "A Theoretical Framework for Personality and Social Behavior." *American Psychologist* 6: 476-483; 1951.
[5] Miller, G. A. *Language and Communication.* New York: McGraw-Hill Co., 1951.
Miller, G. A. "Communication." *Annual Review of Psychology.* Stanford, California: Annual Reviews, 1954. pp. 401-420.
Miller, G. A. "What Is Information Measurement?" *American Psychologist* 8: 3-11; 1953.
Carnap, R., and Bar-Hillel, Y. *An Outline of a Theory of Semantic Information.* Cambridge: Massachusetts Institute of Technology, 1952.
Hartley, R. V. "The Transmission of Information." *Bell System Technical Journal* 17: 535-550; 1928.
Wiener, N. *The Human Use of Human Beings.* Boston: Houghton Mifflin, 1950.
Shannon, C. E. "A Mathematical Theory of Communication." *Bell System Technical Journal* 27:379-423; 1948.

Characteristics Study, the description of teacher behavior and teacher characteristics was approached in several stages:

1. In order to obtain information basic to the description of teacher behavior, there was the two-pronged need to develop instruments for recording assessments of teacher activities in the classroom and to perfect observation procedures. Teacher assessments, it was decided, would be made by trained observers. The staff pursued for a long period the refinement of observation methods to provide maximum reliability and validity of the assessments obtained. Employing the assessment instruments and the observation procedures that had been developed, large numbers of teachers, together with their classes, were observed. (This stage of the Study represented an effort to determine the kinds of behaviors which could be observed in the classroom and the most effective methods for observing and assessing them.)

2. Having conducted extensive observations and having obtained what appeared to be analytical, factual assessments of certain classroom characteristics of teachers, the Study next sought the determination of the major patterns of observed teacher behavior that might emerge through factor analysis of the intercorrelations of assessments of the various observed teacher dimensions. (This was done separately for teachers at the elementary and secondary levels of teaching.)

3. Concurrently with the observation and analysis of teacher behavior, the Study attempted the development of questionnaire-type instruments for tapping other teacher-characteristic domains which could not be most efficiently assessed by direct observation in the teacher's classroom. These were direct-inquiry, self-appraisal instruments developed to obtain estimates of: (a) teachers' attitudes (attitudes toward pupils, attitudes toward parents, attitudes toward colleagues, attitudes toward administrators); (b) teachers' educational viewpoints (academic-centered school program vs. school programs stressing other objectives, rigid school program vs. flexible school program involving pupil and parent participation, and teacher-directed learning in traditional subject matter fields vs. learning directed by pupil interests and abilities—these referring in aggregate to what frequently are regarded as traditional vs. permissive viewpoints); (c) the verbal intelligence or verbal understanding of teachers; and (d) the emotional adjustment of teachers.

4. Another of the main interests of the Study, and one which consumed a major share of staff time and energy, involved the identification of correlates, or concomitants, of observed teacher classroom behavior patterns. This was a matter of: (a) developing paper-and-

pencil instruments consisting of items hypothetically related to teacher classroom behavior and other personal characteristics of teachers (items having to do with specific preferences, judgments, activities, family and home backgrounds, and the like, which were hypothesized to be concomitants of certain teacher characteristics) and (b) empirically deriving and validating scoring keys for such materials.

5. With the data made available by the systematic observation of teachers and the administration of the paper-and-pencil test and inventories, numerous comparisons were made of teacher groups and of teachers classified with respect to various aspects of status.

The results of the research conducted in connection with the Teacher Characteristics Study have been reported in a number of sources and will not be reviewed here, although the reader's attention is called to a few of the study's publications which are listed in the accompanying footnote. The most general statement describing the study as a whole is found in the book *Characteristics of Teachers*[6] published by the American Council on Education. Of particular interest to some readers will be the findings relating to one research carried out and reported in *Characteristics of Teachers* as Chapter 8, "Some Characteristics of Outstanding Teachers." Certain aspects of the research, including investigations of the relationship of teacher behavior and pupil behavior, which were not treated in detail in *Characteristics of Teachers* are indicated in the footnote.[7]

What Is Meant by the "System" Concept?

The concept of the "system," including definitions and assumptions, has been described in the references to the work of Bertalanffy and Miller indicated in a preceding footnote. . . .

In this discussion, a "system" will be defined simply as any identifiable

[6] Ryans, D. G., *op. cit.*

[7] Ryans, D. G. "Inventory Estimated Teacher Characteristics as Covariants of Observer Assessed Pupil Behavior." *Journal of Educational Psychology* 52: 91-97; 1962.

Ryans, D. G. "Some Concomitants of Inventory Estimated Emotional Maturity of Experienced Teachers." *California Journal of Educational Research* 11: 106-109, 144; 1960.

Ryans, D. G. "Some Validity Extension Data Relative to Empirically Derived Predictors of Teacher Behavior." *Educational and Psychological Measurement* 18: 355-370; 1958.

Ryans, D. G. "A Note on Activities of Teachers During their Childhood and Adolescence." *California Journal of Educational Research* 9: 57-59; March 1958.

Ryans, D. G. "Teacher Characteristics in Relation to Marital Status of the Teacher." *California Journal of Educational Research* 10: 68-72; March 1959.

assemblage of complexity organized elements or subsystems (e.g., which may be behavior variables characterizing an individual person, individual persons forming an identifiable group, etc.) which are *inter*dependent and united by a common information network, which are characterized by a regular (i.e., lawful or orderly) form of interaction, and which function as an organized whole to attain some objective or produce some effect or end product uniquely characteristic of the system operating as a unit.

Because of the necessary exchange of information among elements or subsystems of a given system and between the system and other systems in its environment, any system may be thought of as an "information-processing" system. Information-energy exchanged among the elements of a system, or transmitted from one system to another (as from teacher to pupil), may be described as "communication" or "information flow."

This concept of a "system" assumes: (1) an observable end product or "output" of the system, (2) produced by the system to fulfill some defined objective, (3) the output being postulated to be associated with certain necessary conditions or "inputs" to the system, and (4) there being some sort of mediation in the input-output flow of information within the system (i.e., orderly interaction or information flow among the system inputs, both internal and external, and the elements or subsystems comprising the system under consideration, such interaction being unique to the particular system and being controlled by identifiable, though modifiable, combinations and sequences of operating principles). The operating rules or controlling principles relative to this mediating functioning of the system usually must be *inferred*. They usually cannot be directly observed but are inferred from analysis of the observable inputs, outputs, concomitants, and known subsystems and their discernible interdependence.

It is our contention that the teacher may be conveniently described from the standpoint of both research and teacher education as such a "system." (Similarly, the pupil may be described as a system; and the teaching-learning process involving the teacher and pupil, or pupils, also may be defined in terms of systemic functioning.)

THE CONCEPT OF "INFORMATION"

In our model of teacher behavior which views the teacher as an information system, the term "information" is used to refer to any set of symbols that convey meaning. That is, information signifies something that is potentially subject to common identification by the source-transmitter (e.g., the teacher) and the receiver-destination (e.g., the pupil) of the information.

"Information," then, is used in this information system theory of instruction to refer to communicable facts, concepts, and rules that possess meaning for the pupil—thus making the pupil, as well as the teacher, necessarily an active and integral element of the communication process if it is to achieve its goals of both transmitting information and facilitating its integration into the information hierarchy of the pupil. Information as thus defined possesses meaning for the receiver-destination in the sense that the facts or rules communicated either (a) provide a meaningful context, or fit into some existing context possessed by the receiver-destination, and (b) provide associations and cues for their choice or selection upon need for retrieval for application to future behavior or future courses of action.

"Information processing," as this term is used in describing either the teacher or the pupil as an "information-processing system," refers to the selection, the preparation for transmission, and the forwarding or communication of some meaningful message.

Teacher information processing may be hypothesized to involve a five-phase sequence of activities engaged in by the teacher consisting of:

1. The sensing, identifying, and classifying of both internal (i.e., internal to the teacher) and environmental inputs;
2. The evaluating of possible courses of action in light of the pupil behavior domain involved, the content of the information to be communicated, the pupil behavior goal with respect to the activity of the moment, and the information form and channel consistent with the intended pupil use of the information;
3. The making of decisions by the teacher, involving the selecting of appropriate information content, appropriate media to facilitate learning, and appropriate transmission channels;
4. The programming, or the logical-psychological ordering and arranging of the intended information output (i.e., teacher behavior); and
5. The transmission of appropriate information via appropriate channels (i.e., teacher behavior) in order to assure receipt of the information by the pupil and to facilitate its integration into his behavioral background.

Communication of information by the teacher may take any one of several forms. It is especially important that this be observed, lest the reader perceive the "information system" theory of behavior and instruction as involving the transmission of facts alone. Instead, the transmission of information also may involve concepts and rules. And while the communication of facts, concepts, and rules may involve verbal symbols as in spoken or written language, it may be accomplished with a set of quantitative symbols. Or it may take the form of physical gestures, facial expressions, or personal-social behaving styles of the teacher. Or it may be effected by a demonstration (either in the limited sense that a chemistry experiment is demonstrated by a teacher, or from a broader point of view in which the individual teacher serves as a "model" whose behavior may be imitated by his pupils or students).

The information transmitted by a teacher also may be related to any of several kinds of content. It may have to do with cognitive-type materials (e.g., knowledge, concepts, etc., relating to some "subject matter" content). It may have to do with affective content (e.g., attitudes and values, temperamental-emotional characteristics, etc.). Or the information may have to do with psychomotor skills it is intended that the pupil acquire.

The purposes for which information is processed and communicated by the teacher also may vary. The information may serve the purpose simply of "reporting" as in the case of "news" that is printed or broadcast. The information may perform a direction-giving or a command and control function. The information may be intended to describe or to clarify some policy. It may be employed for the purpose of coordinating action that requires mutual exchange of information. It may be employed by the instructor simply to clarify issues or problems. It may be used to summarize or to classify facts or concepts that may be recombined in different forms to promote new discoveries.

It has been noted that in the teaching-learning process the immediate purpose for which information is processed and transmitted is to facilitate the acquisition of knowledge, understanding, skills, procedures, attitudes, etc., on the part of pupils. It should be kept well in mind, however, that simply because some particular item of information is transmitted, and even if it is effectively "received" by the pupil, this does not in itself imply acquisition of knowledge or skill. Such acquisition depends on the *active response* of the learner and on the existing conditions affecting the learner as an information-processing system when the information is received.

It also should be observed that the same information content, communicated by the teacher in the same way, may have different "meaning" for different pupils. The implication of such individual differences among the pupils who receive the information is that the teacher often must give attention to supplying preliminary information which will provide the necessary base and preparatory "set" from which to proceed.

Further description of the teacher as an information system will be omitted. Figure I provides a schematic representation of the teacher as an information-processing system, but no attempt will be made in the present statement to go into details that are either explicit or implied. However, it is important to note certain implications of this "information system" theory of teacher behavior for teacher education.

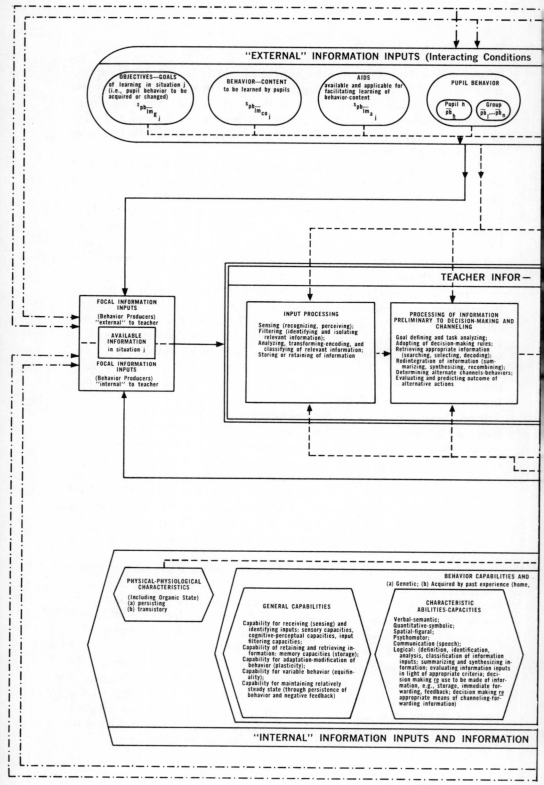

Teacher Information Processing System

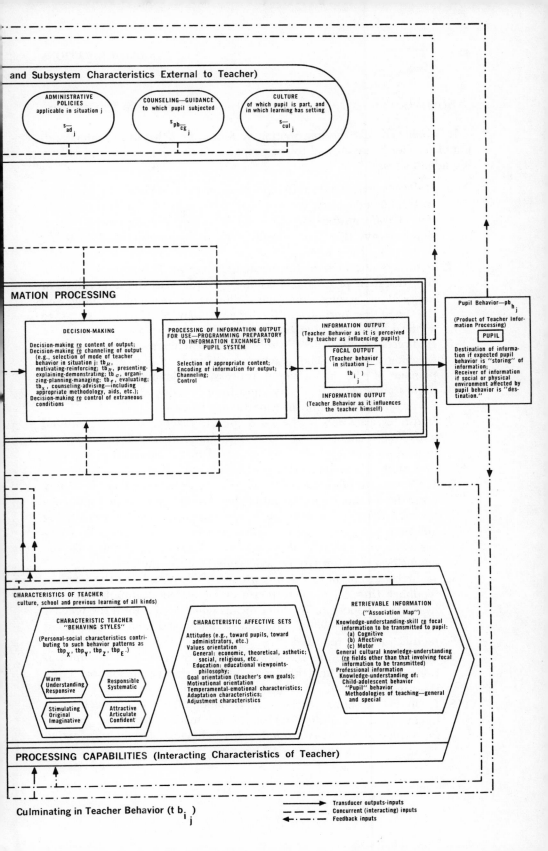

SOME IMPLICATIONS OF THE THEORY FOR TEACHER EDUCATION

It is believed that the information system approach to the understanding of teacher behavior and to the preparation of teachers has the following advantages;

1. It directs attention to the importance of the communication process, so teacher education courses may focus upon the important problem of transmitting cognitive, affective, and psychomotor information in ways that will maximize its understanding and facilitate its learning by students.

2. It directs attention to the "systemic" nature of instruction and of the education process as a whole; it emphasizes the importance of interactions among conditions influencing teaching-learning and the need for optimizing the organization of teaching so as to achieve better the objectives of instruction.

3. It directs attention to the role of the teacher as a coordinator of teaching-learning. The teacher is viewed as the organizer and planner of the instructional process, employing whatever techniques and media that may contribute best to achievement of the purposes of instruction in a particular situation.

4. It directs attention to the need for the teacher to be acquainted with the technology of education (i.e., with the principles of individual learning, with programmed instruction or auto-instruction, with educational data processing, etc.).

5. It directs attention to the teacher as a decision-maker. Not only must the teacher be cognizant of the various inputs which influence his own behavior, but he must recognize the need of considering alternate procedures and courses of action and making decisions regarding content as well as procedure in an effort to maximize the acquisition of information, or learning, by the pupil.

6. It directs attention to the importance of "feedback" to the teacher; feedback through pupil response and reactions, through tests and evaluative devices, or by other means which will inform the teacher of the effectiveness of procedures employed and permit their modification as required.

7. It directs attention to the interplay of instruction with administration, with counseling, and with other instructional-support functions in the over-all school or college system.

8. It directs attention to the several major channels of teacher behavior (i.e., the *motivating-reinforcing* teacher behavior, *presenting-explaining-demonstrating* teacher behavior; *planning-organizing*

teacher behavior; *evaluating* teacher behavior; and *counseling-guiding* teacher behavior).

9. It directs attention to the need for knowledge about learning aids and media and how to use them, and to the media and procedures best suited to each of the major classes of teacher behavior noted under 8 above.

10. It directs attention to the importance of the behaving styles of teachers (i.e., warm-understanding teacher behavior, responsible-systematic teacher behavior, stimulating-imaginative teacher behavior, etc.) in facilitating information transmittal and subsequent pupil learning.

11. It directs attention to the search for the most appropriate ways of transmitting various kinds of information with which the school is concerned (i.e., the appropriateness of different system techniques and learning aids for transmitting particular kinds of information, such as knowledge and understanding, psychomotor skills, attitudes, etc.).

12. It directs attention to information transmission that is organized to create an appropriate "set" or readiness for learning on the part of the pupil.

The above list is a partial one, but it will serve to illustrate the kinds of advantages that may accrue from turning attention to the information system nature of teacher behavior. . . .

3. Selected Concepts of Communication as a Basis for Studying Mental Health in the Classroom

Wilbert W. Lewis

One of the most serious obstacles to the investigation of mental health problems has been an absence of commonly accepted criteria by which change may be judged. Although concepts such as "repression," "withdrawal," and "denial" have been used with some success in describing persons who have serious problems of adjustment, they have proved to be inappropriate when used with those who are presumed to be normal or nearly so.

Reprinted with permission of the National Society for the Study of Communication from *The Journal of Communication*, 11: 157-162, September, 1961.

An area in which this difficulty is keenly felt at the present time is research on the mental health ramifications of classroom teaching procedures. Especially in the elementary grades, where the children are young and impressionable and their contact with one teacher is extensive, a relationship between a teacher's behavior and pupils' psychological well-being seems likely. The purposes of the present paper are (1) to analyze the communication process with a view to developing concepts relevant to investigations in mental health and (2) to discuss these concepts as they may apply to teacher-pupil interaction in a school classroom. The choice of communication as a major concept around which to focus descriptions of human interaction is an attempt to mitigate the valuing tendencies implicit in the concepts associated with mental health. The teacher-pupil interaction seems particularly amenable to description as a communication process, if the process is defined as one which includes exchange of feelings and attitudes as well as concepts and information.

A DEFINITION AND TWO ASSUMPTIONS

The definition of communication which this paper employs is at a rather high level of abstraction: *Communication is a process by which a person reduces the uncertainty about some state of affairs by the detection of cues which seem to him to be relevant to that state of affairs.* This statement does not specify the content of communication, the media through which it occurs, or even how many persons it involves. The intention is simply to indicate a general point of vantage for viewing human interaction.

An examination of two important assumptions implicit in this definition suggests some of the reasons that communication concepts may be useful in studying the effects of the teacher upon the mental health of her pupils. First, *the continuous flow of experience to which every individual is subjected is not inherently structured or meaningful, but is given meaning by the person who experiences it.* This statement does not imply the extreme subjectivist view that there is no reality except in the "mind," but it does recognize that meaning depends largely upon the personal interpretations which individuals give to "objective" events. It implies, too, that responses to incoming messages and the nature of outgoing messages can be used as the basis for judgments about personality processes in the participants. More specifically, predictions of future events reveal perceptions of past events which the pupil sees as similar to the event being predicted, and the way categories are used by an individual to classify events shows the subjective probabilities which he associates with the categories. In other words, communication reveals beliefs—beliefs about what the world, including oneself is "really" like—and beliefs in turn afford clues to mental health.

Second, *beliefs are constantly being tested by the stimuli an individual receives from the events in which he is a participant.* Thus, a belief is strengthened, modified, or rejected according to its usefulness in helping an individual "make sense" of the events in his life. This process is analogous to that of formulating hypotheses, testing them, and making appropriate revisions. Ideally one approaches psychological maturity by revising beliefs so that they fit reality, but actually most persons are not very precise in testing their personal belief systems.

As a means of studying mental health, a communication model has the merit of allowing us to conceptualize human interaction as an exchange of information relevant to personal belief systems and thus to infer segments of an individual's belief system. Whether the pupil is sending or receiving messages, his beliefs serve as a filter which structures his output of information and which governs his selective use of the information he receives. He responds not to the totality of available stimulation but to those cues or patterns of cues that he sees as relevant to his beliefs. Consequently, analyzing the functioning of beliefs during communication is a means of drawing inferences concerning changes in personality processes which are not accessible for direct observation.

Four Concepts of Communication

Any process extending through time is characterized by an integrity that analysis necessarily violates to some degree, and the present situation is no exception. An analysis simple enough to be workable is certain to neglect some of the important nuances of teacher-pupil interaction, but *receptiveness, accuracy, mobility,* and *responsiveness* are aspects of communication which are both generally important and specifically meaningful to the study of mental health in the classroom. This article is concerned primarily with the observation of these four aspects of communication rather than with their implications for mental health—a complex topic which is beyond the scope of this paper.

RECEPTIVENESS

The receptiveness with which we are concerned is the willingness to find out what another person thinks about a topic of mutual interest. A working knowledge of language and intact audio-perceptual mechanisms for both children and teachers are assumed.

At one level, receptiveness is reflected in one's tendency to remain silent while the other person is talking or thinking about what to say as contrasted with the practice of inundating the other person in a steady stream of words. (It would be naïve not to qualify this assertion, however, since silence may be the result of an active fantasy life rather than of a desire to listen.) Verbal gambits such as inquiring into another's thoughts or feelings about a topic, if accompanied by reduced verbal output, ordinarily indicate an interest in receiving communication from another. In addition, nonverbal cues, such as the direction of one's gaze, facial expression, and bodily posture, enhance the perception that someone is ready to listen. Although these considerations may seem superficial, the absence of observable signs that one is ready to listen may prevent the conversational partner from speaking. The continuation of receptiveness, once the initial attitude has been established, also deserves mention. The recipient of a message emits cues which the communicator may use to determine whether his message is being attended to. Whether the recipient yawns or smiles, for example, may materially influence the communicator in deciding whether to continue or to stop.

In summary, receptiveness includes behaviors that convey to another person the information, "Lines of communication are open between us; I am interested in hearing what you have to say."

ACCURACY

A second aspect of recipient behavior has to do with the accuracy shown in the reception of a message. Here perfection, because of the semantic problems inherent in encoding and decoding, is impossible, but both the degree and the nature of inaccuracy have implications for mental health.

Since accuracy refers to the active use of the information received, it goes beyond receptiveness, which is a relatively passive condition. Although ultimately the accuracy of received communication has a subjective referent—some idea or feeling inside the sender—the receiver's understanding of the idea or feeling can be tested. Can he restate the message in a way which the sender considers satisfactory? Can he predict correctly what the sender will do? Can he do what the sender requests? Can he make the same guess concerning a third party as that which the sender has made?

Accuracy of received communication thus refers to how the receiver uses information relative to a sender's meaning. The receiver may believe he understands the arrangement of events in a concept used by the sender, but the criterion of accuracy requires that understanding be validated through "correct" predictions of additional verbalizations or other behaviors of the sender.

MOBILITY

Mobility refers to the tendency of a sender to move up and down the abstraction ladder in his attempts at communication. If a teacher speaks of both courtesy and such specific acts as opening the door for another person, she is demonstrating mobility in her communication. On the other hand, if she relates "courtesy" to "kindness" and other abstractions, or if she refers only to behaviors, "Jimmy, open the door for Sally," etc., she is nonmobile, although at different levels of abstraction. The inclusion of elements representing different levels of abstraction is one means of providing "redundance." A speaker cannot assume that his listener categorizes a given set of events in the same way that he himself does, nor can he assume that the listener imposes the same conceptual significance on a particular event. A speaker should explicitly bridge the gap between concept and event in order to maximize the probability that the message will have approximately the same meaning for the listener as for himself. The use of mobility may show only that the speaker is a skillful communicator, but it may also serve as a datum for an inference relevant to the mental health of the individual. It seems likely that a person who speaks primarily to reduce tension or to combat an inner disturbance will demonstrate less mobility than will one who is simply attempting clear communication. In other words, a consistent reduction in mobility suggests a negatively valued inference in regard to the mental health aspects of the communicator's behavior, whereas increases in mobility have positive implications.

RESPONSIVENESS

A second condition of sending behavior with implications for mental health is the sender's "taking audience reaction into consideration." The information concept of feedback is relevant here. Both speaker and listener are involved, for responsiveness designates both the corrective information which the receiver of the message emits and the sender's adjustments to that information. The relevance of the sender's message to the receiver's need for information can be judged by the responses of the receiver as he "listens"—an affirmative nod, a glassy stare, or a shift to another topic as soon as the sender pauses for breath. A teacher demonstrates responsiveness to this kind of feedback when she alters the pace of the lesson, makes a digression from the lesson plan, or otherwise responds to expressed needs by altering the pattern of communication.

Responsiveness thus pertains to modifications in the pattern of the sender's behavior which reflect his detection of changing interests, feelings, abilities, etc., in the receiver. These modifications may be looked upon as an interaction of the sender's intent to make the message as clear as possible and the cues from receivers indicating that the message was not clear.

IMPLICATIONS FOR RESEARCH

Although these four concepts relevant to communication have been stated rather positively, they presently have only heuristic value and are subject to revision or rejection depending on their utility. The next step is to create and to test hypotheses utilizing the communication approach to the study of mental health in the classroom. The possible significance of such an investigation is beyond dispute, and the writer believes that this method of study is an improvement over one which borrows concepts of abnormality from clinical psychology.

Possible interrelationships of the four concepts also deserve experimentation because of their implications for both teaching and the theory of communication. For example, receptiveness in a teacher may be accompanied by accuracy in understanding the points of view which children express, mobility in sending may have a positive relationship to accuracy in receiving, and mobility and responsiveness in the teacher may have effects on mobility and responsiveness in students.

The most difficult work remains. Communication-oriented concepts must be translated into operational definitions, hypotheses must be developed, and methods of observation must be evolved. Nevertheless, the communication approach seems promising, and the writer hopes that this article may serve as a first step toward the asking of some answerable questions about mental health in our school classrooms.

4.   An Analysis of Classroom Patterns of Communication

W. W. Lewis, John M. Newell and John Withall

The purpose of this paper is to (a) describe the origins and use of a set of observational categories for studies of interaction in the classroom and (b) report the sensitivity of these categories to the classroom com-

Reprinted with permission of authors and publisher: Lewis, W. W., Newall, J. M., and Withall, J. "An Analysis of Classroom Patterns of Communication." *Psychological Report*, 1961, 9: 211-219.

munication behaviors of two instructors teaching according to two predetermined instructional methods or foci. Although a number of systems for this purpose are already available (1, 3, 6), they are structured around concepts like dominative-integrative or teacher-centered versus learner-centered behavior. The studies being described here are rather specifically oriented toward the description of classroom interaction as a process of communication acts (4).

Communication acts are defined broadly to include the exchange of information, directions, concepts, or evaluations between two or more persons. It seemed desirable to develop a set of categories that would be primarily descriptive rather than evaluative. The descriptive categories were intended to minimize the degree of inference by an observer in recording the interaction in a classroom. At the same time it seemed necessary to use a set of categories comprehensive enough to cover any communication act likely to occur in a classroom. The Bales Interaction Process Analysis categories (2) seemed to hold some promise in meeting those needs. However, the use of the Bales categories in recording behavior in elementary and secondary school classrooms suggested some serious limitations, primarily the large proportion of responses being categorized as "asking for orientation" and "giving orientation." In order to make finer discriminations in this behavioral setting, new categories were added and some of the old ones were dropped or redefined. Following several revisions, 13 categories were selected. There is no relationship implied among any of the 13 categories except that they are mutually exclusive. That is, there is no continuum, such as "asking—giving" or "thinking—feeling," underlying the numbering of the categories.

In order to test the usefulness of the observational categories in discriminating activity characteristics in classrooms, two small experimental classes, each with a different instructor, were formed. The general objective of both classes was to help classroom teachers understand children's behavior. However, each instructor intentionally used a different instructional method to achieve his objective. The observational categories were used systematically with both classes to see what differences could be demonstrated.

Method

THE INSTRUCTIONAL APPROACHES

The two instructional methods will be referred to as (a) the case-study method and (b) the student-centered method. The stated intent of the instructor using the case-study method was to employ case studies, done by the students in his class, to develop and elaborate concepts relevant to an understanding of children's behavior in the school classroom. The initiation of activities, pacing, and evaluation of learning experiences in the case-study approach were controlled largely by the instructor. He assigned readings, case histories, and a final examination to the students in his group.

The stated intent of the instructor using the student-centered method was to provide an opportunity for his students to discuss their pupils, themselves, or issues of importance to them personally. He attempted to respond at a level of personal significance to whatever material was raised spontaneously by members of the class. Topics for discussion, readings, and tasks related to the discussions were not assigned by the instructor using the student-centered method, but were left to the initiative of the individual students.

The students in the two groups were all enrolled for credit in a graduate course at the University of Wisconsin dealing with guidance practices in the public school. All were employed full time as teachers or administrators in a suburban community of Madison, Wisconsin. In one group there were 6 elementary teachers, 2 elementary principals, and 1 high school teacher; 3 men and 6 women. In the other group were 4 elementary teachers, 1 music teacher, 1 elementary principal, and 1 high school teacher; 2 men and 5 women. The students had been assigned to one of the two instructional groups by shuffling their course cards and dealing the cards into two piles. The two groups met in separate rooms at the same building, at the same hour, and for the same length of time. There were 14 meetings, each lasting approximately 150 minutes, for each of the groups.

THE OBSERVATIONAL CATEGORIES

The 13 categories are designed to be applied during the process of communication in the classroom, either in a live observation of an actual classroom, or to tape recordings of classroom behavior. An observer is asked to make a series of judgments about the dominant intent of the initiator of each act of communication. He is asked to project himself into the role of the recipient of the communication act and decide what was the dominant intent of the person speaking. Both verbal and non-verbal aspects (where detectable) of the behavior are used in making the judgment. An arbitrary time interval, 10 sec., is used as the unit of behavior which is judged by the observer.

A brief description and illustrations of each of the categories follow.

1. *Asks for Information.* An act having as its major intent the eliciting of a response which presumably may be evaluated for accuracy, either by objective operation, general acceptance, or reference to an authority (such as the teacher or a text book).

Examples.—Asks question about content of lesson; asks for report; asks for confirmation of response previously given; asks for repetition of what has been said; offers incomplete statement with the expectation that another will finish it; asks any question in such a way as to imply that there is a "right" answer; asks name of an object; asks for definition; asks for enumeration.

2. *Seeks or Accepts Direction.* An act implying willingness to consider suggestion or direction from another, or if suggestion or direction has already been offered, an act or statement indicating compliance.

Examples.—Asks how to begin an assigned task; asks what to do next; asks which procedure to follow; asks for volunteers; follows directions of another; agrees with suggestion or direction; indicates that direction will be followed at some future time; asks for permission for a specific act.

3. *Asks for Opinion or Analysis.* An act intended to elicit problem-structuring statements from others, either affective-evaluative or cognitive-interpretive.

Examples.—Asks for opinion, wish, feeling, belief, or preference; asks for evaluation of behavior; requests for interpretation or explanation of some phenomena without implying that there is one "correct" answer; requests for elaboration or examples of a concept; requests for statement of relationships between concepts; non-directive leads or questions to facilitate self-exploration by others; reflection of feeling or alternate meaning of what another has said for purposes of clarifying meaning; asks for interpretation of another's personal experience (as distinguished from asking for a report of experience).

4. *Listens.* Five seconds or more out of any 10-sec. interval where an individual is listening or attending to another individual is given a listening score (less than 5 sec. is not scored).

5. *Gives Information.* An act intended to convey, confirm, or infirm "facts" which may be evaluated by objective operation, general acceptance, or reference to an authority.

Examples.—Giving data such as names, dates, speed, capacity, etc. relevant to a topic under discussion; attempting to provide information requested by another; confirming the accuracy of others' responses; denying the accuracy of others' responses; gives report on what one has seen, heard, read, etc.; gives repetition of what has been said; names object; gives definition; gives enumeration.

6. *Gives Suggestion.* An act intended to structure action or indicate alternatives for others which, at the same time, implies autonomy for others by providing more than one alternative or allowing for refusal.

Examples.—Offering a procedure in a tentative way; offering two or more procedures, leaving choice to others; stating a preferred behavior without indicating that the preference holds for others; volunteers own services.

7. *Gives Direction.* An act intended to structure some action of another in which compliance seems to be taken for granted, or in which non-compliance would probably elicit some form of disapproval.

Examples.—Calling class to attention; calling attention to some detail; getting attention of another by calling his name; routine administrative directions or orders; stating expectation of behavior to be followed; setting limits on behavior; stating consequences of behavior; granting a request; denying a request.

8. *Gives Opinion.* An act intended to structure or give direction to a topic under discussion by use of speaker's internal, private, or unstated criteria.

Examples.—States opinions, wish, feeling, belief, or preference; makes a statement or asks a question reflecting a personal point of view; verbalizes introspective processes; gives criticism or evaluation of a behavior or concept; agrees or disagrees with opinion voiced by another.

9. *Gives Analysis.* An act intended to structure or give direction to a topic under discussion by reference to a frame of reference or a criterion that is explicitly stated and external to speaker's personal point of view.

Examples.—Gives interpretation or explanation of some phenomena without implying that it is the only "correct" way of looking at it; elaborates or gives examples of a concept; points out relationships between examples and concepts or between two or more concepts; points out discrepancies between concept and examples; proposes hypothetical example or case to illustrate a point or raise a question.

10. *Shows Positive Feeling.* An act which implies positive evaluation of some behavior or interaction in the observational field, regardless of whether the referent is the self or some other person.

Examples.—Any friendly act or overture, such as greeting or responding to a greeting; praising, approving, encouraging, rewarding, or showing active attention to others; sharing or sympathizing with others, expressions of satisfaction, enjoyment, or relief; joking or laughing "with" others.

11. *Inhibits Communication.* An act which implies unwillingness or inability to engage in the ongoing process of communication, regardless of whether the act stems from negative evaluation, internal te on, or disinterest.

Examples.—Does not respond when response would ordinarily be expected; is cool, aloof, or disinterested in what is going on; is inattentive to or ignores a question or request; does not comply with a request; shows tension by blocking, "fright," etc.; accepts criticism or rebuff without reply.

12. *Shows Negative Feeling.* An act which implies active negative evaluation of some behavior or interaction in the observational field, regardless of whether the referent is the self or some other person.

Examples.—Disapproving, disparaging, threatening, discouraging another's behaviors; lowering another's status; defending or asserting self; poking fun, belittling, or laughing "at" others; expressing fear, rage, hostility, disappointment, discouragement, displeasure, unhappiness, etc.

13. *No Communication.*[1] The behavior occurring in the classroom is not relevant to teacher-pupil communication during a 10-sec. interval.

PROCEDURE IN APPLYING CATEGORIES

The observer makes his judgments sequentially, as they occur in the classroom interaction, assigning at least one category score to each 10-sec. interval within a predetermined length of time. When there is a shift in the inferred intent of the communicator within any given 10-sec. interval, the interval is assigned an additional category score, or more if necessary. After the observer completes his recording for a time sample, he tabulates the number of occurrences of each category and makes a summary of the communication pattern during the time of observation in the form of frequencies for each category.

The observational categories were used on selected samples from both instructional approaches. Sessions 3, 7, and 12 were arbitrarily designated as early, middle, and late segments of the course. Within each of these sessions, for each instructional approach, a 24-min. sample was taken at a point beginning 10 min. after the session started, and another 24-min. sample was taken at a point beginning 10 min. after a coffee break midway through the session. Following this procedure, each 48-min. sample is used to represent the communication pattern in the early, middle, and the late stages of each groups development. The observers worked from tape recordings which were collected routinely in all of the group meetings.

Two independent category records were made on each time sample, one on the communication acts of the instructor in the class, the other on the communication acts of the students in the class. In this way, three records of category frequencies, representing early, middle, and late sessions, were collected for each instructor, and three records of category frequencies were collected for the students as a group in each class.

An estimate of inter-judge reliability was obtained by having two observers independently categorize 24-min. samples from tape recordings of three different instructors, the two reported on here and one other. The frequency of use of the 13 categories was tabulated for each in-

---

[1] Since the completion of this study, an additional category, 14, Perfunctory Agreement or Disagreement, has been added.

structor. The agreement between the two observers, quantified as rank-order correlation coefficients for each of the three instructors, was .99, .97, and .98.

ANALYSIS OF THE DATA

An attempt to assess the overall similarity of the communication patterns of the two instructors, between sessions for the same instructor and between instructors for the same session, was carried out by comparing the ranking of category use by each instructor. Each session was treated separately to establish ranking of categories. The rankings were compared by means of Spearman's *rho* (5, pp. 202-213). Since the frequency of occurrence of some of the 13 categories was not large, the rank-order correlation coefficients for the instructors are based on categories $1 + 5$, 3, 4, $6 + 7$, 8, and 9, and for the students on categories 1, $2 + 3$, 4, 5, $6 + 7$, 8, 9, and 10.

TABLE 1

RHOS SHOWING SIMILARITY OF CATEGORY FREQUENCIES IN EARLY, MIDDLE
AND LATE SESSIONS FOR CASE-STUDY GROUP

Sessions	Instructor	Students
Early-Middle	.94*	.96**
Early-late	.89*	.82*
Middle-late	.94*	.90**

*$p < .05$ **$p < .01$

Table 1 shows high inter-session consistency for the case-study instructor, indicating little change in his overall pattern of communication from session to session. Table 2 shows low inter-session consistency for the student-centered instructor, suggesting that his pattern of communication, at least in its broad outlines, was somehow different in the early

TABLE 2

RHOS SHOWING SIMILARITY OF CATEGORY FREQUENCIES IN EARLY, MIDDLE
AND LATE SESSIONS FOR STUDENT-CENTERED GROUP

Sessions	Instructor	Students
Early-middle	.26	.73*
Early-late	.56	.96**
Middle-late	.81	.73*

*$p < .05$ **$p < .01$

TABLE 3

RHOs SHOWING SIMILARITY OF CATEGORY FREQUENCIES BETWEEN
GROUPS DURING THE SAME SESSION

Sessions	Instructor	Students
Early	.89*	.89**
Middle	.49	.85*
Late	.24	.78*

*$p < .05$ **$p < .01$

session from what it was in the middle session, and that the late session
was still different from either the early or middle one. The data reported
in Table 3 confirm the impression of change in the pattern of communication by the student-centered instructor. In the early session, both instructors were alike in their communication patterns but they became
progressively dissimilar in the middle and late phases of the group
meetings.

A comparison of communication patterns of students in the two groups
was also based on ranking of category use. For students, the *rhos*, also
reported in Tables 1, 2, and 3, do not reflect any change. Each group was
alike in use of communication categories in early, middle, and late sessions,
and the groups were similar to each other in each of the three sessions.

Differences of content in the communication patterns of the two groups
were analyzed by comparing the proportion of the total responses for
each category during a single session. The third and twelfth sessions
were arbitrarily designated as the early and late samples in the series of
meetings. Categories for which significant differences in proportions were

TABLE 4

SIGNIFICANT DIFFERENCES IN USE OF CATEGORIES BY INSTRUCTORS
IN EARLY AND LATE SESSIONS (PROPORTION OF TOTAL RESPONSES)

	Case-Study	Student-Centered	Z	p
Early Session				
Listening	.60	.73	4.41	<.01
Asking For and Giving				
Information	.16	.08	3.09	<.01
Giving Analysis	.15	.09	2.33	<.05
Late Session				
Listening	.58	.71	3.37	<.01
Giving Directions and				
Suggestions	.09	.01	4.64	<.01
Giving Opinion	.03	.10	3.86	<.01
Giving Analysis	.10	.02	3.48	<.01

TABLE 5

SIGNIFICANT DIFFERENCES IN USE OF CATEGORIES BY STUDENTS
IN EARLY AND LATE SESSIONS (PROPORTION OF TOTAL RESPONSES)

	Case-Study	Student-Centered	Z	p
Early Session				
Listening	.33	.16	5.28	<.01
Giving Opinion	.16	.28	3.80	<.01
Late Session				
Listening	.28	.14	5.12	<.01
Giving Information	.24	.52	8.20	<.01

obtained between the case-study and the student-centered classes are reported in Table 4 for the instructors and in Table 5 for the students. The categories that are not included in the two tables are those in which the proportion of responses did not differ significantly or in which the category's proportion of the total number of responses for the session was so small that differences appeared to be spurious.

Table 4 shows that, although both instructors spent over half of their time listening, in both sessions sampled, the student-centered instructor spent a significantly greater proportion of his time listening than did the other instructor, both in the early and late sessions. He also gave more opinions in the late session. The case-study instructor asked for and gave more information in the early session, gave more directions and suggestions in the late session, and gave more analysis in both sessions.

The responses of the students in both groups, in Table 5, seem to suggest again that differences between instructors are more marked than differences among their students. For example, the proportion of students' listening responses in both sessions simply mirrors the greater verbal activity of the case-study instructor on both occasions.

DISCUSSION

The two procedures used in analyzing observational data on the two instructional groups, namely, (a) ranking category usage in each group and (b) proportional usage of each category by both groups, reflect expectations based on the stated intent of the instructors. The case-study instructor intended to structure the interaction of his group around the analysis of material collected by his students on children in their classrooms. The student-centered instructor's intent was to pursue the personal meaning of whatever questions were raised spontaneously by members of his class.

The analysis of broad communication patterns showed that both instructors started out in about the same way, and that the case-study instructor continued the same pattern into middle and late sessions of the group meetings. The student-centered instructor progressively modified his pattern of communication through the middle and late sessions. No such change was noticeable in the broad communication patterns of the students in either group. Another method of analysis of the communication categories indicated more specifically some of the differences between the two groups. While both groups were in fact "discussion" groups, as indicated by the consistent categorization of over half of both instructors' behaviors as listening, the student-centered instructor did more listening, in both early and late sessions, than the case-study instructor. The higher level of verbal activity by the case-study instructor and perhaps his concern with the cognitive structuring of the discussions, are shown in his more frequent use of the categories of asking for and giving information, giving directions and suggestions, and giving analysis. A clue to the nature of the changing behavior of the student-centered instructor is given in the difference between the two instructors in the late session that was not present in the early session. The student-centered instructor gave more opinions than the case-study instructor, and more opinions than he himself had given in the early session, which suggests that he was moving out of the role of discussion "leader" as the sessions progressed and into the role of "participant," while the case-study instructor was maintaining his role of moderator or director of the discussion throughout the sessions. There is very little evidence of differences between the two groups of students, or of change by students within either group, that cannot be interpreted as a reflection of differing levels of verbal activity of the instructor in the group.

The 13 observational categories seem to be useful in making discriminations between instructional groups in which it may be presumed that different patterns of communication are occurring. The two methods of analyzing data based on the observations, (a) looking at relative use of all categories and (b) comparisons of use of each category, suggest interpretations that are consistent with each other and that are consistent with the intent of each of the instructors. The next step in the use of the categories is to apply them to undergraduate courses in teacher education where the method of instruction is intentionally varied from one class to another.

SUMMARY

This is a report on the development of a set of observational categories for the study of classroom interaction and on the reliability of these categories in describing the classroom communication behaviors of two instructors teaching according to two predetermined and describable instructional foci. The study was conceived within the framework of viewing classroom interaction as a series of communication acts, verbal and non-verbal, between teacher and learners.

REFERENCES

1. ANDERSON, H. H., & BREWER, H. M. Studies of teachers' classroom personalities: I. Dominative and socially integrative behavior of kindergarten teachers. *Appl. Psychol. Monogr.*, 1945, No. 6.
2. BALES, R. F. *Interaction process analysis.* Cambridge, Mass.: Addison-Wesley, 1950.
3. FLANDERS, N. A. *Interaction analysis in the classroom: a manual for observers.* Univer. of Minnesota, College of Education, August, 1960.
4. LEWIS, W. W. Selected concepts of communication as a basis for studying mental health in the classroom. *J. Communication*, in press.
5. SIEGEL, S. *Nonparametric statistics for the behavioral sciences.* New York: McGraw-Hill, 1956.
6. WITHALL, J. The development of a technique for the measurement of social-emotional climate in classrooms. *J. Exp. Educ.*, 1947, 17, 347-361.

5.   Cybernetics, Information Theory and the Educative Process

C. Kyle Packer and Toni Packer

Norbert Wiener coined the word *cybernetics* to designate ". . . the entire field of control and communication theory, whether in the machine or in the animal. . . ."[1] This science and the closely related field of information theory have brought about a sharpening of concepts and rapid development of new ideas as well as a mushrooming of applications, usually in the direction of automation.

But do the concepts that are basic to cybernetics and to information theory have any relevance to education?

One might first think of automatic computing machines and of the fact

Reprinted with permission from *Teachers College Record*, 61:134-142, December, 1959.
[1] Wiener, Norbert. *Cybernetics* (Cambridge: Technology Press, M.I.T., and New York: John Wiley & Sons, Inc., 1948), p. 19.

that some theorists have attempted to draw parallels between these machines and the human brain. This sort of thing will not be attempted here. Rather, it will be suggested that certain concepts taken from cybernetics and from information theory do appear to have a relevance to the teaching-learning process. This is in the nature of a preliminary study which appears to show that further work in this field might bear fruit.

These concepts may bear on the teaching-learning process in several ways: (a) on our *theory* of the process; (b) on our *study* of the process—our experimentation; (c) on our *knowledge* of the process; and (d) on our *attitude* as participants in the process.

We shall take certain concepts singly, in so far as possible, and, though not attempting a survey of cybernetics and of information theory, try to explain the concepts and their potential significance.

FEEDBACK

Feedback is a term that antedates the term cybernetics. Classical examples of feedback are the governor of a steam engine (Watt, 1788) and the household thermostat. Essentially, including feedback in a system means that we use part of our output (the power of our steam engine or the heat of our furnace) to cause a change (in the flyballs of the governor or in the contacts of the thermostat) which, in turn, causes our system to stay within certain bounds.

To make this form of control clearer, contrast it with, say, an automatic washing machine. There is no control which judges the performance (in terms of cleanliness) and determines whether to continue or to stop the washing process. We set the controls according to our intentions. We must then judge the results and reset the controls if necessary. We, that is, are the means by which feedback does in some measure occur. Thus with a push-button radio, we can set the push button to bring in rather accurately a certain station. When we want that station we push that button. Since there is no feedback by which the actual performance of the radio changes in any manner the setting, no further change in setting will occur. If we wish to tune the station better, we have to do it, perhaps at the same time recalibrating our push button.

The very usefulness of the push-button radio, however, shows that this method of control is quite satisfactory in certain systems.

Wiener has cited a dramatic example of feedback in the control system of an elevator. The obvious conclusion of what is essential in such a system very well illustrates the principle of feedback:

It is important that the release for opening the door be dependent on the fact that the elevator is actually at the door; otherwise something might have detained it, and the passenger might step into the empty shaft. This control of a machine on the basis of its *actual* performance rather than its *expected* performance is known as *feedback. . . .*[2]

Immediately preceding this example, Wiener states this generalization:

For any machine subject to a varied external environment to act effectively it is necessary that the information concerning the results of its own action be furnished to it as a part of the information on which it must continue to act.[3]

Tustin, using the familiar thermostat as an illustration, contrasts a feedback loop with an open control sequence, by considering the placement of the thermostat in one case indoors, and in the other outdoors.[4] In the open control sequence, with the thermostat outside, the room temperature may not stay within the desired range. The two systems may be diagrammed as in Figures 1 and 2.

FIGURE 1

Open Control Sequence

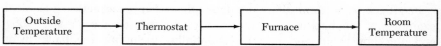

Feedback, diagrammed in Figure 2, shows a circularity which may be described as its characteristic feature.

FIGURE 2

Feedback Loop

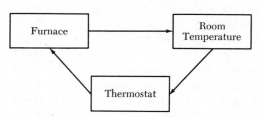

It would appear that feedback, especially in the light of Wiener's generalization quoted above, may be a concept useful to a theory of the

[2] Norbert Wiener, *The Human Use of Human Beings,* Rev. Ed. (Boston: Houghton-Mifflin, 1954), p. 24.

[3] Wiener, *op. cit.,* p. 24.

[4] Arnold Tustin, "Feedback," in *Automatic Control,* by the editors of *Scientific American* (New York: Simon & Schuster, 1955), pp. 11-13.

teaching-learning process. Clearly the learner needs information concerning the results of his behavior furnished to him as part of the information on which he continues to act. It is not enough that he *intended* to act thus; he needs to know how he *actually* performed.

This difference between the intended pattern of performance and the actual pattern of performance becomes a new input which changes both the amount and the direction characteristics of the pattern of performance so that it approximates more closely the pattern desired.[5]

The feedback principle reveals the kind of information needed for improved performance even more explicitly than does the principle of "immediate knowledge of results." Not only the correctness or incorrectness, but the deviation, the amount and direction of error, is essential to the system involving feedback.

There are, indeed, cases in which the knowledge of results implies the amount and direction of corrective action, but it is only this implied information which makes feedback successful, not merely the correct model itself. It is thus clear that marking, grading, testing, and so on are rather poor feedback designs in the teaching-learning system.

We have spoken only of the learner, but the concept of the teaching-learning process which has been accepted as the framework for these ideas from cybernetics implies a close link between teacher and learner. This will be referred to later, but here, in relation to feedback, it should be emphasized that the teacher is often the "mechanism" by which the feedback loop is completed.

We are thus contrasting a system which might be diagrammed as in Figure 3 or Figure 4 with the system shown in Figure 5.

FIGURE 3

Open Control Sequence in Main and Subsystems

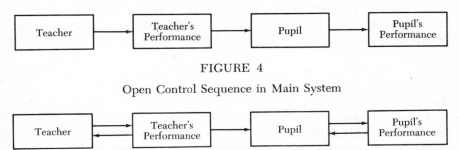

FIGURE 4

Open Control Sequence in Main System

That is to say, in a system involving feedback (Figure 5) the pupil's performance is taken as part of the information on which the teacher

[5] Wiener, *Cybernetics*, p. 13.

FIGURE 5

Feedback Loop in Main and Subsystems

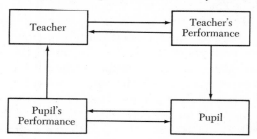

continues to act, and some of this information, coming back to the pupil, is the difference between the pupil's actual performance and the given pattern.

The role of information and messages is the very heart of cybernetics, for as Wiener states,

> Control . . . is nothing but the sending of messages which effectively change the behavior of the recipient.
>
> It is this study of messages, and in particular of the effective messages of control, which constitutes the science of *Cybernetics*. . . .[6]

And in referring to the link between communication and control, Wiener emphasizes that feedback is essential, for effective control necessitates our receiving messages that our orders have been received, understood, and obeyed.[7]

Without here discussing control or degree of control in the teacher-learner relationship, the need for these return messages in this relationship is patently clear. Certain examples of bad teaching—from emotional outbursts such as "That's the third time he's done these problems and he still hasn't solved them right!" to the almost emotionless ramblings of the absent-minded professor in the lecture hall—show that basically we realize that complete lack of feedback results in a poor teaching-learning situation.

Feedback, in its very simplest form, may be a sort of right or wrong criticism which leaves the figuring out of the pattern to the learner. Parental do's and don'ts may function at this rather simple level. The child may, of course, be getting incidentally other clues which do facilitate his learning. This predisposition to learn is not an in-built characteristic of machines, however, and Wiener has contrasted systems utilizing the

---

[6] Wiener, *The Human Use of Human Beings* (Boston: Houghton-Mifflin, 1950), pp. 8-9.

[7] See Wiener, *The Human Use of Human Beings,* 1954, p. 16.

simple feedback of the control engineers with systems constructed on the basis of his more generalized conception of feed-back:

If . . . the information which proceeds backward from the performance is able to change the general method and pattern of performance, we have a process which may well be called learning.[8]

Perhaps we could contrast the controlling methods and teaching methods by contrasting feedback of the right-wrong, do-don't type with feedback which gives information as to how the performance could be modified so as to achieve the correct performance.

Conditions may be such that feedback causes oscillation or "hunting," and a breakdown of the system.[9] This may well have a parallel in certain teacher-pupil situations which result in poorer pupil performance, but these considerations will not be elaborated in this discussion.

Some guideposts to the further study of feedback are provided by both Nagel[10] and Tustin,[11] and we may apply their suggestions to the teacher-pupil situation in somewhat the following way: We need to know how to measure performance or to compare it to some standard and, in a sufficiently short time to be effective, alter our methods so as to effect a change in the conditions under which the pupil or student is performing. We must know how to transmit information effectively, know the conditions under which breakdown may occur, and develop ways to predict outcomes in order to prevent such oscillatory behavior from developing.

"Bits" of Information, or Halving Uncertainty

Modern digital computers operate on the binary number system, a number system based on two rather than on the customary ten. In information theory too the binary digit has become the essential unit; the term binary digit being contracted to the word *bit*, which is defined precisely so as to provide an exact standard with which to measure the amount—not the quality—of information. Essentially, if there exists uncertainty and we receive information which *halves* that uncertainty, we have received one *bit* of information.

The nurse's first remark to the nervous father waiting outside the delivery room reduces his uncertainty by one-half. Of the two possibilities, a boy or a girl, her remark that "It's a boy" halves the uncertainty, thus

---

[8] Wiener, *The Human Use of Human Beings*, 1954, p. 61.
[9] Wiener, *Cybernetics*, p. 14.
[10] Ernest Nagel, "Self-Regulation," in *Automatic Control*, by the editors of *Scientific American* (New York: Simon & Schuster, 1955), pp. 3-4.
[11] Tustin, *op. cit.*, p. 14.

providing one *bit* of information.* Of course this is a simplified view of
the situation for the purpose of an example. Other uncertainties exist for
the nervous father, and other information is contained in the nurse's
remark. Her statement tells that the birth process is complete, her manner
may show that all is well, and so on.

In this example, halving the uncertainty made for complete certainty.
This is the unusual case. If one hundred possibilities exist, information
reducing the uncertainty to fifty would convey one *bit* of information, but
would not provide complete certainty. Thus if we know that something
appears in a 100-page book, the statement that it is on a right-hand page
provides one *bit* of information.

Although we may not be in position to measure precisely the amount
of information contained in each statement we make, the concept of
reducing uncertainty is a useful one in a theory of the teaching-learning
process. For the process of teaching and of learning is a process of
reducing uncertainty. Furthermore, it will be clear that in order to reduce
uncertainty surely and efficiently, the teacher must know some of the
uncertainties in the minds of students, know the subject well enough to
differentiate among the set of possible messages which includes the misconceptions, and have the skill to communicate in such a manner as to
reduce these uncertainties.

These three factors already have been given attention by skilled
teachers. Certain features can be brought out in the light of the concepts
taken from information theory. First of all, no matter how well organized
a certain body of knowledge is, the uncertainties to be considered are
primarily those of the student. Ashby states that ". . . the act of 'communication' necessarily implies the existence of a *set* of possibilities, i.e.,
more than one. . . ."[12] Further:

> . . . we must give up thinking . . . about "this message." We must become scien-
> tists, detach ourselves, and think about "people receiving messages." And this
> means that we must turn our attention from any individual message to the set of
> all the possibilities.[13]

The fact that two and two are four seems clear and definite, and may be
communicated and explained by a few well-chosen examples. However,
if one is aware of the need to know the uncertainties in the pupils' minds,
one should observe carefully the various thrusts, guesses, and inaccuracies
made by the pupils. The pupil must be given ample chance to express his
own thinking, not for grading or marking, but so that the teacher gets
information on the pupil's uncertainties in order to reduce them.

* The logarithmic relation of uncertainty to possibility is seen in the fact that *one*
possibility means *no* uncertainty: the logarithm of one is zero.

[12] W. Ross Ashby, *An Introduction to Cybernetics* (London: Chapman & Hall,
Ltd.; New York: John Wiley & Sons, 1956), p. 123.

[13] *Ibid.*, p. 124.

We do not, in fact, convey any information unless we reduce the uncertainty in the pupil's mind. Statements, no matter how well chosen, convey information only when they reduce uncertainties. That is to say, the information is not contained in the statement *per se*.

It is clear that a statement made to a class of thirty students conveys, in all likelihood, a different amount of information to each. A statement about a deciduous conifer would convey a different amount of information to those who knew something about conifers, but not about the larch, from that conveyed to those who knew about the larch.

The set of possible messages has variety to the extent that the elements of the set are distinguishable. However, the variety in a set is in part determined by the powers of discrimination of the observer.[14] The discriminations made by one pupil will not be the same as those made by another. Their two sets of discriminations being different means that different amounts of information are contained in what appears to be the same message. Some people seem to get more out of puns, poetic allusions, or coded messages than others do, owing to differences in their powers of discrimination. In certain cases, satisfactory communication may necessitate altering either the sender's message or the receiver's powers of discrimination.

This presents a different-from-the-usual picture of the communication problem in the teacher-learner situation. *The set of possible messages* is a different base of operation from *the message*. Clearly, then, the teacher's function includes knowing not merely the subject, or message, but the other possibilities—the set—from which this message is selected. The various responses and questions of pupils assume a new significance as clues to this set from which we are selecting our message.

This concept of the teacher's function may, in part, account for the fact that a scholar well versed in his field may be a poor teacher. If he is so oriented toward his subject matter and all of its ramifications that he fails to observe the uncertainties of his students, he may make statements which, though they would be highly informative to certain persons, only slightly reduce the uncertainties of his students and hence convey little information to them. On the other hand, knowing his field well, he may be in a better position to detect crucial uncertainties in his students' thinking and to reduce these with particularly apt and informative remarks.

Moreover, good teachers know that parroted statements do not prove learning. They contain little information because they do not reduce the teacher's uncertainty about the uncertainty of the pupil. In "Mending Wall," Robert Frost speaks of the proverbial masking understanding and preventing investigation:

[14] *Ibid.,* pp. 124-26.

He moves in darkness as it seems to me,
Not of woods only and the shade of trees.
He will not go behind his father's saying,
And he likes having thought of it so well
He says again, "Good fences make good neighbours." [15]

COUPLING

In the foregoing remarks on feedback and on *bits* of information, it is clearly evident that the teacher and the student are linked in a system in which reciprocal communication is of utmost importance.

This process has been described as "coupling." According to Ashby,

The coupling is of profound importance in science, for when the experimenter runs an experiment he is coupling himself temporarily to the system that he is studying.[16]

If this is true, then the teacher-student or teacher-class coupling is certainly a vital concept in studying the teaching-learning process.

When individual components are coupled, each affects the conditions or the input of the other. The resultant combination is a *new system*. The teacher-class system must be regarded as a system of coupled components, not as two unrelated systems operating by chance along the same time-scale.

This concept is useful in studying the teaching-learning process or in studying a particular teacher-class system. It should be helpful in reforming the teacher's attitudes toward his role in the classroom.

Coupling which results in a system in which each component affects the other is coupling with feedback. This is in contrast to the system in which one component dominates the other; that is, a system in which one component affects the other without the other affecting it.

Systems with interacting components were considered in the section on feedback. Again, in the discussion on bits of information, coupling was indicated to be essential to the communication process. There it was pointed out that reducing uncertainty of pupils involved getting information as to their uncertainties; that is, information must be communicated back and forth between teacher and student. Thus conceived, mistakes of the students are not unfortunate circumstances, but part of the information on which the teacher bases his teaching.

Further, the instructor who examines the total system in which he and the students are coupled will observe different relationships from those

---

[15] From *Complete Poems of Robert Frost*. Copyright, 1930, 1949, by Henry Holt and Company, Inc. By permission of publishers.

[16] Ashby, *op. cit.*, p. 48.

observed by the instructor who examines the students as an independent, non-coupled system. Observations on the teacher or parent as part of a coupled system have been made by Davis and Dollard,[17] based upon Hull's concept of "circular reinforcement,"[18] and by Porter.[19]

ENTROPY AND DISORGANIZATION

Here we shall be concerned with an apparent law with which human beings are battling in their whole efforts to achieve organization: the law that disintegration is constantly occurring. This is certainly true in any system of communication and should be taken for granted in the class-room. It may well bear on our attitudes as participants in the teaching-learning process, for, if nothing else, the expected can be approached with forethought and planning.

As long ago as 1824 Carnot showed that while the energy changes in a steam engine resulted in no loss of energy, they did result in a state in which that part of the energy of the steam going to the condenser was no longer available for work. The thermodynamic processes of even the most efficient heat engine result in this "unavailable energy." Clausius, in formulating mathematically the unavailable energy (1854) as the product of two factors, introduced the term "entropy" for the one factor, "tem-perature" being the other. It has been shown that entropy must either remain constant (and then only under theoretically ideal conditions) or increase, but it could never decrease. That is to say, the entropy of the universe increases, hence the universe is "dying" because more and more energy becomes unavailable. These ideas have been promulgated by and been the concern of many workers since the second law of thermody-namics was stated, following the work of Carnot.

At the risk of oversimplification, the essential ideas are that in practice all energy changes are accompanied by some energy being converted into heat. Further, heat cannot be transformed completely into other forms of energy, with the result that it becomes unavailable: it is and will re-main heat. Heat does not flow from a colder to a hotter body, but only in the reverse direction. As a result of all this, the temperature will tend to reach an average, a uniform level, a state of equilibrium. In terms of probability: the improbable, the ordered, states will disappear and only the more probable, random, or disordered states will persist in the

[17] Allison Davis and John Dollard, *Children of Bondage* (Washington, D. C.: American Council on Education, 1940), pp. 281–85.

[18] Clark Hull, Abstract of S-R Sessions of Monday-Night Group, 1938-39 (Institute of Human Relations, Yale University, 1939), p. 4. Mimeographed.

[19] E. H. Porter, Jr., *Therapeutic Counseling* (Boston: Houghton Mifflin Co., 1950), pp. 45-48.

universe. Entropy thus has been viewed as a measure of randomness, of disorganization, of the "most probable states."

Shannon and Wiener pointed out the similarity of the form of probability calculations of the information in a message with the formula for entropy as a measure of thermodynamical probability. Our approach in making analogies and comparisons should be cautious, but the relevancy to our undertaking crops out in many statements of authorities. For example, Wiener stated:

That information may be dissipated but not gained, is, as we have seen, the cybernetic form of the second law of thermodynamics.[20]

And again:

. . . we can show by general observations that phonetic language reaches the receiving apparatus with less over-all information than was originally sent, or at any rate with not more than the transmission system leading to the ear can convey; and that both semantic and behavior language contain less information still.[21]

This tendency toward deterioration is part and parcel of the act of communication; hence our concern in education. Wiener points out that

The commands through which we exercise our control over our environment are a kind of information which we impart to it. Like any form of information, these commands are subject to disorganization in transit. They generally come through in less coherent fashion and certainly not more coherently than they were sent. In control and communication we are always fighting nature's tendency to degrade the organized and to destroy the meaningful; the tendency, as Gibbs has shown us, for entropy to increase.[22]

Educators should not be surprised at this natural tendency being in action in the classroom. It falls largely to us to fight this; enlisting the aid of the pupil if we can, but in no case blaming him for this natural phenomenon.

The implication to education may be even broader:

As entropy increases, the universe, and all closed systems in the universe, tend naturally to deteriorate and lose their distinctiveness, to move from the least to the most probable state, from a state of organization and differentiation . . . to a state of chaos and sameness. . . . But . . . there are local enclaves whose direction seems opposed to that of the universe at large and in which there is a limited and temporary tendency for organization to increase.[23]

Education, in perpetuating the culture of the group, may tend to aid the increase of entropy—to increase, that is, the sameness of cultural patterns. However, to the extent that it provides centers for the birth and

[20] Wiener, *The Human Use of Human Beings,* 1954, p. 78.
[21] *Ibid.,* p. 81.
[22] *Ibid.,* p. 17.
[23] *Ibid.,* p. 12.

growth of these local enclaves in which organization and differentiation increase, it tends to cause entropy to decrease. The dual aspects of culture and of education—stability and change—have been pointed out by others.[24]

THE FIELD OF CYBERNETICS

In his work *On Human Communication*, Colin Cherry writes:

. . . it was apparent during the years immediately preceding the Second World War that the ideas, basic concepts, and methods of communication engineering were of wide applicability to other specialized branches of science. The lead was taken by Norbert Wiener who, with Rosenblueth, called attention to the great generality of the concept of *feedback*, which had been studied intensively by communication engineers for twenty years, and emphasized that this concept provided a useful relationship between biological and physical sciences. They referred to this general study as *cybernetics*. . . .[25]

Ashby states that

Cybernetics . . . treats, not things but *ways of behaving*. It does not ask "What *is* this thing?" but *"What does it do?"* . . . Cybernetics deals with all forms of behaviour in so far as they are regular, or determinate, or reproducible.[26]

One must consider whether the teacher-pupil or teacher-class system could be studied from the standpoint of cybernetics as has been suggested in this article. Surely, if such a study is to be fruitful, it must go beyond mere analogies. Further, a good theoretical groundwork should not be compromised by liberties taken to make "applications."

Ashby has described "two peculiar scientific virtues of cyberenetics" which may strengthen claims here presented:

One is that it offers a single vocabulary and a single set of concepts suitable for representing the most diverse types of system. . . .
The second . . . is that it offers a method for the scientific treatment of the system in which complexity is outstanding and too important to be ignored.[27]

There is no doubt that the systems with which we are concerned in the teaching-learning process are extremely complex. Clear concepts expressed in adequate terminology in a framework that is broad enough to encompass the complexity of the systems we study may be the result of the application of the methods and concepts of cybernetics to the teaching-learning process.

[24] Melville J. Herskovits, *Man and His Works* (New York: Alfred A. Knopf, 1952), pp. 40, 491.
[25] Colin Cherry, *On Human Communication* (Cambridge: Technology Press, M.I.T., and New York: John Wiley & Sons, 1957), p. 56.
[26] Ashby, *op. cit.*, p. 1.
[27] *Ibid.*, pp. 4-5.

6.   Nonverbal Communication in Teaching

Charles M. Galloway

1. TEACHER NONVERBAL COMMUNICATION *

Do teachers need to become cognizant of the consequences of their nonverbal messages in teacher-pupil interaction? Can teachers alter and modify the attitudes and meanings that they communicate nonverbally to pupils? Are we overlooking and minimizing the significance of nonverbal cues in our analysis of classroom interaction?

In a study of teacher nonverbal behavior at the elementary school level, teachers differed in their ability and inclination to be encouraging or inhibiting in their communicative contacts with pupils. The evidence suggested that the teachers who were most encouraging tended to reveal their interest in pupils through their listening behavior, their appropriate responsiveness, and their emotional support. Teachers who displayed inhibiting communicative behaviors were disinterested in pupil talk, were inconsistent in their behavioral responses to pupils, and were more likely to express disapproval in their nonverbal contacts with pupils.[1]

CLASSROOM INTERACTION

For the past several years an assumption supporting many studies in education has been that the pattern of communication existing in a classroom represents a major datum for research activity. Investigators have centered on the direction and amount of verbal communication occurring in the classroom between the teacher and pupils with supposedly little attention devoted to nonverbal communication. To be sure, major reasons for such a lack of concern with the nonverbal can be traced to the difficulties of categorization, the elusiveness of the meaning of nonverbal messages, and the seemingly subordinate function the nonverbal plays to the verbal in classroom settings.

Indeed, observational procedures that provide faultless descriptions of verbal interaction have not been fully developed and such research needs to continue. For these reasons and perhaps more, the nonverbal dimen-

* Reprinted with permission of the Association for Supervision and Curriculum Development and Charles M. Galloway, from *Educational Leadership*, 24:55-63, October, 1966. Copyright © 1966 by the Association for Supervision and Curriculum Development.
[1] Charles M. Galloway. "An Exploratory Study of Observational Procedures for Determining Teacher Nonverbal Communication." University of Florida, Gainesville, 1962. (Unpublished doctoral dissertation.)

sion has been minimized, underplayed, and sometimes overlooked in teacher-pupil research.

During ordinary classroom talk between a teacher and pupils it may appear that an exchange of information is occurring exclusively at the verbal level, but a freightage of meanings is interchanged at the nonverbal level also. There are an indefinite number of signs and signals that serve the purpose of what we may term nonverbal language. Such a conclusion can be stated because pupils are reading the meaning of the expressions and conduct of a teacher whether the teacher likes it or not. Sometimes the glance of an eye or a facial expression may reveal what the meaning is—indeed, a message communicated in this way may be quite informative.

In everyday classroom interaction the communicative aspects of meaning between the teacher and pupils are fraught with elusiveness and complexity. Verbal language assumes the tremendous burden for the coherency of communication between human beings. And verbal language serves us well for it has an infinite flexibility in expressing thought forms and concepts. Indeed, it is almost too obvious to state that teachers rely overwhelmingly upon words to state and clarify the ideas and meanings they intend to transmit. After all an exchange of information and ideas between the teacher and pupils must be transmitted somehow and verbal vehicles represent the primary means of conveyance.

One of the negligent acts man has perpetrated, however, is the assignment of the same definition and meaning to more than one word, and conversely, the assignment of multiple definitions and meanings to the same word. There are other variables that add to the difficulty: the intention of the speaker, the perceptual experience of the listener, the context, and the present feelings and attitudes of the persons at the instant of communication. Even if distortions were consciously avoided in communication, the problems these variables present would be enough to account for serious misunderstandings between teachers and pupils.

WORDS AND MEANING

Words are "slippery customers" when it comes to meaning and the problem of unintentional discrepancies in the use of words while communicating is serious enough to account for profound misunderstandings. Torrance[2] has found that even though teachers vocalize the "right words," purportedly representing certain attitudes, the teacher's "real attitude" was likely to "show through," thereby affecting behavior and emotional reactions on the part of pupils.

To check on the fidelity of verbal statements, pupils read the meanings

[2] E. Paul Torrance. "Teacher Attitude and Pupil Perception." *Journal of Teacher Education* 11:97-102; March 1960.

behind nonverbal expressions and quite frequently place greater store in the validity of the character of the nonverbal. Indeed, among many pupils the nonverbal is heavily relied upon to reveal the authenticity, truth and genuineness of a message communicated by a teacher. For example, a teacher may verbally utter an approval of some seatwork a pupil is doing, yet the pupil may pick up cues which suggest disapproval. Although a teacher may verbally insist with the most persuasive language that he holds a certain belief, a pupil will continually check the teacher's nonverbal expressions to see if a contradiction can be detected.

Throughout the course of a teaching day a teacher may believe that he is communicating, "I enjoy this subject," "Aren't these ideas interesting?" "I like you," when all the time the pupils in the classroom are understanding different meanings. That is, a contradiction exists between what the teacher says and what the teacher communicates. In effect pupils will gauge the true intent or meaning of a teacher's communication by attending to the ungovernable aspects of his expressive behavior as a check on the verbal. If a difference exists between the two expressions, it is the nonverbal that is believed and accepted by the pupil as representing the authentic message.

Indeed, the pupil is in a position to be the most seriously victimized by difficulties in communication since the educative process is highly verbalized with a great premium placed on the printed and spoken word. Overlooked by many of us in our classroom teaching is that pupils may learn more true meanings from nonverbal messages than they do from our verbalizations. For indeed, it is the nonverbal that we turn to for meaning when the verbal appears to be vague and confusing.

THE DISADVANTAGED

Especially important is the notion that nonverbal messages may be more significant to pupils than teacher verbalizations when they attempt to ascertain the teacher's true feelings and attitudes toward them. A prominent example of this phenomenon occurs with linguistically disadvantaged youngsters who are bombarded by the verbal avalanches of teacher talk in classroom settings, and who subsequently have no recourse but to rely upon the nonverbal messages of teacher behavior. The research conducted by Bernstein[3] has shown that youngsters from the lower classes depend almost exclusively upon the nonverbal for the detection of meaning in school situations. These children do not possess the verbal facility to compete in an academically oriented classroom of abstract symbolization, and they most assuredly do not understand the verbal language of culturally different teachers.

[3] Basil Bernstein. "Social Structure, Language, and Learning." *Educational Research* 3:163-76; June 1961.

While the communication process proceeds continuously and simultaneously in all pupils when the teacher is talking, each child attempts to understand the teacher's words, gesture, intonation, action, and silence according to the meaning such signs and signals have for them individually. But, it is the culturally disadvantaged child who understands the *least* amount of information that is transmitted verbally and who reads the *most* meaning into the nonverbal behavior of the teacher. In all fairness, however, many of these youngsters not only read meanings that are not intended by the teacher, but they also misread the true intentions of the teacher. Such an outcome is the consequence of two language worlds and especially of two worlds of reality.

NONVERBAL MEANINGS

In conclusion, it must be stated that the meanings inherent in nonverbal expressions are used by pupils to check on the fidelity of communicative acts, and that such meanings are used by these same pupils to obtain a better picture of the self a teacher proposes to be. By interpreting and inferring from nonverbal expressions pupils may attempt to obtain the full import of a teacher's perceptions and motivations. To gain perceptual clarity and consistency each pupil feels he must be aware of the various nonverbal cues which facilitate obtaining added information. During classroom interaction, the expressive acts of a teacher's activity suggest a promissory character that is assumed by pupils to represent a more accurate reflection of the real self of the teacher.

Within classroom settings it is now recognized that teachers vary considerably in their ability, or in their willingness to communicate effectively when the question of competence in verbal language is raised. Teachers vary widely also in their disposition to communicate favorable feelings and attitudes toward pupils. The travesty is that too many of us are not aware of the feelings which we express toward students in our teaching. More pointedly, it might be stated that teachers are unaware of the consequences of the nonverbal messages they transmit in classroom teaching, not to mention the out-of-classroom interactions. Perhaps a failure to interpret or to be aware of the many "affective" implications of nonverbal language constantly remains a grave handicap and a profound difficulty for truly understanding the impact of one's communication with pupils.

This discussion has attempted to highlight the function nonverbal messages play in classroom interaction between teachers and pupils. Research investigations of the nonverbal dimension are extremely difficult, but the significance of the nonverbal is unquestioned.

2. Categories for Observing Teacher Nonverbal Communication [1]

The investigator constructed seven observation categories for observing a teacher's nonverbal communication with pupils in instructional settings. The purpose of arriving at the categories was to enable observers to make inferences at the time a nonverbal behavior was enacted by a teacher. When a communicative act occurred, which was related to the category system, observers recorded a number representative of the category. . . . In short, seven categories of a teacher's communicative behavior were recognized which were assumed to be heavily influenced by nonverbal expressions. Three of the categories were considered as encouraging communications, and three were considered as inhibiting. The neutral category of pro forma was considered as neither encouraging nor inhibiting. . . .

ENCOURAGING COMMUNICATION

1. *Enthusiastic Support.* A nonverbal expression implying enthusiastic support of a pupil's behavior, pupil interaction, or both. An expression that manifests enthusiastic approval, unusual warmth, or emotional support; being strongly pleased. An expression that exhibits strong encouragement to pupil. Examples of nonverbal determinants are as follows:

    1. *Facial expression.* Any expression that implies support or approval of some behavior or interaction occurring in the classroom. Any facial expression that connotes enjoyment, pleasure, or satisfaction with the pupil, or the topic.
    2. *Action.* Any movement or action that portrays enthusiastic approval and active acceptance in an approving way, e.g., a pat on the back, or a warm greeting of praise. An act that endorses approval of the pupil, and gives strong encouragement.
    3. *Vocal language.* Any voice quality indicating pleasure or warm acceptance. The use of the voice through intonation or inflection suggests approval and support.

2. *Helping.* A responsive act that relates to modifications in the teacher's behavior which suggest a detection of expressed feelings, needs, urgencies, problems, etc., in the pupil. A communicative act that

[1] Reprinted with permission from the author's doctoral dissertation, p. 65, 67-68, 146-149. See footnote 1 part 1 of this article.

performs a function which helps a pupil or answers a need. An act that meets a pupil's request; a nurturant act. This act is the spontaneous reaction that the teacher manifests in the form of an actual response. It may be either intellectually supporting, or problem-centered. Examples of nonverbal determinants:

1. *Facial expression.* An expression that implies, "I understand," or "I know what you mean," which is followed up by some kind of appropriate action. An expression that is consistent and sensitive to the pupil's need. A facial expression that registers an acceptance and an understanding of a pupil's problem.
2. *Action.* A movement or action that is intended to help or perform a function for the pupil. The action of the teacher is consistent with the need expressed by the pupil. Any action that suggests understanding and assistance.
3. *Vocal language.* A vocal utterance that is acceptant and understanding. The voice may be tender, compassionate, or supportive; or it may be a laugh or vocalization that breaks the tension.

3. *Receptivity.* A nonverbal expression that implies a willingness to listen with patience and interest to pupil talk. By paying attention to the pupil, the teacher exhibits an interest in the pupil, and implicitly manifests approval, satisfaction, or encouragement. Such a nonverbal expression implies to the pupil that "lines of communication are open."

1. *Facial expression.* Maintains eye contact with pupil in a systematic fashion, exhibiting interest in pupil, pupil's talk, or both. Facial expression indicates patience and attention. Other expressions suggest a readiness to listen, or an attempt at trying to understand.
2. *Action.* The teacher's demeanor suggests attentiveness by the way the total body is presented and movements used. An expressional pose or stance that suggests alertness, readiness, or willingness to have pupils talk. Teacher may be paying attention to pupil talk, even though eye contact is not established. A moving gesture that indicates the pupil is on the "right track." A gesture that openly or subtly encourages the pupil to continue.
3. *Vocal language.* A vocal utterance or vocalization that augments pupil talk, or that encourages the pupil to continue. An utterance indicating "yes-yes" (um-hm), "go on," "okay," "all right," or "I'm listening." Although in a sense, the utterance can be characterized as an interruption, it in no way interferes with the communication process; indeed, such a vocalization supplements, and encourages the pupil to continue.

4. *Pro forma.* A communicative act that is a matter of form, or for the sake of form. Thus, the nature of the act, whether it is a facial expres-

sion, action, or vocal language, conveys little or no encouraging or inhibiting communicative significance in the contextual situation; a routine act. When the pupil is involved in a consummatory act, or when it is appropriate or unnecessary for the teacher to listen or to respond, pro forma applies.

INHIBITING COMMUNICATION

5. *Inattentive.* A nonverbal expression that implies an unwillingness or inability to engage attentively in the communicative process, thus, indicating disinterest or impatience with pupil talk. By being inattentive or disinterested the teacher inhibits the flow of communication from pupils.
   1. *Facial expression.* Avoids eye contact to the point of not maintaining attention; exhibits apparent disinterest, or impatience with pupil by showing an unwillingness to listen.
   2. *Action.* An expressional pose or movement that indicates disinterest, boredom, or inattention. A demeanor suggesting slouchy or unalert posture. Body posture indicates "don't care attitude," or an ignoring of pupil talk. Postural stance indicates internal tension, preoccupation with something else, or apparently engrossed in own thought. Either a moving or completed hand gesture that suggests the teacher is blocking pupil talk, or terminating the discussion.
   3. *Vocal language.* A vocal utterance that indicates impatience, or "I want you to stop talking."

6. *Unresponsive.* A communicative act that openly ignores a pupil's need, or that is insensitive to pupil's feeling; a tangential response. Display of egocentric behavior or a domination of communication situation by interrupting or interfering in an active fashion with the ongoing process of communicating between pupils, or from pupil to teacher. An annoying, or abusive act; or a failure to respond when a response would ordinarily be expected by ignoring a question or request.
   1. *Facial expression.* An expression that is troubled, unsure, or unenthused about the topic in question. An expression that threatens or cajoles pupils; a condescending expression; as unsympathetic expression; or an impatient expression. An obvious expression of denial of feeling of pupil, or noncompliance of a request.
   2. *Action.* Any action that is unresponsive to or withdrawing from a request or expressed need on the part of the pupil. An action that manifests disaffection or unacceptance of feeling. A gesture that suggests tension or nervousness.
   3. *Vocal language.* A vocalization that interferes with or interrupts

ongoing process of communication between pupils, or from pupil to teacher. Such a vocalization, when it is an obvious interruption, appears unresponsive to the flow of communication and to the pupils.

7. *Disapproval.* An expression implying strong disapproval of a pupil's behavior or pupil interaction. An expression that indicates strong negative overtones, disparagement, or strong dissatisfaction.

   1. *Facial expression.* The expression may be one of frowning, scowling, threatening glances. Derisive, sarcastic, or disdainful expression may occur. An expression that conveys displeasure, laughing at another, or that is scolding. An expression that "sneers at" or condemns.

   2. *Action.* Any action that indicates physical attack or aggressiveness, e.g., a blow, slap, or pinch. Any act that censures or reprimands a pupil. A pointed finger that pokes fun, belittles, or threatens pupils.

   3. *Vocal language.* Any vocal tone that is hostile, cross, irritated, or antagonistic to pupil. The vocalization is one of disappointment, depreciation, or discouragement. An utterance suggesting unacceptance.

The Cognitive Process

OVERVIEW

THE cognitive perspective directs us to seek answers to such questions as: What content is it that teachers and pupils talk about? To what aspect of the topic at hand do teachers and pupils devote their discourse? What are the various types of logical thinking processes manifested in classrooms? How can we empirically specify examples of the operations of the intellect? What types and examples of creative, productive thinking can we locate in classroom discourse? When we say, "This teacher really teaches the pupils how to think," what is it that he teaches the pupils to do? What are the cognitive skills that teachers and pupils perform in their verbal behavior?

In spite of the fact that the development of "good thinking" has always been an aim of teaching (consider the popular phrase "teach the children *how* to think, not *what* to think"), the examination of teaching from this vantage point represents a comparatively new approach. There were several attempts in the first quarter of the century to investigate the use and types of questions that teachers ask, but these were done via questionnaires to teachers as opposed to actual observation. For some unknown reason these studies were not refined during the next thirty years. In the late 1950's educators again began to look at teaching by focusing on the thought processes, logical operations, and content of classroom teaching. The cause for this particular resurgence at that time is difficult to pinpoint. Yet it is probably not coincidental that it came at the time when many Americans began concentrating their demands on the content of teaching as the arms and space races went into high gear.

A careful reading of the selections to follow shows that teaching is complex. Indeed, the central aim of each of the following selections is to shed light on this complexity. These studies define the basic concepts of the cognitive perspective. Gallagher and Aschner write about productive thinking. Smith and his associates discuss logical operations. Maccia considers actual and hypothetical thinking. Bellack and his associates discuss pedagogical, substantive, and instructional meaning. Davis and Tinsley, adapting the work of Bloom and his associates, review knowledge and intellectual skills and abilities. The further significance of four of these selections comes from the categories each has constructed to define the basic concepts operationally. With these well defined categories it is possible to talk meaningfully and specifically about the thinking manifested in classroom discourse. Without such categories, productive thinking, for example, is so general a concept that it is virtually impossible to identify examples of it. Therefore, the reader needs to pay careful attention to these attempts to describe in behavioral terms classroom content, logic, and thinking.

The taxonomy by Bloom and his associates utilized as the foundation for the study by Davis and Tinsley requires special mention. According to the authors their taxonomy arranges the intended behavior of students in the cognitive domain into a sequential and cumulative order. That is, "The classifications of the taxonomy in general range from the concrete to the abstract or intangible" and each includes those that precede it. The two major categories of the cognitive domain are knowledge and intellectual abilities and skills. Davis and Tinsley's category "memory" comes from Bloom's "knowledge," while "translation," "interpretation," "application," "analysis," "synthesis," and "evaluation" stem from Bloom's major category called intellectual abilities and skills and maintain the order of the sub-categories in the taxonomy. The last two categories of affectivity and procedure belong to Davis and Tinsley and are not part of the taxonomy.

As a result of the complexity of this cognitive aspect of teaching, the systems devised to quantify it are themselves intricate. One crucial element of the intricacy is the type of basic unit of analysis employed. None of the selections employs the dimension of time as a methodological means for breaking up the classroom discourse into small units in which to locate and categorize cognitive behavior. Smith and associates use the episode and monolog; Bellack and associates use the pedagogical move; Gallagher and Aschner use the thought unit; and Davis and Tinsley use the teacher's question. As opposed to a simple time unit, such units of analysis require much more skill and training in order to achieve competence and reliability. The investigators have not chosen units based on time since they feel it is inappropriate when focusing on cognitive behavior. They believe that time units divide the discourse into fragments inconsistent with the flow of classroom thinking. The reader, then, must give careful attention to the definitions of the various units of analysis.

In the case of Bellack and Smith the units of analysis take on considerable importance. They become more than just units of discourse. They themselves become concepts with which to view teaching. Bellack therefore devotes much of his article to describing and analyzing his four pedagogical moves. Furthermore, he uses these moves to create a new concept, the teaching cycle, with which it is possible to discuss patterns in classroom teaching. Similarly, Smith spends considerable effort and space in defining his episode and monolog. Especially in these two studies the unit of analysis assumes an importance which matches that of the cognitive categories.

In regard to the systems devised, the reader needs to keep two factors in mind. First, the sets of categories in these selections overlap. For example, Bellack's dimension of meaning labeled substantive-logical is a tighter and simpler version of the logical operations of Smith. In other respects these two studies differ. The evaluative category of Gallagher and Aschner's productive thinking is quite similar to Bellack's opining and justifying, to Smith's evaluating and opining, and to Bloom's evaluation. Yet the concept of productive thinking is not the same as the concept of logical operations. Maccia's hypothetical thinking is similar to Gallagher and Aschner's divergent thinking. Other examples of overlapping will be apparent.

Second, these studies use similar terminology but not always with the same definitions. The overlaps in categories and terminology stem in part from the common area of endeavor and in part from the fact that these investigators are in fairly close contact with each other through their reports, correspondence, and conferences.

All of the selections concentrate on the verbal behavior of teaching. They do so because verbal behavior is the prime medium through which teachers and pupils express their thoughts. Moreover, due to the intricacy of the instruments, these systems rely on tape recordings to preserve the classroom discourse. This method allows for slowing down the pace of the discourse in order to get at its meaning. Live discourse simply occurs too fast to permit the analysis in terms of these multi-faceted concepts.

In light of all these points there is no denying that these instruments for analyzing cognitive behavior are impractical for the day-to-day needs of the untrained classroom teacher. But this does not invalidate the worth of these studies. If these systems do not serve his daily needs, the teacher can use these concepts and categories for informal analysis and as a guide to his planning for classroom activities or he can try to simplify the instruments and the procedures to fit his own peculiar situation. Or he can rely on a corps of trained observers that can serve a group of teachers. These studies may serve as the foundation for less cumbersome instruments in the future. As in other fields, first attempts are often complicated but lead to simpler systems as more people apply their talents to the task.

The multi-dimensional study by Bellack and his associates is included in this section because it is primarily a system for content analysis of classroom language. It analyzes the substantive topic under study and the logical operations performed with that topic. Elsewhere in this book the results of this research are presented as *The Classroom Game*. This is consistent with the notion of the language game that these investigators borrowed from Wittgenstein for their framework, as they themselves explain in the selection here. The flow model of this teaching game, presented in the article entitled *The Flow of Teaching*, provides yet another way to conceptualize the study's results in addition to the notions of the classroom game and the patterning of teaching cycles.

These selections raise questions for research. For example, is it possible to devise an instrument and to train observers to gather data pertinent to Maccia's concepts of actual thinking and hypothetical thinking in the classroom? Surely, if hypothetical thinking is as important to our democracy as Maccia claims, we need to know under what conditions it occurs and can occur most effectively. Similarly, we need to conduct parallel studies to those of Bellack, Smith, Gallagher and Aschner, and Davis and Tinsley but with different age groups to see if the age factor correlates with varying results. Are children of 8 or 10 mature enough to engage in hypothetical thinking or divergent thinking?

We also need to create experimental conditions to see if certain teaching techniques affect the results. For example, what occurs if the teacher deliberately restrains from speaking-reacting moves as categorized by Bellack? What occurs if the teacher deliberately asks fewer questions? What happens if the teacher does not define new terms? These are but a few suggestions of the many follow-up studies that we need to conduct. The alert reader will certainly come up with many more.

7.   The Language of the Classroom

Arno A. Bellack and Joel R. Davitz in collaboration with Herbert M. Kliebard, Ronald T. Hyman, and Frank L. Smith, Jr.

PURPOSE AND PROCEDURES

The purpose of this research was to study the teaching process through analysis of the linguistic behavior of teachers and students in the classroom. Observation of what goes on in elementary and secondary schools reveals that classroom activities are carried on in large part in verbal interaction between students and teachers; few classroom activities can be carried on without the use of language. This study, therefore, focused on language as the main instrument of communication in teaching. The major task was to describe the patterned processes of verbal interaction that characterize classrooms in action. A subsidiary aim, viewed primarily as an exploratory phase of our general line of research, was to study linguistic variables of classroom discourse in relation to subsequent pupil learning and attitude change.

The subjects were 15 teachers and 345 pupils in Problems of Democracy classes studying a unit on international trade. The 15 classes, located in seven high schools in the metropolitan New York area, ranged in size from 15 to 35 pupils, with a mean of 23 pupils. To establish reasonable limits within which the classes could carry on their work and to provide a relatively stable basis both for testing changes in knowledge and for analyzing the substantive meanings of the classroom discourse, a unit of instruction was selected for the participating classes. This unit was based on the first four chapters of the pamphlet *International Economic Problems,* written by Dr. James Calderwood.[1] Teachers were asked to teach in any manner they believed appropriate; no effort was made to control their methods of instruction. The experimental class sessions consisted of four periods on four successive days during the regular school schedule. Transcriptions of tape recordings of four sessions for each of the 15 classes

Reprinted with permission. Selected from *The Language of the Classroom: Meanings Communicated in High School Teaching,* Parts 1 and 2. Part 1, Arno A. Bellack and Joel R. Davitz in collaboration with Herbert M. Kliebard and Ronald T. Hyman; Part 2, Arno A. Bellack in collaboration with Ronald T. Hyman, Frank L. Smith, Jr., and Herbert M. Kliebard. U.S. Department of Health, Education, and Welfare, Office of Education, Cooperative Research Projects No. 1497 and No. 2023. New York, Institute of Psychological Research, Teachers College, Columbia University, 1963 and 1965.
    [1] James D. Calderwood. *International Economic Problems.* Minneapolis, Curriculum Resources Inc., 1961.

served as the basic data for the analysis of the verbal interaction of teachers and pupils.

THEORETICAL VIEW OF CLASSROOM BEHAVIOR

We began with the assumptions that the primary function of language is the communication of meaning and that describing linguistic events in the classroom in terms of the meanings expressed by teachers and students is a potentially fruitful direction for research. Our conception of the nature of meaning was derived in large measure from Wittgenstein's view that "the meaning of a word is its use in the language."[2] Equation of meaning and use suggested that the basic problem was to identify the distinctive functions language actually serves in the verbal interplay between pupils and teachers.

In searching for the meaning of what teachers and students communicate in the classroom, we found it helpful to identify (1) what the speaker was doing *pedagogically* with the words he spoke at a given time; (2) *what* he was saying (i.e., the content of his statement); and (3) the *feeling tone* or emotional meaning conveyed by the communication. That is, in analyzing the utterance of a teacher or of a student at a given point in class discussion, we were first of all concerned with the pedagogical significance of what the speaker was saying—whether, for example, he was structuring the class discussion by launching or focusing attention on a topic or problem, eliciting a response from a member of the class, responding to a question posed by a previous speaker, or reacting to a comment previously made. Second, we were interested in identifying the content of the communication—what topic was under discussion, what information the question called for, what explanation was being offered, or what assignment was being made. Furthermore, in addition to the pedagogical function of the language and the content of the message, we were concerned with both the explicit and the implicit emotional aspects of the speaker's vocal expression.

The basic methodological problem was to devise the means whereby these three dimensions of meaning could be defined operationally. In dealing with this problem, we were again influenced by Wittgenstein's approach to language. In his view, "the *speaking* of language is part of an activity, or a form of life."[3] Language is adaptable to many uses and functions in carrying on activities that are essentially linguistic in nature. Wittgenstein refers to these activities as "language games," a metaphor

[2] Ludwig Wittgenstein. *Philosophical Investigations.* Oxford, Basil Blackwell, 1958. p. 20.
[3] *Ibid.*, p. 11.

used to point up the fact that linguistic activities assume different forms and structures according to the functions they come to serve in various contexts. A game has a definite structure, and there are certain moves that a player is bound to make insofar as he is playing the game at all. These are some of the verbal activities that he identifies as language games:[4]

> Giving orders and obeying them
> Reporting an event
> Forming and testing a hypothesis
> Play acting
> Making a joke and telling it
> Making up a story and reading it

Carrying the game metaphor a step further, Wittgenstein observes that verbal activities in various contexts follow language rules that govern the use of words in these activities. Learning to participate in various types of language activities is therefore very much like learning to play a game. Participants have to learn the rules, the purpose of the rules, and how the various parts of the game are related; only if one learns these rules can he play the game successfully.

Viewing classroom discourse as a kind of language game was a useful approach for purposes of this research, in that it suggested a framework for analysis within which the various dimensions of meaning could be defined in operational terms. Teaching is similar to most games in at least two respects. First, it is a form of social activity in which the players— teachers and pupils—fill different but complementary roles. Furthermore, teaching is governed by ground rules of play which guide the actions or moves made by participants. We reasoned that if we could identify the various types of verbal moves teachers and students make in playing the game of teaching and the rules they implicitly follow in making these moves, we would be in a position to investigate the functions these verbal actions serve in classroom discourse and hence the meanings which are communicated.

Examination of the transcripts of classroom discussions suggested that the actions that characterize the verbal interplay of pupils and teachers could be classified in four major categories. We labeled these basic verbal actions *pedagogical moves* and classified them in terms of the functions they serve in classroom discourse:

Structuring. Structuring moves serve the pedagogical function of setting the context for subsequent behavior by launching or halting—excluding interaction between pupils and teachers and by indicating the

---

[4] *Ibid.*, p. 11-12.

nature of the interaction. For example, teachers frequently begin a class period with a structuring move in which they focus attention on the topic or problem to be discussed during that session.

Soliciting. Moves in this category are designed to elicit a verbal response, encourage persons addressed to attend to something, or elicit a physical response. All questions are solicitations, as are commands, imperatives and requests.

Responding. These moves bear a reciprocal relationship to soliciting moves and occur only in relation to them. Their pedagogical function is to fulfill the expectation of soliciting moves. Thus, students' answers to teachers' questions are classified as responding moves.

Reacting. These moves are occasioned by a structuring, soliciting, responding, or another reacting move, but are not directly elicited by them. Pedagogically, these moves serve to modify (by clarifying, synthesizing or expanding) and/or to rate (positively or negatively) what has been said previously. Reacting moves differ from responding moves, in that while a responding move is always directly elicited by a solicitation, preceding moves serve only as the occasion for reactions. Rating by a teacher of a student's response, for example, is designated a reacting move.

As we proceeded with the analysis of the data in terms of pedagogical moves, it became evident that these moves occur in certain cyclical patterns or combinations which we designated *teaching cycles.* A teaching cycle begins either with a structuring move or with a soliciting move, both of which are *initiating* maneuvers; that is, they serve the function of getting a cycle underway. In contrast, responding and reacting moves are *reflexive* in nature; a responding move is elicited by a soliciting move and a reacting move is occasioned by a preceding move and therefore they cannot begin a cycle. A cycle frequently begins, for example, with a soliciting move by the teacher in the form of a question, continues with a responding move by the student addressed, and ends with a rating reaction by the teacher. A cycle might also get underway with a structuring move by the teacher in which he focuses attention on the topic to be discussed, continue with a question related to this topic, and end with responding moves by one or more pupils. The concept of teaching cycles makes it possible to identify patterns in the verbal exchange between teachers and students and thus to describe the ebb and flow of the teaching process as it develops over time.

In addition to meaning from the viewpoint of the pedagogical significance of what teachers and students communicate, we were also interested in the dimension of meaning represented by the content of the messages communicated. Analysis of the classroom protocols from this point of view revealed that teachers and students communicate four functionally different types of meanings: (1) *substantive meanings* with associated (2) *substantive-logical* meanings; and (3) *instructional meanings* with associated (4) *instructional-logical* meanings.

Substantive meanings refer to the subject matter discussed in the class; that is, specific concepts such as multilateral trade and generalizations involving, for example, the relation between specialization and the factors of production. Substantive-logical meanings refer to the cognitive processes involved in dealing with the subject matter, such as defining, explaining, fact stating, interpreting, opining and justifying. Instructional meanings refer to the social-managerial aspects of the classroom, such as assignments, materials and routine procedures which are part of the instructional process. Instructional-logical meanings refer to distinctively didactic verbal processes such as those involved in rating negatively and positively, explaining procedures, and giving directions.

As we developed techniques for analyzing classroom discourse in terms of pedagogical units, we attempted to develop parallel methods for dimensions of meaning suggested by Osgood, Suci and Tannenbaum:[5] however, did not prove feasible; instead, a procedure utilizing larger time samples of the discourse was developed. This provided a reliable basis for characterizing the emotional style of the discourse in terms of dimensions of meaning suggested by Osgood, Suci and Tannenbaum[5]: (1) valence; (2) strength; and (3) activity.

ANALYSIS OF THE DATA

CODING SYSTEM

The four types of pedagogical moves described above were the basic units of analysis. Within each pedagogical move the four types of meanings described in the preceding section were identified when they appeared in the discourse and were coded according to categories 3 through 8 summarized below.[6]

(1) SPEAKER: indicates source of utterance

   Teacher (T); *Pupil* (P); *Audio-Visual Device* (A)

(2) TYPE OF PEDAGOGICAL MOVE: reference to function of move

   Initiatory Moves

      Structuring (STR): sets context for subsequent behavior, launches, halts/excludes

[5] Charles Osgood, George J. Suci, and Percy H. Tannenbaum. *The Measurement of Meaning.* Urbana, University of Illinois Press, 1957.

[6] Italics indicate actual coding terminology.

Soliciting (SOL): directly elicits verbal, physical, or mental response; coded in terms of response expected

Reflexive Moves

Responding (RES): fulfills expectation of solicitation; bears reciprocal relation only to solicitation

Reacting (REA): modifies (by clarifying, synthesizing, expanding) and/or rates (positively or negatively); occasioned by previous move but not directly elicited; reactions to more than one previous move coded REA

Not Codable (NOC): function uncertain because tape inaudible

(3) SUBSTANTIVE MEANING: reference to subject matter topic (Based on a content analysis of the pamphlet by Calderwood)

Trade (TRA)

Trade—Domestic and International (TDI)

Trade—Money and Banking (TMB)

Trade—Who Trades with Whom (TWH)

Factors of Production and/or Specialization (FSP)

Factors of Production—Natural Resources (FNR)

Factors of Production—Human Skills (FHS)

Factors of Production—Capital Equipment (FCE)

Factors Other Than Natural Resources, Human Skills, and Capital Equipment Occurring in Discussion of Reasons for Trade (FRE)

Imports and/or Exports (IMX)

Foreign Investment—General (FOR)

Foreign Investment—Direct (FOD)

Foreign Investment—Portfolio (FOP)

Barriers to Trade (BAR)

Barrier—Tariffs (BAT)

Barrier—Quotas (BAQ)

Barrier—Exchange Control (BAE)

Barrier—Export Control (BAX)

Barrier—Administrative Protectionism (BAA)

Promoting Free Trade (PFT)

Relevant to Trade (REL)

Not Trade (NTR)

(4) SUBSTANTIVE—LOGICAL MEANING: reference to cognitive process involved in dealing with the subject matter under study

Analytic Process: use of language or established rules of logic

Defining-General (DEF): defining characteristics of class or term with example of items within class explicitly given

Defining-Denotative (DED): object referent of term
Defining-Connotative (DEC): defining characteristics of class or term
Interpreting (INT): verbal equivalent of a statement, slogan, aphorism, or proverb

Empirical Process: sense experience as criterion of truth

Fact Stating (FAC): what is, was, or will be without explanation or evaluation; account, report, description, statement of event or state of affairs
Explaining (XPL): relation between objects, events, principles; conditional inference; cause-effect; explicit comparison-contrast; statement of principles, theories or laws

Evaluative Process: set of criteria or value system as basis for verification

Opining (OPN): personal values for statement of policy, judgment or evaluation of event, idea, state of affairs; direct and indirect evaluation included
Justifying (JUS): reasons or argument for or against opinion or judgment
Logical Process Not Clear (NCL): cognitive process involved not clear

(5) NUMBER OF LINES IN 3 AND 4 ABOVE

(6) INSTRUCTIONAL MEANINGS: reference to factors related to classroom management

Assignment (ASG): suggested or required student activity; reports, tests, readings, debates, homework, etc.
Material (MAT): teaching aids and instructional devices
Person (PER): person as physical object or personal experiences
Procedure (PRC): a plan of activities or a course of action
Statement (STA): verbal utterance, particularly the meaning, validity, truth or propriety of an utterance
Logical Process (LOG): function of language or rule of logic; reference to definitions or arguments, but not presentation of such
Action-General (ACT): performance (vocal, non-vocal, cognitive, or emotional) the specific nature of which is uncertain or complex
Action-Vocal (ACV): physical qualities of vocal action
Action-Physical (ACP): physical movement or process
Action-Cognitive (ACC): cognitive process, but not the language or logic of a specific utterance; thinking, knowing, understanding, listening

Action-Emotional (ACE): emotion or feeling, but not expression of attitude or value

Language Mechanics (LAM): the rules of grammar and/or usage

(7) INSTRUCTIONAL-LOGICAL MEANING: reference to cognitive processes related to the distinctly didactic verbal moves in the instructional situation

Analytic Process: see (4) above

Defining-General (DEF)

Defining-Denotative (DED)

Defining-Connotative (DEC)

Interpreting (INT)

Empirical Process: see (4) above

Fact Stating (FAC)

Explaining (XPL)

Evaluative Process

Opining (OPN): see (4) above

Justifying (JUS): see (4) above

Rating: reference to metacommunication; usually an evaluative reaction (REA)

Positive (POS): distinctly affirmative rating

Admitting (ADM): mild or equivocally positive rating

Repeating (RPT): implicit positive rating when statement (STA) is repeated by another speaker; also for SOL to repeat vocal action (ACV)

Qualifying (QAL): explicit reservation stated in rating exception

Not Admitting (NAD): rating that rejects by stating the contrary; direct refutation or correction excluded

Negative (NEG): distinctly negative rating

Positive/Negative (PON): SOL requesting positive or negative rating

Admitting/Not Admitting (AON): SOL asking to permit or not permit procedure or action

Extralogical Process: SOL expecting physical action or when logical nature of verbal response cannot be determined

Performing (PRF): asking, demanding, explicit directive or imperative

Directing (DIR): SOL with or without stated alternatives; asking for directive, not permission for specific action

Extralogical Process Not Clear (NCL): extralogical process involved not clear

(8) NUMBER OF LINES IN 6 AND 7 ABOVE
Each pedagogical move is coded as follows:

(1)/(2)/(3)/(4)/(5)/(6)/(7)/(8)
 (1) Speaker
 (2) Type of Pedagogical Move
 (3) Substantive Meaning
 (4) Substantive-Logical Meaning
 (5) Number of Typescript Lines in (3) and (4)
 (6) Instructional Meaning
 (7) Instructional-Logical Meaning
 (8) Number of Typescript Lines in (6) and (7)

CODING THE PROTOCOLS

The following excerpt from one of the coded protocols illustrates the coding procedures and interpretation of the coded information.[7]

Excerpt from Protocol

Teacher (Move #1): Now, in order to pacify, or help satisfy, certain groups in American industry and American politics who want high protective tariffs, or who are clamoring for protection, we have inserted into our reciprocal agreements two—what you might call—safeguards which are coming up now as President Kennedy looks for greater authority in the tariff business. (Move #2): What have we inserted in here to give an element of protection or to stifle the outcries of American businessmen who want protection? Two clauses which we call . . . ? Yes?
Pupil (Move #3): The peril point and the escape clause.
Teacher (Move #4): Right. The peril point and the escape clause.

Code

Move #1 T/STR / BAT / XPL / 5 / - / - / -
Move #2 T/SOL / BAT / FAC / 2 / - / - / -
Move #3 P/RES / BAT / FAC / 1 / - / - / -
Move #4 T/REA / BAT / - / - / STA / POS / 1

Interpretation

The teacher focuses on a substantive area by explaining something having to do with tariffs to the extent of five lines (Move #1). He then solicits for two lines with the expectation that a factual response on tariffs will be given (Move #2). A pupil gives a one-line response by stating a fact about tariffs (Move #3). The teacher positively evaluates the statement by the pupil (Move #4).

The entire segment of discourse is an example of a teacher-initiated cycle (STR SOL RES REA).

[7] For a full one-page excerpt see the addendum to this article. RTH, editor.

RELIABILITY

The results . . . indicate a consistently high degree of reliability for all major categories of analysis; agreement ranged from 84 to 96 per cent [between pairs of coders]. Thus, the data strongly support the conclusion that the system devised is this research for a content analysis of classroom discourse is highly reliable.

EMOTIONAL MEANINGS

The semantic differential technique was used to describe each teacher's emotional style in terms of the meanings he conveyed along three dimensions: valence, activity, and strength.[8] Since it seemed reasonable to assume that our interpretations of the emotional meanings expressed by teachers would be quite different from those of the typical high school students who participated in the research, it was decided that emotional meanings should be analyzed from the point of view of student observers. Judges in this part of the study were 11th grade students in a communications class in a senior high school similar to those who participated in the experimental classes. Because of the confidential nature of the tape recordings, ratings were obtained only for thirteen teachers who consented to have recordings of their classes played for persons other than regular members of the research staff. These ratings served as the basis for analyzing the emotional meanings communicated by the teachers. The correlations [of reliability between sets of judges] obtained are valence, r. 81; activity, r. 75, and strength, r. 84. The results thus indicate adequate internal consistency.

RESULTS

Perhaps the most striking aspects of the results are the remarkable similarities among many of the teachers and classrooms and the stability of individual classes over the four sessions. The data reveal a consistent and generally stable pattern of pedagogical discourse.

1. Teachers dominate the verbal activities of the classrooms studied. The teacher-pupil ratio in terms of lines spoken is approximately 3 to 1; in terms of moves, the ratio is about 3 to 2. The volume of total verbal output is thus considerably greater for the teacher than for the pupil.

2. The pedagogical roles of the teacher and the pupil are clearly defined in terms of the frequency of behavior in each category of pedagogi-

[8] Osgood, Suci, and Tannenbaum. *op. cit.*

cal moves. The teacher is responsible for structuring the lesson, for soliciting responses from pupils and for reacting to pupils' responses. The pupil's primary task is to respond to the teacher's solicitation. Occasionally the pupil reacts to preceding moves, but he rarely uses the reacting move to rate previous action. Only infrequently does the pupil solicit a response from the teacher or from another pupil. Seldom does the pupil spontaneously structure the discourse; when he uses a structuring move he frequently presents it as the fulfillment of a specific assignment made by the teacher, which usually involves a debate or a report.

Pedagogical Move		Total	Percentage of moves by teachers	Percentage of moves by pupils	Percentage of moves by audio-visual devices
Soliciting	SOL	100.	86.0	14.0	0
Responding	RES	100.	12.0	88.0	0
Structuring	STR	100.	86.0	12.0	2.0
Reacting	REA	100.	81.0	19.0	0

$$N(SOL) = 5,135$$
$$N(RES) = 4,385$$
$$N(STR) = 854$$
$$N(REA) = 4,649$$

3. Structuring moves account for about six per cent of the discourse in terms of moves spoken. Soliciting, responding and reacting each account for approximately 30 per cent of the moves. The classes vary somewhat from this pattern, but for the four moves the distribution of variations is fairly restricted, with most classes clustering within a few percentage points of each other. Furthermore, in each of the classes the proportion of moves devoted to each of the pedagogical moves tends to be generally stable over the four sessions. This reflects a consistent style of play within each class.

4. Analysis of teaching cycles centers on the dimensions of initiator (teacher or pupil) of the cycle, pattern of pedagogical moves within the cycle, and the rate at which cycles occur. Classes vary in the extent to which teachers initiate teaching cycles; generally, teachers initiate about 85 per cent of the cycles. Analysis of cycle pattern indicates that the basic verbal interchange in the classroom is the soliciting-responding pattern. Teachers often shape and frame this basic pattern with reacting moves and occasionally with structuring moves, although teachers differ in the extent to which they use the structuring and reacting moves. Classes also differ in the rate at which verbal interchanges take place; the average rate is slightly less than two cycles per minute.

5. In approximately two-thirds of the moves and about three-fourths

of the lines speakers refer to or talk about substantive material, that is, the subject matter of international trade. Of all the categories of analysis, classes vary most widely in the substantive meanings expressed. This finding was not anticipated, since the major restriction imposed on the teachers by the research procedure was specification of the substantive material to be covered.

6. With respect to the substantive-logical meanings, approximately one-half of all moves involve empirical meanings (fact stating and explaining). Speakers use the analytic mode (defining and interpreting) and the evaluative mode (opining and justifying) much less frequently; each of these two modes accounts for about one-tenth of the moves in any class. Thus, a major proportion of the discourse in the classes studied is devoted to stating facts about and explaining principles and problems of international trade, while considerably less of the discourse is concerned either with defining terms and interpreting statements or with expressing and justifying personal opinions about economic issues.

7. In almost one-half of the moves and approximately one-fourth of the lines of the discourse, speakers convey instructional meanings. It is chiefly the teacher who expresses the instructional meanings. A large proportion of these meanings might be viewed as metacommunications, in that they involve teacher comments about preceding comments by pupils. Other instructional categories that occur with relative frequency are procedures, materials, and assignments. All other instructional categories account for very little of the discourse.

8. The instructional-logical meanings that occur most frequently involve fact stating, usually about procedures, assignments, and other instructional matters. A substantial proportion of statements in this area also deal with teachers directing pupils to perform various actions. Almost all of the remaining instructional-logical entries involve some form of rating reaction by the teacher.

9. With respect to the analysis of emotional meanings, teachers maintain a relatively stable emotional style, insofar as the dimensions of potency and activity are concerned, and, to a lesser degree, in terms of valence. Teachers thus tend to be consistent over time in the kinds of emotional meanings they convey to students.

The Language Game of Teaching [1]

These results provide a description of the language game of teaching. Despite the fact that the rules of this game are not explicitly stated for

[1] A fuller description of The Language Game of Teaching is presented in Section 5 of this book.

any of the players, teachers and students in the classrooms under study obviously follow a set of implicit rules with few deviations. These rules define the teaching game. Although classes differ somewhat in details, for the purposes of an initial description of the classroom game, the results indicate that common elements underlie much of the teaching game, in that pupils and teachers follow a consistent set of language rules.

The classroom game involves one player called the teacher and one or more players called pupils. The object of the game is to carry on a linguistic discourse about subject matter, and the final "payoff" of the game is measured by the amount of learning displayed by the pupils after a given period of play. In playing the game, each player must follow a set of rules. If one plays the role of teacher, he will follow one set of rules; if one plays the role of pupil, he will follow a somewhat different, though complementary, set of rules. In fact, the first rule, which might be called "the rule of rules," is that if one is to play the game at all, he will consistently follow the rules specified for his role.

Within the general set of rules defining the game, there are individual differences among teachers and classes in style of play. In one classroom, the teacher or pupils may specialize in one kind of move or sequence of moves, while in another class the players may specialize in a slightly different pattern of discourse. Notwithstanding these variations in style and differences in specialization of moves, the game is played by a consistent set of general rules. These rules are rarely made explicit during the course of play; more often, they are defined implicitly by the ways in which teachers and pupils use these moves. It follows then that if one is to understand the rules of classroom behavior, he must study the functions that the pedagogical moves actually serve in the discourse of teachers and pupils.

Another way to interpret these data is to consider the sequence of pedagogical moves that occurs most commonly in the typical game. This sequence is, essentially, the solicitation-response teaching cycle which is shaped and framed by structuring and reacting moves. The most common type of verbal interchange in the classroom involves a teacher's solicitation and a pupil's response, which is usually followed by an evaluative reaction by the teacher. If this sequence does indeed define a general pattern of classroom discourse, it would seem to be important to investigate this sequence of moves in greater detail, to evaluate its pedagogical effectiveness, and to devise methods of increasing the effectiveness and efficiency of both teachers' solicitations and teachers' reactions.

A One-Page Excerpt from a Protocol

T: However, to get back to our main point once more, in talking about the U. S. role in, in all this international trade. Our export trade is vital to us. Our import trade is vital to us, and it would upset and shake American economy to a tremendous extent if we were to stop importing or stop exporting. Let's turn to American investments abroad. You suppose we do invest much money outside of the U. S.?

T|*REA*|IMX|XPL|6|PRC|FAC|2
T|STR°|FOR|-|-|PRC|FAC|1
T|SOL|FOR|FAC|2|-|-|-|

P: Yes.

P|RES|FOR|FAC|1|-|-|-|

T: In what ways, in what fields? How would it be done?

T|SOL▲|FOR|XPL|2|-|-|-|

P: Well, a lot of the big companies here in the U. S. will set up companies over in other countries, and that way they can give the workers over there a chance to work and to sell their products and the foreign countries can get the tax off that.

P|RES|FOD|XPL|7|-|-|-|

T: I think you put the most important thing last, but that's true. The branch office in a foreign country, which involves the exportation of American capital, is so often done to avoid paying what?

T|REA|FOD|-|-|STA|QAL|2
T|SOL■|FOD|XPL|3|-|-|-|

P: Taxes.

P|RES|FOD|XPL|1|-|-|-|

T: What kind of taxes?

T|SOL•|FOD|FAC|1|-|-|-|

[° This move begins a STR-SOL-RES teaching cycle.
 ▲ This move begins a SOL-RES-REA teaching cycle.
 ■ This move begins a SOL-RES teaching cycle.
 • This move begins a new teaching cycle which is not completed in this short excerpt. In the full report it turned out to be an SOL-RES teaching cycle. Editor]

8.   The Flow of Teaching

Ronald T. Hyman

This research[1] provides yet another way of looking at the over-all flow of the classroom verbal behavior. It is indeed possible with the concepts developed in this research project to conceptualize the discourse into a flow model of the teaching game. This flow model is put in graphic form in Figure 1.

We begin with the No-Game State. A class is in the no-game state when no action is taking place. This no-game state ends as a speaker moves the class into activity or activity begins which has been previously specified to take place at a given time.

At the Directive Fork, the teacher or pupil with his discourse either launches or excludes a new game or sub-game. (In our project the language game was taken to be the unit on International Trade which might include, among others, sub-games as debating on the Common Market by two teams of pupils, viewing a film on foreign investments and discussing U.S.-Canadian trade.)

The Launching Path and the Excluding Path indicate the decision of the speaker to either start or bar a game/sub-game. The speaker may do so by either a structuring move or a soliciting move. For example, a speaker may structure with, "Now for our topic of the Common Market." He may solicit with, "To get us started, Jonathan, would you please tell us the date of formation and the members of the Common Market." By such moves the speaker launches. He may exclude a game/sub-game, for example, by a structuring move such as, "Now today we won't be discussing the Outer Seven group at all" or by a soliciting move such as, "Don't talk about tariff policy today or even tomorrow. Wait until Wednesday."

As the speaker launches or excludes, he specifies the Dimensions of the Game. These dimensions include the *Activity* (e.g., debating, testing, discussing), the *Agent* who is to perform the activity (e.g., the entire class, one pupil, a small group of pupils), the *Time* to perform the game/sub-game in terms of beginning point and duration; the *Substantive Topic* (e.g., barriers to trade, factors of specialization, foreign investment), the *Logic Operation* (e.g., defining, explaining, opening), and the *Instruc-*

Reprinted with permission from "The Language of the Classroom: Implications for Supervisors and Teachers." *Journal of Secondary Education*, 42: 106-113, March, 1967.

[1] *The Language of the Classroom* by Bellack, Davitz, Kliebard, Hyman, and Smith. (See previous article. RTH, editor)

FIGURE 1

The Flow of the Teaching Game

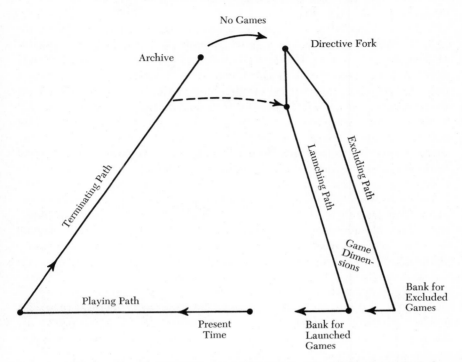

No Games

Directive Fork

Archive

Terminating Path

Launching Path

Excluding Path

Game Dimen-sions

Bank for Excluded Games

Playing Path

Present Time

Bank for Launched Games

tional Aids (e.g., textbook, globes, chalkboard). These dimensions define the particular game/sub-game.

A game that has been launched is stored in the Launching Bank. When the appropriate beginning point in time arrives, it gets underway. Some begin immediately upon being launched, while others await their due time in the Launching Bank. A game that has been excluded is stored in the Excluding Bank. The speaker may change his mind and decide to remove a game/sub-game by first directing it to be launched and then adjusting the time dimension, if necessary. Such a game/sub-game moves to the Launching Bank and follows the same course as all other launchings.

The next position is the Present Time. It is obviously continually changing. A game/sub-game moves to this position when the appropriate time arrives.

The Playing Path represents the game/sub-game as it is played. All the Game Dimensions previously specified come together here. Sometimes more than one game/sub-game occurs simultaneously. This may happen, for example, when some pupils are meeting in small groups planning their panel on tariff policy while others are taking a make-up test. While moving along the Playing Path, a speaker may launch and/or exclude other games/sub-games.

Along the Terminating Path, a game/sub-game is ended. There are several ways to terminate a game/sub-game. A speaker may explicitly *Halt* on-going action by saying, "That's enough now for this panel discussion." A game may simply *Expire* at a given time because it has been pre-decided to do so. A sub-game involving testing that is scheduled for a half an hour expires after its assigned time runs out. A speaker may end a game/sub-game by *Replacing* it with another one. For example, during a discussion on barriers to trade, the teacher may say, "Now let's see this film we have on foreign investments." Thus the sub-game on barriers to trade ends as the one involving viewing a film on foreign investment begins.

In the Archive are stored and recorded all the games/sub-games of the class. The Halting and Expiring methods lead directly to the archive, since they do not lead to further play by themselves. The Replacing method leads to further play and so connects directly with the Launching Path. The dotted line in the diagram represents this. The games/sub-games so ended by this method are also recorded in the archive.

The no-game state begins again when the on-going action is terminated via the Halting and Expiring methods. The Replacing method by-passes this no-game state. The no-game state continues until a previously launched game/sub-game leaves the Launching Bank, or until a speaker begins new activity, as noted already.

This flow model allows us to view the discourse of any classroom at any time and to assess what state the class is in. This model encourages us to conceive of teaching as a recurring dynamic process. It allows us to focus on and examine selected aspects of classroom discourse. The observer can ask whether the teacher structures for the future and loads up the Launching Bank so that the class does not enter the no-game state when an on-going game ends? When does he structure for the future, at the beginning of a new game, during one, or at the end of each particular sub-game? How does a teacher end a game/sub-game? Does the teacher remove games from the Excluding Bank and launch them? What happens to the class when they are in a no-game state? The observer who uses this model has a framework within which to interpret the activity he sees.

9.   A Study of the Logic of Teaching

B. Othanel Smith and Milton Meux

Teaching Behavior

As one observes teaching behavior he sees a variety of activities. The teacher asks questions and listens to and appraises answers; listens and responds to students' questions; and reprimands, approves, or reacts neutrally to students. He tells how to do something or shows how it is done. He listens to students tell how to do something or observes their efforts to do it. All of these activities take place in an orderly fashion, and yet they exhibit no readily observable pattern of development. To identify operations within which such elements of teaching behavior have meaning is one of the main tasks of research.

Teaching is assumed here to be a social phenomenon, fundamentally the same from one culture to another and from one time to another in the same culture. It has its own elements, forms, regularities, and problems. It takes place under what seems to be a relatively constant set of conditions—time limits, authority figures, student ability limits, institutional structures, etc. In its essential features it is a system of social action involving an agent, an end-in-view, a situation and two sets of factors in the situation—one set over which the agent has no control (e.g., size of classroom and physical characteristics of pupils) and one set which the agent can modify with respect to the end-in-view (e.g., assignments and ways of asking questions). The latter set of factors constitutes the means by which ends-in-view are reached. The means, in turn, consists in two types of factors: subject matter and instructional paraphernalia, and the ways of manipulating and maneuvering the subject matter and paraphernalia. The first of these we call material means and the second procedural means. The procedural means have two aspects: large-scale maneuvers which we call strategies, and smaller movements, constituting tactical elements of strategies, which we call logical operations.

"Strategy" refers to a pattern of acts that serve to attain certain outcomes and to guard against certain others. Among the general objectives toward which a strategy may be directed are the following: to insure that certain learnings will be acquired in as brief a time as possible; to induce students to engage in an exchange of ideas; and to minimize the number

Reprinted with permission from *A Study of the Logic of Teaching* by B. Othanel Smith and Milton Meux. U.S. Department of Health, Education, and Welfare, Office of Education, Cooperative Research Project No. 258 (7257). Urbana, Bureau of Educational Research, College of Education, University of Illinois, 1962.

of wrong responses as the student attempts to learn concepts and principles. We are just beginning a study of strategies, and our conception of
them is only in the formative stage.

By "logical operations," which are the focus of our study, we mean the
forms which verbal behavior takes as the teacher shapes the subject
matter in the course of instruction. For example, the teacher reduces
concepts to linguistic patterns called definitions; he fills in gaps between
the student's experience and some new phenomenon by facts and generalizations related in a verbal pattern referred to as explanation; he rates
objects, events, etc., by reference to facts and criteria related in a pattern
called evaluation. If he does not engage in such operations himself, the
teacher either requires his students to do so, or more typically, the teacher
and his students jointly carry on these operations through verbal exchanges.

These operations exhibit a structure which can be observed and described. Of course, the structure as it is exhibited in the classroom is often
incomplete because the operation is formed elliptically. The teacher may
not follow exactly the pattern of a particular type of definition or the
complete outlines of a particular form of explanation. Nevertheless, these
operations are clearly enough outlined in teaching behavior to be identified and described.

Moreover, these operations can be evaluated logically by reference to
rules of validity and correctness, and, while such rules do not describe
how a given operation is to be performed, they do afford checking points
as to the clarity and rigor of the operation's performance. When teaching
behavior takes the form of operations whose patterns can be evaluated
by reference to rules of validity and correctness, it is said to be
logical. . . .

The Unit of Discourse

To analyze the mass and variety of verbal behavior recorded in the transcripts, two kinds of unit were developed: episode and monolog. . . . An
episode is defined as the one or more exchanges which comprise a completed verbal transaction between two or more speakers. The monolog,
on the other hand, consists in the solo performance of a speaker addressing the group. Division of the discourse into these two kinds of units
exhausts the discourse. Where one unit ends the next begins. We shall
now set forth in some detail these two basic forms.

EPISODIC DISCOURSE

In its normal course, a discussion in progress exhibits a characteristic
development. Certain forms of utterances are used to enjoin or invite

immediate reply; other forms are conventionally understood to forestall or prohibit immediate response. A direct question, addressed either to a given person or to the group at large, conventionally demands some kind of responding action on the part of the individual or group addressed. A rhetorical question, on the other hand, is commonly understood to be uttered for its dramatic or rhetorical effect, but some do serve to trigger discussion. When a reply is made to a direct question, it is also a convention that the reply itself be acknowledged in some way, at least by word or gesture if not by further responding commentary or questioning. These and other forms of verbal behavior fall together into definite patterns in the course of a discussion.

We have encountered two patterns of episodic discourse. In each of the patterns there is a remark which serves to launch the verbal transaction. We call the remarks which act in this way entries. In the first pattern, called the *reciprocating pattern*, alternation between two speakers occurs after the entry—back and forth movement so aptly described as reciprocating action. In the other pattern, called the *coordinate pattern*, each successive speaker responds more or less directly to the entry rather than to the remarks of the immediately preceding speaker. Hence each utterance following the entry is coordinate with all the others, with respect to that entry and to the utterance closing the episode.

The following [set of two] episodes[1] illustrates the *reciprocating* pattern.[2]

Episode 1   •T: *Now who do you know who was the first person who discovered the Hawaiian Islands?* Steve?

    Steve: Was it Captain Cook?

    T: That's right. // *Do you know about what time it was,* Steve?

    Steve: 1670 something?

    T: No, it's not that early. Come down about a hundred years.

    Steve: 1770?

    T: Yes. It was 1778, actually during the time of our American Revolution. // *And do you know what he called the islands?* They weren't Hawaii at the time. Anybody know? Oh, I think this is an easy name to remember—especially around noon. Steve?

    Steve: Cook Islands?

    T: No. They weren't Cook Islands. That's a good guess, but that doesn't happen to be it. The Sandwich Islands.

    Steve: Oh.

    T: Do you eat sandwiches at noon, too? // In this particular period, the United States wasn't too interested. Of course,

---

[1] From a U. S. History class, grade 11.

[2] In this excerpt, italics indicate the entry in each episode. Paired diagonal lines have been placed as indicators for the breaking points between episodes.

• 'Teacher' is abbreviated as 'T' throughout the report.

> we were concerned with gaining our freedom from England
> at that particular time, but soon after that . . . etc.

Below is a typical example of an episode corresponding to the *coordinate* pattern. The point under discussion concerns the question of a novelist's use of his story as a medium for propaganda:[3]

Episode 2   T: All right, now, as Carol pointed out, Alan Paton is pleading
        for the alternative solution—that of brotherly love or peaceful co-existence between the races. *Now, what do you think of a novelist who tries to preach a lesson or to promote his point of view through the medium of fiction?* You think of that. Mary?

Mary: I was just going to say that I think it's the type of the novel. I mean it's the way that it is presented that moves us. He could present it in different ways if he wanted to. Not necessarily the—the novel or—oh, something that teaches you a moral lesson.

     T: All right, just as we discussed, it's a short story. Some stories do have a moral lesson to preach and then they become parables rather than just generalized short stories. And others simply are entertaining. Denny?

Denny: Well, I think that more people would be interested in the fiction form of the novel than in just a pamphlet giving specific reasons why the two races should live together in brotherhood. I think it would attract more attention and be more interesting.

Judy: Well, since it's—When people read it, it's more parallel to everyday life. You might be able to understand it a lot better in a novel and so on. Otherwise, you just see these facts and you wouldn't associate yourself and how you would feel and react to it.

     T: All right. // Well, now, the chief function of any kind of fiction is to entertain, isn't it? *Do you feel that in this book, Cry the Beloved Country, the author is actually entertaining you?* . . .

Episodes are determined not by shifts in speakers, but by shifts in what the speakers are talking about, and by the speech forms and patterns of their dealings with the point under discussion. . . . It should be noted, incidentally, that episodes are not always brought through a final or closing phase, as are those presented here to illustrate typical episodic forms. Quite often one episode will be terminated without any explicit closing comment or assent; instead, the transaction is closed tacitly by the advent of a new entry, that is, of an utterance advancing some new point, which, in turn, triggers more response. There is nothing out of the ordinary about a discussion which proceeds through such a series of truncated episodes. They are merely common phenomena of group verbal activity.

[3] From an English class, grade 11.

MONOLOG DISCOURSE

The second form in which units of classroom discourse may be identified embodies the alternate basic element of group verbal behavior: the "solo performance" of a speaker addressing the group. For an example of how monolog discourse typically occurs during class sessions, let us return to the U. S. History class that we observed in a discussion of the Hawaiian Islands. The teacher has been talking with Steve, it will be recalled. She turns from their play on words and launches into the following monolog:

Monolog 1   T: Do you eat sandwiches at noon, too? // In this particular period, the United States wasn't too interested. Of course, we were concerned with gaining our freedom from England at that particular time, but soon after that we began to send people out around the world to trade and, of course, to stop at one of—many of them would stop at the Hawaiian Islands. The first people who went out there to settle, however, were not traders. Do you know what their interest was? Do you remember what their interest was? They went in 1820, the very first Americans in the islands—who settled in the islands. They were missionaries, and they were going out to try and christianize the heathens. Then people who were interested in trade and farming in particular went into the islands and their concern, of course, was the raising of sugar cane.

And that brings us down into the period of history that we have been discussing more recently—when they were trying to make treaties which would make it possible for them to trade with the United States—particularly to get rid of their sugar in the United States. And the first trade treaty was made in the 1870's. It was a reciprocal trade treaty in which one particular product from Hawaii was to be admitted to the United States free. The product was, of course, the one which they had in greatest quantity at that time—sugar. In 1880, they renewed that treaty, and the United States got the right to use a particular coaling base —coaling station there. // Now, do you have any idea which base we acquired in the 1880's—the use of which base? One that you should recognize. A very prominent part in the American defense system today. Tony?

Tony: Pearl Harbor?
T: Pearl Harbor. That's right. And we have had a base there at Pearl Harbor, then, since 1880. // Now, how did the United States first become aware of the problem of . . . ? etc.

The excerpt above stands as almost a model of a teacher's monolog. It is also quite typical of the way in which many teachers move from discussion to lecture and back to discussion again.

Monolog discourse does not reveal phase-like qualities, as in episodic interplay. However, expository monologs in progress exhibit a kind of paragraph-to-paragraph movement. This is seen in the teacher's monolog above—indicated by an indentation—as she shifts from the topic of early settlers of the Hawaiian Islands to that of the trade treaties between the Hawaiian Islands and the United States. A solo speaker often moves from point to point in his exposition, raising it, elaborating at some length, and then proceeding to some further point.

Monologs are usually found in the didactic or expository discourse of the teacher. However, in his role as leader and arbiter of class proceedings, the teacher also delivers in monolog form, upon occasion, announcements, assignments, and sometimes admonishments and moral preachments. Student monologs generally consist in such verbal activity as the presentation of assigned reports.

Monologs occur much less frequently than do episodes, although there is variation from class to class. This is to be expected, since monolog performances are quite normally reserved for special purposes and special occasions in group discussion proceedings.

Although no analysis of monologs has been made for this report, it probably would be useful in further analyses of classroom discourse to take note of these paragraph-like passages in a didactic monolog for the relation their contents may have to prior and subsequent class discussion. . . .

RELIABILITY

Coefficients [of agreement between pairs of judges] range from .62 to .73—a fairly small range—with a median of .70. . . .

ENTRIES AS THE BASIS OF CLASSIFICATION

Episodes can be classified in a number of ways: by the nature of their content, by the number of verbal interactions they involve, by the psychological processes they entail, and so on. In this study episodes are to be classified in terms of their logical features. . . .

As we began the task of working out a classificatory scheme for episodes, the question arose as to whether the entire episode or only a particular part of it was to be considered. We could classify the opening phases and thereby group episodes by these phases. Or we could use either the continuing or the closing phase as the basis of classification. Or again, we could classify the episodes without regard to their parts.

Certain considerations led us to classify episodes by their opening phases. The opening phase always contains a verbal move which evokes at least one, but more often a series of related verbal exchanges. We have called this verbal move an entry. It is always a self-initiating move on the part of the person who makes it and it is followed by responding remarks. The entry thus tends to shape the character of the episode. If the entry calls for the meaning of a word, the continuing phase is apt to consist of statements telling how the word in question is used. Likewise if the entry calls for an explanation, the continuing phase will likely emphasize statements which give reasons for or otherwise account for an action, event, etc. Of course, it is not necessarily the case that the continuing phase will be consistent with the demands of the entry. The student may misunderstand the entry. He may not know how to respond and thereby fumble the verbal exchange. Or for some other reason the student may fail to make an appropriate response. In any event, there is not always a close logical correspondence between what the entry calls for and what the body of the episode contains. For this reason, we chose to use the entry as the cue to the purport of the episode rather than the continuing phase of the unit.

The Development of Categories

At the outset it seemed possible to select ready-made categories from among those found in works on logic. If such selection were possible, the remaining task would consist of devising criteria and procedures for placing episodes in appropriate categories. However, it soon became clear that no such simple solution was possible. The great variety and complexity of symbolic operations demanded by teachers made it quite clear that episodes could not be neatly fitted into ready-made classes. It was necessary to follow a more empirical procedure—to work out categories in terms of the nature of the entries themselves. Of course, conventional categories of logic such as definition, designation, and classification appear in our list of categories. This is necessarily the case. To refuse to use such categories would be to invent a new logic, and that task is not within our domain. But the occurrence of these categories in our list resulted from study of the entries themselves rather than from a priori decisions. . . .

As we began to examine a sample set of entries, and to look at each entry as a whole, we became aware of the fact that the logical character of an entry could be decided by reference to the sort of response it demands. This is the approach which we finally used in the development of the categories. When we speak of response, we of course do not mean the response which the student made and which can be found by examining the continuing phase of the episode. Rather, we appeal to an ideal response. Such a response is a schema. It is a form to which responses to the members of a given class of entries would conform, regardless of the content with which entries deal, were the responses logically correct.

The meaning of an ideal response may be further clarified by reference to examples of entries. The entry "From which state did Mark Hanna come?" demands that a particular political unit be specified. It is not necessary that we know the state from which he came in order to know that the entry requires as an appropriate response that a particular state be indicated. Nor do we need to know the time at which he came from the particular state. Were we asked to give an actual rather than an ideal response, we would want the ambiguity removed from the entry by specifying the time. Mark Hanna might have come from New York, or any one of a number of states, depending upon the occasion. In the sense of nativity he could have come from one and only one state. Furthermore, an ideal response may be made in more than one way. In the present case the particular state could be specified by naming it, by pointing to it on a map, or by sketching its shape, and so on. "Which line is the base of the triangle?" is an entry which likewise requires that a particular something, namely a line, be specified. "What is the word (in the sentence) that is to be modified?" similarly requires that something—a word—be singled out. We can now generalize what we have been doing and say that there is a set of entries which demands as a response schema that particular things be specified by naming, pointing, or whatnot.

In contrast to the foregoing entries are cases in which no object in particular is called for. From the entry "What is some food material that the fish could use?" it is clear that food material is to be indicated. But the phrase "some food material" is a variable. The entry therefore does not demand that a specific food item be indicated. Any one of a number of foods could be named each of which would satisfy the demands of the entry equally well. In cases of this type the response schema consists in naming or otherwise indicating any one of a number of variables satisfying the function of the entry.

Some entries demand more complex response schemata. "How did McKinley happen to be killed?" requires that a sequence of events leading up to and ending in McKinley's death be related. "How did they finally relieve this beleaguered garrison?" is an entry which also demands recounting of a chain of events ending in the relief of the garrison. A similar response is to be made to the entry "In the East, what had Cleveland done that made the Capitalists unhappy?" Here the response consists in narrating the acts of Cleveland that led to dissatisfaction among the financial leaders. Thus, we have a response schema which consists in the narration of a sequence of events leading up to and culminating in a particular state of affairs. This state of affairs is said to be the result or outcome of the events, and the events are said to explain or to account for the outcome. Again, it is not necessary that we know what the actual events were in order to tell that an entry demands the narration of events as a response.

KINDS OF ENTRIES

The foregoing discussion is perhaps sufficient to indicate the way in which we arrived at a set of logical categories. The categories into which the entries were grouped are as follows:

1) *Defining.* Entries making up this group are concerned with how words or other symbols are used to refer to objects (abstract or concrete). These entries vary in form and content, but in general they ask implicitly or explicitly for the meaning of terms.

In some cases, a term is given and a definition or meaning of the term is to be supplied as a response to the entry. In the example, "What does the word 'dorsal' mean?" the question requires that whatever is designated by "dorsal" be indicated.

In other cases, neither the word "mean" nor "define" occurs in the entry. Rather the entry asks what something *is*, for example, "What is a cablegram?" These entries require that the noun appearing in the question be defined, or that the referent of the noun be described.

In a few cases, the noun in the entry is a grammatically proper name. In these cases, the entry requires that the object designated by the proper name be described or otherwise indicated. For example, "Who was Paul Elmer More?" is a question which asks that the person referred to be described unambiguously.

Finally, some entries ask for a term or expression that can be substituted for another term or expression; for example, "What is the symbol for gravity?"

2) *Describing.* To describe is to represent something by words or drawing, to tell about something. Thus, the entries making up this category mention or suggest something and require that an account of this something be given. In the question "What can you tell us about the gill rakers?" we are asked to describe the gill rakers.

However, not all questions which mention or allude to something ask for a description. For example, "What would be some examples of a sense organ?" is a question which names a class of things and asks that instances of it be cited. No description is called for.

In some cases, as in the example just given, it is easy to tell whether the entry requires a description or an identification. But in a large number of entries the intent of the entry in this regard is obscure. "What did

Cleveland find out?" is a question which might be answered by naming whatever it was that Cleveland uncovered. But our expectations would be more nearly satisfied were the question answered by a brief account of what he found out. On the other hand, "What is a common defect of this part (cerebellum) of the brain?" can plainly be answered by naming the defect. But a description of the defect would not be inappropriate as an answer.

3) *Designating.* To designate is to identify something by name—word or other symbol. The name designates the object (abstract or concrete) to which it refers. Thus, this group of entries is made up of items in which something is described or otherwise indicated, and the name used to refer to it or to identify it is asked for. These entries vary widely in form and content. In general, they demand that objects (abstract or concrete) be designated by name or other symbol, or simply by pointing. Consider the question "What do you call a word used to modify a verb?" The question is answered by giving the name of the word, namely, "adverb." The question "What reptile did he show in the film?" is answered in the same way, although the question does not explicitly ask what the reptile is called. Again, "What is the word (in a given sentence) that's to be modified?" is a question which can be answered by pointing to the particular word or by saying it.

4) *Stating.* Entries in this group do not ask for names, descriptions, etc., but for statements of issues, steps in proofs, rules, obligations, theorems, conclusions, ideas, beliefs, promises, threats, etc. For example, the question "What is the conclusion?" asks for a statement of some sort. It can seldom be answered satisfactorily merely by naming.

5) *Reporting.* The entries in this group ask for a report on what a book or document says, for information in the text, or for a summary or review, and the like.

6) *Substituting.* The entries making up this category ask the student to perform a symbolic operation usually of a mathematical nature.

7) *Evaluating.* To engage in evaluating is to estimate the worth, dependability, etc. of something. An entry of this type requires that some object, expression, event, action, or state of affairs be rated as to its value, dependability, desirability, and the like. For example, the question "Is he a good judge?" asks the student to rate a judge who acts in some particular manner.

8) *Opining.* In opining, the body of evidence from which the conclusion is drawn is not explicitly delineated by the entry of the episode, i.e., no explicit conditions are given on which the conclusion is to be based. The person may be required to supply that which is the case, or to affirm or deny what is suggested in the entry as being the case. It is characteristic of such episodes that the conclusion involves an inference from evidence

rather than a report of a single fact. "Do you think that historians will say that Wilson was right in proposing the League of Nations?" is an entry which asks for a conjecture about how historians of the future will judge Woodrow Wilson with respect to a particular set of actions—those involved in proposing the League of Nations.

9) *Classifying*. Each entry in this group makes explicit reference to an instance or class (type, sort, group, set, kind) of things or both. The entry requires that a given instance be put in the class to which it belongs, or that a given class be placed in a larger class to which it belongs as a subclass. For example, "What special type of triangle did you find it to be?" is a question which makes reference by the "it" to a particular triangle. The student is expected to tell what class of triangles this particular one belongs to. As an illustration of questions which ask that a class be placed in a larger class, consider the following: "What group of animals does the jellyfish belong to?" In this question, the term "jellyfish" does not refer to a particular jellyfish but to a subclass. The student is required to name the larger class to which the group of animals called "jellyfish" belongs.

10) *Comparing and Contrasting*. This type of entry requires that two or more things—actions, factors, objects, processes, etc.—be compared. In some cases, the entry specifies two or more things, and asks that either their similarities or differences be noted. In other cases, the entry asks that they be compared with respect to a particular characteristic. The question "What's the difference between probation and parole?" illustrates the first of these cases. The student is asked merely to make a comparison, the points of comparison not being explicitly indicated. The second case is illustrated by the question "Is his (fish's) eye very large compared to the size of the grasshopper's?" Here the eyes of the two different animals are to be compared with respect to size only.

In still other cases, the entry names a thing and requires that another thing similar to it, be indicated. Consider the question "Which one (Canadian house) corresponds to the House of Commons?" The House of Commons is the given object. The question asks that the Canadian house most like it be named. Entries of this kind do not require that differences or similarities be explicitly stated. The student considers the differences or likenesses and selects the object in terms of them, as required by the entry.

11) *Conditional Inferring*. These entries contain an antecedent, that is, the conditional part of a statement. In the sentence "When it rains, the streets are wet" the phrase "When it rains" is the antecedent. The phrase "the streets are wet" is the consequent. Now, the entries which make up this category give an antecedent. Sometimes they give both an antecedent and a consequent. But they never contain a consequent alone.

Here is an example of an entry containing an antecedent only: "How does that (undemocratic handling of colonies) affect the mother country?" The phrase "undemocratic handling of colonies" is the antecedent. It describes the condition of which the effect on the mother country is the consequent. The question asks the student to tell what the consequent is. Take another case: "If that diagonal (in rhombus) is given as 12 and this angle is 60, what is the angle at C and at A?" The antecedent is "if that diagonal (in rhombus) is given as 12 and this angle is 60." The consequent asked for by the question is the size of the angle at C and A. In all cases where the antecedent alone is given, the entry requires that the consequent—effect, result, outcome, subsequent behavior, etc.,—be supplied as the answer.

Consider an example of an entry containing both an antecedent and a consequent: "Did you ever get a headache from sleeping in a draft?" The phrase "sleeping in a draft" is the antecedent, and "get a headache" is the consequent. Now, in entries of this sort, the student is required to affirm the consequent, to deny it, or to say he does not know whether he has ever suffered or enjoyed the consequent under the given condition or not.

12) *Explaining.* There are several types of explanatory entries, but they all have one thing in common. They give a particular consequent and they require that an antecedent be supplied. To explain is to set forth an antecedent condition of which the particular event or process to be explained is taken as the effect, or else, to give the rules, definitions, or facts which are used to justify decisions, judgments, actions, etc. In the example "Why did the light go out?" the consequent is "the light go out." The question asks the student to give a reason (reasons) to account for the fact that the light is out. The reason(s) is the antecedent.

There are six kinds of explanation entries, depending upon the sort of antecedent used to account for the consequent. They are mechanical, causal, sequent, procedural, teleological, and normative. These are described as follows:

12.1) *Mechanical Explaining.* This type of entry gives an event or action which is to be accounted for by describing the way the parts of a structure fit or work together. A sample entry will help to make this category clear: "How (do fish make a sound)?" The action to be accounted for is "fish make a sound." Now, the antecedent consists of some kind of structure which enables the fish to make vibrations. A description of this mechanism would constitute an answer to the entry.

12.2) *Causal Explaining.* Entries of this type give events, situations, or states to be accounted for and ask that a state of affairs be cited of which the given event (or situation or state) is taken to be the result. Consider the example: "What makes a person's muscles sort of twitch-like?" The event to be explained is the twitching of a person's muscles. The explanation consists of a description of the condition of the nerves associated with the twitching.

12.3) *Sequent Explaining.* Entries of this sort ask how something happened. They require that a sequence of events be cited of which the event to be accounted for is the sequel. For example, the question "How did McKinley happen to be killed?" requires the recitation of the events leading up to the assassination of President McKinley.

12.4) *Procedural Explaining.* These entries require that the steps or operations by which a given result or end is attained be described. Here is a sample entry: "How did you get 72 (for an answer)?" It is expected that the student tell the steps he took to obtain this answer.

12.5) *Teleological Explaining.* This type of entry contains descriptions of actions, decisions, states of affairs, or the worth of things. It requires that these be accounted for or justified by reference to purposes, functions, or goals. An entry of this sort is: "Why are you doing those problems?" The consequent to be explained is "doing those problems." The explanation consists in giving a purpose, say, to satisfy an assignment.

12.6) *Normative Explaining.* Entries of this type do either of two things. First, they may mention or assume a decision, judgment, or state of knowing and require that it be justified by citing a definition or characteristic or both. Here is an example: "*Why do we call them* (animals between vertebrates and invertebrates) *the Chordata animal group?*." The consequent is the underscored part of the question. To give the antecedent in this case is to cite a definition of the chordata phylum and to point out that the animals in question have the characteristics called for by the definition.

Second, members of this group of entries cite actions, decisions, or choices (either made or to be made) and require that rules be given as reasons for the decisions, choices, etc. Consider this example: "Why do we use shorter (in comparing two pencils as to length)?" The consequent to be explained is "we use shorter." The antecedent demanded by the question consists of a rule prescribing the use of "shorter" in such cases. Entries of this type usually call for grammatical or mathematical rules.

13) *Directing and Managing Classroom.* Many entries have little or no logical significance. They are designed, not to evoke thought, but to keep the classroom activities moving along. Such entries belong in this category. . . .

RELIABILITY

Coefficients [of agreement between pairs of judges] range from 0.00 to 1.00. The median is .67, and the middle 50% of the coefficients range from .62 to .84—a fairly high percentage of agreement for the present status of the categories. . . .

LOGICAL OPERATIONS IN TEACHING: THEIR OCCURRENCE AND DISTRIBUTION

The purpose of this first phase of our investigation, as indicated earlier, was to determine what logical patterns, if any, are to be found in teaching. To accomplish this end, all entries were classified by the two members of the project staff (the principal investigators) who were responsible for developing the categories. Each entry was placed in one and only one category, no disagreements being permitted. The distribution of entries by logical categories obtained by this procedure is presented in Table 3. The classes have been grouped by subject matter and content areas.

It is clear from examining Table 3 that several distinct types of logical operations are present in teaching behavior. Not only are there different logical operations, but they differ in the frequency with which they occur. There is no clearly appropriate method for obtaining expected frequencies in each of the categories from our data, nor do we have any defensible rational basis for determining the expected frequencies in each category. Therefore, we have not employed a significance test to establish that these categories vary in frequency of occurrence. However, with such a large number of entries, it seems doubtful that any statistical test is required to support the conclusion that the number of entries varies significantly from one category to another. Describing, Designating (3T), and Explaining (12T) are the three most frequently occurring operations in that order, with Directing and Managing Classroom and Conditional Inferring and Stating next. The least frequent operations, aside from subcategories, are Substituting, Reporting, and Classifying. We conclude, then, that we have established that there are logical operations in teaching, and furthermore that some of these operations are more prevalent than others, notably Describing, Designating, and Explaining, in that order.

As shown in Table 3, there are marked differences from class to class in the frequencies of the logical operations. Although the analysis and interpretation of such differences is not central to this study, and was not included in its original purpose and design, some discussion of these differences might be of interest. Since the data were not gathered for the purpose of clarifying the relative effects of teachers, subjects, schools, and grade levels on the nature and frequency of logical operations, these variables are highly confounded. Thus the following discussion is quite speculative.

The schools differ with respect to money expenditure per student, sociocultural characteristics, etc. Such differences would probably influence the logical demands in the classroom mostly through the medium of the teacher, so that school differences probably reduce to differences in teachers. Thus, for the purpose of this discussion, we will ignore differences among schools.

The classes vary from the ninth to the twelfth grades. This variation in grade level, however, occurs in an age range in which the capacity of the average student to handle logical demands probably is roughly the same from one age level to another. On the basis of a great deal of evidence concerning the development of IQ with maturation, it seems that there is little significant increase in the IQ beyond the ninth grade; thus the capacity of the student to handle intellectual operations probably changes very little during the high school years. Also, Piaget's observations have led him to conclude that the handling of propositional logic has been achieved by most normal adolescents by the time they have reached high school. Thus, for the purposes of this discussion, we can ignore not only the differences in schools but the differences in grade levels insofar as maturation of the student is a factor in determining the logical operations at these levels.

However, these assumptions still leave the teacher and subject matter variables confounded. It is unrealistic to assume that neither of these variables has little or no effect on the distribution of logical operations. It is plausible to suspect that teachers will differ in the extent to which they employ different logical operations. Consider two U.S. history classes at the eleventh-grade level that dealt with fairly similar historical periods, labeled in Table 3 as U.S. history$_B$ and U.S. history$_E$. In the U.S. history$_B$ class, there are fewer entries especially in Describing, the 3.14 subcategory of Designating, and Sequent Explaining, but there are more entries in Evaluating, Opining, Causal Explaining, and Directing and Managing Classroom. These differences seem to be attributable to the teachers' ways of handling the material, rather than to differences in the subject matter.

It is also quite plausible that there are differences from subject to subject within a content area (e.g., physics vs. biology in the science area), and from one content area to another. . . .

We may conclude tentatively from this brief discussion, then, that it seems likely that differences may exist in the extent to which the logical operations are employed from teacher to teacher, and from area to area. Adequate answers as to what this extent is, however, cannot be determined from our data, but await further studies designed more specifically to investigate these matters. . . .

TABLE 3

Distribution of Logical Categories by Areas and Subjects

Area	Mathematics	Science				Social Studies ▲				
Subject / Category	Geometry	Physics	Chemistry	Biology	Physiology	U.S. History$_B$	U.S. History$_E$	U.S. History$_A$	World History	Sociology
1. Defining										
1.11	5	2	3	7	11	2	2	0	10	6
1.12	4	1	2	4	14	4	0	0	7	1
1.13	0	0	0	0	0	2	4	0	0	0
1.14	0	10	2	0	1	1	0	0	0	0
1T*	9	13	7	11	26	9	6	0	17	7
2. Describing	97	63	59	110	62	39	82	13	49	35
3. Designating										
3.11	1	0	8	17	11	2	2	0	1	12
3.12	4	1	1	7	6	1	4	0	2	0
3.13	29	7	11	28	27	6	4	1	4	6
3.14	0	0	0	0	14	13	40	8	42	3
3.15	2	2	0	13	6	1	4	0	5	2
3T*	36	10	20	65	64	23	54	9	54	23
4. Stating	58	12	7	5	5	10	16	2	4	4
5. Reporting	6	7	0	9	14	5	6	0	9	13
6. Substituting	4	4	0	0	0	0	0	0	0	2
7. Evaluating	2	4	13	1	4	23	4	2	17	7
8. Opining	6	1	5	3	12	43	27	6	5	8
9. Classifying	11	2	6	20	2	2	4	1	2	2
10. Comparing and Contrasting	11	8	5	23	7	7	6	3	6	5
11. Conditional Inferring	37	26	15	22	19	12	9	2	25	16
12. Explaining										
12.1 Mechanical	0	1	0	12	6	0	0	0	0	0
12.2 Causal	0	6	8	11	14	18	7	3	12	9
12.3 Sequent	0	0	0	5	0	9	17	0	4	2
12.4 Procedural	16	3	10	4	4	0	4	0	4	1
12.5 Teleological	2	0	2	4	5	12	6	4	4	4
12.6 Normative	22	0	6	11	1	8	2	0	2	4
12T*	40	10	26	47	30	47	36	7	26	20
13. Directing and Managing Classroom	39	6	17	12	15	49	7	8	29	9
Total number of entries per subject	356	166	180	328	260	269	257	53	243	151

* Indicates total number of entries in this category.

▲ Subscripts on the subjects in this area indicate the school in which this class was taped.

TABLE 3 (continued)

Area	English[+]			Core Program		
Subject Category	English 9	English 11	English 12	Core Program	Number of entries in the category	Percent of total number of entries
1. Defining						
1.11	11	4	6	0	69	2.0
1.12	1	0	6	0	44	1.3
1.13	1	0	3	0	10	0.3
1.14	0	1	0	1	16	0.5
1T*	13	5	15	1	139	4.1
2. Describing	39	40	15	77	861	25.3
3. Designating						
3.11	15	2	0	0	71	2.1
3.12	7	1	0	0	34	1.0
3.13	38	8	9	14	192	5.7
3.14	2	16	8	4	150	4.4
3.15	6	10	3	3	57	1.7
3T*	68	37	20	21	504	14.8
4. Stating	94	2	7	4	230	6.8
5. Reporting	6	0	6	18	99	2.9
6. Substituting	0	0	0	0	10	0.3
7. Evaluating	7	19	44	9	156	4.6
8. Opining	3	11	37	12	179	5.3
9. Classifying	21	12	11	7	103	3.0
10. Comparing and Contrasting	8	10	11	2	112	3.3
11. Conditional Inferring	9	17	24	15	248	7.3
12. Explaining						
12.1 Mechanical	0	0	1	1	21	0.6
12.2 Causal	4	2	17	3	114	3.4
12.3 Sequent	2	6	4	0	49	1.4
12.4 Procedural	4	3	4	5	62	1.8
12.5 Teleological	4	6	21	5	79	2.3
12.6 Normative	44	4	8	1	113	3.3
12T*	58	21	55	15	438	12.9
13. Directing and Managing Classroom	38	18	22	49	318	9.4
Total Number of entries per subject	364	192	348	230	3397	

* Indicates total number of entries in this category.
+ Subscripts on the subjects in this area indicate the grade level of the class.

10. A Preliminary Report on Analyses of Classroom Interaction[1]

James J. Gallagher and Mary Jane Aschner

The introduction of many innovations in curriculum and methods has changed the face of American education and has increased interest in methods of evaluation of educational programming. The purpose of the present article is to present a new approach—one involving analysis of classroom interaction—which may be useful in arriving at such an evaluation.

The educational literature teems with examples of past evaluations of educational programs, most of them focused primarily upon the *product*. The measure of the success of a given program was the standing of the child at the end of a period of a kind of educational treatment, or the amount of change the child achieved over a given period of time. Such methods of evaluation have been especially common in research evaluating the usefulness of ability grouping or acceleration. Methods of teaching reading have also been frequent objects of evaluation. In a comparison of reading-method X with reading-method Y, one common procedure has been to obtain two groups of children, presumably comparable on important variables, with one group being placed in a classroom where they would receive reading-method X, and the other group where they would receive reading-method Y. The children would be tested on reading skills both at the beginning and at the end of the experiment. Such a procedure has been curiously sterile in producing improvements in reading programs and other areas of educational curriculum and planning as well. Why?

Let us suppose that the group mentioned above, who received reading-method Y, obtained scores on reading ability that were superior to those of the group who underwent reading-method X. We may then conclude that there were certain variables at work in the total environment provided by reading-method Y which were superior to those operative in the environment in which reading-method X was applied. The problem confounding the educator lies in the multitude of possible factors that could have been responsible for the resulting differences in the experimental and control group test scores. Was it the organization of content that brought about the improvement? Was it a superior teacher, or his

Reprinted with permission from the *Merrill-Palmer Quarterly of Behavior and Development*, 9: 183-194, July, 1963.

[1] This research has been supported by the Elizabeth McCormick Fund and the Cooperative Research Branch of the U.S. Office of Education.

enthusiasm for the new method? Or was the change due to one small part of the total instructional method rather than to the whole? Could not the same benefits be obtained perhaps, merely by adopting only one part of program Y?

Yet faced with such results, the educational administrator must often limit his decision to either accepting or rejecting method Y. This, in short, is the basic defect in attempts that have been made to use the product of the program—or the children's achievement gain—as the criterion for the effectiveness of programming.

An alternative method of evaluation consists in analyses of the teaching process as it goes on in the classroom. Such analyses can be accomplished in the examination of teacher-pupil interaction and of the developmental processes of learning. In analyzing these interaction sequences, it is possible to identify—and to describe—fruitful or fruitless teaching procedures in a way that has not been possible under the conventional "pre-post test" type of study.

PRIOR INTEREST IN SEQUENCE ANALYSIS

Interest in the process of verbal interaction is not new; the present study has profited from the experiences of two different lines of investigation. Rogers (1951) and Snyder (1947) pioneered a series of investigations into the process of psychotherapy through the classification of the verbal interactions of client and counselor relationships. Rogers has commented, "Let it be said at the very outset that in the present stage of our knowledge we do not really know what is the essential process of therapy." Practically all counselors and therapists believe that there is a flow and sequence in the process of counseling itself, but it has not been thoroughly investigated.

In a more specifically educational setting, Aschner (1961) using in-class analysis techniques, has discovered certain conventions and ground rules that tend to shape the course and contexts of classroom operation. Smith (1961) has investigated classroom interaction in an attempt to identify the logical dimensions of the teaching process. Smith points out the importance of studying both teacher and pupil behavior, as well as their mutual interaction. His view of the present state of knowledge of the teaching process is quite similar to that expressed by Rogers.

Our knowledge of the act of teaching as well as that of taking instruction is meager. Neither of these acts has been investigated sufficiently to justify from a scientific standpoint fundamental changes in teaching. . . . The act of teaching has received far less attention than its central role in pedagogy would seem to require (pp. 93-94).

There are two major prerequisites to an efficient analysis of the teaching process: (a) some type of classification system which enables the investigator to label teacher-pupil and pupil-pupil interactions, and (b) a theoretical structure which provides a basis for evaluating teacher behaviors in terms of their effectiveness. By using a particular frame of reference or theoretical structure, the investigator can evaluate a given instance of teacher-pupil interaction or a sequence of such interactions to see how closely the observed sample of behavior approximates the theoretical ideal or goal. Other investigators have adopted similar approaches in the study of the classroom or of a particular type of educational program (Flanders, 1960; Spaulding, 1962; and Suchman, 1961).

A RESEARCH PROJECT ON PRODUCTIVE THINKING

The present research is investigating productive thought processes in gifted children, as these are evidenced within the context of classroom verbal interaction. The definition of productive thinking used in this study is similar to that formulated in the theoretical structure developed by Guilford (1956). We define "productive thinking" as consisting in those divergent, convergent and evaluative operations whereby the individual draws upon available past and present acts, ideas, associations and observations in order to bring forth *new* facts, ideas and conclusions. Productive thinking, so defined, includes both the creative and critical-analytic dimensions of reasoning. The basic data for the present study of verbal interaction were obtained through tape recording five consecutive classroom sessions in 12 classes of intellectually superior children of junior high school age, in a variety of subject matters: Social Studies, Mathematics, Science and English.

THE GUILFORD CLASSIFICATION SYSTEM

Guilford's *Structure of Intellect,* (1956), was developed through a series of studies using factor analytic methodology. The parameters of this theoretical structure consist in the *operations* of thinking, the *content* within which these operations are performed and the *products* which result from the performance of these operations upon the content. Guilford has identified four types of content in his theoretical structure: *figural, symbolic, semantic* and *behavioral.* Figural content is represented by geometric patterns and designs which convey no intrinsic meaning. Symbolic content is made up of signs and signals which convey meaning by representing other things, such as numbers or formulae. Semantic content represents meaning as conveyed in spoken and written language. Behavioral content is identified as the physical actions and social behaviors of the individual. The present research concentrates primarily upon the areas of symbolic and semantic content, since these are emphasized in a school setting.

As products of thinking, Guilford lists *units, classes, relations, systems, transformations* and *implications*. For example: The apple *(unit)* is a tree-grown fruit *(class)*. If the wind blows much harder, the roof will be torn off our house *(implications)*. A brick has little in common with an ordinary book *(association)*, but I could use it for a book-end *(transformation)*. The more people there are who want something, the higher the price will be *(system)*. The last three of these product categories represent, in reality, more complex combinations of the first three, placed in various relationships with one another.

The present category system was constructed primarily on the operations of intellect as Guilford has described them. Five primary categories have been developed. These are: cognitive memory *(C-M)*, convergent thinking *(CT)*, divergent thinking *(DT)*, evaluative thinking *(ET)*, and routine *(R)*. The routine category consists in the familiar and conventional interpersonal maneuverings of speakers in the management activities of the classroom setting, and in a number of categories defining behaviors—verbal and otherwise—expressing affect and feeling tone.

In addition to the tape recordings of the classroom proceedings, two observers were present in the classroom during each recorded session, and took extensive notes on the classroom activities. They noted, for example, such things as blackboard diagrams and written material, textbook references, charts, and demonstration apparatus materials. In addition, they tried to identify the more obvious attitudinal dimensions of interaction between teacher and class, such as censure, praise, frustration, humor, etc. Each transcribed classroom session has been classified, unit by unit, by trained judges working with the scoring manual developed for this purpose (Aschner, Gallagher, *et al.*, 1962). These codings are then transferred to a flow chart for more extensive analysis. In order that the reader have some idea of the dimensions of each of these areas of cognitive behavior in the classroom, a brief description is given below.[2]

Cognitive-memory operations represents the simple reproduction of facts, formulae, or other items of remembered content through use of such processes as recognition, rote memory and selective recall. Some examples of cognitive-memory performance would be seen in the following:

T: Will you tell us what is the first question on the guidesheet?
Bill: What is the "spoils system"?

[2] See the addendum to this article for a more complete description of the categories. RTH, editor.

T: What were some of the main points covered in our discussion about mercantilism?

Mary: One of the things we learned was that there was an attempt to keep a favorable balance of trade.

T: Does anybody remember who was the sixteenth President of the United States?

Bob: Abraham Lincoln.

All of the above are examples of teacher-student interchanges that do not require the student to integrate or associate facts; the questions dealt with are all of the kind that can be handled by direct reference to the memory bank. The sole duty of the student is to select the appropriate response from his store of remembered items. While factual information is clearly indispensable to the development of higher thought processes, it is also obvious that it would be a sterile and uninteresting class that dealt exclusively with this type of question, never moving into the challenge and excitement of more complex operations.

Convergent thinking represents the analysis and integration of given or remembered data. It leads to one expected end-result or answer because of the tightly structured framework through which the individual must respond. Some examples of convergent thinking follow:

T: If I had six apples and gave John two, how many apples would I have left?

Bob: Four.

T: Can you sum up in one sentence what you think was the main idea in Paton's novel, *Cry The Beloved Country?*

Pete: That the problem of the blacks and the whites in Africa can only be solved by brotherly love; there is no other way.

Thus, convergent thinking may be involved in the solving of a problem, in the summarizing of a body of material, or in the establishment of a logical sequence of ideas or premises—as, for example, in reporting the way in which a machine works, or in describing the sequence of steps by which the passage of a bill through Congress is accomplished.

Divergent thinking represents intellectual operations wherein the individual is free to generate independently his own data within a data-poor situation, or to take a new direction or perspective on a given topic. Some examples of divergent thinking would be:

T: Suppose Spain had not been defeated when the Armada was destroyed in 1588 but that, instead, Spain had conquered England. What would the world be like today if that happened?

Sam: Well, we would all be speaking Spanish.

Peg: We might have fought a revolutionary war against Spain instead of England.

Tom: We might have a state religion in this country.

These examples represent teacher-stimulated divergent thinking, but it need not always be teacher-generated. In a regular discussion of the "spoils system," a student may come up with the following:

Well, sure, the spoils system might be a good thing when a political party is getting started, but what about when there's no party system—like in the United Nations?

Here the student reveals his ability to take off from an established fact or facts and see further implications or unique associations that have not been requested or perhaps even thought of by the teacher. Instances of this type of self-initiated student behavior would also fall under the general category of divergent thinking.

Evaluative thinking deals with matters of judgment, value and choice, and is characterized by its judgmental quality. For example:

T: What do you think of Captain Ahab as a heroic figure in Moby Dick?
Bob: Well, he was sure brave, but I think he was kind of mean the way he drove the men just because he had this crazy notion of getting back at Moby Dick.
T: Is it likely that we will have a hard winter?
Mary: Well, I think that the pattern of high pressure areas suggests that we will.
T: Who was the stronger President, Jackson or Adams?
Mike: Adams.

In the first of the above examples, the student is asked to construct a value dimension of his own in terms of what he considers "heroic," and then to make a judgment as to where on this value dimension he would place Captain Ahab. In the second response, the student is asked to make an estimate or to give a speculative opinion or assessment or probability. A third possibility involves entering a qualification or disagreement, wherein the respondent would offer a modification of a prior judgment of another student; or he may state a counter-judgment, in which he declares direct opposition to the statement of the previous speaker.

The final category, routine, contains a large number of miscellaneous classroom activities. Included here are the attitudinal dimensions of praise and censure of others and of self. Also present are dimensions of *structuring*, a kind of prefatory remark, telling in advance what the speaker intends to say or do, or what he expects someone else to say or do. Other characteristic occurrences, such as humor, as well as the ordinary, "routine" classroom management behaviors—even to requests to close the door or asking what time it is—are included in this primary category.

The excerpt given below represents about one and a half minutes of recorded classroom activity in a science class. The discussion concerned the relationship between gravitational attraction and the weight of a body in space.

[1] Doug: All right, then, so that if you weighed one-fourth as much as 10 lbs. you'd weigh 2.5 lbs., and since you go 4,000 miles from—and every time to weigh one-fourth as much, you would go 4,000 miles further than 12,000 miles, and that is 16,000.

T: At this point, I weigh 10 lbs., 16,000 miles out from the center of the earth.

[2] Doug: You said from the surface.

T: No, it is measured from the center of the earth. 12,000 miles from the surface would be 16,000 miles from the earth.

Doug: Oh.

[3] T: Are you with me now?

Doug: I thought you said to double the distance. . . . (remainder of Doug's comment unclear.)

T: No, you've got to double that distance every time. So, for example, in order to find out where I would weigh one-quarter as much as I do on the earth, I've got to double that distance. In order to find out where I weigh one-quarter as much as I weigh here, I've got to double that entire distance. So it's . . . . 20 . . . . 32,000 miles from the center of the earth or it's 28,000 miles from the earth's surface. Now, can you see that if I keep on doing this, and you can see that as I keep on doing this, I'll never, never, ever—Don—as you see that I keep on doing this, I'll never get to a point where I'll weigh nothing. [4] It would always be one-quarter of something. It would always be a small number. I can go out there forever and there will still be a small, a small fraction of an ounce that I would weigh. In other words, the gravitational attraction of any object never stops. It just keeps on going out. It gets less very rapidly but it never gets to nothing. Peter?

[5] Peter: Well, it's just like the rabbit who was being chased by the hound and the hound caught up by half as much each time and he never got there but he kept gaining more and more, half as much each time—closer.

[6] T: (Addressing the class) You all understand that problem? / [7] If I'm chasing one of you and every five minutes I get half the distance to you, I'll never reach you. I'll keep getting half the distance to you, but I'll never get there, because there will always be something—some distance between us.

The numbered remarks above represent typical features of teacher-student interaction behavior. These merit a closer consideration:

1. In this instance, Doug is giving a typical example of convergent thinking; he is spelling out the steps that he is following to obtain a solution to the problem.

2. Here, Doug is making a request for clarification, and is also actually questioning the correctness of the teacher's approach. This is a type of response that is usually observed only in the more self-assured students—youngsters who do not hesitate to express their doubts about the correctness of the teacher's position.

3. This type of teacher behavior is classified in the routine category and is called "monitoring-feedback." It is one type of teacher behavior in which the teacher attempts to ascertain whether or not the student or the class as a whole understands the point that he is trying to make.

4. In this instance, the teacher—after a long clarifying explanation—sets forth the general rule or principle underlying the phenomenon that they are discussing. Depending upon one's philosophy, one might suggest, in this instance, that it might have been better for the teacher to elicit the general rule from the students rather than to state it himself.

These are the sorts of points that can be brought under discussion through the use of tapescripts. In this way an experienced teacher, or a teacher-in-training, has the opportunity to examine his own performance and that of the students in the cool and quiet aftermath of the class session. Using tapescripts in this way is not unlike using motion pictures of football games to view on the day after the game, in order to find out why certain plays were successful while others were not. The teacher can profit greatly from a close study of the responses of his students to the ways in which he carries on instruction.

5. Despite the fact that this class sequence centers upon convergent thinking processes, some students, Peter for instance, are irrepressible; such students can be counted upon to come up with unique or unusual associations, as Peter does here by bringing in a highly appropriate analogy. This type of divergent thinking performance is far from commonplace, even among groups of highly talented students.

6. This is an example of teacher clarifying behavior in which he restates the analogy that Peter presented, thus to make sure that the students all grasped the point that Peter was trying to make.

7. The diagonal line between the first and second sentences of the teacher's remarks represent the division between thought units on the tapescript. In addition to being a promising tool for research in classroom interaction, the tapescript also provides, as we have said, an opportunity for the teacher to look over both his own performances and those of his students, in order to detect weak points in his own presentation, and to discover particular student problems that escaped him in the swift moment-by-moment pace of the classroom session itself.

Table 1 shows the total thought units classified in one social studies classroom over five consecutive 56-minute sessions. In this class, the boys seemed to be consistently more fluent verbally, and in the flow of ideas in all expressive areas. Using the Mann-Whitney U test, this difference between boys and girls was significant at the .10 level in the area of divergent thinking and total production, and approximated that level in the three other areas. Despite these differences in production, the proportion of the different thought processes used was quite similar in boys and girls. The interpretation to be applied to these proportions must await further analyses and comparisons with other classroom groups and other teachers.

TABLE 1

SEX DIFFERENCES IN EXPRESSED THOUGHTS IN SOCIAL STUDIES
CLASS FOR GIFTED CHILDREN

| | | Expressed Thought Processes (Five Consecutive Class Sessions) | | | | |
		Cognitive Memory	Convergent Thinking	Divergent Thinking	Evaluative Thinking	Total
Boys (N=10)	Mean	12.8	7.7	8.9	5.6	35.0
	Percent of Total	36	22	25	16	
Girls (N=9)	Mean	8.0	5.1	4.1	3.1	20.3
	Percent of Total	39	25	20	15	
Teacher	Total	262	100	31	107	500
	Percent of Total	52	20	6	22	
Boys vs. Girls* Mann Whitney U		25.5	28.0	24.0	28.5	24.0

* A U of 24 significant at .10 level.

The teacher's proportion of total thought productions (questions and statements) was rather similar to the students. She produced a higher percentage of cognitive-memory and evaluative responses, but a lower proportion in convergent and divergent thinking. Many of the teacher's cognitive-memory responses represented attempts to clarify and add to student statements, rather than a mere doling out of facts.

The low percentage of teacher divergent questions in comparison with student responses is described in more detail in Figure 1. Figure 1 indicates the relationship of the thought processes expressed by the students to the types of teacher questions posed during the five class sessions.

Although divergent production is presented in this figure, similar graphs can be made for each area of cognitive operation. It can be noted that 17 per cent of the teacher's total question-asking activities was done in divergent thinking in class session I, as opposed to 4 per cent in class session II, and 11 per cent in class session III, etc. It is interesting to note that the profile of the divergent production of both girls and boys, follows the same general pattern as that of the teacher. In those sessions during which the teacher asks for more divergent production, the percentages of responses in this area are correspondingly high. When the amount of divergent production requested stays below 5 per cent, the decrease in divergent production by the students is marked.

It may be noted however, that only a slight increase in the teacher's percentage of divergent questions brings forth a large increase in diver-

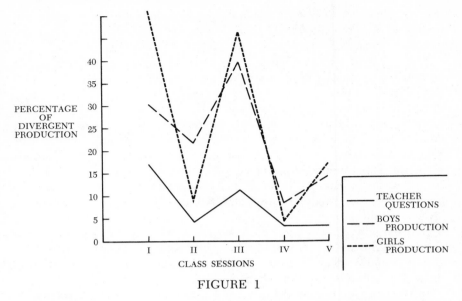

PERCENTAGE
OF
DIVERGENT
PRODUCTION

————— TEACHER
           QUESTIONS

— — — BOYS
           PRODUCTION

------ GIRLS
           PRODUCTION

CLASS SESSIONS

FIGURE 1

Relation of Teacher Questions to Student Divergent Thinking Production.

gent production in the students. This results from the fact that a single question, such as "What would happen if the United States were colonized from the West coast to the East instead of vice versa?", can bring forth as many as fifteen or twenty responses, each related to divergent production on the part of these gifted students.

While the boys produced more divergent responses than the girls, the ratio of their total responses to the divergent area was about the same, as seen in Figure 1. In addition to capturing much of the general flavor of the varieties of intellectual operations that occur in the classroom context, it is also possible to trace profiles of individual children, and to determine whether certain students may have problems in expressing themselves in a given area of intellectual operation. Further analyses will also deal more directly with the sequential patterns of teacher-student interaction, as distinguished from that quantification of total, over-all results, as indicated in Table 1 and Figure 1.

The long range goals of the present research include:

1. The construction of a reliable classification system by means of which the verbal interaction of teachers and pupils can be analyzed in any classroom, regardless of subject matter content or student ability level. It may be possible eventually to investigate the question of whether there are fundamental differences in expected intellectual operations from one subject matter to another—for example, from science to social studies, or

from mathematics to English. Such differences might explain, in part, the reason why some students are able to perform quite well in one subject area and yet perform poorly, or in a mediocre way, in other areas.

2. It is hoped that through an analysis of classroom interaction it will be possible to identify examples of certain kinds of highly desirable intellectual performance. It should then be feasible, working backward from these criterion cases, to see what types of teacher behavior or pupil behavior preceded and hence may have stimulated these desirable outcomes. In this manner it may be possible to gain insight into effective methods of teaching for higher conceptual performance, and thus to lay the groundwork for experimental studies in which teachers could—through the strategic use of certain kinds of behavior—seek to raise the level of intellectual productivity of gifted children and, indeed, of children at all levels of ability.

3. Attempts will be made to relate the in-class performances of the children in this study to a wide variety of measures of intellectual aptitude and personality characteristics, measures which were administered to them prior to tape recording their classroom sessions.

4. Measures of family attitudes and behavior will also be related to individual in-class performances through family interviews and questionnaires designed by the sociologist on the project staff.

The eventual goal of the project is to arrive at a description of the intellectual processes that occur in the classroom and, through this, to acquire not only a greater understanding of the teaching process itself, but also to work out more effective ways of training teachers for the stimulation of productive thought processes.

REFERENCES

ASCHNER, MARY JANE. The language of teaching. In Smith, B. O. and Ennis, R. H. (Eds.), *Language and concepts in education*. Chicago: Rand McNally, 1961.

ASCHNER, MARY JANE, GALLAGHER, J. J., JENNE, W. C., PERRY, JOYCE, FARR, HELEN, & AFSAR, SIBEL. A system for classifying thought processes in the context of classroom verbal interaction. (Mimeographed, Institute for Research on Exceptional Children, University of Illinois, 1962).

FLANDERS, N. A. *Teacher influence, pupil attitudes and achievement*. Minneapolis: U. of Minnesota Press, 1960. (Final report, Cooperative Research Project No. 397).

GUILFORD, J. P. The structure of intellect. *Psychol. Bull.*, 1956, 53, 267-293.

ROGERS, C. R. *Client-centered therapy*. Boston: Houghton Mifflin, 1951.

SMITH, B. O. A concept of teaching. In Smith, B. O. and Ennis, R. H. (Eds.), *Language and concepts in education*. Chicago: Rand McNally, 1961.

SPAULDING, R. L. Some correlates of classroom teacher behavior in elementary schools. Address given at A.E.R.A. meeting, Atlantic City, New Jersey, February 20, 1962.

SNYDER, W. U. *A casebook of non-directive counseling.* Boston: Houghton Mifflin, 1947.

SUCHMAN, J. R. Inquiry training: building skills for autonomous discovery. In Morse, W. C. and Wingo, G. M., *Psychology and Teaching.* Chicago: Scott Foresman, 1961.

ADDENDUM: SECONDARY CLASSIFICATION CATEGORIES[3]

I. ROUTINE (R)

This category includes routine classroom procedural matters such as management of the classroom, the structuring of class discussion and approval or disapproval of the idea or the person.

MANAGEMENT

Mq— *Question:* Requests or invitations to speak; calling for questions, as in "Anybody have a question?"

Mp— *Procedure:* Announcements or procedural instructions, given or requested for individuals or the group as a whole.

Ma— *Aside:* Incidental or parenthetical comment; gratuitous content.

Mnc— *Nose-Counting:* Calling for or responding with a show of hands for a tally or canvas.

Mfb— *Feedback:* Request for or response with signs from group as to whether or not the speaker's actions or remarks are clearly understood.

Mw— *Work:* Non-verbal actions or seatwork going on in connection with current discussion or class proceedings.

X— Unclassifiable response primarily due to technical recording difficulties.

STRUCTURING

Sts— *Self-Structuring:* Conventional prefatory move to signal content and purpose of one's own next remarks or behavior.

Reprinted with permission from *Productive Thinking of Gifted Children* by James J. Gallagher. U.S. Department of Health, Education, and Welfare, Office of Education; Cooperative Research Project No. 965. Urbana, Institute for Research on Exceptional Children, College of Education, University of Illinois, 1965.

[3] The full classification system and instructions are presented in a supplementary publication ASCHNER-GALLAGHER SYSTEM FOR CLASSIFYING THOUGHT PROCESSES IN THE CONTEXT OF CLASSROOM VERBAL INTERACTION, Urbana, Ill. University of Illinois, 1965.

Sto— *Structuring Other*(s): Engineering next speech or actions of others(s). Monitoring other's performance. Pump-priming to keep discussion going on a point already before the class.

Stf— *Future Structuring:* Forecast of future activity, study, learning, etc. beyond this particular class session.

Stc— *Class Structuring:* Focusing class attention on point to be emphasized or taken up; laying groundwork for question or problem; probing, pushing, adding data for bogged-down class (teacher only).

VERDICT

Ver— *Verdict:* (+ or —) Impersonal praise or reproach on quality of *academic* performance of individual or group.

Verp— *Personal Verdict:* (+ or —) Personal praise or reproach of individual. (Occasionally by T on whole class) Negative Verp generally on deportment.

Agr— AGREEMENT: (+ or —) Acceptance or rejection of content; conceding a point; *not* permission-giving nor procedural.

S— SELF REFERENCE: Speaker's personal report or comment upon or about self. Often conventional device; cautionary tactic.

Du— DUNNO: Explicit indication that one does not know.

Mu— MUDDLED: Speaker confused, mixed up, flustered.

Hu— HUMOR: Remark of evident witty, humorous, or comic intent; response (usually laughter) to same.

II. COGNITIVE-MEMORY (C-M)

C-M operations represent the simple reproduction of facts, formulas and other items of remembered content through use of such processes as recognition, rote memory and selective recall.

Scr— SCRIBE: Giving a spoken or written spelling or exemplification of a work or expression.

RECAPITULATION

Req— *Quoting:* Rote recitation or literal reading from text, paper or notes in hand.

Rep— *Repetition:* Literal or nearly verbatim restatement of something just said.

Rec— *Recounting:* Narration of past extra-class occurrence.

Rev— *Review:* Recitation of material which occurred or was discussed in current or past class session.

CLARIFICATION

Clm— *Clarifying Meaning:* Rendering a previous statement more intelligible either by (a) restating or rephrasing or (b) adding informative details.

Clq— *Clarifying Qualification:* Render a previous statement more accurate either by (a) "Entering a rider" upon the remark or (b) entering an explicit correction.

FACTUAL

Fs— *Fact Stating:* Requests for and recitations of items taken to be matters of fact.

Fd— *Fact Detailing:* Spinning out further a prior assertion of fact or other statements (As, Exr) in which factual items were mentioned.

Fm— *Factual Monologue:* Reporting of factual material in the form of a monologue during which verbal exchange is conventionally excluded.

III. CONVERGENT THINKING (CT)

Convergent thinking is thought operation involving the analysis and integration of given or remembered data. It leads to one expected result because of the tightly structured framework which limits it.

TRANSLATION

Tr— *Translation:* Shift of conceptual material from symbolic or figural content to semantic, or vice versa.

ASSOCIATION

As— *Association:* Involving likenesses and differences; degrees of comparison; and relationships of direction, spatial position and/or classification, etc.

EXPLANATION

Exr— *Rational Explanation:* Asking or telling why X is the case; why Y caused X, etc. Substantiating a claim or conclusion by citing evidence.

Exv— *Value Explanation:* Asking or telling why X is good, bad, useful, important, etc. Justifying a rating, viewpoint, or value-based judgment by giving reasons why.

Exn— *Narrative Explanation:* Step-by-step account of how something is done, how a mechanism works, or of what led up to an event or given outcome.

CONCLUSION

Gen— *Generalization:* Integration of prior remarks by slightly more general reformulation.

Cons— *Summary Conclusion:* Summary reformulation, often serial or enumerative, of material treated in discussion or reading.

Conl— *Logical Conclusion:* Calling for a deductively drawn implication from material presented.

IV. EVALUATIVE THINKING (ET)

Evaluative thinking deals with matters of value rather than matters of fact and is characterized in verbal performance by its judgmental character.

UNSTRUCTURED

Ura— *Unstructured Rating:* A value judgment produced or requested on some idea or item in terms of a scale of values provided by the respondent.

Uju— *Unstructured Judgment:* A value judgment produced or requested on some idea or item wherein the value dimension has already been provided.

STRUCTURED

Svp— *Structured Probability:* An estimate or speculative opinion is given or requested as to the likelihood of some occurrence or situation.

Svc— *Structured Choice:* Speaker calls for or declares his position as a choice between alternatives (not between *Yes or No* answers).

QUALIFICATION

Qj— *Qualified Judgment:* An offer or request for a rider or modification to a prior value judgment. Also, attempts to make more precise the value dimension discussed.

Q-c— *Counter Judgment:* Speaker declares a directly opposed position with respect to value statement of a previous classroom speaker.

V. DIVERGENT THINKING (DT)

In a Divergent Thinking sequence, individuals are free to independently generate their own ideas within a data-poor situation, often taking a new direction or perspective.

El— ELABORATION: Structured or free (s or f). Building upon a point already made; filling out or developing a point, but not shifting to a new point, often by concocting instances or examples.

Ad— DIVERGENT ASSOCIATION: (s or f) Constructing a relationship between ideas, casting the central idea into sharper and often unexpected perspective, by comparisons, analogies, etc.

Imp— IMPLICATION: (s or f) Extrapolation beyond the given, projection from given data—typically by antecedent—consequent or hypothetical construction—to new point(s) of possibility.

Syn— SYNTHESIS: Spontaneous performance, tying in, integrating the current central idea with an entirely new point or frame of reference. May be a variation or reversal of a previous conclusion.

Double Paired Ratings: The complex nature of verbal classroom interaction often requires the combination of more than one of the above described categories.

11. Hypothetical Thinking in Education

George S. Maccia

The rude awakening brought about by recent advances in Russian technology has brought on a flood of charges and counter-charges about the condition of education in the American schools. It has been said often that schools are developing a "group-mindedness" among our youth which depreciates individual excellence and effort. As a remedy some are calling for a return to hard "facts" and the so-called mind-sharpening disciplines of mathematics and science. Against the sound and fury of current controversies, I suggest that the solution to the problem for education in democracy does not lie in the reemphasis of certain specific subject contents severly taught. Furthermore, it lies only partially in social

"Hypothetical Thinking in Education" by George S. Maccia is reprinted with permission from *Educational Theory*, 10: 182-186, July, 1960.

adjustment. It lies, rather, in the development of the quality of thinking on the part of individual students.

Whether shaping satellites or democracy, individuals who think creatively and build co-operatively are necessary. Creative thinking employs both analysis and synthesis. Analysis and synthesis form part of the activities in which students are engaged in our nation's schools. In our classrooms experience is examined, distinctions are noted, categories are proposed, concepts are formed, concepts are related, and re-formed. Yet, creative thinking, unfortunately, is not emphasized in any great measure either in current educational practices or in current proposals for improvement. Certainly, individual differences in physiological equipment, cultural backgrounds, and in motivation do account in part for the small measure of creative thinking achieved in our schools. One might argue, indeed, as many do, that only a few are gifted. Nevertheless, I aver that there is a mind-set in much of our current methodology which shackles thought.

In our current methodology we have come to prize two notions about formal education both of which have been shaped to operate within a machinery of mass production. On the one hand we assert the primacy of subjects rooted in traditions of classical literature which we call the Humanities. On the other hand we assert the primacy of subjects rooted in traditions of naive empiricism which we call the Sciences. In the Humanities we dish out the gems of the past in order to preserve our heritage and to provide models for 'liberal' thinking. In the Sciences the most abstract conceptions are forced into ill-fitting models of actual experience in order to support the contention that experience teaches. Such methods, unfortunately, assure that meanings are confined to what is said to be actual, e.g., the descriptions of the writings of yesterday's creative thinkers and the quantitative relating of particular events. In both cases we cripple our youth by building around them a wall of actual experience too high for them to see what lies beyond. The creative man must re-make his experience. He must leap the wall and explore the region of the possible.

The thesis of this paper is that thinking analytically at any level of human discourse involves not only thinking in terms of what is actual, but also thinking in terms of experience which is not actual. In other words, thinking in terms of possibles is equally involved and is of utmost importance. The earth satellites remind us every ninety minutes or so of the necessity to think the possible.

If credence is to be given the claim that our current methodology in education cripples our youth, further explanation of what I mean by *thinking in terms of what is actual* and *thinking in terms of what is possible* is in order.

Thinking What Is Actual

Thinking in terms of the actual is the thinking we do when we describe particular objects or events. Our thoughts about the actual take the form, "Here is a . . ." That is to say, they are expressed in categorical statements. For instance, "Here is a black crow" is such a statement. Furthermore, thinking in terms of the actual leads us to summarize our descriptions about experience. We set forth descriptive generalizations such as, "All crows are black." When descriptive generalizations are a part of science, they are known as empirical laws. Boyle's law—"At constant temperature, the volume of a gas varies inversely with the external pressure" is an example from the physical sciences.

Thinking what is actual is, of course, a necessary skill for the isolation of objects and events from experience and for the grouping together of isolates of like kind. Descriptive generalizations are important tools in analytical thinking. They are used widely in every day affairs, as well as in science. Descriptive generalizations, unfortunately, are often regarded as the essence of thinking and of science. Consider the following statements: "Science," one student reported on an examination paper, "is a factual study built on definite concrete knowledge"; "The study of science is a purely physical task," reported another. How often have you read or heard similar statements about science? If more evidence is required that descriptive generalizations are often regarded as the essence of science, I refer the reader to any of the several textbooks in the teaching of elementary science methods. And for evidence that it is not uncommon in education to place a premium upon thinking in terms of what is actual, I suggest that the reader examine the current crop of textbooks on audiovisual methods in education.

Thinking What Is Possible

Thinking what is possible is hypothetical thinking. Such thinking is characterized in part by the employment of conditional propositions which are of the form, "if p then q." A proposition of this form is suppositional.

In the sciences conditional statements are often about inferred entities —e.g., statements about molecules or atoms or electrons. Consider the following statement: "If the kinetic energy of a gas is increased then molecules travel at a higher rate of velocity." The inferred entity, molecule, which is talked about in the preceding statement differs from an

actual entity. It is derived, not observed. Thus, the statement is suppositional rather than actual.

Hypothetical thinking also employs the contrary-to-fact statement which
differs from the conditional statement in being expressed in the subjunc-
tive mood. For example, the chemist states: "If the temperature were to
fall to − 273°C there would be zero volume." This statement does not
relate directly to what is actual. All known substances solidify at a
temperature above − 273°C, thereby fixing observable volume at some
definite value greater than zero. Every schoolboy and every physical
scientist uses the concept of Absolute Zero, a concept which is derived
from the proposition just stated. Although the schoolboy may be, the
scientist is not disturbed by the obvious discrepancy between his thinking
and his experience of the actual. The scientist knows that he can describe
the actual with greater certainty by considering what is possible, rather
than by solely considering what is actual.

HYPOTHETICAL THINKING AND PROBLEM SOLVING

We have seen that analytical thinking has, at least, two characteristics:
description of the actual and consideration of the possible. It is now my
intention to point out that problem solving relies more on hypothetical
thinking than it does on description of particulars and descriptive
generalizations.

Much is made of the importance of contact between the thinker and
something actual. Emphasis is placed upon experience of the actual. It
must be noted that the experience of the possible is justifiable in science,
only so far as it is rooted in what is actual. Such a prescription is necessary
if wild speculation is to be avoided. Some educators place too high a
premium, however, on description and descriptive generalizations. Problem solving is looked upon merely as a guess concerning the conclusions
of the study which are to be expressed in the form of descriptive generalizations. Such a procedure would never conclude with a derived entity
such as Absolute Zero, for the particulars which could be observed say
nothing directly about it—indeed, they are all against such a formulation.
Absolute Zero is a hypothetical entity, remains a hypothetical entity, but
it provides, nevertheless, part of the means for solving certain kinds of
problems.

The function of hypothetical thinking in problem solving has been
minimized. The emphasis upon particulars tends to restrict thinking to
that which is descriptive of what is actual and places a premium upon
the weighting of hypothetical thinking on the side of the greatest number

of particulars. I am not suggesting that particulars be ignored. I am suggesting that we can value particulars too highly, and may fall into the error of Comté. As Peirce put it: "Comté's own notion of a verifiable hypothesis was that it must not suppose anything that you are not able directly to observe. From such a rule it would be fair to infer that he would permit Mr. Schlieman to suppose he was going to find arms and utensils at Hissarlik but would forbid him to suppose that they were either made or used by any human being, since no such beings could ever be detected by direct percept. He ought on the same principle to forbid us to suppose that a fossil skeleton had ever belonged to a living ichthyosarus." (V.579)[1]

The history of science reveals that frequently in theory construction fruitful hypothetical thinking runs counter to what is suggested by the greater body of particulars. We are all now aware of the tremendous impact of Einstein's hypothetical thinking in our everyday world. His thinking grew out of the findings of the Michelson-Morley experiments and these, in turn, ran counter to the greater body of particulars then known about physical phenomena. Consider also De Broglie, who turned his back on the particulars and hypothesized phase waves which are mathematical devices not directly related to particulars, but which make possible mathematical reconciliation of waves and particles existing together in mechanical motion. Schroedinger, in developing his generalized wave mechanics, likewise hypothesized special conditions that are totally absurd in so far as our actual spatial experience is concerned. He postulated nine dimensions for the helium atom and 279 dimensions for an atom of uranium, thereby resolving some of the contradictions in the wave-particle theory of matter.

Dirac's solution was even further removed from the particular than either De Broglie's or Schroedinger's. His mathematical symbols were completely general and did not define or represent any actual conditions or events. Algebraic axioms, some restrictive assumptions, the deductions from these assumptions, and the relations between the equations evolved from the entire set of building blocks for his solution to the wave-particle problem. Dirac's solution for the integration of scattered and contradictory data provides a case for problem solving which is greatly removed from the naive conception of problem solving often propounded in what is called the "Method of Science."

Doing things and being done by things is not the be all and end all of problem solving. Seeing possible relations within a system of thought seems to provide significant contributions to the solutions of problems.

---

[1] *Collected Papers of Charles Sanders Peirce*, ed. by Hartshorne and Weiss.

HYPOTHETICAL THINKING AND EDUCATION

In requesting that a closer look be given to hypothetical thinking and its role in the solving of problems, I do not suggest that counting angels on pinheads is a fruitful educational exercise. Thinking about the actual is one aspect of analytical thinking. It is a necessary aspect, for it anchors hypothetical thinking ultimately to experience to which all men can attest. What I would warn against is the tendency to think what is actual so rigidly that only one possible set of relations is seen. In order to solve problems, analytical thinking must include what is possible. The thinker must not only allow for different relationships, but must break the bonds of conventional relationships and alter patterns of thinking which have become habitual or which follow exclusively the suggestions which appear to be called for by particulars.

In order to illustrate my meaning, consider the following example:

Problem

You are asked to connect the dots in the figure by means of four straight lines drawn continuously. In order to accomplish this integration, the individual must surmount certain conventions or patterns of integration which are suggested by the apparent relation of the dots:

(1) the dots mark off the area within which the lines are to be drawn,

(2) each line must pass through the same number of dots, and

(3) the figure is completely closed within the configuration of the dots. The solution to this particular problem requires thinking which considers relationships which are not suggested by the dots themselves. A reorientation is required. The solver of this problem must think what is possible. In other words, hypothetical thinking is required, as the solution reveals.

If the foregoing analysis of the nature of hypothetical thinking has merit certain conclusions follow for education. More emphasis should be placed upon hypothetical thinking. Students should be confronted by situations which call for the reorientation of his experience. He must be

Solution

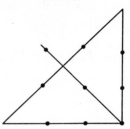

asked to see possible relations. He should be encouraged to think suppositionally.

Some steps in this direction have been taken in the physical sciences. Students are asked to solve problems of the following sort:

(1) You have a closed box which contains an infinite supply of oxygen. In the box is a lighted candle which is fastened to the bottom of the box. The box is dropped off a cliff and falls freely for several thousand feet. What would happen inside the box?

(2) You are falling freely in space. In each hand you hold a bar of the same kind of metal. One of the bars is a magnet. How can you tell which bar is the magnet?

In order to solve these problems, the student must think what is actual. He must know the particulars of science in their ordinary relationships. But it is not the knowledge of particulars alone which brings the solution. The student must think in terms of a world of experience in which there is no gravity and deduce what is possible in such a world. In other words, the student must think hypothetically.

Reorientation of thinking seems to be the first step to thinking creatively. Once reorientation occurs, habitual patterns of thinking are no longer relied upon exclusively. Insights about possible relationships, hitherto undreamed, are allowed. The thinker, whether he be a scientist or a poet, becomes free to create new theories or new language forms. In this way a new world of experience is synthesized.

Thus, it appears that education has a twofold task. First, activities should be provided which enable the student to acquire mastery of the tools, methods, and relationships which have been developed for ordering experience. Second, the student should be involved in activities which will enable him to obtain a sensitivity to possible relationships which are outside the experience in which he normally operates. The student must deal with the possible.

12. Cognitive Objectives Revealed by Classroom Questions Asked by Social Studies Student Teachers[1]

O. L. Davis, Jr., and Drew C. Tinsley

Questions posed in the social studies classroom for over half a century have been recognized as emphasizing memory as the most important cognitive operation (*e.g.*, Adams, 1964; Barr, 1929; Stevens, 1912). Yet, during this period, the attention of the social studies has been focused repeatedly on admonitions to foster pupils' critical thinking and, especially in recent years, discovery procedures. Common also has been the belief that classroom questions of "fact" and "thought" productively might be distinguished. Consequently, more appropriate social studies objectives have been thought possible by teachers stressing "thought" questions.

In the past decade considerable progress has been made in the analysis of cognitive operations (Bloom, 1956; Guilford, 1956) and "memory" and "knowledge" have come to be seen more adequately as essential and prerequisite to thinking. Cognitive processes, misunderstood as "thought" in general, have been identified in hierarchical complexity. Use of these systems as criteria has proved powerful in understanding a variety of educational matters. With respect to instructional objectives, the *Taxonomy of Educational Objectives: Cognitive Domain* (Bloom, 1956) has been particularly influential. For example, objectives revealed in social studies textbook questions have been analyzed (Davis and Hunkins, 1966) as have classroom examinations (Pfeiffer and Davis, 1965) and Jarolimek (1962) has demonstrated the *Taxonomy*'s value in planning differentiated instruction.

The *Taxonomy*, however, has not been applied to an analysis of questions in classroom interaction. Previous studies of teaching have considered questions in their analyses . . . but the questions of both teachers and pupils have not been studied against the criteria of the *Taxonomy*.

This study, then, was designed to determine the range of cognitive objectives manifest in secondary school social studies classrooms by questions asked by student teachers and their pupils.

This paper was presented at the annual meeting of the American Educational Research Association, New York, February, 1967, and is reprinted with permission of the authors and the *Peabody Journal of Education*.

[1] The authors gratefully acknowledge the cooperation of Don Edwards, Jean McMillan, and Gregg Millett for their assistance in data collection and to Luke Davis, III, and Cathy Hennan for help in data processing.

METHOD

Participating in the study were 44 individuals enrolled in secondary student teaching of the social studies at The University of Texas during the fall semester, 1966. Of these, 32 taught at the senior high school level and 12 taught in junior high schools.

A *Teacher-Pupil Question Inventory* (TPQI) was developed by the investigators and was the source of data analyzed in this study. The TPQI schedule requires a classroom observation of 30 minutes divided into alternating five-minute periods. At each instance of a question asked by either the teacher or a pupil, the observer decides which category in which the question may be classified and marks a tally in a provided space. Questions are judged by attention to their form and inferred intent as well as the nature of the response elicited and its reception by the pupil or teacher. The TPQI has nine categories, seven of which are based on the Bloom *Taxonomy* and the formulations of Sanders (1966). The remaining two classifications include non-cognitive questions. The nine categories are as follows:

1. *Memory*—The one questioned recalls or recognizes information (facts, generalizations, etc.);
2. *Translation*—The one questioned changes information into a different form (linguistic, symbolic, image, etc.);
3. *Interpretation*—The one questioned states relationships between various types of data;
4. *Application*—The one questioned solves a realistic problem requiring the identification of the crucial issue or points and the selection and use of appropriate knowledge and skills;
5. *Analysis*—The one questioned answers with explicit attention to the relationship(s) between the ideas expressed and with obvious awareness of the process employed in the reasoning.
6. *Synthesis*—The one questioned suggests answers to a problem that is original, speculative, or creative;
7. *Evaluation*—The one questioned makes a judgment according to explicit criteria (external or internal);
8. *Affectivity*—The one questioned responds with a statement of feeling, emotion, or opinion without a standard of appraisal;
9. *Procedure*—The question relates to classroom organization, student behavior, or instructional management.

Each student teacher was observed at least twice by their regular university supervisor. Prior to the observations and following a design similar to one used by Flanders (1963), the supervisors underwent a period of training in the use of the TPQI and procedures to be followed in the study. By the end of training, the observers reached almost unanimouse agreement on classification of questions in the training (audiotaped) materials. Midway during the observation period, observers met again for another training session. Consequently the reliability of observations may be considered adequate.

RESULTS

TPQI item frequencies were determined for the entire group; means of individual teachers' item totals were computed and medians of these means were determined (see Table I).

TABLE I

TOTAL QUESTIONS AND MEDIANS AND RANGES OF MEAN NUMBERS
OF QUESTIONS ASKED BY SOCIAL STUDIES STUDENT TEACHERS
AND THEIR CLASSES (N=44)

Question Category	TEACHERS			PUPILS		
	Total	Median	Range	Total	Median	Range
Memory	1313	11.25	.67-36.33	714	0.25	0-5.00
Translation	187	1.00	0-8.00	123	0	0-4.00
Interpretation	391	3.70	0-10.00	401	0.33	0-4.33
Application	40	0	0-5.00	0	0	0
Analysis	66	0	0-6.00	3	0	0-.50
Synthesis	10	0	0-4.00	5	0	0-2.00
Evaluation	136	.70	0-11.00	15	0	0-1.50
Affectivity	78	0	0-8.00	4	0	0-.50
Procedural	299	2.50	0-11.0	118	0	0-6.00

Inspection of these data reveals that both teachers and pupils asked more "memory" questions than all other questions combined. The next largest number of questions fell in the "interpretation" and "translation" categories. "Procedure" questions for both teachers and pupils and "evaluation" questions for teachers followed as less frequently asked. The medians of zero (0), as well as the low item frequencies, indicated that questions asking for expressions of "affectivity" and the higher cognitive processes were seldom noted overall and, when observed, were evidenced by only a few of the teachers and their pupils. The types of questions asked by teachers and pupils were highly correlated (rs = .90).

Questions of junior high and senior high student teachers were further analyzed by categorizing, for each item, individuals whose item mean fell above and below the group median for that item. On only three items were there obtained significant differences: "translation" (*chi square* = 5.47, p < .05); "evaluation" (*chi square* = 18.05, p < .001); and "procedure" (chi square = 4.05, p < .05). These results indicate that a larger proportion of junior high student teachers asked more questions in these categories than did senior high student teachers.

The number and percents of the student teachers and their classes which asked no questions in the question categories are presented in Table II.

TABLE II

NUMBER AND PERCENT OF SOCIAL STUDIES STUDENT TEACHERS AND THEIR CLASSES (N=44) ASKING NO QUESTIONS IN QUESTION CATEGORIES

| Question Category | TEACHER | | | | | | PUPIL | | | | | |
| | All (N=44) | | Sr. Hi. (N=32) | | Jr. Hi. (N=12) | | All (N=44) | | Sr. Hi. (N=32) | | Jr. Hi. (N=12) | |
	N	%	N	%	N	%	N	%	N	%	N	%
Memory	0	0	0	0	0	0	20	45	17	53	3	25
Translation	18	41*	14	44	4	33	29	66	24	75	5	42
Interpretation	1	2	0	0	1	8	19	43	17	53	2	17
Application	34	77	24	75	10	83	44	100	32	100	12	100
Analysis	28	64	22	69	6	50	41	93	31	97	10	83
Synthesis	42	95	31	97	11	92	42	95	30	94	12	100
Evaluation	17	39	15	47	2	17	37	84	32	100	5	42
Affectivity	29	66	25	78	4	33	42	95	32	100	10	83
Procedure	7	16	5	16	2	17	28	64	25	78	3	25

* Rounded to nearest percent.

Not one of the student teachers failed to ask a "memory" question; all but one asked an "interpretation" question; and less than one-sixth did not ask a "procedure" question. Over one-half of the student teachers in both groups asked *no* questions categorized as "application," "analysis," and "synthesis," and, for the senior high group alone, "affectivity." Pupils in most classes observed failed to ask other than "memory," "procedure," and "translation" questions. Pupils in *no* class asked an "application" question and pupils in most classes did *not* ask questions of the teacher requiring "translation," "analysis," "synthesis," "evaluation," "affectivity," or even "procedure." The types of questions *not* asked by teachers and by pupils were closely related (junior high: rs = .93; senior high: rs = .76).

DISCUSSION

Memory or the acquisition of knowledge was the major cognitive objective apparent in teachers' and pupils' verbal questions in these social studies classes. Indeed, when the "translation" and "interpretation" categories are combined into "comprehension" (Bloom, 1956), no other cognitive objective seems to have been effectively operational in these 44 social studies classrooms. As a result, the intellectual atmosphere of these social studies classes can only be characterized as meager.

These findings are remarkably similar to those reported by Gallagher (1965). He noted that "cognitive-memory" was the most dominant thought process for both teachers and pupils in social studies. Also, an overwhelming emphasis upon acquisition of knowledge and a neglect of other cognitive objectives has been reported in an analysis of ninth-grade social studies examinations (Pfeiffer and Davis, 1965).

The accumulating evidence indicates persuasively that the major objectives guiding secondary school social studies classes are those emphasizing "memory" and "comprehension." Since Bloom (1965) described "comprehension" as the lowest form of intellectual activity, the operational objectives cannot be considered any but having a low congitive level. This conclusion is particularly depressing in light of the generally held objective for the social studies to foster critical thinking, certainly involving high-level cognitive operations. Too, that student teachers evidenced behaviors typical of the field is surely cause for concern. At least two major observations seem viable.

One, more deliberate attention to different cognitive objectives in social studies' classrooms is necessary. To be sure, questions requiring memory will be essential, for knowledge is prerequisite to thinking. If other and higher level cognitive objectives *are* considered desirable, the types of questions employed in the classroom must be altered. Not only, but certainly, must social studies' teachers change the use of their own language (questions), but also must the type of questions be changed in classroom tests and in instructional materials (Davis and Hunkins, 1966). These suggestions are patently practical for Hunkins (1966) demonstrated that by changing the cognitive emphasis of questions in instructional materials to higher levels, pupil achievement was increased.

Two, specific understandings and skills of classroom questioning and the purposes of questions need major attention in the pre-service and in-service education of teachers. Apparently, any consideration, if any, of these important learnings by teacher candidates, at least those in this study, was not realistic and specific enough for them to be incorporated as behaviors. If social studies objectives are to emphasize higher thinking processes in practice, such a condition cannot be tolerated. Use of micro-teaching techniques (Allen, 1966), a study program based on classroom-tested materials (*e.g.*, Sanders, 1966), and feed-back and discussion of information obtained with the TPQI are reasonable possibilities. As a beginning, certainly, courses in social studies methods and student teaching could incorporate a component dealing specifically with questions, their cognitive emphases, and candidates' ability to vary their use of questions in classroom discourse.

REFERENCES

ADAMS, THOMAS H. *The Development of a Method for Analysis of Questions Asked by Teachers in Classroom Discourse.* Doctor's thesis, New Brunswick, New Jersey: Rutgers, The State University, 1964. 149 pp.

ALLEN, DWIGHT W. "A New Design for Teacher Education: The Teacher Intern Program at Stanford University." *The Journal of Teacher Education* 17: 296-300; Fall 1966.

AMIDON, EDMUND. "Interaction Analysis: Recent Developments." Unpublished paper read at American Education Research Association. Chicago, Illinois: February, 1966. 10 pp. (mimeographed).

BARR, ARVIL S. *Characteristic Differences in the Teaching Performance of Good and Poor Teachers of the Social Studies.* Bloomington, Illinois: Public School Publishing Co., 1929. 127 pp.

BELLACK, ARNO A. AND JOEL R. DAVITZ. *The Language of the Classroom: Meanings Communicated in High School Teaching, Part I.* USOE Coopera-tive Research Project #1497, New York: Institute of Psychological Research, Teachers College, Columbia University, 1963. 200 pp.

BLOOM, BENJAMIN S. (editor). *Taxonomy of Educational Objectives; Handbook I: Cognitive Domain.* New York: David McKay, Inc., 1956. 207 pp.

DAVIS, O. L., JR. AND FRANCIS P. HUNKINS. "Textbook Questions: What Think-ing Processes Do They Foster?" *Peabody Journal of Education* 43: 285-292; March, 1966.

DODL, NORMAN R. "Questioning Behavior of Elementary Classroom Groups." *The California Journal of Instructional Improvement* 9: 167-179; October, 1966.

FLANDERS, NED A. "Intent, Action, and Feedback: A Preparation for Teach-ing." *Journal of Teacher Education* 14: 251-260; September, 1963.

GALLAGHER, JAMES J. "Expressive Thought by Gifted Children in the Class-room." *Elementary English* 42: 559-568; May, 1965.

GALLAGHER, JAMES AND MARY JANE ASCHNER. "A Preliminary Report: Analysis of Classroom Interaction." *Merrill-Palmer Quarterly of Behavior and Develop-ment* 9: 183-194; July, 1963.

GUILFORD, J. P. "The Structure of Intellect." *Psychological Bulletin* 53: 267-293; July, 1956.

HUNKINS, FRANCIS P. *The Influence of Analysis and Evaluation Questions on Critical Thinking and Achievement in Sixth Grade Social Studies.* Doctor's thesis. Kent, Ohio: Kent State University, 1966. 301 pp.

JAROLIMEK, JOHN. "The Taxonomy: Guide to Differentiated Instruction." *Social Education* 26: 445-447; December, 1962.

MEDLEY, DONALD M. "OScAR: Still Developing." Unpublished paper read at American Educational Research Association, Chicago, Illinois: February, 1966. 12 pp. (mimeographed).

PFEIFFER, ISOBEL AND DAVIS, O. L., JR. "Teacher-Made Examinations: What Kind of Thinking Do They Demand?" *NASSP Bulletin* 49: 1-10; September, 1965.

SANDERS, NORRIS M. *Classroom Questions: What Kinds?* New York: Harper & Row, 1966. 176 pp.

SLOAN, FRED A., JR. AND ROBERT T. PATE. "Teacher-Pupil Interaction in Two Approaches to Mathematics." *The Elementary School Journal* 67: 161-167; December, 1966.

SMITH, B. O. AND M. O. MEUX. *A Study of the Logic of Teaching.* USOE Co-operative Research Project #258. Urbana: University of Illinois, 1962. 231 pp.

STEVENS, ROMIETT. *The Question as a Measure of Efficiency in Instruction.* Teachers College Contribution to Education No. 48, New York: Teachers College, Columbia University, 1912. 95 pp.

TABA, HILDA; LEVINE, S. AND ELZEY, F. *Thinking in Elementary School Children.* USOE Cooperative Research Project #1574. San Francisco, California: San Francisco State College, 1964. 207 pp. (mimeographed).

The Emotional Climate

OVERVIEW

TEACHERS have long looked at teaching from the vantage point of psychology. To study teaching, they have used such concepts as anxiety, hostility, interpersonal relationship, and withdrawal. They have conducted investigations of the teacher's personality traits, especially those of the "effective" teacher. As part of their certification program, they have studied the principles of educational psychology as these relate to teaching. In short, the emotional perspective for the study of teaching is very familiar and widely accepted.

The reason is fairly obvious. The achievement of any goal is facilitated by a favorable emotional atmosphere, and the goal of gaining knowledge and skills is no exception. Furthermore, as shown by other articles in this book, learning of this type is only one goal of teaching. It is not surprising, then, that Rogers, Stavsky, Macdonald and Zaret, and Withall all point to the necessity for a good emotional tone in teaching and to the need for a favorable interpersonal relationship between the teacher and the student. Withall's brief statement is an excellent summary of this point: "learning, as change in behavior, is most likely to occur when there is a non-threatening situation, when the learner interacts in a wholesome social milieu." Stavsky claims that without a positive interpersonal relationship teaching is relatively ineffective. Bills[1] cites research which shows that when the teacher creates a favorable interpersonal relationship, that is, when the teacher is process-like, to use Bills' term, the students feel more positive toward other students in the class. Also, this process-like behavior is seen by students as helpful to them in their fuller development. Furthermore, the process-like teacher shares decision-making with his students.

Because of these insights, the analysis of teaching from the emotional vantage point is fundamental. This analysis takes three forms in the following section: (1) the categorizing of classroom verbal behavior; (2) the rating of statements about teaching; and (3) the expository analyzing of teaching based on experience and previous research.

In the first type, the article by Withall is already a classic, for it was the first attempt to establish a category system for describing classroom discourse from the emotional perspective. Withall does not present data relating emotional climate to learning, for his purpose was first to establish that the climate of the classroom can be empirically detailed. And he did do this. He builds on the work by Anderson and Lippitt and in turn influences the work of Flanders and many others who do relate classroom climate to learning. (It is suggested that the reader compare the definitions of climate offered by Withall and Flanders. See Section Four of this book for "Teacher Influence, Pupil Attitudes, and Achievement" by Flanders.)

Macdonald and Zaret also develop a system for categorizing the verbal behavior of the teacher and students. As opposed to Withall's continuum, which proceeds from learner-centeredness to teacher-centeredness, these two investigators use a process continuum going from opening behavior to closing behavior. Their categories are more complicated because they analyze both teacher and pupil talk and use different categories for each. For Withall the unit is a teacher statement, and for Macdonald and Zaret it is the question-answer response flow occuring within a critical incident.

The article "The Concept of an Ideal Teacher-Student Relation-

---

[1] Robert E. Bills. "Insights for Teaching from Personality Theory: Intelligence and Teaching." *The Nature of Teaching.* Ed. by Louise M. Berman. Milwaukee, University of Wisconsin-Milwaukee, 1963. p. 49-64.

ship: A Comparison and Critique," focuses on the interpersonal relationship created in teaching. The instrument is an adaptation of one originally used to rate the psychotherapeutic relationship. The study deals with the ideal, not the actual, teaching relationship. As the article notes, though the instrument has limitations with regard to rating the teaching relationship, it still provides data which drive home the importance that teachers ascribe to a good relationship with their pupils.

In an unpublished thesis, Giladi[2] reports that the concepts of the most ideal and least ideal teaching relationship held by a group of Israeli teachers and high school students are in high agreement and are also similar to those reported in "The Concept of an Ideal Teacher-Student Relationship: A Comparison and Critique." Before reading the latter article completely, the reader may wish to use the instrument himself to generate his own data on teaching. This will then allow him to compare his data with those published here from the five groups studied.

The two other selections by Rogers and Stavsky consider teaching non-empirically. Rogers bases his article on his extensive experience and writings as a practicing psychotherapist, teacher of psychotherapists, and researcher. He, more than any other contemporary psychotherapist, has encouraged teachers to apply therapeutic concepts and principles to teaching. In a manner similar to Phenix in the section on the vantage point of games, Rogers first sets forth the goals and conditions of learning in psychotherapy as he conceives it. Then he discusses the implications of these points for teaching. (He uses the word *education* here as a synonym for classroom teaching.) The reader will quickly notice that several of Rogers' ideas run counter to current teaching practices found in our schools, e.g., testing and lecturing.

Stavsky first considers the role of anxiety in the lives of children and then specifically treats the role of anxiety in teaching children in the classroom. He acknowledges that he regards teaching as similar to psychotherapy and therefore easily applies therapeutic

[2] Moshe Giladi. A Study of the Concept of the Ideal Teacher-Student Relationship in a Kibbutz School. Unpublished Master of Education Thesis. New Brunswick, Graduate School of Education, Rutgers—The State University, 1967.

notions to teaching. His definition of teaching is obviously a clear utilization of the psychotherapeutic vantage point. The reader is alerted to Stavsky's point about the role of discipline in teaching, for his opinions seem quite different from prevailing ideas.

The articles in this section tie in with other sections. As noted elsewhere, the article by Hallman serves as an excellent bridge between the psychological and aesthetic perspectives. Indeed, Hallman draws heavily on Rogers' writings to show the importance of psychological concepts for creativity and creative teaching. Similarly, Curran's demand for the removal of the humdrum in teaching as a condition for making teaching artistic parallels Rogers' plea that teaching should put students in real contact with life's problems so as to bring about the desire to create. It is clear, then, that these perspectives, psychological and aesthetic, center around sets of emotions which have considerable overlap and that the reader will be able to compare these emotions by carefully examining the various articles.

But this section has its closest ties with the one on classroom social climate. Indeed, the connection between the two is shown in the term "social-emotional climate." Flanders readily acknowledges that he builds upon the work of Withall. He employs Withall's concept of social-emotional climate but defines it somewhat differently. An examination of Flanders' ten categories will show how he relies on this psychological perspective. Even the style of analyzing the data is similar, as will be shown by a comparison of Withall with Flanders and Chapline. It is only fair to note that one significant difference from Withall is Flanders' lack of a continuum and scale in the categories defining influence.

The need for the teacher to accept and support the pupil, a need that is stressed in every article in this section, is seen in Hughes as well as Flanders. Two of Hughes' seven functions of teaching deal with affectivity; and in her model of good teaching, cited in the overview to Section 4, she calls for a high range of 10-20 per cent for positive affectivity. Yet she does not eliminate negative affectivity completely. This position may be in line with Schwab's view that teacher correction of the pupil is a positive characteristic when done within the context of an overall face-to-face relationship. The teacher, according to these authors, should praise and support the student but not indiscriminately.

This is the point of Macdonald and Zaret's comment about a teacher being locked in an open position. That is, some teachers may exhibit only one type of behavior pattern; and though it may be the open, or positive, position, it may not be always desirable. In the light of Flanders' firm statement that students who achieved the most learning were in classes exposed to flexible patterns of teacher influence, it is necessary to give added thought to this point. Whether explicit or implicit, the call for mixed behavior seems prevalent. The reader may wish to compare this type of behavior mixture with the one labeled transactional by Getzels and Thelen in their article in Section 4.

A brief note on the relation between this section and the cognitive and communications vantage points is in order. The Macdonald and Zaret article reveals that connection most clearly, for they incorporate categories from Gallagher and Aschner. Furthermore, in their report of results, Macdonald and Zaret point out that the teacher gets the responses he solicits. This, they note, is corroborated by Gallagher and Aschner. Similarly, the data in other articles indicate that good communications is extremely important to the realization of an ideal teacher-student relationship.

How adequate is the psychotherapeutic framework for analyzing teaching? Since psychotherapy is most often a voluntary relation between one therapist and one client (to use Rogers' term), the question is whether the concepts and principles of psychotherapy, which are based on that kind of relationship, can be applied usefully to classroom teaching. If not directly applied, can they still be used to guide our analysis. Is it meaningful to talk about teaching in such terms as Rogers' "significant learning"? If so, is it possible for classroom teachers to bring about "significant learning"? Is it meaningful to talk about teaching in such terms as anxiety, interpersonal relationship, transference, and hostility? In what ways does the employment of these concepts give us insight into teaching? Obviously, the authors in this section are convinced that such concepts are relevant to the study of teaching, as Macdonald and Zaret explicitly state at the end of their article. Many readers may wish to carry the discussion further.

There is little point here in suggesting further research questions, for Withall's are more than adequate as a start. Much more research is needed, however, about the effect of different emotional climates, not only on the pupil's learning but also on his verbal and nonverbal behavior patterns.

13.   Significant Learning: In Therapy and in Education

Carl R. Rogers

Presented here is a thesis, a point of view, regarding the implications which psychotherapy has for education. It is a stand which I take tentatively, and with some hesitation. I have many unanswered questions about this thesis. But it has, I think, some clarity in it, and hence it may provide a starting point from which clear differences can emerge.

SIGNIFICANT LEARNING IN PSYCHOTHERAPY

Let me begin by saying that my long experience as a therapist convinces me that significant learning is facilitated in psychotherapy, and occurs in that relationship. By significant learning I mean learning which is more than an accumulation of facts. It is learning which makes a difference—in the individual's behavior, in the course of action he chooses in the future, in his attitudes and in his personality. It is a pervasive learning which is not just an accretion of knowledge, but which interpenetrates with every portion of his existence.

Now it is not only my subjective feeling that such learning takes place. This feeling is substantiated by research. In client-centered therapy, the orientation with which I am most familiar, and in which the most research

Reprinted with permission of the Association for Supervision and Curriculum Development and Carl R. Rogers from *Educational Leadership*, 16: 232-242, January, 1959. Copyright © 1959 by the Association for Supervision and Curriculum Development.

has been done, we know that exposure to such therapy produces learnings, or changes, of these sorts:

The person comes to see himself differently.

He accepts himself and his feelings more fully.

He becomes more self-confident and self-directing.

He becomes more the person he would like to be.

He becomes more flexible, less rigid, in his conceptions.

He adopts more realistic goals for himself.

He behaves in a more mature fashion.

He changes his maladjustive behaviors, even such a long-established one as chronic alcoholism.

He becomes more acceptant of others.

He becomes more open to the evidence, both to what is going on outside of himself, and to what is going on inside of himself.

He changes in his basic personality characteristics, in constructive ways.[1]

I think perhaps this is sufficient to indicate that there are learnings which are significant, which do make a difference.

SIGNIFICANT LEARNING IN EDUCATION

I believe I am accurate in saying that educators too are interested in learnings which make a difference. Simple knowledge of facts has its value. To know who won the battle of Poltava, or when the umpteenth opus of Mozart was first performed, may win $64,000 or some other sum for the possessor of this information, but I believe educators in general are a little embarrassed by the assumption that the acquisition of such knowledge constitutes education. Speaking of this reminds me of a forceful statement made by a professor of agronomy in my freshman year in college. Whatever knowledge I gained in his course has departed completely, but I remember how, with World War I as his background, he was comparing factual knowledge with ammunition. He wound up his little discourse with the exhortation, "Don't be a damned ammunition wagon; be a rifle!" I believe most educators would share this sentiment that knowledge exists primarily for use.

To the extent then that educators are interested in learnings which are functional, which make a difference, which pervade the person and his actions, then they might well look to the field of psychotherapy for leads or ideas. Some adaptation for education of the learning process which takes place in psychotherapy seems like a promising possibility.

[1] For evidence supporting these statements see references (6) and (8).

THE CONDITIONS OF LEARNING IN PSYCHOTHERAPY

Let us then see what is involved, essentially, in making possible the learning which occurs in therapy. I would like to spell out, as clearly as I can, the conditions which seem to be present when this phenomenon occurs.

FACING A PROBLEM

The client is, first of all, up against a situation which he perceives as a serious and meaningful problem. It may be that he finds himself behaving in ways which he cannot control, or he is overwhelmed by confusions and conflicts, or his marriage is going on the rocks, or he finds himself unhappy in his work. He is, in short, faced with a problem with which he has tried to cope, and found himself unsuccessful. He is therefore eager to learn, even though at the same time he is frightened that what he discovers in himself may be disturbing. Thus one of the conditions nearly always present is an uncertain and ambivalent desire to learn or to change, growing out of a perceived difficulty in meeting life.

What are the conditions which this individual meets when he comes to a therapist? I have recently formulated a theoretical picture of the necessary and sufficient conditions which the therapist provides, if constructive change or significant learning is to occur (7). This theory is currently being tested in several of its aspects by empirical research, but it must still be regarded as theory based upon clinical experience rather than proven fact. Let me describe briefly the conditions which it seems essential that the therapist should provide.

CONGRUENCE

If therapy is to occur, it seems necessary that the therapist be, in the relationship, a unified, or integrated, or congruent person. What I mean is that within the relationship he is exactly what he *is*—not a façade, or a role, or a pretense. I have used the term congruence to refer to this accurate matching of experience with awareness. It is when the therapist is fully and accurately aware of what he is experiencing at this moment in the relationship, that he is fully congruent. Unless this congruence is present to a considerable degree it is unlikely that significant learning can occur.

Though this concept of congruence is actually a complex one, I believe all of us recognize it in an intuitive and common-sense way in individuals with whom we deal. With one individual we recognize that he not only means exactly what he says, but that his deepest feelings also match what he is expressing. Thus whether he is angry or affectionate or ashamed or enthusiastic, we sense that he is the same at all levels—in what he is experiencing at an organismic level, in his awareness at the conscious level, and in his words and communications. We furthermore recognize that he is acceptant of his immediate feelings. We say of such a person that we know "exactly where he stands." We tend to feel comfortable and secure in such a relationship. With another person we recognize that what he is saying is almost certainly a front or a façade. We wonder what he *really* feels, what he is really experiencing, behind this façade. We may also wonder if *he* knows what he really feels, recognizing that he may be quite unaware of the feelings he is actually experiencing. With such a person we tend to be cautious and wary. It is not the kind of relationship in which defenses can be dropped or in which significant learning and change can occur.

Thus this second condition for therapy is that the therapist is characterized by a considerable degree of congruence in the relationship. He is freely, deeply, and acceptantly himself, with his actual experience of his feelings and reactions matched by an accurate awareness of these feelings and reactions as they occur and as they change.

UNCONDITIONAL POSITIVE REGARD

A third condition is that the therapist experiences a warm caring for the client—a caring which is not possessive, which demands no personal gratification. It is an atmosphere which simply demonstrates "I care"; not "I care for you *if* you behave thus and so." Standal (10) has termed this attitude "unconditional positive regard," since it has no conditions of worth attached to it. I have often used the term acceptance to describe this aspect of the therapeutic climate. It involves as much feeling of acceptance for the client's expression of negative, "bad," painful, fearful, and abnormal feelings, as for his expression of "good," positive, mature, confident and social feelings. It involves an acceptance of and a caring for the client as a *separate* person, with permission for him to have his own feelings and experiences, and to find his own meanings in them. To the degree that the therapist can provide this safety-creating climate of unconditional positive regard, significant learning is likely to take place.

AN EMPATHIC UNDERSTANDING

The fourth condition for therapy is that the therapist is experiencing an accurate, empathic understanding of the client's world as seen from the inside. To sense the client's private world as if it were your own, but without ever losing the "as if" quality—this is empathy, and this seems essential to therapy. To sense the client's anger, fear, or confusion as if it were your own, yet without your own anger, fear, or confusion getting bound up in it, is the condition we are endeavoring to describe. When the client's world is this clear to the therapist, and he moves about in it freely, then he can both communicate his understanding of what is clearly known to the client and can also voice meanings in the client's experience of which the client is scarcely aware. That such penetrating empathy is important for therapy is indicated by Fiedler's research in which items such as the following placed high in the description of relationships created by experienced therapists:

The therapist is well able to understand the patient's feelings.

The therapist is never in any doubt about what the patient means.

The therapist's remarks fit in just right with the patient's mood and content.

The therapist's tone of voice conveys the complete ability to share the patient's feelings. (2a)

FIFTH CONDITION

A fifth condition for significant learning in therapy is that the client should experience or perceive something of the therapist's congruence, acceptance, and empathy. It is not enough that these conditions exist in the therapist. They must, to some degree, have been successfully communicated to the client.

THE PROCESS OF LEARNING IN THERAPY

It has been our experience that when these five conditions exist, a process of change inevitably occurs. The client's rigid perceptions of himself and of others loosen and become open to reality. The rigid ways in which he has construed the meaning of his experience are looked at, and he finds himself questioning many of the "facts" of his life, discovering that they are only "facts" because he has regarded them so. He discovers feelings of which he has been unaware, and experiences them, often vividly, in the therapeutic relationship. Thus he learns to be more open to all of his experience—the evidence within himself as well as the evidence without. He learns to *be* more of his experience—to be the feelings of which he has been frightened as well as the feelings he has regarded as more acceptable. He becomes a more fluid, changing, learning person.

THE MAINSPRING OF CHANGE

In this process it is not necessary for the therapist to "motivate" the client or to supply the energy which brings about the change. Nor, in some sense, is the motivation supplied by the client, at least in any conscious way. Let us say rather that the motivation for learning and change springs from the self-actualizing tendency of life itself, the tendency for the organism to flow into all the differentiated channels of potential development, insofar as these are experienced as enhancing.

I could go on at very considerable length on this, but it is not my purpose to focus on the process of therapy and the learnings which take place, nor on the motivation for these learnings, but rather on the conditions which make them possible. So I will simply conclude the description of therapy by saying that it is a type of significant learning which takes place when five conditions are met:

When the client perceives himself as faced by a serious and meaningful problem;

When the therapist is a congruent person in the relationship, able to *be* the person he *is;*

When the therapist feels an unconditional positive regard for the client;

When the therapist experiences an accurate empathic understanding of the client's private world, and communicates this;

When the client to some degree experiences the therapist's congruence, acceptance, and empathy.

IMPLICATIONS FOR EDUCATION

What do these conditions mean if applied to education? Undoubtedly the reader will be able to give a better answer than I out of his own experience, but I will at least suggest some of the implications.

CONTACT WITH PROBLEMS

In the first place it means that significant learning occurs more readily in relation to situations perceived as problems. I believe I have observed evidence to support this. In my own varying attempts to conduct courses and groups in ways consistent with my therapeutic experience, I have found such an approach more effective, I believe, in workshops than in regular courses, in extension courses than in campus courses. Individuals who come to workshops or extension courses are those who are in contact with problems which they recognize as problems. The student in the regular university course, and particularly in the required course, is apt to view the course as an experience in which he expects to remain passive or resentful or both, an experience which he certainly does not often see as relevant to his own problems.

Yet it has also been my experience that when a regular university class does perceive the course as an experience they can use to resolve problems which *are* of concern to them, the sense of release, and the thrust of forward movement is astonishing. And this is true of courses as diverse as Mathematics and Personality.

I believe the current situation in Russian education also supplies evidence on this point. When a whole nation perceives itself as being faced with the urgent problem of being behind—in agriculture, in industrial production, in scientific development, in weapons development—then an astonishing amount of significant learning takes place, of which the Sputniks are but one observable example.

So the first implication for education might well be that we permit the student, at any level, to be in real contact with the relevant problems of his existence, so that he perceives problems and issues which he wishes to resolve. I am quite aware that this implication, like the others I shall mention, runs sharply contrary to the current trends in our culture, but I shall comment on that later.

I believe it would be quite clear from my description of therapy that an overall implication for education would be that the task of the teacher is to create a facilitating classroom climate in which significant learning can take place. This general implication can be broken down into several sub-sections.

THE TEACHER'S REAL-NESS

Learning will be facilitated, it would seem, if the teacher is congruent. This involves the teacher's being the person that he is, and being openly aware of the attitudes he holds. It means that he feels acceptant toward his own real feelings. Thus he becomes a real person in the relationship with his students. He can be enthusiastic about subjects he likes, and bored by topics he does not like. He can be angry, but he can also be sensitive or sympathetic. Because he accepts his feeling as *his* feelings, he has no need to impose them on his students, or to insist that they feel the same way. He is a *person*, not a faceless embodiment of a curricular requirement, or a sterile pipe through which knowledge is passed from one generation to the next.

I can suggest only one bit of evidence which might support this view. As I think back over a number of teachers who have facilitated my own learning, it seems to me each one has this quality of being a real person. I wonder if your memory is the same. If so, perhaps it is less important that a teacher cover the allotted amount of the curriculum, or use the most approved audio-visual devices, than that he be congruent, real, in his relation to his students.

ACCEPTANCE AND UNDERSTANDING

Another implication for the teacher is that significant learning may take place if the teacher can accept the student as he is, and can understand the feelings he possesses. Taking the third and fourth conditions of therapy as specified above, the teacher who can warmly accept, who can provide an unconditional positive regard, and who can empathize with the feelings of fear, anticipation, and discouragement which are involved in meeting new material, will have done a great deal toward setting the conditions for learning. Clark Moustakas, in his book, *The Teacher and the Child* (5), has given many excellent examples of individual and group situations from kindergarten to high school, in which the teacher has worked toward just this type of goal. It will perhaps disturb some that when the teacher holds such attitudes, when he is willing to be acceptant of feelings, it is not only attitudes toward school work itself which are expressed, but feelings about parents, feelings of hatred for brother or sister, feelings of concern about self—the whole gamut of attitudes. Do such feelings have a right to exist openly in a school setting? It is my thesis that they do. They are related to the person's becoming, to his effective learning and effective functioning, and to deal understandingly and acceptantly with such feelings has a definite relationship to the learning of long division or the geography of Pakistan.

PROVISION OF RESOURCES

This brings me to another implication which therapy holds for education. In therapy the resources for learning one's self lie within. There is very little data which the therapist can supply which will be of help since the data to be dealt with exist within the person. In education this is not true. There are many resources of knowledge, of techniques, of theory, which constitute raw material for use. It seems to me that what I have said about therapy suggests that these materials, these resources, be made available to the students, not forced upon them. Here a wide range of ingenuity and sensitivity is an asset.

I do not need to list the usual resources which come to mind—books, maps, workbooks, materials, recordings, work-space, tools, and the like.

Let me focus for a moment on the way the teacher uses himself and his knowledge and experience as a resource. If the teacher holds the point of view I have been expressing then he would probably want to make himself available to his class in at least the following ways:

He would want to let them know of special experience and knowledge he has in the field, and to let them know they could call on this knowledge. Yet he would not want them to feel that they must use him in this way.

He would want them to know that his own way of thinking about the field, and of organizing it, was available to them, even in lecture form, if they wished. Yet again he would want this to be perceived as an offer, which could as readily be refused as accepted.

He would want to make himself known as a resource-finder. Whatever might be seriously wanted by an individual or by the whole group to promote their learning, he would be very willing to consider the possibilities of obtaining such a resource.

He would want the quality of his relationship to the group to be such that his feelings could be freely available to them, without being imposed on them or becoming a restrictive influence on them. He thus could share the excitements and enthusiasms of his own learnings, without insisting that the students follow in his footsteps; the feelings of disinterest, satisfaction, bafflement, or pleasure which he feels toward individual or group activities, without this becoming either a carrot or a stick for the student. His hope would be that he could say, simply for himself, "I don't like that," and that the student with equal freedom could say, "But I do."

Thus whatever the resource he supplies—a book, space to work, a new tool, an opportunity for observation of an industrial process, a lecture based on his own study, a picture, graph or map, his own emotional reactions—he would feel that these were, and would hope they would be perceived as, offerings to be used if they were useful to the student. He would not feel them to be guides, or expectations, or commands, or impositions or requirements. He would offer himself, and all the other resources he could discover, for use.

THE BASIC MOTIVE

It should be clear from this that his basic reliance would be upon the self-actualizing tendency in his students. The hypothesis upon which he would build is that students who are in real contact with life problems wish to learn, want to grow, seek to find out, hope to master, desire to create. He would see his function as that of developing such a personal relationship with his students, and such a climate in his classroom, that these natural tendencies could come to their fruition.

SOME OMISSIONS

These I see as some of the things which are implied by a therapeutic viewpoint for the educational process. To make them a bit sharper, let me point out some of the things which are not implied.

I have not included lectures, talks, or expositions of subject matter which are imposed on the students. All of these procedures might be a part of the experience if they were desired, explicitly or implicitly, by the students. Yet even here, a teacher whose work was following through a hypothesis based on therapy would be quick to sense a shift in that desire. He might have been requested to lecture to the group (and to give a *requested* lecture is *very* different from the usual classroom experience), but if he detected a growing disinterest and boredom, he would respond to that, trying to understand the feeling which had arisen in the group, since his response to their feelings and attitudes would take precedence over his interest in expounding material.

I have not included any program of evaluation of the student's learnings in terms of external criteria. I have not, in other words, included examinations. I believe that the testing of the student's achievements in order to see if he meets some criterion held by the teacher, is directly contrary to the implications of therapy for significant learning. In therapy, the examinations are set by *life*. The client meets them, sometimes passing, sometimes failing. He finds that he can use the resources of the therapeutic relationship and his experience in it to organize himself so that he can meet life's tests more satisfyingly next time. I see this as the paradigm for education also. Let me try to spell out a fantasy of what it would mean.

In such an education, the requirements for many life situations would be a part of the resources the teacher provides. The student would have available the knowledge that he cannot enter engineering school without so much math; that he cannot get a job in X corporation unless he has a college diploma; that he cannot become a psychologist without doing an independent doctoral research; that he cannot be a doctor without knowledge of chemistry; that he cannot even drive a car without passing an examination on rules of the road. These are requirements set, not by the teacher, but by life. The teacher is there to provide the resources which the student can use to learn so as to be able to meet these tests. There would be other in-school evaluations of similar sort. The student might well be faced with the fact that he cannot join the Math Club until he makes a certain score on a standardized mathematics test; that he cannot develop his camera film until he has shown an adequate knowledge of chemistry and lab techniques; that he cannot join the special literature section until he has shown evidence of both wide reading and creative writing. The natural place of evaluation in life is as a ticket of entrance, not as a club over the recalcitrant. Our experience in therapy would suggest that it should be the same way in the school. It would leave the student as a self-respecting, self-motivated person, free to choose whether he wished to put forth the effort to gain these tickets of entrance. It would thus refrain from forcing him into conformity, from sacrificing his creativity, and from causing him to live his life in terms of the standards of others.

I am quite aware that the two elements of which I have just been speaking—the lectures and expositions imposed by the teacher on the group, and the evaluation of the individual by the teacher, constitute the two major ingredients of current education. So when I say that experience in psychotherapy would suggest that they both be omitted, it should be quite clear that the implications of psychotherapy for education are startling indeed.

PROBABLE OUTCOMES

If we are to consider such drastic changes as I have outlined, what would be the results which would justify them? There have been some research investigations of the outcomes of a student-centered type of teaching (1, 2, 3), though these studies are far from adequate. For one thing, the situations studied vary greatly in the extent to which they meet the conditions I have described. Most of them have extended only over a period of a few months, though one recent study with lower class children extended over a full year (3). Some involve the use of adequate controls, some do not.

I think we may say that these studies indicate that in classroom situations which at least attempt to approximate the climate I have described, the findings are as follows: Factual and curricular learning is roughly equal to the learning in conventional classes. Some studies report slightly more, some slightly less. The student-centered group shows gains significantly greater than the conventional class in personal adjustment, in self-initiated extra-curricular learning, in creativity, in self-responsibility.

I have come to realize, as I have considered these studies, and puzzled over the design of better studies which should be more informative and conclusive, that findings from such research will never answer our questions. For all such findings must be evaluated in terms of the goals we have for education. If we value primarily the learning of knowledge, then we may discard the conditions I have described as useless, since there is no evidence that they lead to a greater rate or amount of factual knowledge. We may then favor such measures as the one which I understand is advocated by a number of members of Congress—the setting up of a training school for scientists, modelled upon the military academies. But if we value creativity, if we deplore the fact that all of our germinal ideas in atomic physics, in psychology, and in other sciences have been borrowed from Europe, then we may wish to give a trial to ways of facilitating learning which give more promise of freeing the mind. If we value independence, if we are disturbed by the growing conformity of knowledge, of values, of attitudes, which our present system induces, then we may wish to set up conditions of learning which make for uniqueness, for self-direction, and for self-initiated learning.

SOME CONCLUDING ISSUES

I have tried to sketch the kind of education which would be implied by what we have learned in the field of psychotherapy. I have endeavored to suggest very briefly what it would mean if the central focus of the teacher's effort were to develop a relationship, an atmosphere, which was conducive to self-motivated, self-actualizing, significant learning. But this is a direction which leads sharply away from current educational practices and educational trends. Let me mention a few of the very diverse issues and questions which need to be faced if we are to think constructively about such an approach.

In the first place, how do we conceive the goals of education? The approach I have outlined has, I believe, advantages for achieving certain goals, but not for achieving others. We need to be clear as to the way we see the purposes of education.

What are the actual outcomes of the kind of education I have described? We need a great deal more of rigorous, hard-headed research to know the actual results of this kind of education as compared with conventional education. Then we can choose on the basis of the facts.

Even if we were to try such an approach to the facilitation of learning, there are many difficult issues. Could we possibly permit students to come in contact with real issues? Our whole culture—through custom, through the law, through the efforts of labor unions and management, through the attitudes of parents and teachers—is deeply committed to keeping young people away from any touch with real problems. They are not to work, they should not carry responsibility, they have no business in civic or political problems, they have no place in international concerns, they simply should be guarded from any direct contact with the real problems of individual and group living. They are not expected to help about the home, to earn a living, to contribute to science, to deal with moral issues. This is a deep seated trend which has lasted for more than a generation. Could it possibly be reversed?

Another issue is whether we could permit knowledge to be organized in and by the individual, or whether it is to be organized *for* the individual. Here teachers and educators line up with parents and national leaders to insist that the pupil must be guided. He must be inducted into knowledge we have organized for him. He cannot be trusted to organize knowledge in functional terms for himself. As Herbert Hoover says of high school students, "You simply cannot expect kids of those ages to determine the sort of education they need unless they have some guidance."[2] This seems so obvious to most people that even to question it is to seem somewhat unbalanced. Even a chancellor of a university questions whether freedom is really necessary in education, saying that perhaps we have overestimated its value. He says the Russians have advanced mightily in science without it, and implies that we should learn from them.

Still another issue is whether we would wish to oppose the strong current trend toward education as drill in factual knowledge. All must learn the same facts in the same way. Admiral Rickover states it as his belief that "in some fashion we must devise a way to introduce uniform standards into American education. . . . For the first time, parents would have a real yardstick to measure their schools. If the local school continued to teach such pleasant subjects as 'life adjustment' . . . instead of French and physics, its diploma would be, for all the world to see, inferior."[3] This is a statement of a very prevalent view. Even such a friend of forward-looking views in education as Max Lerner says at one point, "All that a school can ever hope to do is to equip the student with tools which he can later use to become an educated man" (4, p. 741). It is quite clear that he despairs of significant learning taking place in our school system, and feels that it must take place outside. All the school can do is to pound in the tools.

One of the most painless ways of inculcating such factual tool knowledge is the "teaching machine" being devised by B. F. Skinner and his associates (9). This group is demonstrating that the teacher is an outmoded and ineffective instrument for teaching arithmetic, trigonometry, French, literacy appreciation, geography, or other factual subjects. There is simply no doubt in my mind that these teaching machines, providing immediate rewards for "right" answers, will be further developed, and will come into wide use. Here is a new contribution from the field of the behavioral sciences with which we must come to terms. Does it take the place of the approach I have described, or is it supplemental to it? Here is one of the problems we must consider as we face toward the future.

I hope that by posing these issues, I have made it clear that the double-barrelled question of what constitutes significant learning, and how it is

[2] *Time*, December 2, 1957.
[3] *Ibid.*

to be achieved, poses deep and serious problems for all of us. It is not a time when timid answers will suffice. I have tried to give a definition of significant learning as it appears in psychotherapy, and a description of the conditions which facilitate such learning. I have tried to indicate some implications of these conditions for education. I have, in other words, proposed one answer to these questions. Perhaps we can use what I have said, against the twin backdrops of current public opinion and current knowledge in the behavioral sciences, as a start for discovering some fresh answers of our own.

REFERENCES

1. FAW, VOLNEY. "A Psychotherapeutic Method of Teaching Psychology." *American Psychologist* 4: 104-09, 1949.
2. FAW, VOLNEY. "Evaluation of Student-Centered Teaching." Unpublished manuscript, 1954.
2a. FIEDLER, F. E. "A Comparison of Therapeutic Relationships in Psychoanalytic, Non-directive and Adlerian Therapy." *Journal of Consulting Psychology* 14: 436-45, 1950.
3. JACKSON, JOHN H. "The Relationship Between Psychological Climate and the Quality of Learning Outcomes among Lower-status Pupils." Unpublished Ph.D. thesis, University of Chicago, 1957.
4. LERNER, MAX. *America as a Civilization.* New York: Simon & Schuster, 1957.
5. MOUSTAKAS, CLARK. *The Teacher and the Child.* New York: McGraw-Hill Book Company, 1956.
6. ROGERS, C. R. *Client-centered Therapy.* New York: Houghton Mifflin Company, 1951.
7. ROGERS, C. R. "The Necessary and Sufficient Conditions of Therapeutic Personality Change." *Journal of Consulting Psychology* 21: 95-103, 1957.
8. ROGERS, C. R., and R. DYMOND, editors. *Psychotherapy and Personality Change.* Chicago: University of Chicago Press, 1954.
9. SKINNER, B. F. "The Science of Learning and the Art of Teaching." *Harvard Educational Review* 24: 86-97, 1954.
10. STANDAL, STANLEY. "The Need for Positive Regard: A Contribution to Client-centered Theory." Unpublished Ph.D. thesis, University of Chicago, 1954.

14.   Using the Insights of Psychotherapy in Teaching

William H. Stavsky

What insights have come from the social, psychological, and medical sciences to help us understand the disturbed child? The greatest gain, in my opinion, has been our increased interest in, and comprehension of, the problem of anxiety and its role in the etiology of the child's current behavior. The importance of anxiety in the life of the child and of the adult has been increasingly recognized as psychotherapy has continued to expand. As therapies have developed since Freud, the aim of the psychotherapist, regardless of the kind of psychotherapy used, has always been to bring about an alteration in his patient's anxiety and thus to help his patient mature.

This article stresses the role of anxiety in the behavior of children because greater understanding of its nature, its causes, and its susceptibility to change can mean greater advancement in psychotherapy for the disturbed child. Improved understanding may also suggest new prophylactic measures against undue mental stress and its undesirable effects: the psychoses, neuroses, crime, delinquency, divorce, and other conduct disorders. Finally, to come to the main problem of this discussion, understanding the role of anxiety will help orient our understanding of the child in the learning situation (the classroom).

THE NATURE OF ANXIETY IN CHILDREN

The problem of anxiety in children is similar to that in adults. Children have anxieties that are caused by the situations in which they are placed. The anxieties will clear up if the children are removed from the situation or if the situation is altered in some way. Children also have anxiety about things of which they are not conscious or aware. When this anxiety is great, it tends to show up in aberrational behavior. Some persons not only suffer from anxiety of whose cause they are unaware but also suffer from anxiety, induced by situational problems, which can affect and stimulate that anxiety of whose determining content they are unconscious.

When symptomatic behavior has become a definite part of a child's life, anxiety itself may not be obvious, either to the child or to the teacher

"Using the Insights of Psychotherapy in Teaching," by William H. Stavsky, is reprinted from *The Elementary School Journal*, 58: 28-35, October 1957, by permission of The University of Chicago Press. Copyright © 1957 by The University of Chicago Press.

or the parent. In such a case the symptomatic behavior has in some way either eliminated or reduced the feeling of anxiety to a point where it is not readily observable to the outsider and is seemingly not apparent to the child himself. This is nature's way of alleviating pain (anxiety). However, the symptoms themselves may, in turn, bring on fresh anxiety if they collide with the demands of reality; but this anxiety is not so great as that which has been hidden by the symptoms. This picture suggests the complicated role that anxiety may play in the behavior of the child.

What, however, of the disturbed child? If we assume mental life to be a continuum, differences may be approached as a matter of degree rather than of quality. For example, a child so disturbed as to be psychotic represents, on the surface, a difference in quality when compared to the normal child. Yet psychotherapeutic research often shows the difference to be in degree rather than in kind. In the case of the disturbed child the difference may be a difference in the amount of anxiety present. If this hypothesis is correct, a child who is so unfortunate as to have a great deal of anxiety, conscious or unconscious, is the disturbed child.

How the child acquired this excess anxiety is an interesting question. It may possibly be that the child is born to be *unduly* anxious; that at birth he is constitutionally, *unusually* responsive to anxiety-inducing stimulation. For example, the young child is excessively anxious when frustrated in his basic needs—such as his needs for sucking, tenderness, warmth, cuddling, biting, or movement. On the other hand, the child may become unduly anxious because of unfortunate traumatic experiences, such as being mothered or fathered by an anxiety-inducing mother or father. Again, there may be a lack of mothering or fathering, or he may have other excessive and sustained traumatic experiences that exert a frightening pressure on him. Or he may develop excessive anxiety because of a *combination* of constitutional factors and experience. All three are theoretically possible.

The outstanding fact is that anxiety, in varying degrees, is present in all children. In some children it is intolerable. Anxiety is a most unpleasant experience. Whatever the dynamisms that underlie the arousal of anxiety, the child, as he develops, seeks to avoid or reduce or control this anxiety so that he will be as free of it as possible. This process begins in infancy, perhaps in pre-infancy, and continues until death.

A child who is unable to reduce or control his anxiety by normal movement or behavior must try other kinds of behavior. For example, an infant who has been seriously neglected may incline toward apathy, as if being apathetic had proved successful in alleviating the tremendous anxiety set up by lack of tender motherly handling. Nature has helped him control his anxiety, but his behavior is already reminiscent of the later detached reaction of some psychotic adults. We can see that all behavior in the developing child is always in the direction of controlling anxiety. When normal behavior proves ineffective because anxiety is excessive, symptomatic behavior develops to help him reduce or control the anxiety.

Such symptomatic behavior may take the form of severe and frequent temper tantrums, refusal to eat, inability to learn in school (that is, to profit on the basis of his talents), withdrawing in autistic fashion into a world of his own, becoming difficult to control, truancy or other conduct disorders, bullying, overdependency and childishness at a level below his chronological age, or other symptomatic behavior (not directly caused by physical factors and theoretically curable by the elimination of the physical factors). It is as if the normal responses of life in mastering anxiety are insufficient and a palliative must be added to help lessen the hurt. This palliative or symptom makes the child more comfortable and is nature's last way (other than death) of reducing anxiety when the more normal, healthy ways have failed. However, these symptoms interfere with happy living, and they call for measures that will enable healthy and positive behavior to function instead.

In psychotherapy with children, as with adults, the object is to find the anxiety and its sources. Although the anxiety dealt with in psychotherapy has a history as long as the life of the individual, it is generally "worked through" mainly in its *current* manifestation. In this sense, psychotherapy repeats the development of the child. In addition, for greater self-understanding by the patient, both emotionally and intellectually, the historical determinants of his anxiety are given consideration wherever they show up. Also in treatment, anxiety caused by the patient's current situation must be dealt with, particularly in the case of a child, since he is less able than an adult to alter his environment. For example, a child living with a psychotic mother might be better placed in a foster home or in an institution, particularly if the psychotic mother is obviously mothering the child with anxiety-inducing patterns of behavior.

ALLEVIATING ANXIETY IN THE CLASSROOM

A problem child or a disturbed child is certainly one with excessive anxiety (conscious or unconscious). Consequently, in order to understand troublesome behavior in the classroom, the teacher must appreciate its roots in anxiety, as the therapist *must* in therapy. In what way does psychotherapeutic understanding help the teacher in his relations with his pupils, with the undisturbed as well as the disturbed children?

First and foremost, psychotherapy and teaching both embody an *interpersonal relationship* between an adult and a child. This interpersonal relationship is called "transference" in the psychotherapeutic situation.

There is no reason why we cannot also think of transference as a class-room phenomenon, since its dynamics are definitely in existence there. In fact, without a positive transference or a positive interpersonal relationship, teaching is relatively ineffective. As the interpersonal relationship develops in psychotherapy, the basis for reducing or controlling anxiety exists and change can proceed. As it develops in the classroom, the basis for the advancement of learning is laid.

This brings us to a second analogy between psychotherapy and teaching. As I have stated, psychotherapy through the interpersonal relationship must alter the anxiety in the child in such a manner that its unpleasantness is reduced or becomes more controlled. When this is achieved, psychotherapy has then created the possibility for normal growth. Now we can note that the teacher, like the therapist, utilizes techniques that are *intrinsically anxiety-reducing or anxiety-controlling techniques*. The teacher's techniques are not those of the therapist, who, by interpreting the child's play associations, dreams, slips of the tongue, gestures, and remarks, gradually exposes the child's anxiety and eventually renders it more controllable. With the teacher, the techniques are, to put it simply, the common teaching techniques. They are, for example, knowing how to motivate for learning, showing sincere interest in children, showing respect for individualism, developing ever increasing skill in teaching, using proper disciplinary measures, utilizing patience, avoiding ridicule, sustaining the teaching program, using sensible praise, avoiding partiality, and possessing the capacity to forget past unpleasant relationships with the child. These techniques are actually approaches which reduce or control anxiety, and, if successfully used, result in a teacher-pupil relationship that is relatively free of anxiety and in the establishment of a comparatively secure road for the development of the learning process. We might add that, though both therapeutic and teaching techniques reduce or control anxiety, the psychotherapist works mainly through the unconscious dynamisms of anxiety, while the teacher works along an ego-building level.

For the sake of clarity, let us consider several of the teaching techniques and note how they help reduce anxiety and promote learning. The friendly, sympathetic teacher naturally promotes a feeling of well-being and security, and the pupil is encouraged to face the anxiety-inducing tensions of a new learning situation. A child learns arithmetic faster when the situation is friendly and sympathetic than when the attitude is blatantly the reverse or is *implicitly* not friendly to him. Arithmetic, for example, can mean much more to a child than numbers which, when put in certain relationships, give certain mathematical results. To a child, numbers may also mean failure (anxiety), being unable to compete with his friends (anxiety), losing face or status at home (anxiety), not being as capable as father or mother (anxiety), being inferior to a sibling (anxiety), the unconscious fear of losing mother and father (anxiety), the unconscious fear of being unable to become a capable man or woman (anxiety), the unconscious fear of his own sex impulses. Consequently, learning arithmetic is more than an intellectual feat. It is also an overcoming of the anxiety that numbers may somehow provoke in the child. The teacher, utilizing the teaching skills enumerated above, in most instances is capable of helping the child through this anxious experience, so that the youthful ego can integrate and assimilate the experience. With time, skill in the use of numbers develops, and the probability that numbers will arouse anxiety is reduced. The teacher's understanding of the role of anxiety in learning, particularly in learning arithmetic, is important because failure to integrate and assimilate anxiety in arithmetic is, unfortunately, responsible for many a child's refusal to continue in the field of mathematics even though he has the natural talent to develop in this area.

What has been said of arithmetic also applies to reading or to any learning situation. I have stressed numbers difficulties instead of reading difficulties because the latter is a more conspicuous difficulty from a social standpoint and has caused more concern than has failure to perform well in arithmetic. In a scientific age, however, indifference to mathematics is obviously a serious loss.

Discipline is another example of a technique that can reduce or control anxiety. Ordinarily we think of discipline as an anxiety-inducing, rather than as an anxiety-reducing, experience. Nevertheless, when used properly, objectively, and fairly—for the purpose of maintaining a harmonious environment and not for the sake of punishment as such—the anxiety-reducing effects of discipline are great and promote learning. In a loosely controlled situation a young child can easily be stimulated to impulsive behavior which, if unchecked, induces anxiety in him. He will then continue to misbehave in response to newly aroused anxiety. The child is testing to see how much the teacher will let him "get away with."

Basic, however, in this testing behavior is the fact that, when a child resorts to impulsive behavior (acting smart, bullying, teasing, showing off, defiance, sly trickiness), he is expressing a need to dominate and unconsciously is expressing a desire to be the adult, the parent. For many reasons, to play the part of the authoritative adult can be, and is, an anxiety-inducing situation, depending on how much of the parent's role the child unconsciously wants to take over. In the classroom the child may get support from the other children who laugh at him (they are experiencing the same need and are also expressing anxiety). However, once he starts off in this direction, his anxiety must continue to increase, because to be that authoritative is an adult experience and he is not ready for it. Yet his unpleasant inner tensions drive him on, since he is not aware of what he is really trying to achieve by such behavior. The anxiety caused by these tensions can be resolved only when the child either becomes the adult or yields to be the child again. Of course, for a child to be an adult is an impossibility. If he is successful in usurping the authority of the adult, he becomes what some people call a "monster." In this guise he is frightening, not only to adults, but also to himself. His own anxiety has not been resolved. Only when maturation has been completed and his experiences have been thoroughly assimilated through growth, can the child actually become the adult and not experience undue anxiety. The child's best solution in such a situation is to be reduced to the status of a child again and to get the satisfaction of being a child. Here discipline is needed, to stop the child's nonsense, to reduce his anxiety, and to enable him to satisfy his childish need. The manner in which this is done is the badge of the skilled teacher.

The teacher who can stop this kind of behavior in a way that is reassuring rather than anxiety-inducing is helping the child to control or handle his anxiety. Objectivity, interest in the child, a firm insistence that he behave, and the proper use of restrictions which will impress on the child that nonsense will not be permitted—these not only are desirable in a classroom situation but also are therapeutically desirable in helping the child master (integrate and assimilate) anxiety tensions. In the classroom situation, discipline is important and, when properly used, in an anxiety-reducing function.

One of the main functions of teaching, then, is to reduce or to control anxiety in order that the goal of the class—learning (and development) —may be reached. Some of the techniques that are effective in the pursuit of that goal have been enumerated above, and there are many more. In fact, good teaching methods and devices are also anxiety-reducing techniques. These include such things as trips, school projects, games, songs, plays, visual aids, visiting other classes, prizes, special classes, and many other successful techniques and approaches that have been introduced and used in the teaching curriculum over the ages. *From a psychotherapeutic point of view, teaching is basically an interpersonal relationship, which, with its proper techniques and devices, helps reduce or control anxiety and so promotes learning.* Psychotherapy, with its own peculiar techniques, is also an interpersonal relationship and seeks to achieve the same effect: the reduction or control of anxiety and the promotion of the individual's development. The psychotherapist, however, sets up the emotional potentials for, rather than bringing about, learning.

The conscious and extensive elaboration of this view of teaching is hardly necessary to accomplish effective teaching. Through the ages, good teaching has been accomplished largely because good teachers intuitively do the very things discussed here. They create a situation which is relatively free of anxiety, and teaching proceeds without too much let or hindrance. On the other hand, there is no doubt that a not inconsiderable portion of teaching has always been sterile because of the failure of some teachers to foster the appropriate interpersonal relationship and to create a classroom atmosphere that is relatively secure. While this holds true at all levels of teaching, its lack in the lower grades is particularly harmful. In these grades, failure to create a teaching situation that is relatively free of anxiety will condition, around learning, feelings of anxiety that persist with many children. Eventually many children who develop such anxiety give up and drop out of school when they reach the required legal age. If we face the problem realistically, we may say that children shy away from learning only because they feel too insecure in the learning process. While many factors may create anxiety in the classroom and while good teaching is no guaranty against all anxieties, there is no question that poor teaching —a poor interpersonal relationship—always creates insecurity (anxiety) in the classroom and for many children a loss in, and a fear of, learning.

ANXIETY IN THE SERIOUSLY DISTURBED CHILD

The good teacher also has his failures. And perhaps he is more interested in finding out why he must fail with some of his pupils than why he is successful with most. I do not intend to dwell on failures in learning that result from our present-day overcrowded classrooms. Obviously the interpersonal relationship approaches a vanishing point in overcrowded classrooms. Insecurity among children in such a learning situation is excessive, and many of them will suffer irreparably.

Neither am I emphasizing the failure of a child who cannot keep up with others because of low mental age. Children who learn as much as their native ability enables them to are not failures. It is important, however, to know whether they are actually achieving to the full capacity of their talents; for here, too, the factor of anxiety may enter. Slow children may be slower because of excessive unconscious anxiety. It is also probable that most slow children are *additionally* slower because of the feelings of inferiority (conscious anxiety) they experience in not being like other children in learning ability. The anxiety factor—conscious, unconscious, or both—in the slow child can well be an additive factor in his slow learning process.

The teacher who fails with his pupils is encountering an anxiety situation in the children. This may have been brought about by circumstances beyond the teacher's control. At times it may reflect a failure on the part of the teacher to introduce the proper interpersonal situation. In the case of the seriously disturbed child, however, more often than not it is the child rather than the teacher who is the crux of the matter. The seriously disturbed child is different from the others in his consistent pattern of behavior. He is hard to control, he is difficult to interest, to stimulate. He may be withdrawn from the classroom situation. He may be "smart-alecky," sly, defiant, and even hostile and overtly abusive.

Whether the child has been disturbed by situational circumstances (such as a traumatic family setup), by excessive constitutional anxiety, or by a combination of the two, the fact remains that the normal methods of teaching in the classroom are not adequate to relieve his anxiety. He is characterized by restlessness or hyperactivity, tenseness, aggressiveness, or withdrawal. Failure to achieve academically may also be present. Such children disturb a classroom and cause the teacher to be disturbed. It is not difficult to spot these children, over a period of time, since they are the ones who do not become integrated with the learning situation of the classroom and who continue to present the same problems from one classroom to another. Do the insights gained from psychotherapy suggest what the teacher can do with these children?

The teacher must recognize that these children are not wilfully evading the responsibilities of the classroom because of a particular, voluntary animus. They are like other children in their aspirations and wants, but they are unable to achieve their desires and needs through normal responses. They cannot take easily to learning because they cannot like it; behind the learning there is too much anxiety. They cannot respond to discipline because normal discipline does not dissipate or remove their anxiety. The normal child respects the teacher who insists on order, because in an orderly situation the child feels relatively free of anxiety. The disturbed child, however, is not always free of anxiety in an orderly situation. Order may be helpful, but the influence of orderliness is not enough to make a significant difference in his anxiety processes. It is true that forceful coercion will often bring a seriously disturbing child into line temporarily, but no teacher can function, or wants to continue to function, in a coercive atmosphere. Furthermore, the tensions (anxiety) which are now outwardly controlled by coercion will sooner or later find an outlet in some other tensive activity, such as an act of vandalism in the school building. As long as the underlying anxiety exists, the normal techniques used in the school will not be adequate to effect much change. This fact is generally recognized, and the schools themselves have pioneered in new techniques for handling the disturbed child. For example, special classes and schools have been established for disturbed children, where techniques other than those available in the ordinary classroom are utilized. Social-work contact at home, guidance departments, and a change in the curriculum to place more emphasis on concrete doing rather than abstract thinking are other examples of innovations to help the disturbed child.

The journey to a psychotherapist is the end phase of dealing with a disturbed child's anxiety. When a child is so disturbed that everything has failed, the psychotherapist takes over and applies his special techniques to help the child gain control over his anxiety. To the extent that the therapist is successful, the child can, after a period of time, begin to reflect and utilize the responses and behavior that make for normal development and learning.

CONCLUDING REMARKS

The psychotherapeutic view, applied in the classroom, can help the teacher achieve a greater understanding of his role as teacher. If he sees himself as a person in a relationship that helps children master anxiety in order to develop educationally (and egoistically), he is at once aware that a child's failure to learn is the result of an inadequate interpersonal relationship. It then behooves him to study the interpersonal relationship and determine what factors in the relationship are provoking anxiety. If he has ruled himself out as a possible factor and has already utilized all available teaching devices and means to control anxiety and promote learning, he remembers that the problem is still anxiety and that other anxiety-controlling techniques must be found.

If the teacher ponders and develops his understanding of the role of anxiety that is implicit in the learner in the learning situation, he adds to his professional status as a teacher. Obviously the teacher will not become a therapist by grasping the concept of anxiety in the school situation, any more than one becomes a physician by understanding the nature of modern medicine. On the other hand, when a teacher notes that children lack the appropriate attitude and approach toward learning and feels, at the same time, that they respond as they do in order to avoid inner anxiety, he is not only *not* discouraged with himself as a teacher but is challenged to make better use of his teaching skills in order to do more for the pupils. Even where this is not possible in terms of teaching, understanding the concept of anxiety leads a teacher to find more pertinent plans of action for the sake of an anxious child.

The teacher is in a key situation with respect to handling the problem of anxiety as it affects a child. Since the teacher spends the greater part of the child's year in an interpersonal relationship with the child, he becomes, in effect, a mental barometer of the child's development. The teacher, more than the parent (because the teacher is not forced to *defend* a child's emotional problems), is the *first* important person to be able to evaluate a child's development. These evaluations can often be the basis for redirecting a child's life, if the child is helped or is referred for help. Of course the teacher should not put diagnostic labels on the child. Nor should he utilize anxiety-reducing techniques that go beyond the teaching level. He can and should, however, raise pertinent questions about the reality adjustment of many of his pupils.

This connotes, of course, the importance of the clinical approach in teaching. First, there is the basic understanding that teaching and psychotherapy have a common objective. Both are intimately involved in an interpersonal relationship with children, and both utilize techniques to reduce or control a child's anxiety. If the objective is reached, the child is enabled to progress—toward attainment of knowledge with the teacher, toward attainment of maturation with the therapist. Further, the implications of the anxiety concept in the learning situation not only place the teacher in the position of grasping their significance for the learning process but point to the teacher as a significant observer of the child's state of mental health. In his interpersonal relationship with the child, the teacher is a participant observer of whether the child is adjusting or not—not only in school work, but also in personality.

How effective an observer the teacher is will depend on the significance he attributes to the emotional factor in learning. If he agrees that learning is as much a matter of feeling as it is of brains, the obvious implication is that the teacher must continue to add to his teaching skills an increasing professional understanding of the psychology of maladjustment. The effect is twofold. First, there is a significant gain for the teaching and learning process. Second, the teacher can be properly helpful in alerting against unrecognized and undue inner stress in the child. While this is not the teacher's primary function, it is obviously a pertinent one, for the school and for the normal development of the child.

15. The Concept of an Ideal Teacher-Student Relationship: A Comparison and Critique

Ronald T. Hyman

Currently there is renewed interest in the topic of teaching. Philosophers from the Oxford School of linguistic analysis are now busy applying their skills and techniques to teaching. Communications experts are now

An expansion of an earlier article reprinted with permission from the *Research Bulletin* (New Jersey School Development Council), 11:18-24, Winter, 1966.

investigating teaching as one instance where messages are sent between people. The use of their concepts is shedding light on the teaching situation. These two types of specialists are recent entrants to the group of people investigating teaching. Perhaps the most well-known and established group studying teaching is the psychologists. One segment of the group has concentrated its efforts on examining the relationship between teacher and pupil. These psychologists have employed their insights about the self, anxiety, hostility, transference, and other pertinent concepts to aid teachers in the conduct of their work. Teachers have therefore looked to psychologists as a source of concepts and data helpful to them in their work with students.

The purpose of this study is to focus on this interpersonal relationship between teacher and pupil as an area of continuing concern of educators. Stavsky claims that "teaching is basically an interpersonal relationship which, with its proper techniques and devices, helps reduce or control anxiety and so promotes learning." (7:32.) The central question, then, is what kind of teacher-pupil interpersonal relationship is best. Writers like Bills (1), Hargadon (5), Rogers (6), Stavsky (7), Hallman (4), and Combs (2) are all helpful in answering this question in general terms. They draw from the psychotherapists in answering the question but do not offer any empirical method for answering this question which, it is felt, is needed.

To empirically describe the teacher-pupil interaction the instrument described by Louise L. Tyler (8) was chosen since it focuses on the interpersonal relationship. Tyler developed the instrument by borrowing from Fiedler (3) who studied the therapist-patient relationship. Tyler adopted Fiedler's instrument by changing the wording of his statements "so that they were appropriate for a teaching situation" (8:113). In this way, Tyler's instrument consists of 75 statements about the teacher-student relationship divided into three dimensions, communication and understanding, emotional distance, and status. Each dimension consists of 25 statements divided evenly into five levels with five statements on each level. The 75 statements are to be sorted into seven categories of 1, 7, 18, 23, 18, 7, 1 items along a continuum from the most to the least ideal teacher-pupil relationship. The breakdown of dimensions and statements are listed below:

DIMENSIONS

Communication

    1–16–31–46–61—No communication is possible.
    4–19–34–49–64—Communication is poor.
    7–22–37–52–67—Some communication exists.

10–25–40–55–70—Communication and understanding is good.
13–28–43–58–73—Communication and understanding is excellent.

Emotional Distance

2–17–32–47–62—Teacher draws away from or rejects student.
5–20–35–50–65—Teacher is somewhat cool toward student.
8–23–38–53–68—Teacher is emotionally neutral.
11–26–41–56–71—Teacher tends to draw emotionally close to student.
14–29–44–59–74—Teacher tends to be too close, is sticky.

Status

3–18–33–48–63—Teacher feels very inferior and insecure.
6–21–36–51–66—Teacher tends to look up and defer to student.
9–24–39–54–69—Teacher maintains peer relationship with student.
12–27–42–57–72—Teacher tends to look down on student.
15–30–45–60–75—Teacher feels very superior to student.

STATEMENTS

1. The teacher cannot explain things so that a student understands.
2. The teacher feels disgusted by the student.
3. The teacher treats the student like an honored guest.
4. The teacher often flounders around before getting the student's meaning.
5. The teacher is somewhat cool toward the student.
6. The teacher is hesitant about asking questions of the student.
7. The teacher reacts with some understanding of the student's ideas.
8. The teacher is interested but unemotionally involved.
9. The teacher sees the student as a co-worker on a common problem.
10. The teacher is usually able to understand what the student is saying.
11. The teacher likes the student.
12. The teacher is overprotective of the student.
13. The teacher's comments are always right in line with what the student is attempting to convey.
14. The teacher responds warmly to the student's ideas.
15. The teacher talks down to the student.
16. The teacher shows no comprehension of the ideas the student is trying to communicate.
17. The teacher is hostile toward the student.
18. The teacher tries to sell herself.
19. The teacher often misses the point the student is trying to get across.
20. The teacher at times draws emotionally away from the student.
21. The teacher readily accedes to the student's requests.
22. The teacher is able to keep up with the student's ideas much of the time.
23. The teacher's feelings do not seem to be aroused by student's remarks.
24. The teacher gives and takes in the classroom situation.
25. The teacher really tries to explain ideas clearly to the student.
26. The teacher is pleasant to the student.
27. The teacher readily dismisses the student's ideas.
28. The teacher is able to understand completely what is being communicated.
29. The teacher showers the student with affection and sympathy.

30. The teacher acts in a very superior manner toward the student.
31. The teacher somehow seems to miss the student's meaning time and again.
32. The teacher rejects the student.
33. The teacher frequently apologizes when making a suggestion to the student.
34. The teacher is unable to understand the student on any but a purely superficial level.
35. The teacher occasionally makes the student angry.
36. The teacher assumes an apologetic tone when reacting to the student's ideas.
37. The teacher understands the student's ideas when they are in agreement with her own.
38. The teacher accepts all of the student's comments in a disinterested fashion.
39. The teacher treats the student as an equal.
40. The teacher always follows the student's line of thought.
41. The teacher is pleased by the student's behavior.
42. The teacher looks down upon the student.
43. The teacher is never in any doubt about what the student means.
44. The teacher expresses great liking for the student.
45. The teacher frequently ridicules the student's ideas.
46. The teacher's own ideas completely interfere with his understanding of the student's.
47. The teacher is punitive toward the student.
48. The teacher is pleased when the student indicates approval of her ideas.
49. The teacher finds it difficult to think along the student's lines.
50. The teacher occasionally makes the student tense and on edge.
51. The teacher tries to please the student.
52. The teacher is able to permit the student's expression of ideas much of the time.
53. The teacher shows little hostility or liking for the student.
54. The teacher responds in neither a superior nor submissive manner toward the student.
55. The teacher is well able to understand the student's ideas.
56. The teacher responds warmly to the student's behavior.
57. The teacher frequently ignores the ideas and suggestions of the student.
58. The teacher's explanations fit in correctly with the student's ability and knowledge.
59. The teacher is greatly moved by the student's reactions.
60. The teacher gives an impression of "holier than thou."
61. The teacher reacts in terms of his own ideas.
62. The teacher is unpleasant to the student.
63. The teacher treats the students with much deference.
64. The teacher's comments tend to disrupt the student's trend of thought.
65. The teacher occasionally feels tense and on edge.
66. The teacher complies with the student's suggestions.
67. The teacher's explanations are understood to some extent.
68. The teacher maintains some distance between students and herself.
69. The teacher responds to the student's ideas in an accepting manner.
70. The teacher reacts in terms of relevant ideas.
71. The teacher is sympathetic about the student's problems.
72. The teacher generally directs the student's ideas.
73. The teacher's manner conveys the ability to accept controversial ideas.

74. The teacher greatly encourages and reassures the student.
75. The teacher ignores ideas coming from the student.

PROCEDURE AND SUBJECTS

For this study four groups of college students were asked to sort the 75 statements into the seven categories according to the manner established by Fiedler and Tyler. In this way, all 75 statements were accounted for and sorted. The students were not told about the three dimensions nor the levels within each dimension. The ratings by the students were then tabulated for each item for each category. This procedure was followed to permit comparison with the two sets of results reported by Fiedler and Tyler. Indeed the purpose of this study is accomplished by comparing the descriptions of the concepts of the ideal teacher-pupil relationship held by prospective teachers in college, by teachers in the field, and by college students not involved in the teaching field with the published descriptions held by professors. These in turn are compared with the published description of the concept of the ideal therapeutic relationship.

The groups of students were members of four classes at The Graduate School of Education of Rutgers—The State University of New Jersey, The School of Education of Hofstra University, Queens College of the City University of New York, and Union Junior College in New Jersey. The group at Union Junior College was studying English literature while the others were all studying Education. Table 1 presents data about these students along with data about the Fiedler and Tyler raters taken from their articles. The differences among the groups are obvious.

RESULTS

Table 2 presents the eight statements chosen by each group as characteristic of the most ideal relationship. There is slightly more "intra-agreement" among the groups concerned with teaching than "inter-agreement" between the teaching and the therapeutic groups. Only one statement, 9, is common to all six groups. Table 3 shows that in the eight statements characteristic of the least ideal relationship there is also more intra-agreement than inter-agreement. Two statements, 2, 17, 32, 45 and 75 are common to the five teaching groups.

Table 4 presents the most ideal relationship in terms of the dimensions and levels conceived of by Fiedler. Four of the six groups, or four of the five teaching groups, have the same pattern, five communications, two

TABLE 1

Description of the Raters According to Number, Occupation and Academic Training

Group	Number of Raters	Occupation	Academic Training
Rutgers	21	Graduate Students who are Teachers	14 B.A., 6 M.A., 1 PH.D.
Hofstra	17	Graduate Students (mainly teachers; others prospective teachers)	B.A.
Union Jr.	21	Undergraduates	1 Year College
Queens	30	Undergraduate Prospective Teachers	2 Years College
Tyler	10	Professors and a Physician	1 M.D., 8 PH.D., and 1 ED.D.
Fiedler	10	Psychiatrists, Psychologists and Laymen	2 M.D., 2 PH.D., 3 M.A., 1 R.N., 1 E.E., 1 PH.B.

TABLE 2

Eight Statements Which Characterize the Most Ideal Teacher-Student and Most Ideal Therapist-Patient Relationships for Each Group

	Teacher-Student					Therapist-Patient
	Rutgers	Hofstra	Union Jr.	Queens	Tyler	Fiedler
	9	9	7	9	9	9
	11	13	9	24	24	13
	14	24	10	25	25	25
	24	25	24	28	55	28
Statements	52	28	25	43	58	39
	58	52	52	55	70	40
	73	58	58	58	71	55
	74	74	74	74	73	73

status, and one emotional distance statements. The Rutgers pattern is different from the others. All the groups have two status statements and they are the same two, 9 and 24, which according to Fiedler, characterize a peer relationship. Their communication statements selected come mainly from the good or excellent levels. Their emotional distance statements come from the close or very close levels. Except for Rutgers, the communication dimension then is the most heavily weighted and the most ideal teacher-student relationship may be summarized as good or

TABLE 3

EIGHT STATEMENTS WHICH CHARACTERIZE THE LEAST IDEAL
TEACHER-STUDENT AND LEAST IDEAL THERAPIST-PATIENT
RELATIONSHIPS FOR EACH GROUP

	Teacher-Student					Therapist-Patient
	Rutgers	Hofstra	Union Jr.	Queens	Tyler	Fiedler
Statements	2	1	1	1	1	1
	15	2	2	2	2	2
	17	16	15	16	17	16
	32	17	17	17	32	17
	42	32	32	32	45	30
	45	45	45	45	46	46
	62	46	60	46	47	47
	75	75	75	75	75	62

TABLE 4

PATTERNS OF THE EIGHT STATEMENTS CHARACTERIZING THE
MOST IDEAL RELATIONSHIP FOR EACH GROUP
ACCORDING TO DIMENSION

	D I M E N S I O N		
Group	Communication	Status	Emotional Distance
Rutgers	3 (exists or excellent)	2 (peer)	3 (close or very close)
Hofstra	5 (exists, good, or excellent)	2 (peer)	1 (very close)
Union, Jr.	5 (exists, good, or excellent)	2 (peer)	1 (very close)
Queens	5 (good or excellent)	2 (peer)	1 (very close)
Tyler	5 (good or excellent)	2 (peer)	1 (close)
Fiedler	6 (good or excellent)	2 (peer)	0

excellent communications in a peer relationship which is emotionally close or very close.

There is also agreement among the groups as to the constitution of the least ideal relationship, as shown in Table 5. There is no one pattern of dimensions which is common to the groups like there is in the lists of the top eight. Yet weighting appears on the emotional distance dimension at the level where the teacher draws away from the pupil. Inspection of the data in the table reveals that the least ideal teacher-student relationship may be summarized as no communication in a relationship where the teacher draws away from the pupil emotionally and feels very superior to him.

TABLE 5

PATTERNS OF THE EIGHT STATEMENTS CHARACTERIZING THE
LEAST IDEAL RELATIONSHIP FOR EACH GROUP
ACCORDING TO DIMENSION

| | D I M E N S I O N | | |
Group	Communication	Status	Emotional Distance
Rutgers	0	4 (very superior or looks down)	4 (draws away)
Hofstra	3 (none)	2 (very superior)	3 (draws away)
Union Jr.	1 (none)	4 (very superior)	3 (draws away)
Queens	3 (none)	2 (very superior)	3 (draws away)
Tyler	2 (none)	2 (very superior)	4 (draws away)
Fiedler	3 (none)	1 (very superior)	4 (draws away)

DISCUSSION

From the data presented one highly significant finding is that there is more agreement about what constitutes the least ideal teacher-student relationship than about what constitutes the most ideal one. The finding is borne out by the greater intensity of agreement and the narrower range of statements used in describing the least ideal relationship. Just why more agreement occurs at this extreme of the continuum is not known. Perhaps it is so because in general people more readily agree about what is bad than about what is good. That is, it is easier to criticize and find fault than it is to locate and suggest positive factors. If this more general condition is true, then an explanation for it being so needs to be offered. As yet, no acceptable explanation for this appears available. Of course, it may still be true even though we cannot show why it is true. In any case, the implication of this finding is that as educators we need to encourage discussion about the most ideal teacher-pupil relationship so as to make explicit our beliefs and achieve an understanding about various views on teaching that is necessary if we are to work together.

The data also show high agreement among the groups concerned with the ideal teacher-student relationship according to the items, the dimensions, and the levels within the dimensions. Further, there is much similarity between the description of the ideal teacher-student relationship and the ideal therapist-patient relationship. It is possible to attribute the agreement among the teaching groups to a consensus in our country about teaching. Indeed, there is no great schism among educators concerning the need for the teacher and pupil to communicate with each other, to work together, and not to be "hostile" or "disgusted" with each other.

Also, the similarity between therapy and teaching can be attributed to some overlap of these fields for there appears to be an element of therapy in teaching and an element of teaching in therapy.

But both of these attributions are shallow. Rather, it seems, that both types of agreement stem from the same source. That is, the ideal therapist-patient relationship and the ideal teacher-student relationship are but special cases of an ideal person-person relationship. No one, whether his role be therapist or teacher or mother or employer, can have a good relationship with another person if he does not communicate with him, or if he feels disgusted by him, or if he feels very superior to him. Furthermore, neither Fiedler nor Tyler shows that the statements in the instrument are unique to therapy or to teaching. The instrument in essence is measuring the general ideal human relationship. What is ideal for therapy in this instrument is ideal for teaching for their specific natures have not been delineated. It is, therefore, not surprising that there is agreement among professors, teachers, prospective teachers, therapists, and laymen for they all have a common base.

One other finding is significant in that it, too, leads to a criticism of the instrument developed by Fiedler and Tyler. Rutgers emphasizes the emotional distance dimension in characterizing the most ideal relationship and de-emphasizes the communication dimension in characterizing the least ideal relationship. This is in contrast to all the other teaching groups. The explanation for this finding lies in the overlap of the three dimensions as shown by examining closely the statements included in each. The categories are simply not discrete. Some status items can easily fit into the emotional distance dimension, for example. In a separate, parallel study a group of nine people was asked to sort the 75 statements into the three dimensions. Only 67 per cent of the status items, 80 per cent of the emotional distance items, and 86 per cent of the communication items were sorted into the categories as conceived by Fiedler. Several items like number 48 and 12 (status) were placed into the emotional distance category six out of nine times. In short, what one group considers to be emotional distance, for example, may not be the same as another group. On account of this, comparisons of the groups regarding data on dimensions are rather shaky. Therefore, it is questionable if Rutgers is different from the other groups.

Conclusion

All of this implies that we must be most sensitive to the limitations of this instrument as a means of describing the ideal teacher-pupil relationship. We must acknowledge its general character as opposed to its uniqueness for teaching. We must be careful also not to make too strong a case for the significance of the findings based on the three dimensional aspect of the statements.

However, even in general terms and without complete agreement about which items are in these dimensions, the findings drive home the importance in teaching of good communication, of eliminating to some degree the superior-subordinate relations, and of responding warmly to the students. These are not new claims. But the instrument does have the ability to mirror them back to us in such a way as to make them meaningful for teachers. Not only are they meaningful, but experience in using the instrument in classroom discussions clearly demonstrates that sorters quickly and intensely respond to the tabulations for they themselves have in essence created them.

Furthermore, some of the findings do not involve the element of dividing the statements into three dimensions. The fact remains that the groups did choose identical items without even being aware of the dimensions envisaged by the researchers. This is significant agreement among people even if we grant that these identical items have different meanings to the various sorters. (Different meanings for the same statement is something we can never avoid when using language.) The fact also remains that with the items *qua* items there was greater agreement about the least ideal than about the most ideal teacher-student relationship. This is worthy of our attention and would not have been known without the employment of this instrument however general it is. These facts warrant further investigation formally and informally.

Undoubtedly in order to benefit more from such an analysis of teaching we need to construct statements so as to describe teaching more specifically. We need to add to or modify the dimensions so as to conceptualize teaching as specifically as possible. These needs became evident only from using the instrument, examining and comparing the data, and seeking acceptable interpretations for the findings.

The implications arising from this study are many but two stand out. First, teachers must carefully consider the type of interpersonal relation they create with their pupils. Teachers need to strive to make the actual relationship correspond with their concept of ideal one. Second, we need to continue the study of teaching from this perspective but with a better instrument whether or not it be reconstruction of the one used here.

References

1. Bills, Robert E. "Insights for Teaching from Personality Theory: Intelligence and Teaching." *The Nature of Teaching.* Ed. by Louise M. Berman, Milwaukee, University of Wisconsin-Milwaukee, 1963, p. 49-64.

2. COMBS, ARTHUR W. "The Personal Approach to Teaching." *Educational Leadership,* 21:369-377, 399, March, 1964.
3. FIEDLER, FRED E. "The Concept of an Ideal Therapeutic Relationship." *Journal of Consulting Psychology,* 14:239-245, August, 1950.
4. HALLMAN, RALPH J. "Principles of Creative Teaching." *Educational Theory,* 15:306-316, October, 1965.
5. HARGADON, B. KEVIN. "Transference: A Student-Teacher Interaction." *School Review,* 74:446-452, Winter, 1966.
6. ROGERS, CARL R. "Significant Learning: In Therapy and Education." *Educational Leadership,* 16:232-242, January, 1959.
7. STAVSKY, WILLIAM H. "Using the Insights of Psychotherapy in Teaching." *Elementary School Journal,* 58:28-35, October, 1957.
8. TYLER, LOUISE L. "The Concept of an Ideal Teacher-Student Relationship." *Journal of Educational Research,* 58:112-117, November, 1964.

16. The Development of a Technique for the Measurement of Social-Emotional Climate in Classrooms

John Withall[*]

Rationale.—In the study[1] proper a brief overview of current theories of learning from the associationist and field-theorist point of view precedes a statement of the major concepts, gleaned largely from the field-theorists, that guide the study. Certain postulates regarding the motivational factors in personality and regarding learning conditions are proposed. The primary motivational force of human behavior is postulated to be a drive toward self-actualization. This drive is said to be influenced by:

1. Need for self-consistency
2. Interaction in terms of an internal frame of reference

Reprinted with permission of the author and the *Journal of Experimental Education,* 17:347-361, March, 1949. (Numbering has been retained as it appeared in the original article.)

[*] The author is indebted to several members of the faculty of the Department of Education at the University of Chicago for their counsel and constructive criticisms during the carrying out of the study reported here. He is particularly grateful to both Dr. Herbert A. Thelen of the Department of Education and the Department of Psychology, and to Dr. Carl R. Rogers of the Department of Psychology, University of Chicago, for their facilitation of the experimenter's efforts to make the study as scientifically sound and as theoretically fruitful as possible.

[1] John Withall, *The Development of a Technique for the Measurement of Social-Emotional Climate in Classroom.* Unpublished Ph.D. dissertation, Department of Education, University of Chicago, 1948.

3. Self-directive behavior
4. Achievement of personal significance and private meanings in a social milieu.

It is postulated that learning (changes in behavior) is most likely to occur when experiences are both

1. *meaningful to the learner,* that is, are perceived by the learner as pertinent to his needs and purposes, are consistent with his personality organization, and are associated with self-directive behavior; and

2. *occur in a non-threatening situation,* that is, the learner is free from a sense of personal threat, interacts with others in a wholesome social milieu, and is helped to evaluate himself on the basis of objective criteria.

Since condition number 1 is postulated to be dependent on condition number 2, some knowledge of the psychological atmosphere represented by number 2 is necessary. Little objective evidence exists regarding psychological atmospheres either in learning or other situations. It was decided, therefore, to attempt to develop a technique to measure social-emotional climate in the classroom through a categorization of teacher-statements. It seems reasonable to assume that the teacher's behavior influences the conditions of learning since she is placed in the classroom by society to manipulate the conditions so as to facilitate learning.

Assumptions and hypothesis.—The basic assumptions of the study are (1) that the social-emotional climate is a group phenomenon; (2) that the teacher's behavior is the most important single factor in creating climate in the classroom, and (3) that the teacher's verbal behavior is a representative sample of her total behavior.

The hypothesis to be tested is that by means of a categorization of teacher-statements a valid and reliable index of social-emotional climate can be obtained.

Work Previously Done in Area of Climate

Some work has been done in the area of climate, notably by Ronald Lippitt at Iowa University and Harold H. Anderson at Michigan State College.

LIPPITT'S STUDY

Lippitt's work in social climate is best represented by his doctoral study.[2] In that study he organized four clubs of five boys each and gave

[2] Ronald Lippitt, *An Analysis of Group Reaction to Three Types of Experimentally Created Social Climate.* Unpublished Ph.D. dissertation, University of Iowa, 1940.

each club successive experiences with an "autocratic" and "democratic" leader during three consecutive six-week periods. Several leaders were used to head each of the clubs. The leaders were required to employ different leadership styles with each successive group. The leadership styles were implemented in accord with certain specific criteria drafted to guide the club leaders. Records of social interaction between group members and leader, stenographic records of conversation in each club, analysis of activity subgroupings, and a running account of psychologically interesting interaction in each group were among data collected by observers of each club session.

The major conclusions of Lippitt's study were:

1. That different leadership styles produced different social climates and resulted in different group and individual behaviors;
2. That conversation categories differentiated leader-behavior techniques more adequately than social-behavior categories;
3. That autocratic leadership elicited either an aggressive rebelliousness towards the leader or an apathetic submission to the leader;
4. That leadership style was the primary factor in producing climatological differences and that club personnel was of secondary importance.

Lippitt's work represents one of the earliest and most significant attempts to observe and control the climate variable in a group situation. His findings regarding the value of categorizing verbal behavior as a means of assessing the quality of group life provides a sound basis for the methodology of this study which utilizes a categorization of teachers' verbal behaviors as its major technique.

ANDERSON'S WORK

Harold H. Anderson, Joseph E. Brewer and others have conducted at Michigan State College investigations[3] into the influence of teachers' classroom personalities on children's behavior, particularly at the primary and elementary school levels. In order to obtain objective measurements of teachers' classroom personalities and concomitant children-behavior, Anderson and Brewer developed twenty-six teacher-behavior categories and twenty-nine children behavior categories by which both teacher and pupil verbal and non-verbal behavior might be categorized. Anderson divided teacher-behaviors into two main kinds—Integrative Teacher Behavior and Dominative Teacher Behavior. Integrative behavior was that which expanded the children's opportunities for self-directive and

[3] Harold H. Anderson, et al. *Studies of Teachers' Classroom Personalities,* Applied Psychology Monographs, Nos. 6, 8, and 11 (Stanford, California: Stanford University Press).

cooperative behavior with the teacher and their peers; dominative behavior tended to restrict children's activities and to lead to distracted, aggressive, non-cooperative conduct. Anderson demonstrated that children's behaviors were consistent with the kind of personality the teacher displayed in the classroom.

Anderson's studies bring out evidence that is highly pertinent to the hypothesis that the main direction of influence in the classroom is from the teacher to the pupil. He has demonstrated too, that reliable patterns of teacher and pupil-behavior can be obtained in the classroom through categorizations of their overt behaviors.

DEVELOPMENT OF CLIMATE INDEX

The concept of climate or psychological atmosphere has been used by others in the area of psychology and education besides Lippitt and Anderson. Lewin, Prescott and Rogers, for example, have made considerable use of the concept. However, no clear-cut definition of the concept can be cited and for the purpose of more effective communication and clearer understanding of the notion as used here, a definition of the term "social-emotional climate" is offered.

Definition of social-emotional climate.—Climate is considered in this study to represent the emotional tone which is a concomitant of interpersonal interaction. It is a general emotional factor which appears to be present in interactions occurring between individuals in face to face groups. It seems to have some relationship to the degree of acceptance expressed by members of a group regarding each other's needs or goals. Operationally defined it is considered to influence: (1) the inner private world of each individual; (2) the *esprit de corps* of a group; (3) the sense of meaningfulness of group and individual goals and activities; (4) the objectivity with which a problem is attacked, and (5) the kind and extent of interpersonal interaction in a group.

Procedure for identifying categories.—Proceeding from our assumption that climate is largely determined by the teacher's behavior, we undertook an analysis of the teacher's verbal-behaviors contained in sound recordings of regular class sessions. A teacher's verbal-behavior is assumed to represent adequately her total behavior. Guided by the postulates regarding individual motivation and conditions of learning, teacher-statements were analyzed in order to ascertain whether the teacher was utilizing behaviors likely to create the postulated conditions for learning. Individual teacher-statements tended to fall into about twenty-five types of responses, e.g.:

1. Reproof statements made with the apparent intent of halting the pupil's present behavior and modifying future behavior;

2. Questions seeking further information from pupil about problem;
3. Statement offering simple administrative information, e.g., about place of next class meeting;
4. Questions containing reproof and a plea for cooperation;
5. Statement approving pupil's behavior and commending him;
6. Statement urging a particular course of action on the learner; and so on.

These twenty-five kinds of responses were soon found to overlap and to be not mutually exclusive. They were reduced to thirteen and finally to seven categories. These categories seemed to encompass all the types of statements which teachers utilized in classrooms. The categories are:

1. Learner-supportive statements that have the intent of reassuring or commending the pupil.
2. Acceptant and clarifying statements having an intent to convey to the pupil the feeling that he was understood and help him elucidate his ideas and feelings.
3. Problem-structuring statements or questions which proffer information or raise questions about the problem in an objective manner with intent to facilitate learner's problem-solving.
4. Neutral statements which comprise polite formalities, administrative comments, verbatim repetition of something that has already been said. No intent inferrable.
5. Directive or hortative statements with intent to have pupil follow a recommended course of action.
6. Reproving or deprecating remarks intended to deter pupil from continued indulgence in present "unacceptable" behavior.
7. Teacher self-supporting remarks intended to sustain or justify the teacher's position or course of action.

It seemed that more than one continuum was identifiable in the seven categories; for example, a continuum from problem-centeredness to person-centeredness might be discerned, a continuum from objectivity to subjectivity or a continuum from learner-centeredness to teacher-centeredness. The latter continuum was accepted as useful in applying the categories to teachers' verbal behaviors. Categories 1, 2, and 3 were said to be learner-centered and categories 5, 6, and 7 were said to be teacher-centered. The neutral category had no influence on either bloc. Certain conventions were suggested for interpreting patterns of verbal behavior; for instance, if the proportion of statements falling into one or more of the first three categories outweighed the proportion falling into one or more of the last three categories, the teacher was said to be learner-centered. If the proportion were reversed, the teacher was said to be teacher-centered. Similarly, if the proportion of statements falling into category 3 outweighed the proportions falling into either categories 1 and 2 combined or categories 5, 6 and 7 combined, then the teacher was said to be more problem-centered than learner or teacher-centered. If the largest proportion fell into the combination of either categories 1 and 2 or categories 5, 6, and 7, then the teacher was said to be more highly learner-centered or more self-centered as the case might be. Once the seven categories had been identified and procedures developed for facilitating their application to data, the next step was to ascertain the objectivity, reliability, and validity of the technique. . . . The climate index was shown to have objectivity, reliability, and validity.

APPLICATION OF CLIMATE INDEX TO EXCERPTS FROM FIVE DIFFERENT CLASSES

To test the applicability of the index categories to regular classroom sessions, samples were drawn from the sound recordings of five regular classes held in the laboratory classroom. These classes included a 7th grade mathematics class, two 8th grade social science classes, an 8th grade art class, and a 9th grade Latin class. The classes met regularly in the classroom three or four times a week and were conducted by the regular class teacher in her usual manner.

Sampling.—Eight random samples, each seven minutes in length, were drawn from the recorded class sessions of the art, mathematics, and Latin class. In addition, one full class session was taken from each of the three aforementioned classes as well as from the two social science classes. A total of 23 seven-minute excerpts (one sample from the Latin class was unusable) and five full class sessions were available from classes at the secondary school level. These excerpts from the sound records of the several class sessions were typed-up and the seven categories applied to the teacher-statements contained in the protocols.

Patterns of statements for each of the four teachers were obtained and an attempt was made, largely for illustrative purposes, to interpret these patterns. A mean pattern of distribution of statements among the seven categories was obtained for each of teachers A, B, and C from the several excerpts from their respective classes. A pattern of statements for teacher D in classes W and Z, respectively, was also obtained from two full class sessions of the social science classes. (See Table 8)

Comment regarding teachers' patterns of statements.—Teacher B appears to use a larger proportion of learner-centered statements (categories 1, 2, and 3) than the other three. Teachers A, C, and D_z seem to use a somewhat similar proportion of teacher-centered remarks; teacher B

TABLE 8

PERCENTAGE OF STATEMENTS LOCATED IN EACH OF THE CLIMATE
INDEX CATEGORIES FOR TEACHERS A, B, C, AND D

	Teacher				
	A	B	C	D_w	D_z
Category	Mean %	Mean %	Mean %	Mean %	Mean %
1	18.2	20.3	8.6	2.5	4.7
2	5.2	7.8	2.8	0.0	0.9
3	28.8	39.7	30.7	53.0	41.1
Total	52.2	67.8	42.1	55.5	46.7
4	10.4	22.2	20.2	21.4	16.8
5	14.8	6.8	23.9	13.7	20.6
6	9.1	1.6	8.9	6.8	10.3
7	13.5	1.6	4.9	2.6	5.6
Total	37.4	10.0	37.7	23.1	36.5
Grand Total	100.0	100.0	100.0	100.0	100.0
	N=497	N=408	N=525	N=117	N=107

uses a low proportion of teacher-centered remarks (categories 5, 6, and 7). Teacher D in both sessions uses a slightly larger proportion of problem-structuring remarks (category 3) that the other three teachers and teacher A uses the lowest percentage of such comments. Teacher B uses the largest proportion of category 1 statements and of category 2 remarks. In the teacher-centered area, teacher D_z and teacher C use the largest proportion of directive (category 5) statements, and teacher B the lowest proportion of such statements. Teacher B uses the lowest proportion of reproving (category 6) remarks and of self-supportive (category 7) statements.

A possible interpretation of B's pattern of statements.—Teacher B would appear to be an individual who would offer verbal support and encouragement to the pupils (category 1) and would attempt, to a lesser extent, to convey to them her understanding of them and of their point of view. She possibly tries to keep the objective problem clearly defined and attempts to keep it the central object of attention and concern (category 3). She appears to utilize a small proportion of hortative statements (category 5). Her negative evaluations of pupil-behavior appear to be minimal (category 6). She appears to feel slight need for indulging in self-supportive

TABLE 9

PERCENTAGES OF PROFESSOR E's STATEMENTS FALLING INTO EACH OF THE SEVEN CATEGORIES

Category	Seminar 1 (N=102) Percent	Seminar 2 (N=84) Percent
1	2.0	3.6
2	4.9	8.3
3	70.6	59.5
Total	77.5	71.4
4	8.8	11.9
5	5.9	1.2
6	0.0	0.0
7	7.8	15.5
Total	13.7	16.7
Grand Total	100.0	100.0

and defensive comments. Here is a teacher, we might infer, whose methodology for facilitating learning is (1) to keep the learners well oriented to the objective problem, and (2) to maintain a helpful and understanding attitude towards them. At the same time, she would seem to be able to keep her own needs well in the background.

APPLICATION OF CLIMATE INDEX TO A HIGHER LEVEL OF INSTRUCTION

To test the applicability of the climate index categories to a level of instruction beyond the secondary school level, typescripts derived from recorded sessions of a graduate seminar and from a counselor-training program were processed.

PATTERN OF STATEMENTS DERIVED FROM A CATEGORIZATION OF PROFESSOR E'S VERBAL BEHAVIOR

The protocols containing Professor E's verbalizations are based on two 2-hour seminar meetings of graduate students. These were two consecutive sessions that were recorded and upon which the typescripts were based. (Table 9)

Comments on Professor E's pattern of statements.—A high degree of problem-orientation is evidenced in these two class situations by the large

TABLE 10

PERCENTAGE OF INSTRUCTOR F'S STATEMENTS FALLING
INTO EACH OF THE SEVEN CATEGORIES

Category	Session 1 (N=36) Percent	Session 2 (N=62) Percent	Session 3 (N=52) Percent
1	0.0	8.0	0.0
2	63.9	58.1	69.2
3	22.2	21.0	15.4
Total	86.1	87.1	84.6
4	0.0	11.3	15.4
5	2.7	0.0	0.0
6	5.6	1.6	0.0
7	5.6	0.0	0.0
Total	13.9	1.6	0.0
Grand Total	100.0	100.0	100.0

proportion of problem-structuring comments (category 3). Positive evalu-ations (category 1) are minimal and negative evaluations (category 6) are non-existent. Some verbal expression of acceptance of the students' ideas and feelings is in evidence on the basis of the percentages falling into category 2. The proportion of hortative statements (category 5) is not large. However, some evidence of a need to sustain himself and to be concerned about his status appears from the comparatively large (in relation to the rest of the pattern) proportion of category 7 statements in both sessions.

PATTERN OF STATEMENTS DERIVED FROM
CATEGORIZATION OF PROFESSOR E'S VERBAL BEHAVIOR

The protocols of Instructor F's sessions were based on three 1½ hour sessions. They were random selections from a group of eight available typescripts. The paucity of statements by the instructor, 150 in all for the entire three sessions, is both striking and interesting. (Table 10)

Comments regarding Instructor F's pattern of statements.—Instructor F uses a large proportion of clarifying and acceptant statements (category 2) in all three sessions. Encouraging and reassuring statements (cate-gory) 1 are at a very minimum. Slightly less than ⅕ of his remarks are problem-structuring comments. Directive, reproving, and self-supportive statements are rarely used and are nearly all confined to session 1; the fact that the bulk of F's self-concerned statements fell into session 1 may be "explained" by the fact that it was the first meeting of the class. The whole pattern of F's verbal behavior is explicable largely in terms of his adherence to the principles of client-centered psychotherapy. Counselors of that persuasion place great emphasis on the creation of permissive and acceptant atmosphere by the use of clarifying and acceptant statements and other appropriate procedures. Instructor F clearly transferred his counseling orientation into the classroom situation.

It would appear from the analysis of both Professor E's and Instructor F's statements that the climate index categories are applicable to a higher level of instruction other than the secondary school level.

Summary, Conclusions, and Implications

Summary.—A technique has been developed for assessing the social-emotional climate in a classroom by categorizing teacher-statements contained in typescripts made from sound records of class sessions. The technique has been shown to have objectivity, reliability, and validity.

Conclusions.—

1. Climate can be assessed and described.
2. Several individuals can be trained to use the criteria of the climate index and achieve an adequate measure of agreement among one another in categorizing statements in typescripts.
3. A valid measure of social-emotional climate of groups is obtainable through a categorization of teacher-statements.
4. Within the limits of behavioral and personality variations of the climate index gives us a consistent pattern of verbal behavior for a given teacher from day to day.
5. Different patterns of verbal behavior used by several teachers can be identified.
6. Statements categorized by the climate index as likely to produce "positive" feelings tend to be similarly categorized by impartial observers and tend to be reacted to with "positive" feelings by the individuals to whom they are addressed.
7. Statements categorized according to the climate index as likely to produce "negative" feelings tend to be similarly categorized by impartial observers and tend to be reacted to with "negative" feelings by the individuals to whom they are addressed.

Some revision of the climate index seems in order as a result of insights arising out of its application to several typescripts and to "live" classroom situations. These improvements should include:

1. Clarification of category 1 in order to distinguish between objective and subjective positive evaluation of pupil behavior; the former may be genuinely learner-supportive; the latter doesn't appear to perform that function; clarification of category 5.
2. More rigid definition of statements to be placed in category 4 which should contain perhaps only verbatim repetitions, polite formalities and administrative comments.
3. Differentiation between types of problem-structuring statements.
4. Considering the possibility of sub-dividing five of the seven categories (not 4 and 7) into "A" and "B" areas. The "A" area would represent little or no element of self-concern on the part of the teacher; the "B" area would represent a considerable element of self-concern and result in tingeing the statement with some affect.

Implications for further research.—Some questions that arise out of this study are:

1. What is the relationship between climate and the quality of the learning that occurs in a classroom?
2. To what extent is the climate in a given classroom a function of the personality of the teacher?
3. To what extent do peer-group relationships influence the classroom climate?
4. Of what value is the climate index to teachers in analyzing their own teaching methods?
5. How applicable is the climate index to the "live" classroom situation?

The study described above represents an attempt to develop a technique for the measurement of social-emotional climate to the end that, ultimately, fuller understanding and control may be achieved of one of the factors hypothesized to influence learning.

References

ALLPORT, GORDON W. "Psychology of Participation," *Psychological Review,* LII (1945), 117-132.

ANDERSON, HAROLD H., and BREWER, HELEN M., "Studies of Teachers' Classroom Personalities, I. Dominative and Socially Integrative Behavior of Kindergarten Teachers." *Applied Psychology Monograph,* No. 6, American Psychological Association (Stanford, California: Stanford University Press, 1945), 157 pp.

ANDERSON, HAROLD H., AND BREWER, JOSEPH E., "Studies of Teachers' Classroom Personalities, II. Effects of Teachers' Dominative and Integrative Contacts on Children's Classroom Behavior." *Applied Psychology Monograph,* No. 8 (Stanford, California: Stanford University Press, 1946), 128 pp.

ANDERSON, HAROLD H., and others. "Studies of Teachers' Classroom Personalities, III. Follow-up Studies of the Effects of Dominative and Integrative Contacts on Children's Behavior." *Applied Psychology Monograph,* No. 11 (Stanford, California: Stanford University Press, 1946), 156 pp.

ANGYAL, ANDRAS. *Foundations for a Science of Personality* (New York: Commonwealth Fund, 1941), 398 pp.

BROTEMARKLE, R. A. "Clinical Point of View in Education," *Training School Bulletin,* XLIV (October 1947), 102–110.

CANTOR, NATHANIEL. *Dynamics of Learning* (Buffalo, New York: Foster and Stewart Publishing Corp., 1946), x + 282 pp.

DEWEY, JOHN. *Experience and Education* (New York: Macmillan Co., 1946), xii + 116 pp.

HILGARD, ERNEST R. *Theories of Learning* (New York: Appleton Century Crofts Inc., 1948), x + 409 pp.

JERSILD, ARTHUR T., and others. "Studies of Elementary School Classes in Action, II: Pupil Participation and Aspects of Pupil-Teacher Relationships," *Journal of Experimental Education,* X (December 1941), pp. 119–137.

JOHNSON, MARGUERITE WILKER. "Verbal Influences on Children's Behavior," *School of Education Monographs in Education,* No. 1 (Ann Arbor, Michigan: University of Michigan, 1939), ix + 191 pp.

LECKY, PRESCOTT. *Self-Consistency: A Theory of Personality* (New York: Island Press, 1945), 154 pp.

LEWIN, KURT. "Psychology and the Process of Group Living," *Journal of Social Psychology,* XVII (1943), 113–131.

LEWIN, KURT, and others. *Changing Behavior and Attitudes.* Publication No. 3 of Research Center for Group Dynamics (Cambridge, Massachusetts: Massachusetts Institute of Technology, 1945).

LIPPITT, RONALD. "An Analysis of Group Reaction to Three Types of Experimentally Created Social Climate." Unpublished Ph.D. dissertation, University of Iowa, 1940.

OLSON, WILLARD C., and others. "Teacher Personality as Revealed by the Amount and Kind of Verbal Direction Used in Behavior Control," *Educational Administration and Supervision,* XXIV (February 1938), 81-93.

SNYDER, WILLIAM U. "An Investigation of the Nature of Non-Directive Therapy," *Journal of General Psychology,* XXXIII (1945), 193–223.

The Psychology of Learning. Edited by Nelson B. Henry. Forty-First Yearbook of the National Society for the Study of Education, Part II (Bloomington, Illinois: Public School Publishing Co., 1942), xiv + 463 pp.

WICKMAN, E. K. *Children's Behavior and Teachers' Attitudes* (New York: Commonwealth Fund, 1929), x + 868 pp.

17.   A Study of Openness in Classroom Interactions

James B. Macdonald and Esther Zaret

BACKGROUND OF THE STUDY

What is essential to understanding the nature of teaching? How should teaching be conceptualized? These questions and others like them lead to a basic concern of many educational researchers and theorists. Behind these questions lies the desire to understand the nature of teaching in order that we may improve the selection, education, and performance of teachers; ultimately, improving the quality of learning in our schools. . . .

What is needed is a dynamic conceptualization which deals with human behavior in terms of a general dimension; a general dimension that can move freely among the levels of the teacher as a behaving person, the interactive context, and the children as behavers. Only when a concept of this order is available will it be possible to move freely in the analysis of teaching.

In recent years the behavioral sciences have discovered exciting new ways of looking at human behavior which have direct implications for our concern. One such approach found, for example, among the writings of Rogers (3), Schachtel (4), Rokeach (5), etc. gives promise for providing a conceptualization of the power, usefulness, and generality needed. Essentially, this is the idea of arranging behavior on a process continuum of openness as contrasted with compensatory and/or defensive behavior. Within this framework teacher and pupils as behaving persons, and the interactions between each, may be conceptualized. . . .

The open-closed analytical framework to be applied to classroom interaction in the present study has been developed from a general theoretical background based on the works of Allport (18), Kubie (19), Rogers (3), Rokeach (5), and Schachtel (4). . . .

RATIONALE OF THE STUDY

The proposed process continuum framework differentiates opening and closing teacher behavior in verbal interaction with learners.

At one end of the continuum, the open teacher, in process, exhibits maximal awareness and acceptance of the learner's frame of reference and his readiness to respond. Teacher interchanges with the learner will

Reprinted with permission from *A Study of Openness in Classroom Interactions*. This investigation was supported (in part) by PHS research grant—MH 07563-01 from the National Institute of Mental Health, Public Health Service. (Numbering has been retained as it appeared in the original article.)

be differentiated and transaction-oriented, relating to the realities of the immediate interaction context, resulting in expanded opportunities for variations in learner behavior.

At the opposite end of the continuum, teacher behavior characterized by rigidity and judgmental authority is "closing" in two crucial aspects of teacher-learner interchanges: first, it limits the teacher's perceptual awareness of the learner's frame of reference and his readiness to respond; and, second, it restricts opportunities for variations in learner behavior.

It is hypothesized that the more "open" teacher, functioning at the optimal level of perceptual awareness of the learner, is more likely to make an effective spontaneous decision in direct response to the learner— a decision which will expand opportunities for variations in the learner's productive behavior. And further, an examination of these decisive teacher responses will reveal characteristic patterns of behavior which may be differentiated on a process continuum of opening to closing/defensive behavior. . . .

This study has focused on the interactive verbal behavior of teachers and learners in a specific instructional context—a social studies discussion and/or planning session. . . .

Figure 2 shows a diagrammatic sketch of an analytical framework which was derived from the theoretical perspective presented above, and further developed during the study. Essentially, this schema contrasts opening behavior with closing behavior on one process continuum in the classroom.

The descriptive behavioral terms in the diagram include representative responses found in interaction studies which appear to be most logically related to the framework of the process continuum. Similar descriptive terms were projected as guides for observation and analysis; in the course of the study modifications and additions were made resulting in the descriptive list found in Figure 2. . . .

The interaction flows primarily from teacher decisions, since almost all classroom behavior is either initiated by the teacher or is learner initiated behavior which is then accepted or rejected by the teacher. A relationship has been postulated between the teacher's mediating responses and possibilities for variations in the learner's ensuing responses. Thus, transaction-oriented teacher decisions would permit productive learner behavior; role-expectancy oriented decisions would promote reproductive learner behavior.

ASSUMPTIONS AND DEFINITIONS OF CONCEPTS

The overall rationale and the definitions of concepts are based on several *assumptions about teaching behavior:*

Revised Analytical Framework

FIGURE 2

CLASSIFICATION OF VERBAL BEHAVIOR IN THE CLASSROOM

OPENING

	Teacher	Learner	
Transaction Oriented Decisions	Stimulating Supporting Clarifying Facilitating Elaborating Evaluating °Monitoring °Chairing Accepting	Discovering Exploring Experimenting Elaborating Qualifying Evaluating Synthesizing Explicating Deriving implications Divergent association Counter-responding	Productive Behavior
Role-expectancy Oriented Decisions	Directing Judging (Verdicts) Reproving Rejecting Ignoring Probing or priming °Monitoring °Chairing Factual dialogue (telling) Affirming	Guessing Confirming Acquiesing Following Parroting Counter responding (directing, judging, reproving rejecting, defending) Reproducing facts Reasoning based on given or remembered data	Reproductive Behavior

CLOSING

° Monitoring—calling on a student to respond; recognizing a volunteer response.
° Chairing—keeping a discussion going; no teacher talk.

A. The teacher is the major agent of influence in the classroom.
B. Every teacher develops expectations regarding learner behavior; these expectations may be general or specific; these expectations may be explicitly or implicitly defined by the teacher.
C. The teacher continually makes decisions, either explicitly or implicitly expressed, which are compatible with his expectations for learner behavior, and which have a decisive effect on the course of action and interaction in the classroom.

D. Any area of teacher decision-making may be examined for fuller understanding, within a consistent and comprehensive framework of analysis.

The significant concepts to be defined are *critical incidents* and *critical shifts* in teaching behavior; *transaction oriented decisions* versus *role expectancy oriented decisions* in the teacher's mediating behavior; *productive* versus *reproductive* responses in learner behavior.

1. CRITICAL INCIDENTS AND CRITICAL SHIFTS

In describing "The Critical Incident Technique in the Study of Individuals" (21) John C. Flanagan has set forth a general definition of "critical incident":

> By an incident is meant any observable type of human activity which is sufficiently complete in itself to permit inferences and predictions to be made about the person performing this act. To be critical, an incident must be performed in a situation where the purpose or intent of the act seems fairly clear to the observer and its consequences are sufficiently definite so that there is little doubt concerning its effects.

In classroom verbal interaction the *critical incident* may be conceptualized as one or a series of related critical shifts which represent a readjustment in teacher strategy to facilitate learning. Harootunian (22) has recently called attention to the frequency of such critical shifts in teacher behavior and has emphasized the potential strategizing inherent in such teacher shifts. . . .

2. ANALYTICAL SCHEMA FOR CLASSIFYING VERBAL BEHAVIOR IN THE CLASSROOM

2.1 *Transaction-oriented* versus *Role-oriented* teacher decisions. The study focused on a conceptualized "question-answer-response" flow of verbal action. In this sequence (QAR) the teacher's mediating response to the learner's answer was assumed to be the decisive factor in evoking or limiting productive learner behavior.

In responding to the learner the teacher reflects his decision to continue the flow of action, or to shift and reorient classroom action to facilitate learning in accordance with his expectation for learner behavior.

In classifying teacher responses to the learner an attempt was made to differentiate between transaction-oriented and role expectancy-oriented teacher decisions. The conceptualized distinction is summarized as follows:

Transaction-oriented decisions were conceived as:
   (1) reflecting flexible teacher expectations.
   (2) accepting and expanding the learner's meanings (as revealed in his responses to teacher questions and statements).
   (3) promoting divergent, evaluative, and choice-making learner behavior.

Role expectancy-oriented decisions were conceived as:
   (1) reflecting rigid teacher expectations.
   (2) rejecting or proscribing the learner's meanings (as revealed in his responses to teacher questions and statements).
   (3) promoting convergent, non-evaluative learner behavior.

2.2 *Productive* versus *Reproductive* learner behavior.
   The continuum of the range of variations in learner behavior includes four categories of the Aschner-Gallagher System (23), an adaptation of the Guilford structure of intellect model, for classifying productive thinking processes in the context of classroom verbal interactions.

   In the present study *Productive* learner behavior includes the Aschner-Gallagher categories of evaluative and divergent responses; *Reproductive* learner behavior includes cognitive memory and convergent responses.

RESEARCH PLAN

The specific aim of this study was an examination of classroom interactions from the viewpoint of the proposed process continuum of openness as contrasted with defensive and/or compensatory behavior in order to see if the behavior observed can be reliably identified, categorized, and analyzed in these terms.

The long term goal is to utilize the tested framework to generate hypotheses for large scale intensive studies involving increased effectiveness in teaching. . . .

Nine teachers, and their classrooms of students, from the Campus Elementary School of the University of Wisconsin-Milwaukee comprised the sample for the study.

Each classroom was visited during a planning and/or discussion period in the Social Studies program. The duration of this visit was from twenty to fifty minutes in each case. Tape recordings were made of these periods.

The tape recordings were transcribed and analysis of the data was made in terms of the analytical framework developed (Figure 2). The researchers' analysis was checked for reliability by submitting selected material to instructed judges for separate analyses. . . .

ANALYSIS AND RESULTS OF THE STUDY

Reliability of the categorization process was checked by comparing trained and independent observers' responses to the categorization task in the areas of 1) critical shifts; and, 2) classroom verbal behaviors. . . . Having obtained acceptable reliability in classification, the transcripts were analyzed to see what kinds of patterns of interaction were in evidence.

Each teacher-pupil response sequence within each critical shift was analyzed and classified in terms of its closing or opening quality. The results of this analysis provided suggestive data concerning the following questions:

(1)—When teacher solicitation behavior is closed in nature will student response be closed? (and the reverse)

(2)—Can classroom interaction of individual teachers be characterized as essentially open or closed?

1. Analysis of the Teachers As A Group

Each teacher's shifts and the ensuing verbal behaviors of teachers and pupils within shifts were analyzed to see whether closed behavior on the part of the teacher (or open behavior) resulted in closed (or open) behavior on the part of students. A total of 147 shifts were identified in the nine transcripts. Analysis of paired or congruent (open-open or closed-closed) instances of verbal behavior revealed 127 cases of congruent behavior on the part of both teacher and pupil and 20 cases where there was a lack of congruence. Thus, congruence was found in 86% of the cases. Application of the sign test to the ratio of 124-23 shows that the ratio could occur by chance alone once every thousand times. (.001 level of significance).

2. Analysis of Individual Teacher's Patterns

A two by two table was constructed for each teacher after examination of their transcripts. Critical shifts were noted and the pairing of teacher-pupil behavior was made. Four categories for any pairing within a critical shift were possible. Figure 3 shows the possible categories.

FIGURE 3

POSSIBLE PAIRING OF TEACHER-PUPIL VERBAL BEHAVIORS

TEACHER

		Role	Transaction
LEARNER	Reproductive (role)		
	Productive (transaction)		

Thus, any set of paired responses within a critical incident could be categorized in one of four ways as shown in Figure 2.

1—teacher role—learner reproductive
2—teacher role—learner productive
3—teacher transaction—learner reproductive
4—teacher transaction—learner productive

The "pure" or expected cases, representing the 86% noted above which fall in the teacher role-learner reproductive and teacher transaction-learner productive categories, are pointed out by the diagonal line arrow in Figure 3. . . .

3. Conclusions drawn from the analysis of Individual Teachers' Classroom Classifications. Three general conclusions should be noted:

1. Significant (.05 level or beyond) congruence of pairs was found in 8 of the 9 individual teacher classrooms.
2. Teacher behavior was by and large, characterized to a significant degree (.05 level or beyond) by either transaction or role oriented behavior. Three teachers were significantly role oriented; four teachers were significantly transaction oriented; and, two teachers were mixed (i.e. not significantly oriented).
3. Learner behavior was, by and large, characterized to a significant degree (.05 level or beyond) by either reproductive or productive behavior. In five cases productive behavior was significantly (.05 level) present; in three cases reproductive behavior was characteristic, and in one case mixed behavior was characteristic.

DISCUSSION

The results of this exploratory study must be held tentatively until further validation is forthcoming. Nevertheless, the percentage of agreement among those classifying behaviors would indicate that the classification system of the process continuum (opening—closing) is a promising tool for interaction research in classrooms.

This model of analysis was originally pursued, as mentioned earlier, with the hope that a global quality of classroom interaction could be identified to utilize across levels of teacher personality, social interaction, and other areas of teacher planning and operating in the classroom. The first step, an analysis at the social interaction level here, appears promising.

There is little doubt that behavioral phenomena are complex and the researchers do not wish to suggest otherwise. On the other hand, there would seem to be very little opportunity for effective utilization of verbal concepts by teachers in monitoring their behavior; or, for that matter, by researchers to make coherent sense out of complicated or partial analytic schemes unless classroom phenomena can be symbolized in relatively global and related terms.

The opening-closing process continuum does have theoretical corrolaries in personality and interaction dimensions, across grade levels, subject areas, and kinds of teacher decisions. As such, it would appear useful in light of the results of this study to pursue this conceptualization further.

Results of the patterns found among the nine teachers have little generality because of the nature of the sample. There is, however, some reason to suggest that these findings are indicative of promising hypotheses. Aschner and Gallagher (23), Guzak (24), and others have also found that teachers elicit the kinds of responses they ask for (in terms of level of thinking). The high percentage of congruent pairs noted in this study is in agreement with these findings in the sense that like begets like. Thus, open teacher (transaction oriented) behavior did appear to elicit open student (productive) behavior, and the reverse.

Though hardly startling as a finding this does at least underline the crucial significance of the teacher's role. The specific nature of the open learner behaviors which were (apparently) readily elicited by teachers is encouraging, inasmuch as they reflect a body of items classifiable loosely as inquiry or creative behaviors. The crucial significance of the development of learner inquiry and creative abilities has been fully expressed in much recent educational literature.

A further hopeful sign may be found in the variance among teachers in the study. Much recent research in classrooms has revealed the similarity in teacher patterns of behavior. Hughes (7), for example, reported the predominance of structuring activities, and the findings of Bellack (25), Flanders (6), and Perkins (10) illustrate a single teacher talk-content focus orientation. At least the present study suggests that teachers are capable of radically different behavior (transaction oriented versus role and needs oriented); and that this behavior can be said to characterize their interactions with learners. Whether some teachers are characteristically "open" in public school settings, however, remains to be seen.

The existence of mixed interactions in two cases raises a further point of interest. Flanders (26) hypothesizes that flexible teacher behavior (in his direct and indirect matrix) may be the most productive. It is worth reflecting upon whether teachers may, in terms of the proposed framework, be exhibiting behavior classifiable as "locked in an open position" as well as essentially opening or closing behavior.

A number of research possibilities appear to be opened by the study. Studies of comparative results with other frameworks, for example, seem to be in order. Further, studies utilizing this framework in relation to criterion variables in classrooms are feasible and desirable. One advantage this framework may have here, as suggested earlier, is that the model would seem to be predisposed to relate to non-achievement variables, such as self-direction, as well as to achievement criteria.

This study, then, is seen by the researchers as an initial exploratory attempt with highly tentative results, although the classificatory model appears to be feasible and useful. It would be less than truthful, however, if we failed to communicate the encouragement found in these results, and our positive convictions about the potential meaning and implications of the model.

REFERENCES

1. TURNER, RICHARD and FATTU, NICHOLAS. "Skill in Teaching, A Reappraisal of Concepts and Strategies in Teacher Effectiveness Research," Bulletin of the School of Education, Indiana University, Vol. 36, No. 3, Bloomington, Indiana.

2. BARR, ARVIL S., et al. "Wisconsin Studies of the Measurement and Prediction of Teaching Effectiveness—A Summary of Investigations," Dembar Publications, Inc., Madison, Wisconsin, 1961.

3. ROGERS, CARL. On Becoming a Person, Houghton Mifflin Company, Boston, 1961.

4. SCHACHTEL, ERNEST G. Metamorphosis, Basic Books, Inc., New York, 1959.

5. ROKEACH, MILTON. The Open and Closed Mind, Basic Books, Inc., New York, 1960.

6. FLANDERS, NED. Teacher Influences on Pupil Attitudes and Achievement: Studies in Interaction Analysis, Cooperative Research Project. No. 397, Minneapolis, Minnesota, University of Minnesota, 1960.

7. HUGHES, MARIE and Associates. A Research Report, University of Utah, 1959.

8. SMITH, B. OTHANEL and others. A Study of the Logic of Teaching: A Report on the First Phase of a Five-Year Research Project, Urbana, Bureau of Educational Research, University of Illinois, 1960.

9. WRIGHT and PROCTOR. *Systematic Observation of Verbal Interaction as a Method of Comparing Mathematics Lessons.* Cooperative Research Project #816, U.S. Office of Education, Department of Health, Education and Welfare, St. Louis, Washington University, 1961.

10. PERKINS, HUGH. "A Procedure for Assessing the Classroom Behavior of Students and Teachers," *American Educational Research Journal.* Vol. I., No. 4 and Vol. 2, No. 1, November, 1964 and January, 1965; pp. 249-260, and pp. 1-12.

11. MEDLEY, DONALD. "Experiences with the Oscar Technique," *Journal of Teaching Education,* Vol. XIV, No. 3, September, 1963. pp. 267-273.

12. ANDERSON and BREWER. *Studies of Teachers' Classroom Personalities II: Effects of Teacher's Dominative and Integrative Contacts on Children's Classroom Behavior.* Applied Psychology Monographs, 1946, No. 8.

13. HEIL, POWELL and FEIFER. Characteristics of Teacher Behavior Related to the Achievement of Children in Several Elementary Grades. Cooperative Research Project #7285, U.S. Office of Education, Department of Health, Education and Welfare, New York, Brooklyn College, 1960.

14. WAIMON, MORT. *Feedback in Classrooms: A Study of the Corrective Responses Made by Teachers as They Interact in the Teaching-Learning Process.* Paper presented at the American Educational Research Association Annual Meeting, February 1961, Atlantic City, New Jersey.

15. WITHALL, JOHN. "The Development of a Technique for the Measurement of Social-Emotional Climate in Classrooms." *Journal of Experimental Education,* 1949, 17: 347-361.

15a. NEWELL, LEWIS and WITHALL. "Use of a Communication Model to Study Classroom Interactions." Paper presented at American Educational Research Association, Annual Meeting, February 1961, Chicago, Illinois.

16. BILLS, ROBERT. "Being and Becoming." Paper presented at the Annual Meeting of the Association for Supervision and Curriculum Development, Las Vegas, Nevada, March 1, 1962.

17. ANDERSON, H. H. "Creativity and Education," Association for Higher Education College and University Bulletin, Volume 13, No. 14, Special Issue, National Committee on General Education, May, 1961.

18. ALLPORT, GORDON. *Pattern and Growth in Personality,* Holt, Rinehart, and Winston, New York, 1961.

19. KUBIE, LAWRENCE. "Research on Protecting Preconscious Functions in Education." Paper presented at Research Institute, Association for Supervision and Curriculum Development, Washington, D. C., 1961.

20. ROGERS, CARL R. "A Process Conception of Psychotherapy." Paper presented at the Annual Conference of the American Psychological Association. New York, September 1957. (Mimeographed).

21. FLANAGAN, JOHN C. "The Critical Incident Technique in the Study of Individuals." *Modern Educational Problems,* pp. 61-70, Seventeenth Educational Conference, New York City, October 1952 (Washington, D.C. American Council on Education).

22. HAROOTUNIAN, BERJ. "The Teacher as Problem Solver: Extra-Class Decision-Making." Paper presented for *Symposium Curriculum and Instruction: A Dialogue on the Reconstruction of Theory.* 50th Annual Meeting, American Educational Research Association, February, 1966.

23. ASCHNER, MARY JANE and GALLAGHER, JAMES, et al. "A System for Classifying Thought Processes in the Context of Classroom Verbal Interac-

tion." Champaign, Illinois: Institute for Research on Exceptional Children, 1965.
24. GUZAK, J. FRANK. "A Study of Teacher Solicitation and Student Response Interaction About Reading Content in Selected Second, Fourth, and Sixth Grades." Doctoral Dissertation, University of Wisconsin, June, 1966.
25. BELLACK, ARNO, and DAVITZ, JOEL R., et al. *The Language of the Classroom.* New York: Institute of Psychological Research, Teachers College, Columbia University, 1953. (Mimeographed).
26. FLANDERS, NED. "Teacher Influence in the Classroom." *Theory and Research In Teaching,* Arno Bellack (ed.) Teachers College, Columbia University Press, 1963, pp. 37-52.

APPENDIX

Following is a sample classroom transcript and analysis of the flow of verbal interchange for one teacher.

The classroom transcript shows the numbers (e.g. 1) of each unit and the critical shifts (marked /).

The analysis sheet shows how the flow was analyzed and classified. A plus (+) indicated a transaction orientation of a unit; A minus (−) indicates role orientation; and zero (0) refers to monitoring or chairing teacher behavior (classified as neutral).

Teacher #3 was classified as predominantly transaction oriented.

RECORD 3

1 TEACHER: Our plans for living things—the way we might be sharing
2 our information—could we do that now. You are just going to tell us
  your plans—you are not going to tell us anything of how—you are
3 just going to tell us how you plan to do it. You may even change your
  plans if you find you can't do everything the way you want it. / Now
  let's have some people tell us how you plan to share your information
4 about your animal or your living things— / Doug.
5 STUDENT: Well, I'm going to give some movies about the—the
6 likenesses and differences between a salamander and myself. And I'm
  setting for a movie already—I have done the likenesses and differences
  —not too many yet and I have seen how many legs on a salamander
  that we have now and if it is one that goes in water or lives on land
  or in water.
7 TEACHER: You are studying our salamander—our own salamander
  and how—
8 STUDENT: And how it gets its babies.
9 TEACHER: / You mentioned something about your photography—

10 STUDENT: Yes, and I will take the pictures with my camera of it to
   see how it acts when it is eating—I will try to get a picture of that—
11 of it eating, and, should I ask about an earthworm?
12 TEACHER: It's up to you.
13 STUDENT: / Could anyone bring an earthworm for the salamander.

Teacher No. 3

Analysis of Verbal Interchanges

Verbal Unit #	Speaker	FLOW OF VERBAL ACTION Ongoing ⟷ Shifting		Critical Incident	Classification of Verbal Behaviors	
1	T	Opening Statement		Opening	Intro-focusing	—
2	T	Opening Statement			Directing	—
3	T	Opening Statement			Elab-facilitating	+
4	T		T—State	1	Direct-monitoring	0
5	S	Answer			Reporting progress	+
6	S	Answer			Synthesizing	+
7	T	T—R—Q			Accepting	+
8	S	Counter R			Elaborating	+
9	T		T—R—Q	2	Support	+
10	S	Answer			Elaborating	+
11	S		⎧ S—Q		Permission for exploring	+
12	T		⎨ T—Answer		Support-facilitating	+
13	S		⎪ S—Q	3	Counter-facilitating	+
14	T		⎩ T—Monitoring ⎭	4	Monitoring	0

The Social Climate

OVERVIEW

$\mathbf{E}$DUCATORS who view teaching from the vantage point of class-room social climate employ such concepts as leadership, power, influence, authority, and role. They ask such questions as: How does the teacher manifest his leadership position in the classroom? In what ways does the teacher use his power? What patterns of teaching influence can we identify in the classroom? Who is recognized as having the authority for making classroom decisions? In what ways do teachers respond to the social needs of the students? What roles does the teacher perform as he teaches?

Of all the vantage points for studying teaching, this one of class-room climate is by far the most common one taken by educators. More empirical studies have been made on teaching from this per-spective than from any other. This background of research gained strength in the 1930's from the work on the dynamics of youth groups done by Kurt Lewin and his associates, Lippitt and White. The early leading researcher on teaching was H. H. Anderson, who, with his associates, studied "dominative" and "integrative" contacts in nursery school. Most of the subsequent research on classroom climate (and youth groups as well) utilizes these two categories of

209

behavior established years ago. This debt is evident in the material included in this section.

Flanders, in summarizing research projects on social classroom climate, has presented a short and insightful synthesis of these two teacher behavior patterns labeled Integrative Pattern and Dominative Pattern.

Integrative Pattern	*Dominative Pattern*
a. Accepts, clarifies, and supports the ideas and feelings of pupils	a. Expresses or lectures about own ideas as knowledge
b. Praises and encourages	b. Gives directions or orders
c. Asks questions to stimulate pupil participation in decision-making	c. Criticizes or deprecates pupil behavior with intent to change it
d. Asks questions to orient pupils to schoolwork	d. Justifies own position or authority[1]

The selections that follow demonstrate the significance of understanding social climate. In our democratic society citizens learn how to use and deal with authority, power, and leadership, in large measure, from their school experiences. Outside the home, the classroom is the one group, and adult-led at that, which each person must join at one time or another. The student learns social values by being personally involved with the teacher and his classmates and by observing the interactions of others about him. He learns how power is used, for example, and what the consequences of power are. In short, the interaction with the teacher and his classmates teaches the pupil social skills, knowledge, and values.

This perspective has yet another significance. For years many people have been claiming that the climate of the classroom, which is set by the teacher, affects the cognitive achievement of the students. Many claim that when a teacher follows a more "democratic" pattern of behavior the students achieve more. Although the empiri-

[1] Ned A. Flanders. *Teacher Influence, Pupil Attitudes, and Achievement.* Cooperative Research Monograph no. 12. U.S. Department of Health, Education, and Welfare, Office of Education. Washington, D.C., 1965.

cal research on this point is inconclusive,[2] we can say that different teachers have different patterns of behavior and that these patterns result in varying student behaviors. That is, certain types of teacher action facilitate certain pupil action. Besides, the democratic pattern, even if it does not yield more cognitive achievement may yield more emotional and aesthetic growth. A need therefore exists to study the relationship between teacher behavior that involves authority, power, influence, and leadership and the cognitive, emotional, and aesthetic behavior of pupils.

R. S. Peters,[3] the British philosopher of education, has clearly demonstrated the various uses of the word *authority* in educational matters. He distinguishes between a teacher who is *in authority* for purposes of social control within the social structure of the schools and a teacher who is *an authority* because of his special competence in a subject or skill area. He further distinguishes being *in authority* from *being authoritarian,* which he claims is a repressive form of the use of social authority. In the selections included here, the reader should note which of these three forms of the word *authority* is being used by the authors.

Three of these selections—Flanders, Hughes, and Perkins—are empirical studies dealing with this matter of authority and influence. They present their instruments and their results, all based on the concepts of teacher power, the superior-subordinate relationship in the classroom, and teacher-pupil interaction.[4] Flanders studied junior high school classes, while Perkins and Hughes studied classes in elementary school. Flanders categorized behaviors occurring in two-minute samples of observation, and Hughes employed the concept of functions performed by the teacher for the pupil for her unit of analysis. The studies were conducted in three different sections of the country (Utah and a west coast state by Hughes, Minnesota by

---

[2] Richard C. Anderson, "Learning in Discussion: A Resume of Authoritarian Democratic Studies." *Harvard Educational Review,* 29:201-215, Summer, 1959. Note that Flanders' study here does claim more achievement for pupils with teachers who are indirect (democratic). The second part of the study by Perkins in the *American Educational Research Journal* (January, 1965) also makes this claim.

[3] R. S. Peters. "The Authority of the Teacher." *Comparative Education,* 3:1-12, November, 1966.

[4] See the Overview to the Communications section for additional comment on the concepts utilized here.

Flanders, and Maryland by Perkins) and in different years. Perkins categorized teacher and pupil behavior, learning activity, and role; Flanders categorized teacher and pupil behavior; and Hughes categorized only teacher behavior. Flanders categorized only verbal behavior, while Perkins and Hughes used both verbal and nonverbal behavior. Hughes drew up narrative records and categorized them afterwards, while Flanders and Perkins categorized behavior "live" in the classroom.

The study by Flanders is no doubt the most well-known one on classroom observation today. His Interaction Analysis instrument is widely used by other researchers because of its simplicity and the ease in obtaining acceptable observer reliability. It is unique in that as the identified categories are paired off, the observer can readily plot the patterning of a class' verbal behavior in a matrix, or a ten-by-ten table, showing the hundred possible sequences of category pairs. Flanders' category system is presented along with the selection by Chapline, which is an illustrative analysis of a matrix plotted from an actual junior high school social studies class.

The reader should be alerted to one category in Marie Hughes' study in particular. Development of content is defined as the response the teacher makes to the data put into the situation by the pupil. The teacher may elaborate on, clarify, add to, accept, stimulate further, and even evaluate material offered by the pupil. In this way, Hughes' "content" category is unique. It is quite different from other content as categorized in studies in this chapter and other chapters. Her other categories, such as positive affectivity and negative affectivity, are similar to others, as shown in the article by Perkins in which he compares his own study with Flanders' and Hughes'. It is significant that, with all their many differences, these studies present similar data.

The three other selections by Getzels and Thelen, Jensen, and Jenkins are non-empirical investigations of classroom teaching from the vantage point of social climate. Much of the same terminology is used but with slightly different meanings. For example, influence for Flanders is not the same as influence for Jenkins. The reader should also be alerted to Jenkins' distinctions among power, authority, and influence. These three selections discuss such concepts as conflict, role, need satisfaction, values, expectations, and personality, for they explicitly draw from anthropology, political science, biology, and psychology, as well as sociology.

These three articles range from the fairly uncomplicated set of concepts employed by Jenkins to the complex framework established by Getzels and Thelen. Jensen presents seven categories for describing how classroom participants relate to one another. It would, of course, be interesting and helpful to be able to use these studies as bases for instruments for direct classroom observation with trained, reliable observers. Jensen's set of dimensions would perhaps be the easiest to develop into a usable instrument. At this point, they provide only the bases for informal diagnoses and observation.

Jensen's point that the teacher must constantly analyze the classroom situation is clearly reminiscent of Dewey in *Democracy and Education*, both in thought and terminology. Dewey asserted that the teacher must know his subject matter so well that he can focus on diagnosing the ongoing discussion.

> When engaged in the direct act of teaching, the instructor needs to have subject matter at his fingers' ends; his attention should be upon the attitude and response of the pupil. To understand the latter in its interplay with subject matter is his task, while the pupil's mind, naturally, should be not on itself but on the topic at hand. Or to state the same point in a somewhat different manner: The teacher should be occupied not with the subject matter in itself but in its interaction with the pupils' present needs and capacities.[5]

In their transactional style, Getzels and Thelen submit that in this ideal-type model of the classroom as a social system "each individual *identifies* with the goals of the system so that they become part of his own needs." This is remarkably similar to R. S. Peters' suggestion for a way to ease the difficulty in resolving the apparent problems arising from being *in authority* and being *an authority*. Pupils have no direct say regarding the appointment of their teacher and may not consent to his being in authority. Also, pupils are

[5] John Dewey. *Democracy and Education.* New York, Macmillan Company, 1961. p. 183.

compelled to attend school and may oppose the efforts of the teacher. For Peters the appropriate approach "is basically to get the pupils to identify themselves with the aims of the school, to share the teacher's concern for what is being handed on. . . . A more appropriate approach for a teacher is to behave and becomes a person who is an authority on something, to be true to his calling. A person who is genuinely an authority about something invests it with an aura. His enthusiasm for his chosen activity or form of awareness and his mastery of its intricacies lures others to be initiated into its mysteries."[6]

Suggestions for further work leap forth from these six selections. One will suffice here to demonstrate that vast numbers of research projects are still needed. Flanders states that no teacher has a pure pattern of influence in the classroom. That is, no teacher manifests only direct influence or indirect influence over the pupils. Rather, each teacher mixes his behavior, and the variations among teachers is the degree to which they mix their verbal influence. Hughes, on the basis of her notion of what kind of people she would like pupils to become[7] and of what the impact of the teacher on the pupils is, has outlined in her full report as a model of good teaching:

Controlling Functions	20–40%
Imposition	1–3%
Facilitating	5–15%
Content Development	20–40%
Personal Response	8–20%
Positive Affectivity	10–20%
Negative Affectivity	3–10%

The question then becomes what pattern or mixture of teacher-influence behavior is most likely to bring out the desired learning in the classroom? This question, no matter which of the six following frameworks we use, is but one of the many significant problems that will necessitate great amounts of energy and ingenuity from investigators.

[6] R. S. Peters. *op. cit.* p. 7.
[7] See the selections by Rogers, Hallman, Gallagher and Aschner, and Maccia for views expressing approaches virtually the same as Hughes'.

18.   Characteristics and Functions of Leadership in Instructional Groups

David H. Jenkins

INTRODUCTION

Leadership is a concept for which there are several definitions. Sometimes it is seen as the behavior of people who are in a position of leader; sometimes it is seen as a particular set of behaviors; at still other times it is viewed as a set of personal characteristics. For gaining further understanding into some of the problems and processes of present-day instructional groups, it is defined here as follows: *Leadership is behavior which affects the instructional group.* Ordinarily, the effects of the behavior will be intended by the person who is acting, but sometimes particular behavior has marked effect on the group without any such intention on the part of the originator of that behavior.

This definition does *not* imply that leadership is behavior which is helpful to the group. Although helpfulness is the desired end, some of the problems of the instructional group arise from the fact that the person in the position of the leader of the group, the teacher, exerts an influence inimical to the basic needs and purposes of the group. Neither is leadership defined as behavior which is exhibited by the person in the position of leader, for student behavior can have a telling effect on the class.

Leadership in the classroom, which has its source in the teacher, gives rise to somewhat different problems than does that which is derived from the students. We will deal with the leadership of both the teacher and the group and then attempt to describe some of the issues which arise in the classroom as the leadership springing from one source impinges upon that deriving from the other.

THE TEACHER AS LEADER

The teacher is ordinarily the individual with greatest influence in the classroom. His behavior is intended to have effect on the pupils; he is more likely, in one way or another, to exercise influence upon the group. It is our purpose here to state some of the important factors underlying this teacher-pupil situation—factors which, if not understood, can lead to

Reprinted with permission from Chapter 8 of *The Dynamics of Instructional Groups,* The Fifty-ninth Yearbook of the National Society for the Study of Education, Part II. Chicago, University of Chicago Press, 1960.

confusion on the part of the teacher with respect to his conception of his leadership role.

THE BASES OF LEADERSHIP OF TEACHERS

Much of the literature and research on teacher behavior and its effects on children has indicated that there is some relationship between what the teacher does and the responses of the group. However, when a particular teacher attempts to apply the findings of research in his classroom, he may discover that he does not obtain the expected results. What is overlooked is the fact that, even though he carries out the same acts, they have a different meaning for the children because his relationship with them is different from that which existed between the adult and the children involved in the original research.

The meaning we assign to behavior arises from the context in which the acts occur as well as from the nature of the acts themselves. The particular behavior of the teacher gains its meaning for the students from the particular relationship which they sense the teacher has with them. Let us examine some elements of this relationship and their correlates.

The Authority of the Teacher. One of the basic aspects of group life is decision-making. The issue is freedom versus control. Freedom is felt when people may make decisions for themselves; control is felt when they are subject to the decisions of others. The need for autonomy is an important human need, one to which adolescents are particularly sensitive. *Authority is the ability to make decisions which affect other people.*

The authority of the teacher does not arise from the instructional group.[1] It arises from the school as an organization and derives its authority from the community at large. In practice, the community vests authority in the school board; certain areas of authority remain under the jurisdiction of the board, and others are passed on to the administrator, who retains authority over some areas and distributes authority over other areas to the teachers concerned. The teacher acquires his authority through this channel, with his areas of authority more or less clearly designated by his administrator.

The teacher gets his authority in the same manner that a foreman in a factory acquires authority over his work crew. If the class is to be allowed to make any decisions for itself, the teacher has to give it that responsibility. It is unrealistic to deny the nature of authority in the school; no organization can exist long without authority of this kind.

[1] Herbert A. Thelen, *Dynamics of Groups at Work.* Chicago: University of Chicago Press, 1954.

How the teacher uses his authority is the major issue for consideration.[2]

Because the issue of freedom versus control is so fundamental in human relations, most behaviors of leaders are watched closely by group members to determine how the leader is using his authority.[3] Students learn to listen for the teacher's real desires whenever the teacher offers them a choice. They have learned, sometimes through bitter experience, that the teacher is not always giving them freedom, in fact, when he says he is doing so. He may say, "Do what you like with this assignment," when he really means "Do what I would like to have you do!" The teacher's wish to be "democratic" tends to drive him to *say* that the students have freedom of choice, but he may not be willing or able to give the students that freedom.

This issue pervades and confuses a host of relationships betweeen teachers and students. The authority implication is clouded or often overlooked by the adult, but the students are aware of its importance and look for it.

The Power of the Teacher. It is evident that, many times, the person in authority must make decisions which restrict certain freedoms of the student. These decisions can only be enforced if the authority carries with it sufficient power to maintain them. *Power is the capability of augmenting or impeding need satisfaction.* One person has power over another when he can control the rewards and punishments which that person receives.

Power becomes an issue when the decisions which are made by the person in authority require the subordinate to do something he resists doing. There is no issue if the person in authority is letting the subordinate do what he wants to do. If the students' attention to uninteresting or apparently purposeless activities is required, power does become an issue in many teacher-class relationships. The community uses its power to require the students' attendance at school, and the teacher uses his power to restrict their behavior in the classroom.

It must be immediately evident that without power the school could

[2] Many interpretations in the educational literature of the research on democratic, autocratic, and laissez-faire leadership (See Ronald Lippitt and Ralph K. White, "An Experimental Study of Leadership and Group Life," in *Readings in Social Psychology*, pp. 340-54. Edited by Guy E. Swanson, Theodore M. Newcomb, and Eugene L. Hartley. New York: Henry Holt & Co., 1952.) have overlooked the fact that the adult leader under each condition has the *same* authority based on adult and organizational status. The conditions of the study demonstrated the effects of different ways of using that authority; under autocracy, the leader kept all decisions to himself; under democracy, he gave certain relevant decisions to the group; under laissez-faire, he gave all decisions to the group.

[3] Henry Clay Lindgren, *Mental Health in Education*. New York: Henry Holt & Co., 1954.

not function, nor could the classroom. Yet it must be equally clear that if the dominant element in the relationship between the teacher and his class is power, the stress of conflict will impede productive learning activities. The power relationship replaces the teaching-learning relationship.

There are many ways in which the teacher can exercise power over the student, none of which is directly related to the learning process. The most obvious is the use of physical force; thrashing is still permitted in many schools. Other methods may be employed: threatening to lower grades, sending students to the office, invoking parents as threats, keeping after school, punishments designed to force students to accept the decision of the teacher. When the teacher's threat dominates the teacher-student relationship, the student comes to fear the situation or to reject the relationship.

Let us turn back, for the moment, to the statement of our concept of leadership and the idea that the task of the teacher is to make the instructional group a unit for learning. It is necessary in some situations that the teacher use power to create proper conditions for learning. At times a teacher would be remiss if he did not make use of his power; not to do so would make the students increasingly insecure, since they would feel that there was nothing that they could depend upon. They want to sense that the teacher *can* control the situation through power if necessary.

However, power is sometimes invoked, not because it is needed to manage the learning situation, but because the teacher needs to demonstrate to himself that he has power over other people. His own personal need for power takes precedence over his responsibilities to teach. When such a situation exists, the students are put under conditions of fear, and their most important task is to placate the power figure, the teacher. The student must give first consideration to his own security. Under these conditions he will not be able to give complete attention to the learning experience.

A portion of the threat embodied in power is related to the severity of the punishments which the teacher uses. Some punishments may be severe because of the immediate suffering which they impose either through pain or denial. Physical punishment and restriction of highly desired privileges are examples. Other punishments may be severe because of the future consequences which they entail. Reducing grades in order to enforce compliance with instructions is an example. Of the two, the punishments which are carried to completion immediately and under the control of the teacher are undoubtedly the more desirable. Punishments which involve future consequences are indeterminable—a teacher does not know, by lowering a grade arbitrarily, what punishment he is administering. It may affect a college scholarship a few years hence, or a job. Neither is the student sensitive to the nature of the punishment which is being administered. If, in later years, he is told why the scholarship was denied or his first job application was rejected, he will understand the significance of the punishment and his reaction will be that of resentment. In every instance, responsible use of punishment requires that the person administering punishment of any kind be aware of the consequences of that punishment.

Not only is the threat involved in power related to the severity of the punishments but it is also related to the students' ability to predict whether and under what conditions the teacher will use punishment. If the rules regarding punishment are clearly stated, so that the student knows what behavior will be punished, he can be relatively secure; he knows the choices and the consequences of those choices. If he breaks the rules, he expects to be punished; but, if the punishment is not administered, he will lose respect for the teacher.

Students' concepts of strictness and fairness relate to these issues. They consider a teacher strict who enforces a rather specific set of rules. A teacher is considered fair who administers punishments and rewards objectively according to an explicit statement of rules and the consequences of their violation. A teacher is considered unfair if he is unpredictable or unreasonable.

We have discussed the concepts of power and authority because they are so directly involved in the relationship between the teacher and his class. It does no good for the teacher to close his eyes to this fact. Power and authority are factors that must be understood because they give meaning to the behavior of the teacher.

How does this show itself in the everyday teaching relationships? Repeatedly the teacher finds himself explaining materials and ideas to his students. He often wishes to test how well he is understood and to ask, "Are there any questions?" Yet, how often are questions forthcoming? The students may well have learned that to ask questions about the material will invoke punishment from the teacher. It may be sarcasm, ridicule, or withholding of privileges because they have not studied or do not understand. It is much safer not to ask any questions. The threat of the teacher's power and how he will use it directly blocks the learning process.[4]

In other cases, the teacher may do his best to suggest ideas and ways of work to the students, hoping that his suggestions will serve to stimulate the child to develop his own ways of work. But, unfortunately, all the child senses is "teacher wants me to do it that way, and I'd better do it." Some teachers avoid this situation with success by making two suggestions, so the student has to make a choice, and then by supporting him in making his own decision.

[4] Harold H. Kelley, "Communication in Experimentally Created Hierarchies," *Human Relations*, IV (1951), 30-56.

It makes little difference what the teacher's intentions are and how "good" the methods are that he uses; if he fails to see what meaning his behavior has for the students, he will not be able to understand their reactions to him.

Let us say again that the teacher working with the instructional group must have the necessary authority and power to work with the group. And there are times in which both should be used to create productive learning situations. But we suggest that, if the student-teacher relationship is dominated by these two issues, it is not likely that either a productive or a satisfying classroom atmosphere will develop.

Influence of the Teacher. There is a third type of relationship which can exist between the teacher, as leader, and the students. This is the condition in which the teacher and the students are open to influence from one another. The student pays attention to the teacher because he *wants* to. He sees his relationship with the teacher as one which will result in further satisfaction. He also believes that the teacher is interested in him and willing to give him the attention needed. If the student feels that he will be listened to by the teacher and that what he says will be seriously considered, he will feel greater security in the classroom. *Power and authority are much less of a threat when the teacher who possesses them is willing to be influenced by those who are subject to them.*

If this type of relationship exists, there is likely to be a feeling of mutual trust and respect. The teacher trusts the students and respects them, and they, in turn, come to trust and respect the teacher. The teacher can demand submission and conformity, but he must earn the students' respect.

The influence relationship is important because it reflects a set of human values relating to the effects we have on other people. It is especially important in the instructional group because communication is highly affected by the relationship which exists between the person who is attempting to communicate and the person who is receiving the communication. When the primary elements of the relationship are those of mutual trust and respect, the communication which is attempted is much more likely to be relevant to the needs of the parties involved and is more likely to be understood by them. Students will be more willing and able to let the teacher know about their problems and concerns. With this information, the teacher can more effectively focus his teaching activities.[5]

We have described in this section three factors which are present in the relationship between the teacher and the student: authority, power, and influence. How the teacher handles these three elements will have a significant effect on how his leadership behavior is interpreted by the students.

[5] Some conditions under which an influence relationship may be established are suggested in the final section of this chapter.

THE FUNCTIONS OF LEADERSHIP OF TEACHERS

The teacher has two essential functions as leader: (*a*) creating conditions in the classroom so that work can be accomplished and (*b*) organizing work activities so that appropriate learnings may be achieved. How well these two responsibilities are carried out becomes the chief criterion of effective leadership behavior for teachers.

Creating Conditions for Work. The first task requires that the teacher have knowledge of the different kinds of behavior which are needed to make work on different tasks productive. He is aware that certain tasks can be achieved most effectively by quiet, undisturbed work, but that satisfactory achievement of other tasks requires active participation and free interaction of students. His leadership job is to establish the conditions needed to enable students to carry out the essential work activities.

Necessary conditions toward which the teacher can direct his leadership behavior may be listed as follows:

1) Physical and physiological conditions
   a) Ready availability of materials and tools. On the basis of industry's time and motion studies, it is reasonable to assert that making tools and materials easily accessible to the students will increase their work efficiency.
   b) Freedom from unnecessary tensions and fatigue. It would be profitable in many schools to examine the nature of the school day, as students experience it, to determine what could be done to reduce the amount of nonwork-oriented tension and fatigue which build up. Too brief lunch periods, little chance for physical activity, insufficient variety of types of work activity within a given class period—all of these contribute to strain.
   c) Sufficient time for the tasks. Elementary teachers usually have an advantage over secondary teachers in scheduling work activities. If students are repeatedly frustrated by a bell which terminates a meaningful activity in which they are highly involved, they may learn to avoid getting intimately involved in the learning tasks.
2) Social conditions and work organization. It seems axiomatic that different tasks may be most profitably performed by two people, others may require three, four, or five; but no more participants should be involved than necessary to supply the resources needed for the completion of the task. The more persons involved, the greater the problems of communication and work management. It seems quite obvious that under most conditions thirty-five students cannot work together effectively. Subgroup organization is required.

Because learning is primarily an individual matter, there are times when the student must be able to work alone, protected from all interference. When all students are productively involved in work activities, interference is less likely because the students quickly relate to one another in such manner that a contact is not an interference at all. But, if only a portion of the group is work-oriented, the teacher may have to act to insure that those who are working are protected from outside interference.
3) Emotional conditions
   a) Security and freedom from threat. The teacher's behavior, how he uses

his authority and power, will determine in large measure whether the children within the class feel safe and secure or whether they will be continually "on edge." If the teacher uses threats and punishment indiscriminately or too frequently, the pupil will discover that his major classroom problem is keeping out of trouble.

The term "security" has some important connotations in the classroom situation. A breakdown in a feeling of security will show itself immediately in a restriction of communication. Statements to the teacher may become more guarded. Students will interact less frequently. They will search for acceptable things to say, unless they choose to be openly hostile. They will avoid communicating to the teacher that which he most needs to know: the nature of their learning problems and difficulties, and how they are thinking and feeling about the material at hand. Blocked communication from students deprives the teacher of the data necessary for an adequate diagnosis of learner needs and the development of more effective teaching.

b) Morale and motivation to work. It is not enough, if the purposes of the classroom are to be accomplished, for the students to be present in a situation which provides the necessary conditions for learning. There has to be some on-going motivation to become personally related and involved as learners in the necessary learning tasks. We are using the term *morale* to describe the attitude and behavior which denotes willingness to be involved.

The following five elements of morale toward which the leadership behavior of teachers can be directed are based on an article by Watson.[6]

(1) A sense of positive direction—an accepted goal. One of the most crucial tasks of the teacher is to lead, to help the students discover a direction which has some meaning to them. When activity in the classroom is segmented, its purpose may be lost in the doing. The leadership behavior of the teacher must constantly demonstrate, clarify, illustrate, and rediscover with the aid of students the developing goals toward which they work.[7] Without a sense of purpose, activity seems useless, and students will not become involved in it.

(2) A sense of mutual support. If we have a sense of purpose, it is strengthened by the knowledge that there are others about us who share the purpose and are working toward its achievement. If several students are involved in a purposeful project, they probably will feel a greater sense of support than if they worked on unrelated activities.

(3) A sense of contribution. It enhances our sense of participation and involvement if, as we are working together in a meaningful direction, we find that as individuals we can make a relevant and useful contribution to the task. The leadership of the teacher and of the class members can be profitably utilized to help members find ways of making individual contributions in performing the tasks and toward achieving the purposes of the group. Leadership must also see that contributors are made aware of and rewarded for their contribution.

[6] Goodwin Watson, "Five Factors in Morale," in *Civilian Morale*, pp. 30-47. Edited by Goodwin Watson. Second Yearbook of the Society for the Psychological Study of Social Issues. New York: Houghton Mifflin Co., 1942.

[7] E. Paul Torrance, "The Behavior of Small Groups under the Stress Conditions of 'Survival,'" *American Sociological Review*, XIX (December, 1954), 751-55.

It is very difficult for a person to know whether his contribution has been found important and useful by others unless they inform him that such is the case.

(4) A sense of progress. Unless work and energy seem to be directed toward a goal, student morale begins to drop. It is important that ways and means be found to demonstrate that progress toward the goal is being made. Progress is measured by determining how much distance must be covered to reach the goal. Unfortunately, far too much of the teacher's leadership behavior and evaluation emphasizes the *lack of achievement* rather than the *amount of progress*. Yet, there is a great difference in the effect of these two emphases on morale; the former dooms the person to defeat, the latter emphasizes his success.

Because of his perspective and position, the teacher is for students a major source for evaluating their progress. Some of the teacher's most effective leadership behavior will be in reminding the group of how much it has progressed and in demonstrating in detail the nature of its progress. Students are thus made to feel themselves successful and are led to return to work with renewed enthusiasm.

(5) A sense of challenge. The task which is set must be big enough to warrant striving for it. Very likely a small task simply doesn't demand enough of the students to get them to work. If they are less sure that they can accomplish the task, the struggle becomes critical, and eventual achievement is a greater success. If the job presents a challenge, it is worth doing. Recent programs for gifted children recognize this fact by putting tasks before the children which require them to put forth their best efforts.

All aspects of morale can be directly affected by the leadership behavior of the teacher. The students' willingness to give their energy to the task at hand is directly affected by how the teacher sets up the tasks, gives encouragement, participates with the students, and makes them aware of success.

Setting Work Activities. Because the basic purposes of the classroom and school are established not by the students but by the community and are interpreted by the professional personnel, the teacher is not free to let the students select their own activities. His leadership responsibility includes making certain that the students engage in activities which will lead toward the achievement of the school's purposes. This is a very useful role to a group, especially when the person in the leadership role makes clear to the group that he is a resource to be used in meeting the demands which he is transmitting to them.[8]

These work demands must be of such nature that the students are motivated to work toward them without loss of morale. The leadership behavior of the teacher requires skill in presenting the requirements in such a way that they can be understood and accepted, while at the same time not making undue use of his power or authority.

[8] Thelen, *op. cit.*

The leader makes clear the demands the group faces but does not force upon them a methodology which seems irrelevant, inappropriate, or frustrating. He encourages students to take responsibility for planning their own participation in the learning. Of course, initial attempts along these lines by a teacher with an inexperienced class will be clumsy, but, as students learn how to employ a variety of methods of work and become sensitive to the unique contribution to the various methods, they can quickly suggest workable approaches to the task. Since the methods are understood by them, they will have the skills for their execution.

The chapters in Section III of this yearbook deal specifically with some of the problems involved in setting suitable learning tasks for the students and with the difficulties that arise when they are performed.

THE SKILLS OF LEADERSHIP

If the leadership behavior of the teacher is to be effective, it must be suitable and useful to the needs of the classroom in which he is working. The skills of leadership are those which permit the leader to act in the necessary ways to help the instructional group proceed most economically to its goals. There are two areas of knowledge and two areas of performance which relate to skills.

The first area of knowledge is that of the behavior of children and of groups of children. This area of knowledge and understanding supplies the raw material from which the leader can make his diagnosis of the children's behavior and of the group situation in which he is working.

The second area of knowledge is that of one's self as a person and as a group leader. The teacher has to recognize the needs and feelings he has in the situation in order to get accurate cues on how to behave. His insight into the nature of the leadership role as well as an understanding of organizational and group work lends perceptiveness to his leader decisions.

One set of skills are those required to direct his own behavior toward leadership ends. All the knowledge in the world is of little help to the teacher if he cannot interpret it usefully through his own behavior. The concept of "using one's self as an instrument of change" is one that is not frequently heard in the field of education, although it is common in the field of social work.[9] A teacher would increase his flexibility as a leader if he were to make more use of the behavioral skills which he finds successful in his other interpersonal relations.

A person can learn, through practice, different modes of behavior and response. Practicing a variety of ways of carrying through different acts

[9] Gertrude Wilson and Gladys Ryland, *Social Group Work Practice*. New York: Houghton Mifflin Co., 1949.

and of saying the same things gives the teacher a wider range of behavioral skills upon which he can draw at any given instant.

Another set of skills are those necessary to determine if the desired ends are being achieved. It is essential that the leadership of the group be able to tell whether or not the progress of the group is toward the goals and purposes established for the group. Evaluation is necessary for diagnosing the productivity of the class in order to plan future activities.

19. The Classroom Group as a Unique Social System

Jacob W. Getzels and Herbert A. Thelen

A CONCEPTUAL FRAMEWORK FOR THE STUDY OF THE CLASSROOM GROUP AS A SOCIAL SYSTEM

THE GENERAL MODEL

We may begin a description of our model with a consideration of the most general context of interpersonal or group behavior, i.e., a given social system.[5] The term "social system" is, of course, conceptual rather than descriptive and must not be confused with society or state, or as somehow applicable only to large aggregates of human interaction. So, within this framework, for one purpose a given community may be considered a social system, with the school a particular organization within the more general social system. For another purpose, the school itself or a single class within the school may be considered a social system in its own right. The model proposed here is applicable regardless of the level or size of the unit under consideration.

We initially conceive of the social system as involving two classes of

Reprinted with permission from Chapter 4 of *The Dynamics of Instructional Groups*, The Fifty-ninth Yearbook of the National Society for the Study of Education, Part II. Chicago, University of Chicago Press, 1960.

[5] The same general set of concepts and categories have been applied to other areas of the school, notably administration, and portions of this section are paraphrased or taken verbatim from the following: J. W. Getzels, "A Psycho-Sociological Framework for the Study of Educational Administration," *Harvard Educational Review*, XXII (1952), 235-46; J. W. Getzels and E. G. Guba, "Social Behavior and the Administrative Process," *School Review*, LXV (1957), 423-41; J. W. Getzels, "Administration as a Social Process," in *Administrative Theory in Education* (edited by Andrew W. Halpin, Midwest Administration Center, University of Chicago, 1958). Our debt to the work of Talcott Parsons will be self-evident. (Footnote numbering has been retained as it appeared in the original article.)

phenomena which are at once conceptually independent and phenomenally interactive. First, there are the institutions with certain roles and expectations that will fulfil the goals of the system. Secondly, there are the individuals with certain personalities and need-dispositions inhabiting the system, whose observed interactions comprise what we call social or group behavior. We shall assert that this behavior can be understood as a function of these major elements: institution, role, and expectation, which together constitute what we call the *nomothetic* or normative dimension of activity in a social system; and individual, personality, and need-disposition, which together constitute the *idiographic* or personal dimension of activity in a social system. In a sense, the one may be thought of as the "sociological" level of analysis, the other the "psychological" level of analysis.

To understand the nature of observed behavior and to be able to predict and control it, one must understand the nature of the relationships of these elements. We shall briefly make four points of definition in this connection:

1. All social systems have certain imperative functions that are to be carried out in certain established ways. Such functions as governing, educating, or policing within a state may be said to have become "institutionalized," and the agencies carrying out these institutionalized functions for the social system may be termed "institutions."

2. The most important analytic unit of the institution is the role. Roles are the "dynamic aspects" of the positions, offices, and statutes within an institution, and they define the behavior of the role incumbents or actors.[6]

3. Roles are defined in terms of role-expectations. A role has certain privileges, obligations, responsibilities, and powers. When the role-incumbent puts these obligations and responsibilities into effect, he is said to be performing his role. The expectations define for the actor what he should or should not do so long as he is the incumbent of the particular role.

4. Roles are complementary. They are interdependent in that each role derives its meaning from the other related roles. In a sense, a role is a prescription not only for the given role-incumbent but also for the incumbents of other roles within the institutions and for related roles outside the institutions. Thus, for example, the role of teacher and the role of pupil cannot be defined or implemented except in relation to each other. It is this quality of complementarity which fuses two or more roles into a coherent, interactive unit and which makes it possible for us to conceive of an institution (or group) as having a characteristic structure.

This dimension of the social system may be represented schematically as follows:

[6] Ralph Linton, *The Study of Man*. New York: D. Appleton-Century Co., 1936.

Social System→Institutions→Roles→Expectations→Institutional Goal-behavior

Within this framework then, the class may be conceived as a social system with characteristic institutions, roles, and expectations for behavior. The class as a social system is related to the school as a social system, which in turn is related to the community as a social system, and so on. Ideally, the goal-behaviors of one social system are "geared in" to the goal-behaviors of the other related social systems. Within the class itself, goal-behavior is achieved through the integration of institutions, the definition of roles, and the setting of expectations for the performance of relevant tasks. In performing the role-behaviors expected of him, the teacher "teaches"; in performing the role-behaviors expected of *him,* the pupil "learns."

So far we have examined the elements constituting the nomothetic or normative aspects of group behavior. At this level of analysis, it was sufficient to conceive of the role incumbents as only "actors," devoid of personalistic or other individualizing characteristics, as if all incumbents were exactly alike and as if they implemented a given role in exactly the same way. This is not, by any means, to derogate the power of this level of analysis. Indeed, for certain gross understanding and prediction of behavior, this is exactly the right level of abstraction. For example, if we know the roles in a given educational institution, we can make some rather accurate predictions of what the people in these institutions do without ever observing the actual people involved.

But roles are, of course, occupied by real individuals, and no two individuals are alike. Each individual stamps the particular role he occupies with the unique style of his own characteristic pattern of expressive behavior. Even in the case of the relatively inflexible military roles of sergeant and private, no two individual sergeants and no two individual privates fulfil their roles in exactly the same way. To understand the observed behavior of *specific* sergeants and *specific* privates, or of *specific* teachers and *specific* pupils, it is not enough to know only the nature of the roles and expectations—although, to be sure, their behavior cannot be understood apart from these—but we must also know the nature of the individuals inhabiting the roles and reacting to the expectations. That is, in addition to the nomothetic or normative aspects, we must consider the idiographic or individualizing aspects of group behavior. We must, in addition to the sociological level of analysis, include the psychological level of analysis.

Now, just as we were able to analyze the institutional dimension into the component elements of role and expectation, so we may, in a parallel manner, analyze the individual dimension into the component elements of personality and need-disposition. We may briefly make two points of definition in this connection:

1. The concept of personality, like institution or role, has been given a variety of meanings. But for our purposes, personality may be defined as the dynamic organization within the individual of those need-dispositions that govern his *unique* reactions to the environment and, we might add, in present model, to the expectations in the environment.

2. The central analytic elements of personality are the need-dispositions, which we can define with Parsons and Shils as "individual tendencies to orient and act with respect to objects in certain manners and to expect certain consequences from these actions."[7]

This dimension of the social system may be represented schematically as follows:

Social System→ Individuals→ Personalities→ Need-Dispositions→ Individual Goal-behavior

Returning to the example of the sergeant and private, we can now make an essential distinction between two sergeants, one of whom has a high need-disposition for "submission" and the other a high need-disposition for "ascendance"; and a similar distinction between two privates, one with a high need-disposition for "submission" and the other for "ascendance," in the fulfilment of their respective roles, and for the sergeant-private interaction. And we may make similar distinctions in the role-fulfilment and interaction among teachers and pupils of varying personality types.

In short, as we have remarked before, to understand the behavior and interaction of specific role-incumbents in an institution, we must know both the role-expectations and need-dispositions. Indeed, needs and expectations may both be thought of as *motives for behavior*, the one deriving from personalistic sets and propensities, the other from institutional obligations and requirements.

By way of summarizing the argument so far, we may represent the general model pictorially as follows:

Nomothetic Dimension

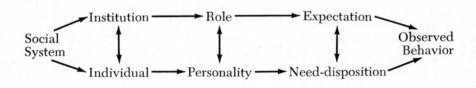

Idiographic Dimension

[7] Talcott Parsons and Edward A. Shils, *Toward a General Theory of Action*, p. 114. Cambridge, Massachusetts: Harvard University Press, 1951.

The nomothetic axis is shown at the top of the diagram and consists of institution, role, and expectation, each term being the analytic unit for the term preceding it. Thus, the social system is defined by its institutions, each institution by its constituent roles, each role by the expectations attaching to it. Similarly, the idiographic axis is shown at the lower portion of the diagram and consists of individual, personality, and need-disposition, each term again serving as the analytic unit for the term preceding it.

A given act is conceived as deriving simultaneously from both the nomothetic and idiographic dimensions. That is to say, social behavior results as the individual attempts to cope with an environment composed of patterns of expectations for his behavior in ways consistent with his own independent pattern of needs. Thus, we may write the general equation: $B = f(R \times P)$, where B is observed behavior, R is a given institutional role defined by the expectations attaching to it, and P is the personality of the particular role incumbent defined by his need-dispositions.

The proportion of role and personality factors determining behavior will, of course, vary with the specific act, the specific role, and the specific personality involved. The nature of the interaction can be understood from another graphic representation as follows:

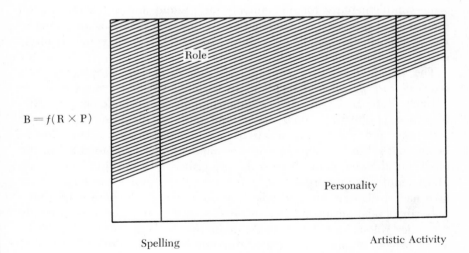

$B = f(R \times P)$

Role

Personality

Spelling   Artistic Activity

A given behavioral act may be conceived as occurring at a line cutting through the role and personality possibilities represented by the rectangle. At the left, the proportion of the act dictated by considerations of personality is relatively small. At the right, the proportions are reversed, and considerations of personality become greater than considerations of role-expectations. In these terms, the participants in the classroom situation may define their overt activity along a continuum between two modes of operation from primary emphasis on *role-relevant* performance to primary emphasis on *personality-relevant* performance. Thus, some tasks require maximum adherence to role-expectations, e.g., learning to spell; others permit greater freedom of personal spontaneity, e.g., artistic activity. We may presume that each educational objective calls for a characteristic proportion or balance between these two types of performance.

In any case, whether the proportion tends toward one end or the other, behavior in the classroom group remains a function of both role and personality, although in different degree. When role is maximized, behavior still retains some personal aspect because no role is ever so closely defined as to eliminate all individual latitude. When personality is maximized, group behavior still cannot be free of some role prescription. Indeed, the individual who divorces himself from such prescription is said to be autistic, and he ceases to communicate with the group.

The major problem of social or group behavior involves exactly this issue of the dynamics of the interaction between the externally defined role-expectations and the internally defined personality-dispositions. To put the problem concretely, we may ask: How is it, for example, that some complementary role-incumbents understand and agree at once on their mutual privileges and obligations, while others take a long time in reaching such agreement and, quite frequently, do not come to terms either with their roles or with each other?

The essential relevant concept we should like to propose here is *selective interpersonal perception*. In a sense, we may conceive of the publicly described normative relationship of two complementary role-incumbents—the prescribed means and ends of the interaction as set forth, say, in a table of organization or in a curriculum of instruction—as being enacted in two separate private interactions, one embedded in the other. On the one hand, there is the prescribed relationship as perceived idiosyncratically and organized by the one role-incumbent in terms of his own needs, dispositions, and goals; on the other hand, there is the same prescribed relationship as perceived idiosyncratically and organized by the other role-incumbent in terms of his needs, dispositions, and goals. These private situations are related through those aspects of the existential public objects, symbols, values, and expectations, which have to some extent a counterpart in the perceptions of both individuals.

When we say two role-incumbents (such as a teacher and a pupil or a teacher and several pupils in the classroom group) understand each other, we mean that their perceptions and private organization of the prescribed complementary expectations are congruent; when we say they misunderstand each other, we mean that their perceptions and private organization of the prescribed complementary expectations are incongruent.

Like all theoretical formulations, the present framework is an abstraction and, as such, an oversimplification of "reality"—some factors in the classroom have been brought into the foreground, others put into the background. By focusing on the sociological dimension with the central concept role and on the psychological dimension with the central concept personality, we have omitted other dimensions contributing to classroom behavior. We should like to mention, however briefly, two other relevant dimensions.

There is first the *biological* dimension, for just as we may think of the individual in personalistic terms, we may also think of him in constitutional terms. The individual's personality is embedded, so to speak, in a biological organism with certain constitutional potentialities and abilities. The need-dispositions of the personality are surely related in some way to these constitutional conditions, probably as mediating between constitutional and nomothetic factors. In this sense, we must bear in mind that underlying the psychological dimension is a biological dimension, although the one is not reducible to the other. We may represent this dimension schematically as follows:

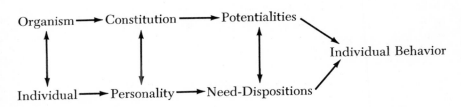

Secondly, there is the *anthropological* dimension. Just as we may think of institutions in sociological terms, we may also think of them in cultural terms, for the institution is embedded in a culture with certain mores and values. The expectations of the roles must in some way be related to the ethos or cultural values. The pupil cannot be expected to learn Latin in a culture where knowledge of Latin has little value, nor can he be expected to identify with teachers in a culture where teachers have little value. In this sense, we must bear in mind that interacting with the sociological dimension there is an anthropological dimension, although again that one is not immediately reducible to the other. We may represent this relationship schematically as follows:

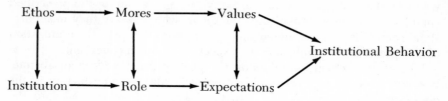

If we may put all the dimensions together into a single, and we are afraid rather unwieldy, pictorial representation, the relationships would look something like this:

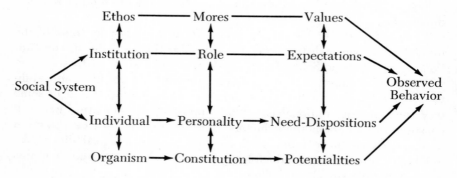

It is our belief that the model can help clarify and systematize the issues we raised in the first section. By way of illustration, we should like to apply the model to two of these issues, notably the issues dealing with the *nature and sources of conflict* and with the *nature of teacher choices in changing classroom behavior.*

APPLICATIONS OF THE MODEL I: CLASSROOM CONFLICT

We may identify for present purposes four major types of conflict, although these do not necessarily exhaust the list:

1. *Conflict between the cultural values outside the classroom and the institutional expectations within the classroom.* Consider the following instance with respect to the motivation for achievement in the classroom, assuming only the substantive data regarding the state of present values to be as people like Riesman and Wheelis have described it.[8] It is expected by the school that the child will work hard in the classroom in order to achieve to the fullest extent of his potentiality. Accordingly, the

[8] See David Riesman *et al., The Lonely Crowd* (New Haven: Yale University Press, 1950); Allen Wheelis, *The Quest for Identity* (New York: W. W. Norton & Co., 1958).

child must be motivated to strive and sacrifice present ease for future attainment. But recent studies suggest that our cultural values are coming more and more to prize sociability and hedonistic, present-time orientations, rather than achievement, as goals. In this sense, the criteria of worth in the classroom and in society at large are incongruent, and to this extent the child is subject to conflict with respect to his classroom behavior. Or consider the potential conflict of the so-called gifted or creative child or *teacher* in the classroom. If the potentially creative person is to be productive and inventive, the cultural values must encourage, or at least be receptive to, personal independence and autonomy. If these people are to express their exceptional talents, they must be able to maintain firm commitments to their own standards and to their own beliefs. But again recent studies suggest that our values are coming to prize conformity more than autonomy, moral relativism more than commitment. We are not here arguing the validity of the substantive data—we are illustrating one potential source of conflict in the classroom, i.e., the incongruity between values and expectations.

2. *Conflict between role-expectations and personality-dispositions.* Conflicts of this type occur as a function of discrepancies between the pattern of expectations attaching to a given role and the pattern of need-dispositions characteristic of the incumbent of the role. Recall again our example of the individual with high need-dispositions for "ascendance" placed in the role of an army private. Or more specifically, consider the issues we raised with respect to the "accidental" and compulsory nature of the classroom group. Particular children have not been chosen for particular roles, or particular roles for particular children. There may be mutual interference between the nomothetic or normative expectations for the "bunch" and the idiographic or differentiated dispositions of each child. In effect, the child is in the classic conflict situation and he must choose whether he will fulfil individual needs or institutional requirements. If he chooses the latter, he is liable to unsatisfactory *personal integration* in the classroom; he is frustrated and dissatisfied. If he chooses the former, he is liable to unsatisfactory *role adjustment* in the classroom; he is ineffective and inefficient as a pupil. In practice, there are usually compromises and accommodations, but the point we want to make here is that the nature of the classroom group activity is quite different when the expectations and the dispositions are incongruent than when they are congruent.

3. *Role conflict.* There is a whole range of conflicts that occur when a role incumbent is required to conform simultaneously to a number of expectations which are mutually exclusive, contradictory, or inconsistent so that adjustment to one set of requirements makes adjustment to the

other set of requirements impossible or at least difficult.[9] It is essentially these types of conflict that are illustrative of the issues we raised in the first section regarding the multiple group and institutional memberships of the participants in the classroom. Role conflicts are evidence of dislocation in the nomothetic dimension of the social system and may arise in several ways.

a) Disagreement within the referent group defining the role. For example, the principal of the school may be expected, by some teachers, to visit them regularly to give constructive help and, by others, to trust them as professional personnel not in need of such supervision. Or, the pupil may be expected by some teachers to emphasize the mechanics of writing, the substance being useful only for the practice of correct form; by other teachers, to emphasize the content and substance, the form being merely an incidental vehicle for the communication. Or perhaps at a more fundamental level, the pupil may be expected by some teachers within the school to conceive of learning as essentially the rote remembrance of information provided by the teacher, and by other teachers as essentially the solution of problems meaningful to the pupil himself.

b) Disagreement among several referent groups, each having a right to define expectations for the same role. To use an example outside our immediate context, the university faculty member may be expected by his department head to emphasize teaching and service to students but by his academic dean to emphasize research and publication. Although these two sets of expectations for the same role do not necessarily conflict, it is clear that the time given to implementing the one set can be seen as taking away time from implementing the other, and to this extent, they *do* conflict.

c) Contradiction in the expectations of two or more roles which an individual is occupying at the same time. It is here that we have all those problems arising from the fact that pupils and teachers are members of numerous different groups in addition to the classroom group. Each group has expectations for its members, and these expectations may be incongruent so that conformity to the expectations of one group may mean nonconformity to the expectations of the other group. Consider here the simple instance of a teacher who is attempting to be, simultaneously, a devoted mother and wife and a successful career woman in her profes-

[9] There are numerous empirical studies in the area of role conflict. See, for example, Samuel A. Stouffer, "An Analysis of Conflicting Social Norms," *American Sociological Review*, XIV (1949), 707-17; Samuel A. Stouffer and Jackson Toby, "Role Conflict and Personality," *American Journal of Sociology* LVI (1951), 395-406; J. W. Getzels and E. G. Guba, "Role, Role Conflict, and Effectiveness: An Empirical Study," *American Sociological Review*, XIX (1954), 164-75; J. W. Getzels and E. G. Guba, "The Structure of Roles and Role Conflict in the Teaching Situation," *Journal of Educational Sociology*, XXIX (1955), 30-40.

sion. Although the expectations of these roles need not inevitably clash, there is the possibility that attending conferences on teaching may get in the way of keeping up with the progress of her children and husband.

4. *Personality conflict.* This type of conflict occurs as a function of opposing needs and dispositions within the personality of the role incumbent as a function of unresolved discrepancies between his needs and his potentialities. The effect of such personal disequilibrium is to keep the individual at odds with the institution either because he cannot maintain a stable relationship with a given role or because he habitually misperceives the expectations placed upon him in terms of his autistic reactions. In any case, just as role conflict is a situational given, personality conflict is an individual given and is independent of any particular institutional setting. No matter what the situation, the role is, in a sense, detached from its institutional context and function and is used by him to work out personal and private needs and dispositions, however inappropriate these may be to the goals of the social system as a whole.

APPLICATION OF THE MODEL II:
CLASSROOM LEADERSHIP IN CHANGING BEHAVIOR

We wish, finally, to apply the terms and categories of our model of the classroom group as a social system to the problem of changing behavior in the teaching-learning situation. In the terms of our model, changing behavior may involve, at one extreme, adaptation of idiographic personality-dispositions to nomothetic role-expectations. We may call this the *socialization of personality.* At the other extreme, changing behavior may involve the adaptation of nomothetic role-expectations to idiographic personality-dispositions. We may call this the *personalization of roles.* In attempting to achieve change, i.e., learning in the classroom, the teacher as the formal group leader always works within these extremes, emphasizing the one, the other, or attempting to reach an appropriate balance between the two. The way the possibilities between socialization of personality and personalization of roles is handled in the classroom determines the kind of group that is achieved and the kind of learning that results.

In this context, we may identify three types of group leadership or, more specifically, three teaching styles:

1. *The nomothetic style.* This orientation emphasizes the nomothetic or normative dimension of behavior and, accordingly, places stress on the requirements of the institution, the role, and the expectation rather than on the requirements of the individual, the personality, and the need-disposition. Education is defined as the handing down of what is known

to those who do not yet know. In the equation $B = f(R \times P)$, P is minimized, R is maximized. It is assumed that, given the institutional purpose, appropriate procedures can be discovered through which the role is taken, despite any personal dispositions of the learner to the contrary, so that he will incorporate the expectations. It then follows that if roles are clearly defined and everyone is held equally responsible for doing what he is supposed to do, the required outcomes will naturally ensue regardless of who the particular role-incumbent might be, provided only that he has the necessary technical competence.

2. *The idiographic style.* The orientation emphasizes the idiographic dimension of behavior and accordingly places stress on the requirements of the individual, the personality, and the need-disposition rather than on the requirements of the institution, the role, and the expectation. Education is defined as helping the person know what he wants to know, as it were. In the equation $B = f(R \times P)$, R is minimized, P is maximized. This does not mean that the idiographic style is any less goal-oriented than is the nomothetic style; it means that the most expeditious route to the ultimate goal is seen as residing in the people involved rather than in the nature of the institutional structure. The basic assumption is that the greatest accomplishment will occur, not from enforcing adherence to rigorously defined roles, but from making it possible for each person to seek what is most relevant and meaningful to him. This point of view is obviously related to particular individuals who fill the roles at a particular time, and expectations must be kept vague and informal. Normative prescriptions of the sort included in typical role-expectations are seen as unnecessarily restrictive and as a hindrance rather than a guide to productive behavior. The teacher frowns upon a priori class "lesson plans," and is not embarrassed to ask the individual pupil, if we may exaggerate the typical case somewhat, "Well, what would you like to do today?"

In short, the emphasis is on what we have called the personalization of roles rather than on the socialization of personality. In many ways, neither the nomothetic nor the idiographic definitions of the teaching-learning situation make any demands on the classroom group as a group—the nomothetic mode emphasizes uniform adherence to a given role, the idiographic mode emphasizes the discrete expression of individual personalities. The fact that the roles and personalities exist in the classroom within a group context is more or less irrelevant.

3. *The transactional style.* This orientation is intermediate to the other two and is, therefore, less amenable to "pure" or even clear-cut definition. Since the goals of the social system must be carried out, it is obviously necessary to make explicit the roles and expectations required to achieve the goals. And, since the roles and expectations will be implemented by the efforts of people with needs to be met, the personalities and disposi-

tions of these people must be taken into account. But the solution is not so simple as it appears from just saying that one should hew to the middle course between expectations and needs, that is, at some midpoint between the nomothetic and idiographic axes. What we are calling the transactional mode is not just a compromise. Instead, the aim throughout is to acquire a thorough awareness of the limits and resources of both individual and institution within which the teaching-learning process may occur (that is, from the nomothetic and to the idiographic extremes) and to make an intelligent application of the two as a particular problem may demand. In the equation $B = f(R \times P)$, R and P are maximized or minimized as the situation requires. Institutional roles are developed independently of the role-incumbents, but they are adapted to the personalities of the actual individual incumbents. Expectations are defined as sharply as they can be but not so sharply that they prohibit appropriate behavior in terms of need-dispositions. Role conflicts, personality conflicts, and role-personality conflicts are recognized and handled. The standard of behavior is both individual integration and institutional adjustment. In short, both the socialization of personality and the personalization of roles is taken into account, and the processes in the classroom may be seen as a dynamic transaction between roles and personalities.

In this mode, the actual balance of emphasis on the performance of role requirements and the expression of personality needs changes as a function of interaction within the classroom group. Account is taken of the common or deviant perceptions of existential objects and roles, and of explicit or implicit agreements on how to deal with conflicts and deviant perceptions. In this sense, the group *qua* group is of crucial significance. It mediates between the institutional requirements and the individual dispositions. On the one hand, it can support the institution by imposing, if necessary, certain normative role-expectations on the group members; on the other hand, it can support the individual in expressing, if necessary, certain idiosyncratic personality-dispositions. In working out this balance between the institution and the individual, the group develops a "culture" or, perhaps better here, a *climate*, which may be analyzed into the constituent *intentions* of the group, and, in effect, the group climate represents another general dimension of the classroom as a social system:

Social System→ Group→ Climate → Intentions→ Group Behavior

The stability and concomitant flexibility of the group in moving between the nomothetic and idiographic extremes depends on the *belongingness* that the individuals feel within the group. The development of this belongingness is accompanied by increased security for all the members of the group. The greater the belongingness, the greater the ease of significant communication between the teacher and the pupils and among the pupils themselves and the greater the shared pride in the achievement of both institutional *and* individual goals. What was an "accidental" and compulsory group becomes a planful and voluntary group. The rigidity of the *platoon* or the *instability* of the *crowd* is changed into the resourcefulness and flexibility of the *team*. They "know" what to expect, what to give, what to take. They find emotional support for their risk-taking, and the consequent increased individual security encourages "open" transactions between personality and role. The boundaries between the private world and the public world become permeable, and the over-lap in the perception of a given situation within the classroom is enlarged. There is, at once, both greater autonomy and heteronomy for the individual. The depth of the person's involvement in the classroom is increased, and, in this sense, learning becomes more meaningful.

Within this framework, this then might be conceived as the ideal-type model of the classroom as a social system: (*a*) Each individual *identifies* with the goals of the system so that they become part of his own needs. (*b*) Each individual believes that the expectations held for him are *rational* if the goals are to be achieved. (*c*) He feels that he *belongs* to a group with similar emotional identifications and rational beliefs.

By way of summarizing the characteristics of the several dimensions presented, we now offer the final pictorial example selected from the categories of goal behavior.

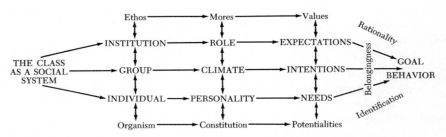

In this final picture we have located the classroom as a social system. From this point of view, the most impressive characteristic of the classroom group, despite its apparent uniqueness, is that it can be studied systematically like *any* other group, be it a board of directors, a neighborhood club, or working team. The fundamental dimensions and concepts remain the same, and in studying any given group within a unified model, we both gain from and contribute to the study of all groups. The dimensions and concepts we have used are derived from the social sciences, and we believe one implication of our effort is that the social sciences have a great deal to contribute to the systematic analysis of education. In so far as there is going to be a "science" of education, it will be related to concepts, findings, and propositions from the whole range of disciplines called social science. It will be an integrative structure of ideas about the ways in which cultural, institutional, group, individual, and organismic factors interact and, in the process of interacting, change and bring about change.

The appropriate application of science to a particular situation is an art. Educational science is translated into educative outcomes through making choices, and this calls for the exercise of judgment. We see the learning group as an emergent reality developing out of the transactions between role and personality in the classroom. The nature of the group is determined ultimately by the way the teacher responds to the specific behavior of the students. But the judgment of the teacher on how to respond depends not merely on his ability to perceive the behavior to which he is responding as an immediate act but to look behind the act and to comprehend the behavior as a transaction within the social system as a whole. For it is within this sort of comprehension that not only the particular group but the particular individual within the group can be most readily understood. And it is through this understanding that the teacher can wisely judge how to respond.

One fundamental concern of teacher and student alike, then, is surely the nature of the group they are establishing. If they are working at cross-purposes, the likelihood of educational achievement is slim, for the chief preoccupation of the individuals will be the problem of dealing with a situation in which they cannot perceive order and consistency—at least not *their* order and consistency. Yet, if the classroom is to be genuinely challenging—and it must be this to be educative—dislocation in goals, expectations, potentialities, needs, and intentions is bound to arise, for the relationships among the various factors in the social system are continually undergoing change, and are, if we may put it this way, always transacting with one another.

It appears to us then that these considerations tell us something about the image of the classroom group that is needed. This is a Utopian ideal. It is not the image of a social system in equilibrium. It is rather the image of a system in motion or, if you will, in dynamic disequilibrium. It is the image of a group continually facing emergent complexity and conflict (if not confusion) and dealing with these realities, not in terms of sentiment but in terms of what the complexity and conflict suggest about the modifications that have to be made in the goals, expectations, needs, and selective perceptions of the teachers and learners. It is through this experience of recognizing and dealing with complexity, conflict, and change in the classroom situation that we can educate children to take their places as creative and autonomous participants in the other social systems that constitute the larger social order.

20. The Social Structure of the Classroom Group: An Observational Framework

Gale E. Jensen

For roughly forty years we have been studying the instructional designs used by or "on" classroom groups to determine their effectiveness as measured by individual achievement and group productivity. Some of these studies have recognized indirectly that the social structure of the classroom in some way influences group performance and individual learning.[1] Some, through the use of sociometric techniques, have studied certain aspects of the social structure directly and have pointed out its influence upon classroom performance and learning.[2] However, little has been done to provide a framework of concepts that could be utilized to formulate and analyze systematically the classroom problems that are in some way related to the social structure of the classroom group.[3] The purpose of this paper is to outline such a conceptual framework.

This framework, it is hoped, will represent a step toward recognizing that the systematic and conscious utilization of conceptual schemes in educational practice is more powerful for dealing with educational problems than are present "common sense" approaches. The framework is not to be taken as "true" or as the only one inferable from existing research data, but rather accepted as something which, while tentative, is necessary for the orderly examination and description of problems of social structure in the classroom. This, of course, means that the framework is subject to reconstruction whenever more adequate concepts can be formulated.

THE CONCEPTUAL FRAMEWORK

The form which a description of the social structure of the classroom group takes should be such that it eventually can be integrated with a descriptive framework for examining the dynamics of the classroom. An

Reprinted from Gale E. Jensen, "The Social Structure of the Classroom Group: An Observational Framework," *Journal of Educational Psychology*, Volume 46, 1955, pp. 362-374. Copyright © 1955 by the American Psychological Association, and reproduced by permission.

[1] Cf. W. S. Monroe, "Methods of Teaching," *Encyclopedia of Educational Research.* New York: The Macmillan Co., 1950, pp. 745-752.

[2] H. H. Jennings, *Sociometry in Group Relations.* Washington, D. C.; American Council on Education, 1948.

[3] Cf. Ronald Lippitt, "Applying New Knowledge about Human Relations in Educational Practice," *Baltimore Bulletin of Education,* March-June, 1952, pp. 23-30.

account, therefore, of the structural aspects of the classroom group should be stated in terms of functional dimensions[4] along which members relate to one another in their attempts (1) to maintain an optimum balance between possible gratifications and deprivations of individual personality needs, and (2) to participate as members concerned with problems both external to the group. Members keep changing their relationships to one another, but always, it is proposed, the changes are along one or more of the dimensions that will be identified. In brief, the dimensions identified indicate all the possible types of functional relationships that individuals can establish between one another *as group members*.[5]

As revealed by the research references cited throughout this article, the dimensions of the social structure of the classroom group represent manifestations of *needs* class members have (a) as individual personalities and (b) as group members. To participate effectively in the tasks or work of the group and to meet their individual needs, members are required to relate to other members in ways that make these accomplishments possible. Stated otherwise, each group member has *need* to establish between himself and the other group members, the kind of relationships that are required for members (1) to work effectively as a group and (2) to maintain a satisfactory balance between the possible gratifications and deprivations of personal needs. These are the basic conditions for a collection of individuals to become and remain a classroom group.

The dimensions along which members seek to relate to one another in a classroom group are seven in number. These are (1) the problem-solving dimension, (2) the authority-leadership dimension, (3) the power dimension, (4) the friendship dimension, (5) the personal prestige dimension, (6) the sex dimension, and (7) the privilege dimension.

The Problem-Solving Dimension.—There are two kinds of problems to which the classroom must continuously devote its energies.[6] One kind pertains to the efforts which the group will expend to organize relations with its external environment. This constitutes the public (or publicly recognized) task of the group. The other kind of problem refers to the efforts of the group to create the kind of intra-group member relationships (its internal socio-psychological environment) that will satisfy members

---

[4] For a more complete statement of the "functional dimensions approach" to social psychology, cf. Jay M. Jackson, "Analysis of Interpersonal Relations in a Formal Organization," unpublished doctoral dissertation, University of Michigan, 1953, pp. 13-17. To be punblished as a Research Center for Group Dynamics monograph. The theoretical development which follows has been influenced by this work.

[5] Cf. Dorwin Cartwright and Alvin Zander. *Group Dynamics: Theory and Research.* Evanston, Illinois: Row, Peterson and Company, 1953, p. 417.

[6] Herbert Thelen, "Educational Dynamics: Theory and Research," *Journal of Social Issues,* Volume 6, No. 2, 1950, pp. 31-32.

to such a degree that the group will have sufficient energies for working on problems arising from relationships between itself and its external environment. These two problems, common to all classroom groups, can best be understood through descriptions of the environmental settings to which they are indigenous.

The *external environment* of the classroom group can be depicted as a field of forces that impinge upon the group and require it to expend some of its time and energies coping with the "outside." These forces at any given time may be psychological, economic, political, psychical, or sociological in character.[7] They are the result of conditions existing between two distinct parts of the external environment of the classroom group. These two parts are identifiable as follows. First, the "school" as a social system encompasses or incorporates the classroom group.[8] As a social system, the "school" represents one part of the external environment of the classroom group. Second, the classroom group is basically a training group for enabling people to become competent for participating in the affairs of their physical, biological, and social worlds. Therefore, the other part of the external environment to which the classroom group must relate is that which lies outside the school and which we generally identify as the "community." The tasks, projects, and problems upon which the group works are to a large extent determined by and selected from this part of the external environment. The content of the school curriculum is composed of our systematized knowledges and perceptions of the phenomena and problems that exist in the "community." These systematized knowledges and perceptions (cultural artifacts) about community phenomena and problems are referred to as school-subjects or disciplines.[9] They are utilized by the school as instructional resources or means for achieving the public goals of the school, *viz.*, to teach school participants (students) to live intelligently and satisfyingly in the community.

The *internal environment* of the classroom group can be presented as the inter-member relations operating within the classroom. The group must expend some of its energies in examining the relationships to be organized and rebuilt from time to time between group members. Because these inter-member relations affect the needs systems of individual group members, the problems they create within the classroom group will usually take priority over any others.[10] Little work on problems

[7] Cf. Clyde B. Moore and William E. Cole. *Sociology in Educational Practice.* New York: Houghton Mifflin, 1952, pp. 33-54.

[8] Gale E. Jensen, "The School as a Social System," *Educational Research Bulletin,* Ohio State University, February, 1954, pp. 38-46.

[9] Clyde B. Moore and William E. Cole, *Op. Cit.,* pp. 330-331.

[10] N. T. Fouriezos, M. L. Hutt, and H. Guetzkow, "Self-Oriented Needs in Discussion Groups." In D. Cartwright and A. Zander, *Op. Cit.,* pp. 354-360. Max Corey, "Interpersonal Relations and the Work of the School," *Baltimore Bulletin of Education,* March-June, 1952, pp. 16-22.

induced by forces of the external environment will be accomplished when internal difficulties are numerous and strong.

If the classroom group is to contribute effectively to the realization of the public goals of the school, it must deal skillfully with the two ever-present or persisting problems that arise in its internal and external environments. Members of the classroom group must develop perceptions and expectations about what is required in one another's behavior for deriving adequate solutions to the problems. They must make certain that the functions attached to "student" and "teacher" rôles[11] for purposes of dealing effectively with group achievement and group maintenance are activated at the right time. In brief, individuals have, as members of the classroom group, a *need* to relate to one another along this dimension or the class will be unable to establish the group stability and unity required for productive class work and individual development. Failure of class members to relate to one another along this dimension frustrate the strong personal needs of some members to learn more about the area of study for which the class is responsible. Under such conditions, these members are likely to withdraw or engage in non-constructive behavior.

In summary, the ways in which classroom group members relate to one another for working on problems induced by the forces of the external and internal environments of the group, represents the problem-solving dimension of the group. The question which reveals the status of this dimension at any one time is: Who engages in or carries on what problem-solving functions with whom to accomplish the public task of the classroom group?

The Authority-Leadership Dimension.—As a classroom group works on its tasks, it is confronted periodically with having to make decisions that affect its progress. The above discussion referring to the problem-solving dimension of the classroom group indicates that the effectiveness with which these decisions are likely to be made is dependent upon having the problem-solving functions activated at the "right" time. To make certain these problem-solving functions are performed at the right time, the group must appoint and/or recognize some members as having the responsibility for and the power to facilitate the problem-solving conditions requisite to making periodic decisions affecting group progress.[12] The status of this authority-leadership dimension in a class for a given time is revealed by the following question. Who is recognized by whom as having the responsibility and power for facilitating the problem-solving conditions necessary for effective decision-making by the class?

[11] Cf. Kenneth Benne and Paul Sheats, "Functional Roles of Group Members," *Journal of Social Issues*, Spring, 1948, pp. 42-47.

[12] Herbert Thelen, "The Experimental Method of Classroom Leadership," *The Elementary School Journal*, October, 1952, pp. 76-85.

By way of example, if the task on which a class is working should change radically, the class will need to consider changes in ongoing and contemplated action. In most instances, one finds that some member of the class is recognized as the responsible person for bringing the class together and calling its attention to certain difficulties with which it may be confronted. This member may carry the designation of "teacher," "chairman," or "leader." He is recognized by class members as the "group convener." He has the power to reconvene the class at the proper time and in a place known to all members.

There are numerous other authority-leadership functions that must be performed to insure the conditions necessary for and conducive to effective decision-making by a group. These functions must be identified by the class and then assigned to members who will assume the responsibility for facilitating their performance at the crucial points of class operation. Along with identifying and assigning the responsibilities for performing authority-leadership functions, the class must identify and assign, either explicitly or implicitly, the prerogatives to be used in carrying out these functions.[13]

To summarize, the members of the classroom group have a *need* to recognize certain members as having the authority and responsibility for facilitating the problem-solving conditions required for effective decision-making at critical points of class work. In terms of the social structure of the classroom group, this means that class members must establish between themselves a network of authority-leader relationships commensurate with the character of the goals and problems with which the group is confronted.

The Power Dimension.—During the operations of the classroom group it becomes apparent that some members have greater ability (1) to influence the direction the class may take and (2) to induce other members to change their thinking and attitudes. The development of these power relationships in the classroom group is inevitable because members can meet their respective needs only through participation in social situations in which varying needs and resources are matched in ways satisfactory to the participating parties.[14] The character of the relationships along this dimension at any given point in class operation can be discovered by asking: Who possesses what means for gratifying or depriving whose needs?

At times this greater ability to influence others may rest with those who are recognized as having certain authorities. At other times the greater

[13] Herbert Thelen, "Engineering Research in Curriculum Building," *Journal of Educational Research*, April, 1948, p. 582.

[14] Herbert Thelen, "Basic Concepts in Human Dynamics," *Journal of the National Association of Deans of Women*, March, 1952, p. 104.

degree of influence is held by those who held no official authority positions. But whether or not this ability to influence rests with those who hold official authority positions is of little importance for the discussion of this dimension. The significant thing is that class members with greater influence are perceived at any given time to have greater resources for gratifying the needs of the group and of individual members.[15] It is this ability to gratify or deprive the needs of others that represents the power an individual member possesses in the class. It is this power as manifested in his ability to gratify or deprive needs that enables a member at any given time to influence the direction the group will take or to induce another member to change his perceptions and attitudes.[16]

This power to gratify and deprive needs may be derived from the crucial position a member holds within the group, or it may be derived from his superior ability as an individual member to perform certain acts, control resources, or solve problems. A particular position in the social structure of the class, particular skills, and particular resources, however, are secondary for determining the power a class member holds. Basically, it is the character of the relationships between his social position, resources and skills, and the needs of other members of the class that determines the power a member may have.

To summarize briefly, the way in which class members align themselves with one another for fulfilling individual and group needs through complementary usage of one another's abilities, social positions, and resources represents the power dimension of the classroom group.

The Friendship Dimension.—In the various situations in which class members find themselves, each develops perceptions and feelings about his ability to insure a satisfactory gratification-deprivation balance. Periodic assessments of group situations are made by individual members to determine the possible gratifications and/or deprivations of needs. These assessments are made particularly when the class is trying to project action and/or come to a decision.[17]

Whenever a situation is perceived or felt to be one which will likely produce an unfavorable gratification-deprivation balance, a group member experiences anxiety and becomes reluctant to express publicly many of his perceptions and feelings. These anxiety feelings may be either consciously or unconsciously experienced. But whether the behavior

[15] Ronald Lippitt, Norman Polansky, Fritz Redl, and Sidney Rosen, "The Dynamics of Power." In D. Cartwright and A. Zander, *Op. Cit.*, pp. 480-481.

[16] J. I. Hurwitz, A. Zander, and Barnard Hymovitch, "Some Effects of Power on the Relations among Group Members." In D. Cartwright and A. Zander, *Op. Cit.*, pp. 491-492.

[17] Herbert Thelen, "Educational Dynamics," *Op. Cit.*, pp. 19-21, and H. H. Jennings, *Leadership and Isolation.* New York: Longman's, Green & Co., 1950, chapter 1.

portrayed is conscious or unconscious in character, many of the perceptions and feelings developed in classroom group situations remain as
privately-held experiences by individual members.[18]

At times the class as a whole may be willing to entertain and attempt
to deal with individual members' feelings and anxieties; but even when
this is true, the group members concerned very often feel that their privately-held perceptions and feelings should not be made public because
they will be too threatening to themselves, other members, or the class as
a whole.

As a means of allaying anxieties and testing perceptions and feelings
being privately held, class members seek to share these perceptions and
feelings with other members in whom they feel they can confide. Stated
otherwise, classroom group members have a *need* to express and test their
privately-held perceptions and feelings with members who will respond
actively and supportingly to them. These members are most often those
designated as "friends," the intimate associates of a clique or coterie to
which they belong.[19]

These relationships which class members seek to develop with one
another in order to share and test private perceptions and feelings
resulting from participation in classroom situations can be identified as
the "friendship" dimension. The question which reveals the status of this
dimension at any given time is: Who in the class shares private feelings
and ideas with whom?

The Personal Prestige Dimension.—In the process of a classroom
group's setting goals for carrying out the learning tasks set by the school
curriculum, individual members make various kinds of contributions to
the group's progress and welfare. In this way, the group discovers the
talents and special worth of its different members.[20]

Each member comes to be valued to some degree by the group. Each
is accorded personal worth commensurate with his talents, personal
characteristics, and contributions to the projects of the group. This
acquisition of personal worth represents the group's approval of a member's contributions and the acceptance of him as a person with membership rights, privileges, and responsibilities. For a given period of class
operation the status of these relationships can be established by determining who is valued by whom by virtue of contributions made to the
welfare of the group and the accomplishment of its goals.

The general approval of him by the group along with the special

[18] Cf. Raymond L. Gorden, "Interaction between Attitude and the Definition of
the Situation in the Expression of Opinion." In D. Cartwright and A. Zander, *Op. Cit.*

[19] Provisions for meeting these needs are sometimes institutionalized in a school
system in the form of a counselling service.

[20] Cf. C. Heinicke, and Robert Bales, "Developmental Trends in the Structure of
Small Groups," *Sociometry*, February, 1953, pp. 7-38.

prestige symbols with which he may be rewarded constitutes the source of one of the most important kinds of psychological rewards a class member receives. "To be wanted," "to belong," "to be approved," or "to win recognition and be honored" is one kind of gratification for which it is common for all people to strive. Without a minimum of this kind of gratification or reward, an individual class member's behavior becomes subject to disorganization, unpredictability, and ineffective problem orientation. Without it a member finds it difficult to continue to take part in the life of the class. In brief, individuals as members of a class have a *need* for being valued by the group.

Briefly stated, the way in which members are related to one another in terms of their being valued by the other group members represents the personal prestige dimension of the classroom group.

The Sex Dimension.—There are two sets of forces that operate so as to make the members of a classroom group relate to one another sexually. First, the society in which members of a classroom group are born and live ascribes or assigns to them different rôles that are based in part upon their sex.[21] People formulate different expectations of one another based on differences in sex and in the classroom these expectations will influence the way in which class members will relate to one another. In almost every kind of situation, formal and informal, in which males and females participate, there are socially defined, common expectations as to (1) what activities are appropriate for the different sexes, (2) how females should behave in the presence of males, (3) how females should behave toward other females, (4) how males should behave when with females, (5) how males should perceive and react to other males. These expectations are brought to the classroom and utilized by members, mostly unconsciously, to relate to one another.

Second, members of a classroom group relate to one another in respect to sex because of certain physiological and psychological forces that affect them as individual organisms.[22] That is, each member has physiological and psychological sex needs which move him or her to seek out other class members who have complementary sex needs and/or who might gratify these needs. In everyday life this relationship is often identified as "love."

The relationships class members endeavor to develop between one another (1) to develop group rôles that take account of culturally defined differences in sex and (2) to satisfy psychological and physiological sex drives represent the sex dimension of the classroom group. The status of the relationships along this dimension at any time is determined by

[21] Kingsley Davis. *Human Society.* New York: The Macmillan Company, 1950, pp. 98-103.

[22] P. Symonds. *The Dynamics of Human Adjustment.* New York: D. Appleton Century Co., 1946, pp. 31-35.

establishing (1) which class members are attempting to define participation in the group according to differences in sex, and (2) which members are relating to one another for purposes of gratifying sex needs?

The Privilege Dimension.—From the first of its history, the classroom group includes at least one member, who because of the rôle he or she holds, receives gratifications (or rewards) in the form of deferences, benefits, advantages, and gifts. The classroom group incorporates this one rôle from the very first of its life because the rôle is assigned to it by the larger social organization of which it is a part, *viz.,* the school. This rôle is that of "teacher."

While the person who is competent to fill the position of "teacher" doubtless makes valuable contributions to the work of the group and achieves personal prestige because of these contributions, he also receives some gratifications by virtue of merely filling the rôle. In brief, the teacher from the first of the group's existence is eligible to receive deferences, benefits, and gifts from members. By virtue of holding the position of "teacher," he has certain privileges that no other member has.

As a class has common experiences, builds a culture for itself, and develops a work structure for effective problem-solving, provisions may be made for rewarding members on a privilege basis in addition to those based on their contributions to the achievement of class goals. The group creates and designates rôles that make members holding them eligible for gratifications in the form of advantages, deferences, and gifts. It seems as though individuals, as group members, have a *need* to insure themselves of a constant receipt of gratifications, especially during those times when they are unable or do not have the opportunity to acquire rewards through making contributions to the work of the class. This attempt to control the "flow" of gratifications seems to represent a sort of "hedging" operation by which members attempt to build into the social structure of the class a sort of "guaranteed set of rewards." The more a group builds a "surplus" of needs-gratifying conditions, the more likely class members will seek to work out privilege relationships between one another. The status of the privilege relationships in a classroom group is determined by discovering who has the right to what gratifications by virtue of the rôle they hold rather than by virtue of the contributions they make to the class goals.

Privilege gratifications may be attached to certain rôles in order to insure that they will be filled by persons who are especially competent in making contributions to the work of the group. They may be assigned to a rôle in recognition of the contributions some group member who presently holds it has made in the past to the welfare and needs of the group. Or these gratifications may be assigned to the rôle as a way of "pointing" to the authority figures of the group. Whatever the reasons may be for attaching these gratifications to certain rôles of the group, the point to be recognized and emphasized is that whatever member fills them becomes eligible for receiving the privilege rewards attached to them.

Application of the Framework to Classroom Group Operation

In the above description of the problem-solving dimension, it was noted that there are two general problems with which classroom groups are continuously confronted. One has to do with building a kind of class organization that will insure high productivity in the sense of (a) effectively accomplishing the tasks set for the class by the school curriculum, and (b) maximizing the growth or achievement of individual members. The other has to do with maintaining the kind of intra-group conditions that enable members to expend their energies upon class work rather than upon the resolution of inter-member or inter-personal difficulties. These two problems of classroom group operation can be identified as the problems of *group productivity* and *group cohesiveness*.

Class productivity and individual achievement decrease whenever either of these two persisting problems remain unresolved for any length of time. The problem which constantly confronts the teacher is that of diagnosing or analyzing the class to determine (1) which of the two general problems besets the class at any given time and (2) what the character of the relationships are that produce the problem.

Without some kind of conceptual framework to indicate "what kind of things to look for" and "how to look at them," it is not likely that the teacher will be able to bring about a resolution of problems induced by the social structure of the class. When this is the case, class productivity and individual achievement falls and the group more or less "bashes" about with little direction given to its efforts. When confronted with these conditions, a teacher tends to feel extremely threatened and is likely to resort to dictatorial or seductive methods in order to gain more security as the main classroom authority. Under these conditions, class members, including the teacher, seldom understand what is happening to them and it is not surprising that they become highly anxious, reject class work, and some become hostile while others take flight or establish extreme dependency relationships with the teacher.

The systematic use of a framework, such as has been outlined, makes it possible for the educational practitioner to avoid being victimized by the situation just described. For example, the conceptual framework of this article identifies for the educational practitioner the dimensions along which members of a classroom group have a *need* to relate to one another. These dimensions of member relationships constitute the factors relevant to problems induced by the social structure of the classroom group. These different kinds of relationships are "what practitioners must look at" to discover what the conditions are that create at a given time either one or both of the two general problems of classroom group operation. The conceptual framework also indicates to the practitioner that the productivity of a class, the achievement of its members as individuals, and the member-satisfaction with life in the class is a function of the relationships within and between the seven different dimensions. This is "how" a classroom group must be conceived in order to analyze or diagnose effectively the conditions that upset class productivity and class cohesiveness.

SUMMARY

This article outlines a seven-dimensional framework that can be used to analyze the two general problems of classroom operation with which teachers are constantly confronted. These problems were identified as class productivity and class cohesiveness.

The seven dimensions contained in the framework represent the different kinds of relationships that members of a classroom group have *need* to establish between themselves. They also identify, for the educational practitioner, the factors relevant to operational problems induced by the social structure of the classroom group. In addition, the framework indicates to the practitioner that the productivity of the class, the growth of its members, and general member-satisfaction with life in the class must be conceived as functions of the member relationships within and between the seven identified dimensions.

The conceptual framework enables the practitioner to recognize that whenever the member relationships along and between these dimensions become (1) inadequate for accomplishing the work of the class as set by the school curriculum and (2) unsatisfactory for meeting member's needs, the class will probably experience a drop in productivity and individual achievement. The most effective group arrangement for restoring a high level of productivity is to systematically utilize a conceptual framework (1) to locate the dimensions containing the inadequate or unsatisfactory relationships and (2) for determining how these relationships are affecting class productivity and class cohesiveness.

21.   Teacher Influence, Pupil Attitudes, and Achievement

Ned A. Flanders

EARLY RESEARCH ON CLASSROOM CLIMATE

The term "classroom climate" refers to generalized attitudes toward the teacher and the class that the pupils share in common despite individual differences. The development of these attitudes is an outgrowth of classroom social interaction. As a result of participating in classroom activities, pupils soon develop common attitudes about how they like their class, the kind of person the teacher is, and how he will act in certain typical situations. These common attitudes color all aspects of classroom behavior, creating a social atmosphere, or climate, that appears to be fairly stable, once established. Thus, the word "climate"[1] is merely a shorthand reference to those qualities that consistently predominate in most teacher-pupil contacts and in contacts among the pupils in the presence or absence of the teacher. . . .

One contribution of research on classroom climate has been the identification of different kinds of verbal statements that the teacher uses. This information has been used in the development of our system of interaction analysis.

A less consistent contribution of this early research concerns the words used to designate patterns of teacher behavior. In fact, there is quite a choice: Anderson—"dominative" and "integrative;" Lippitt and White—"authoritarian," "democratic," and "laissez-faire;" Withall, Flanders, Perkins—"teacher-centered" and "student-centered;" and Cogan—"preclusive" and inclusive."[2] All these come from a short stroll in the conceptual

Reprinted with permission *Teacher Influence, Pupil Attitudes, and Achievement* by Ned A. Flanders. Cooperative Research Monograph No. 12. U.S. Department of Health, Education, and Welfare, Office of Education, Washington, D.C., 1965.

[1] Climate is assessed either by analyzing teacher-pupil interaction and inferring underlying attitudes from the interaction, or by the use of a pupil-attitude inventory and predicting the quality of classroom interaction from the results. Its precise meaning, as commonly used, is seldom clear—just as its synonyms, "morale," "rapport," and "emotional tone," are also ambiguous. To have any meaning at all, the word is always qualified by an adjective, and it is in the choice of adjectives that researchers become reformers and too often lose their objectivity.

[2] "The Measurement of Domination and of Socially Integrative Behavior in Teacher's Contact with Children," *Child Development*, 10,2, 73-89; "Theory and Design of a Study of Teacher-Pupil Interaction," *The Harvard Educational Review*, 26,4, 315-42; "Personal-Social Anxiety as a Factor in Experimental Learning Situations," *Journal of Educational Research*, 45, Oct. 1951; "The Social Climate of Children's Groups," in Barker, R.G., Kaunin, J.S., and Wright, H.F., eds. *Child Behavior and Development*. New York:

garden of psychology; an overnight hike could extend the list indefinitely. Faced with such a choice, we might first pause to discuss the concepts used in this type of research.

Concepts used to describe teacher influence refer to a series of acts occurring during some time period. When a particular series occurs again and again, it becomes familiar to an observer and he can identify it. We call such a series a "pattern" of influence.

It is interesting to distinguish between an influence pattern and the concept of "role," as it is commonly used in the literature of social psychology. The difference is in the degree of behavioral specificity that is implied. For example, it may be said that a teacher plays in the classroom a "democratic" or "authoritarian" role. These concepts not only connote value judgments, but they are so abstract that they fail to denote very much about the behavior of the teacher. If someone tries to create either role, his choice of influence patterns depends primarily on his personal and often unique understanding of the concept. Such a choice involves too many alternatives; specificity is lacking.

The only path through these difficulties is to increase understanding by insisting that the concepts used have explicit behavioral meaning. . . . Certain concepts that refer to the teacher's behavior . . . will be presented. In each instance, a description of behavior in a social setting will be given first. Next, concepts will be used to abstract the behavior events, and in the process, a theoretical definition of the concept will become clear. Finally, the procedures used in this study to measure or quantify the concept will be briefly stated.

The reader may wish to evaluate the development of these concepts by applying the following criteria. First, what are the concepts that are given theoretical meaning by analysis of the behavior that commonly occurs in a classroom? Second, are the procedures used for quantifying behavior that is associated with a concept (a) practical: that is, can they be used in a classroom; (b) representative: that is, do they adequately sample all behavior that could logically be associated with the concept; and (c) reliable: that is, can the error factor be determined and is it low, compared with the differences studied? Third, can the concepts be organized into hypotheses or principles (cause and effect statements) to predict behavior or the consequences of behavior?

CONCEPTS FOR DESCRIBING TEACHER INFLUENCE

Teacher influence exists as a series of acts along a time line. It is most often expressed as verbal communication. In this study we assume that

---

McGraw-Hill,1943,458–508;"Climate influences Group Learning,"*TeachersCollegeRecord*, 61,5, 229-41; "The Development of a Technique for the Measurement of Social-Emotional Climate in Classroom," Journal of Experimental Education, 17, March 1949, 347-61.

verbal communication constitutes an adequate sample of the teacher's total influence pattern. A single act of a teacher occupies a segment of time. Before this act a particular state of affairs exists; after the act is completed, a different state of affairs exists. Some acts are more potent than others and have greater consequences. Furthermore, a long series of similar acts may have more extensive effects than just an isolated few.

A researcher is free to choose concepts that will be used to describe the state of affairs before and after an act, and concepts that will be used to describe the act itself.

Suppose a teacher says, "Please close the door," to a student. The chances are that the student will close the door. Before this act of influence, the student was engaged in some activity, such as thinking or reading. But since he was expected to comply with the teacher's command, he interrupted his train of thought to get up and close the door.

Actually, this sequence of behavior is as complex as we wish to make it. We could theorize about the social expectations that exist when a teacher makes what adults call a reasonable demand of a student. Much could be said, if we had the facts, about how past contacts with other authority figures have helped to form this particular student's reactions to a command. It might be that the student resented this intrusion and chose to push the door so that it slammed, rather than gently closing it. A lesser degree of resentment could be expressed by an audible sigh followed by slow movements.

Because of all the concepts that could be used to describe behavior, there is a choice here along a continuum. The genotypic concepts that describe inner motives or feelings are at one end, and the phenotypic concepts that describe more superficial aspects of behavior are at the other end. The choice should fit the purpose. A psychiatrist would prefer certain concepts for his purposes that would probably be too genotypic for the majority of interpretations that a teacher needs to make.

Our choice in this instance leads to the following explanation. The teacher exerted *direct influence,* which restricted the *freedom of action* of the student, making him momentarily more *dependent* on the teacher. From this illustration we hope the reader will understand that an act of direct influence restricts freedom of action, usually by focusing on a problem and, in this case, it made the student more dependent on teacher influence for a short period of time.

By the way, you the reader may have felt uneasy when you thought of a teacher's restricting the freedom of action of a student. These are terms that often elicit value judgments. However, it seems sensible to assert that a student's freedom of action is restricted when he is told to shut the door. Nevertheless, it is difficult to make an objective description of such events.

Now, suppose the same door is closed, but with a completely different script. The teacher asks, "Does anyone feel a draft in here?" Johnny says, "Yes, it's cold. I think it's coming from this open door." The teacher says, "Well, since it seems cold, please close the door." So Johnny gets up and closes the door.

The second example includes the same command and ultimately leads to the same compliance, yet most of us would agree that the state of affairs would be different at the termination of the episode. Consider, too, differences after a series of such episodes extending over hours, days, weeks, or the school year.

Again we face a choice in conceptualizing the behavior. Our choice is as follows: The command, "Close the door," was modified first by a question, "Does anyone feel a draft in here?" second, by a student response, "Yes, it's cold. I think it's coming from this open door," the latter phrase being a student-initiated idea; and third, by the teacher's acknowledging the student's idea, "Well, since it seems cold . . ." Taken all together, the teacher's acts of influence are more indirect than direct. While the student's freedom of action was restricted, his perception of this restriction was probably modified in the second example because he was solving a problem that he had helped to identify, rather than merely complying with the command of an authority figure. In fact, the teacher's behavior encouraged the student's initiative and, in this sense, his freedom of action was expanded. Later on, after more examples are given, we hope it will become clear that an act of indirect influence expands freedom of action and usually makes a student less dependent on the teacher. He often has greater orientation to a problem, because he helped to identify it.

Most teachers who hear these ideas expressed immediately conclude that indirect influence is superior to direct influence. We believe that the basis of this value judgment lies less in the ideas just expressed than in the social pressures that affect teachers' self-concepts. Most teachers apparently want to believe that they are "indirect teachers," even before they hear how these concepts are defined or are told about any research findings. If being an indirect teacher means consistently using indirect influence, we can state categorically that no such teacher exists, because no teacher employs a pure pattern of influence. All teachers establish some kind of balance based on a combination of direct and indirect influence.

At this point, further objection often arises. It seems obvious that any "intelligent teacher" would prefer to have his students "problem-oriented," as illustrated in the second episode, rather than "authority-oriented," as illustrated in the first episode. (The quotation marks are used here to emphasize how quickly abstract value judgments enter the discussion.) Our experience would suggest that, in the long run, most teachers want the students in their classes to react to the demands of problem-solving rather than to their own authority. Yet does it necessarily follow that indirect influence is superior to direct influence? Is the student in the first illustration any less "problem-oriented" than the student in the second?

Our system of interaction analysis provides an explicit procedure for quantifying direct and indirect influence that is closely related to the teacher behaviors identified by research on classroom climate. Direct influence consists of those verbal statements of the teacher that restrict freedom of action, by focusing attention on a problem, interjecting teacher authority, or both. These statements include lecturing, giving directions, criticizing, and justifying his own use of authority. Indirect influence consists of those verbal statements of the teacher that expand a student's freedom of action by encouraging his verbal participation and initiative. These include asking questions, accepting and clarifying the ideas or feelings of students, and praising or encouraging students' responses. . . .

CONCEPTS FOR DESCRIBING TEACHER FLEXIBILITY AND
HOMOGENEOUS CLASSROOM ACTIVITIES

Anyone who has observed many hours in a classroom soon notices that classroom interaction occurs in a sequence of activity periods. First, there may be a routine 3 to 5 minutes for settling down to work. Next, perhaps, homework is corrected and handed in. Next, a student or group may give a report. This may be followed by a 15-minute discussion, and so on. We have found it advantageous to tabulate interaction analysis data separately for these periods.

The main reason for separating data from different activities is that we can then discover whether a teacher shifts his balance of direct and indirect influence in various activity periods. Is a teacher more indirect when new material is being introduced? Is he more indirect when helping diagnose difficulties? Is he more direct when supervising seatwork? What about evaluating homework or test results?

Identifying activity periods is almost a second system of categorization that is superimposed on the system for classifying verbal statements. In junior-high academic classrooms, we use 5 activity categories: introducing new material; evaluating homework, tests, or learning products; other class discussion; supervising seatwork or group activities; and routine clean-up, passing of materials, or settling down to work. In general, a change from one activity to another is indicated by the statements made, a change of class formation, or a change in the communication pattern.

Tabulating data separately for homogeneous activities permits us to define teacher flexibility and measure it. Teacher flexibility is a measure of the change a teacher makes in his verbal influence from one activity period to another. We measure this by noting the ratio of indirect influence (I) to direct influence (D) in one activity period and comparing it with the corresponding ratio in other activity periods. If we wish to avoid a measure which is a ratio of a ratio, that is, an I/D ratio as a percent divided by a percent, we can compare changes in the percent of indirect influence across different activities, and then make the same comparison for direct influence. Unfortunately, this does not eliminate the statistical problems. Distributions of I/D ratios, comparative percents of indirect statements, and raw tallies all form a "J"-shaped curve. . . .

Hypotheses of Teacher Influence for This Study

In the long run, the purpose of testing hypotheses about teacher influence is to establish principles of teacher behavior that can guide a teacher who wishes to control his own behavior as part of his plan for classroom management. Each principle, if it is to be useful, must be a cause-and-effect statement. Accordingly, this report will express principles in statements that adhere to the following general pattern: if such and such is true, then action "X" will produce result "Y."

This study is concerned with the following hypotheses, which will be stated in terms of the concepts described in the preceding section:

Hypothesis One: Indirect teacher influence increases learning when a student's perception of the goal is confused and ambiguous.

Hypothesis Two: Direct teacher influence increases learning when a student's perception of the goal is clear and acceptable.

Hypothesis Three: Direct teacher influence decreases learning when a student's perception of the goal is ambiguous.

In these three hypotheses, the concept *learning* refers to the development of skills and understandings that can be measured by pre- and post-tests of achievement. In this project, tests were administered before and after a 2-week unit of study, so that an operational definition of learning consists of final achievement, adjusted for initial ability.

By way of brief review, the dynamic explanation of these hypotheses rests on the following reasoning: First, indirect influence increases learning when goals are ambiguous because less disabling dependence develops. During the initial stages of learning, goals are ambiguous. Indirect influence increases student freedom of action, allowing the student the opportunity to question goals and the procedures for reaching them. The net effect of this participation in clarifying goals is less compliance to authority *per se* and more attention to problem-solving requirements, or at least a more balanced orientation for those students who have high dependence-proneness.

Second, direct influence increases learning when goals are clear because the criteria for accepting or rejecting teacher influence as well as various alternative actions can be recognized in terms of the problem-solving requirements. The student is presumably oriented toward the problem; direct teacher influence is likely to be oriented toward the problem and be helpful; and the net effect is more efficient action toward problem solution. Dependence on the teacher remains steady or is decreased as a result of successful progress toward the goal.

Third, direct influence decreases learning when goals are ambiguous because it increases dependence sharply. The primary response of the student is compliance with teacher authority when goals are unclear. This, in turn, develops dependence. Unless the student understands the goal that the teacher has in mind, he has no other acceptable alternative, given our present cultural expectations. The high dependence that quickly develops means that the student is oriented more toward pleasing the teacher than toward meeting the problem-solving requirements.

These hypotheses are generalized predictions across a range of individual differences. The interaction between a teacher and a particular student in a specific situation is modified by unique personality characteristics and situational factors. . . .

CLASSROOM INTERACTION ANALYSIS

The spontaneous behavior of a teacher is so complex and variable that an accurate description of it is most difficult to obtain. Even trained observers struggle with the same biases that distort the testimony of witnesses at the scene of an accident. Too often an observer's preconceptions of what he thinks should happen allow him to perceive certain behaviors but prevent him from perceiving others. Interaction analysis is an observation procedure designed to minimize these difficulties, to permit a systematic record of spontaneous acts, and to scrutinize the process of instruction by taking into account each small bit of interaction.

Classroom interaction analysis is particularly concerned with the influence pattern of the teacher. This might be considered a bias, but it is a bias of purpose and interest. Our purpose is to record a series of acts in terms of predetermined concepts. The concepts in this case refer to the teacher's control of the students' freedom of action. Our interest is to distinguish those acts of the teacher that increase students' freedom of action from those acts that decrease students' freedom of action, and to keep a record of both. The system of categories is used by the observer to separate those acts which result in compliance from those acts which invite more creative and voluntary participation; at the same time, it prevents him from being diverted by the subject matter which is irrelevant to this study.

Interaction analysis is concerned primarily with verbal behavior because it can be observed with higher reliability than most nonverbal behavior. The assumption is made that the verbal behavior of the teacher is an adequate sample of his total behavior; that is, his verbal statements are consistent with his nonverbal gestures, in fact, his total behavior. This assumption seems reasonable in terms of our experience.

THE PROCEDURE

The observer sits in the classroom in the best position to hear and see the participants. At the end of each 3-second period, he decides which of a prescribed set of numbered categories best represents the communication events just completed. He writes this category number down while simultaneously assessing communication in the next period. He continues at a rate of about 20 to 25 observations per minute, keeping his tempo as steady as possible. His notes are merely a sequence of numbers written in a column, top to bottom, so that the original sequence of events is preserved. Occasionally, marginal notes are used to explain the class formation or any unusual circumstances. When there is a major change in class formation, the communication pattern, or the subject under discussion, the observer draws a double line and indicates the time. As soon as he has completed the total observation, he retires to a nearby room and writes up a general description of each separate activity period. This includes the nature of the activities, the class formation, and the position of the teacher. The observer also notes any additional facts that seem pertinent to an adequate interpretation and recall of the total observation period.

THE CATEGORIES

There are 10 categories in the system. Seven are assigned to teacher talk and two to student talk. The 10th category covers pauses, short periods of silence, and talk that is confusing or noisy. The category system is outlined below.

Of the seven categories assigned to teacher talk, categories 1 through 4 represent indirect influence, and categories 5, 6, and 7, direct influence.

Indirect influence encourages participation by the student and increases his freedom of action. To ask a question (category 4) is an invitation to participate and express ideas, opinions, or facts. It is true that a question can be so phrased as to leave very little freedom of action, but at least the student can refuse to answer, a reaction which reflects more freedom than does passive listening. The more general a teacher's question, the greater the opportunity for the student to assert his own ideas.

When the teacher accepts, clarifies, or uses constructively the ideas and opinions of students (category 3), they are encouraged to participate

Categories for interaction analysis, 1959

TEACHER TALK	**INDIRECT INFLUENCE**	1.° ACCEPTS FEELING: accepts and clarifies the tone of feeling of the students in an unthreatening manner. Feelings may be positive or negative. Predicting or recalling feelings are included. 2.° PRAISES OR ENCOURAGES: praises or encourages student action or behavior. Jokes that release tension, but not at the expense of another individual, nodding head or saying "um hm?" or "go on" are included. 3.° ACCEPTS OR USES IDEAS OF STUDENT: clarifying, building, or developing ideas suggested by a student. As teacher brings more of his own ideas into play, shift to category 5. 4.° ASKS QUESTIONS: asking a question about content or procedure with the intent that a student answer.
	DIRECT INFLUENCE	5.° LECTURING: giving facts or opinions about content or procedure; expressing his own ideas, asking rhetorical questions. 6.° GIVING DIRECTIONS: directions, commands, or orders which students are expected to comply with. 7.° CRITICIZING OR JUSTIFYING AUTHORITY: statements intended to change student behavior from unacceptable to acceptable pattern; bawling someone out; stating why the teacher is doing what he is doing; extreme self-reference.
STUDENT TALK		8.° STUDENT TALK—RESPONSE: talk by students in response to teacher. Teacher initiates the contact or solicits student statement. 9.° STUDENT TALK—INITIATION: talk initiated by students. If "calling on" student is only to indicate who may talk next, observer must decide whether student wanted to talk.
SILENCE		10.° SILENCE OR CONFUSION: pauses, short periods of silence and periods of confusion in which communication cannot be understood by the observer.

° There is NO scale implied by these numbers. Each number is classificatory, designating a particular kind of communication event. To write these numbers down during observation is merely to identify and enumerate communication events, not to judge them.

further. Often teachers act as if they do not hear what a student says; to acknowledge and make use of an idea is a powerful form of recognition. To praise or encourage student participation directly (category 2) is to solicit even more participation by giving a reward. The ability to use the feeling tone of a student constructively, to react to feeling and clarify it (category 1), is a rare skill. Teachers with this ability can often mobilize positive feelings in motivation and successfully control negative feelings that might otherwise get out of hand.

All the actions falling into categories 1 through 4 tend to increase and reward student participation, and to give students the opportunity to become more influential. The net effect is greater freedom of action for the students.

Direct influence increases the active control of the teacher and often stimulates compliance. The lecture (category 5) focuses the attention of the students on ideas chosen by the teacher. To give directions or commands (category 6) is to direct the activities of the class with the intent of obtaining compliance. Category 7 refers to criticizing student behavior or justifying the teacher's use of authority. These actions concentrate authority in the hands of the teacher. Direct influence tends to increase teacher participation and to establish restraints on student behavior. The ensuing restriction of freedom may occur in the form of compliance to the teacher or of adjustment to the requirements of problem-solving activities. The net effect is less freedom of action for the students.

The division of student talk into categories 8 and 9 provides an automatic check on freedom of student action within the system of categories. Ordinarily, but not always, a pattern of direct teacher influence is associated with less student talk, which generally consists of responses to the teacher (category 8). A pattern of indirect influence is ordinarily associated with more student talk, which is often initiated by the students (category 9). The use of only two categories to record all kinds of student talk neglects a great deal of information, but the major purpose of these categories is the analysis of teacher influence. The greatest information will accrue from observation if category 9 is used sparingly and only on those occasions when the communication is truly student-initiated.

For example, the act of a student in answering a specific question asked by a teacher obviously falls into category 8. Even the act of giving an oral report may be placed in this category when the student is restricted to a specific outline and is probably responding to the teacher's directions.

Category 9 should be used by the observer only to indicate the student's spontaneous expression of his own ideas. General questions are often a clue that a student may be initiating his own ideas. When a teacher calls on a student who voluntarily raised his hand to speak and asks, "Have you anything to add, Robert?" the chances are that the use of category 9 is correct.

The purpose of category 10 is to record short pauses, silences, and periods of confusion as they occur during classroom interaction. It is not intended to record periods of silence or confusion lasting for more than 2 minutes. The continuous use of this category to designate long periods of silence serves no useful purpose.

The system of categories is designed for situations in which the teachers and the students are actively discussing schoolwork. It is an inappropriate tool when the verbal communication is discontinuous, separated by fairly long periods of silence, or when one person is engaged in prolonged lecturing or in reading aloud to the class. In situations in which two-way communication does not exist and is not likely to exist, the observer should stop and make a note of the exact time at which spontaneous interaction lapsed and the reasons for the interruption. The observer must remain alert to the resumption of spontaneous interaction.

MARKING ACTIVITY PERIODS

Teacher influence is a pattern that is constantly changing over time. The most effective teachers, in fact, have a large repertoire of behaviors, and systematic observation shows that they can present many different influence patterns.

The identification of activity periods is one way that flexibility can be studied. In effect, a second system of categories is super-imposed on the 10 interaction categories; this second system is likely to be different in each research study. For example, it may be sufficient in a study of high school mathematics classes to indicate periods of (a) settling down to work, (b) introducing new material, (c) teacher-directed discussion or work on material that is not new, (d) supervision and direction of individual seatwork, and (e) periods of evaluation, in which homework and test results are discussed.

In an elementary classroom, it would be reasonable to keep interaction data collected during show-and-tell separate from reading instruction, and these in turn from arithmetic, music, games, penmanship, etc.

If interaction analysis is to be used to discover whether a teacher's pattern of influence in planning work with students is different, for example, from his influence pattern while supervising work already planned, then even finer discriminations would be necessary to identify the boundaries of the required time periods. . . .

THE TABULATION OF INTERACTION MATRICES

A trained observer records his data as a series of numbers instead of the hash marks used in early training. For example, the school bell rings and the following interaction occurs. The numbers written down by the observer are indicated in parentheses.

Teacher: "Class! The bell has rung. May I have your attention please! (category 6)

During the next 3 seconds talking and noise diminish. (category 10)

Teacher: "Jimmy, we are all waiting for you." (category 7) Pause.

Teacher: "Now, today we are going to have a very pleasant surprise, (category 5) and I think you will all find it very exciting and interesting. (category 1)

Have any of you heard anything about what we are going to do? (category 4)

Pupil: "I think we are going on a trip in the bus that's out in front." (category 8)

Teacher: "Oh! You've found out! How did you learn about our trip?" (category 4) Etc.

By now the observer has written down 6, 10, 7, 5, 1, 4, 8, and 4. As the interaction proceeds, the observer will continue to write down numbers. To tabulate these observations in a 10×10 matrix, the first step is to make sure that the entire series begins and ends with the same number. The convention we use is to add a 10 to the beginning and end of the series, unless the 10 is already present. Our series now becomes 10, 6, 10, 7, 5, 1, 4, 8, 4, and 10. This procedure is followed in order to produce a finished matrix in which the sum of column 1 equals the sum of row 1, the sum of column 2 equals the sum of row 2, in short, so that the sums of the columns and rows are equal, respectively.

The number 10 is used because it will affect the interpretation of teacher influence the least. One of our less sympathetic critics has suggested, however, that this convention is necessary in order to begin and end an observation in confusion!

The numbers are tallied in the matrix one pair at a time. The row is designated by the first number, and the column is designated by the second number. The first pair is 10–6: the talley is placed in the row 10, column 6 cell. The second pair is 6–10: this is tallied in the row 6, column 10 cell. The third pair is 10–7, the fourth pair is 7–5, and so on. Each pair overlaps with the next and the total number of observations, N, always will be tabulated by $N - 1$ tallies in the matrix. In this case we started a series of 10 numbers and the series produced 9 tallies in the matrix. The tabulation is shown in Figure 2-3.

Each matrix should include all of the observations for the elapsed time of a single activity period, or all the numbers between a double line.

For example, 1 hour's observation in a secondary class may yield a separate matrix for each of the following time periods: first, 5 minutes of routine announcements, getting settled down, taking the roll, etc.; second, 15 minutes of going over homework and reviewing the previous day's assignment; third, 15 minutes for the introduction of some new material and discussion of this material; fourth, 10 minutes to discuss one student's progress on a special assignment; and fifth, 8 minutes of starting on the next day's homework, with the teacher giving help to individual students.

A total matrix for the 53-minute class may also be desirable. In an elementary school, natural units of activity would also be tabulated in separate matrices. A particular research design may require combining matrices of the same activity for subsequent analyses. . . .

Second

	1	2	3	4	5	6	7	8	9	10	Total
1				/							1
2											0
3											0
4								/		/	2
5	/										1
6										/	1
7					/						1
8				/							1
9											0
10						/	/				2
Total	1	0	0	2	1	1	1	1	0	2	9

First

FIGURE 2–3

SUMMARY OF RESULTS

Before summarizing the results of this project, let us review its three main hypotheses, which were first listed on page 256:

(1) Indirect teacher influence increases learning when a student's perception of the goal is confused and ambiguous.
(2) Direct teacher influence increases learning when a student's perception of the goal is clear and acceptable.
(3) Direct teacher influence restricts learning when a student's perception of the goal is ambiguous.

The significant differences in achievement[3] support the generalization that the teaching methods we have called indirect produce more achievement. Our classification of teachers as indirect is based on an above-average proportion of indirect to direct acts of influence over an extended period of time. This evidence alone does not prove or disprove the three main hypotheses, even though it does have important implications for teaching.

The support of hypotheses 1 and 2 comes from the following reasoning. First, students of teachers who used an above-average proportion of indirect to direct acts of verbal influence learn more. Second, teachers

[3] Flanders' project studied 15 seventh-grade social studies teachers (381 pupils) and 16 eighth-grade mathematics teachers (363 pupils) teaching 2-week units of study. RTH, editor.

with an above-average proportion of indirect influence also show more variability in adapting their influence to different types of classroom activities and to the different stages of learning that exist in a 2-week unit of study. Finally, the adaptations made by these more flexible teachers follow the shifts of teacher influence described in hypotheses 1 and 2.

Hypothesis 1 states that indirect teacher influence increases learning when a student's perception of the goal is ambiguous. We assume that learning goals are ambiguous during the initial stages of a 2-week unit of study. The indirect teachers provided more activities that permitted students to express their own opinions and develop initiative during the beginning stages of the unit. Their verbal influence during these stages was much more indirect than their overall 2-week average, and also much more indirect than the initial and overall averages of direct teachers. This evidence clearly supports hypothesis 3.

Hypothesis 1 states that indirect teacher influence increases learning when a student's perception of the goal is clear and acceptable. As learning progressed, the more flexible, indirect teachers decreased their use of activities that expanded student initiative and increased their use of activities that restricted student initiative. At the same time they made adjustments in their own patterns of teacher influence so that they became more direct, compared only to their own average, as learning progressed. This evidence clearly supports hypothesis 2.

Hypothesis 3 has, in one sense, too much evidence to support it. The students whose teachers employed an above-average proportion of direct influence consistently showed less achievement. These teachers showed less flexibility in adapting their influence to different types of classroom activity and to the different stages of learning in a 2-week unit of study. The evidence concerning direct influence is so consistent that the following modification of hypothesis 3 is justified: direct influence decreases learning, except when goals have initially been clarified and made acceptable by the use of indirect influence.

In planning this project, we anticipated that different types of students would react differently to direct and indirect influence. However, no differences were found in achievement between dependent-prone and independent-prone students. We also found that students classified by IQ scores into the top quartile, middle 50 percent, and bottom quartile did not respond differently to teachers whom we classified as direct or indirect. The one exception to this, which occurred in social studies and which indicated that high-IQ students were more sensitive to differences in direct and indirect influence, was not supported in larger samples. The possibility still exists that different types of students develop different attitudes toward teachers who use different patterns of influence. For example, a preliminary analysis of M.S.A.I.[2] scores, not reported here, indicated a significant sex difference.

Perhaps the conclusion that needs to be emphasized most in this summary is that the students who achieved the most and who had significantly higher scores on our revised classroom attitude instrument were in classes which were exposed to *flexible* patterns of teacher influence. This flexible pattern included periods of predominantly direct influence as well as periods of predominantly indirect influence. This characteristic flexibility was associated with a higher overall i/d average. Our data show that a sustained above-average pattern of direct influence restricts learning and produces less desirable attitudes. It is obvious that as teacher influence deviates from this narrow pattern, the overall i/d must increase. These deviations are what we have called flexibility.

22.   A Case Study in Interaction Analysis Matrix Interpretation

Elaine B. Chapline

Interaction Analysis, developed and expanded by Flanders for the analysis of teacher-pupil verbal interactions within the classroom, has a unique form in which data can be described and interpreted. Summarization of class sessions can be made succinctly through the production of ten by ten matrices. Each cell on the matrix depicts the frequency with which a particular verbal sequence occurred during a session. These matrices may be constructed for a part or for all of a class session. In order to interpret matrix data appropriately, additional information which spells out the purposes of the lesson and the nature of the learning activity are important. These extra-matrix cues serve as a frame of reference within which inferences about teacher influence may be drawn.

A matrix (Figure 2) which can serve as a case study in matrix interpretation was developed from an audio-tape recording of a ninth grade social studies class. This lesson took place during a regular forty-five minute class period and was recorded by the classroom teacher. It was the first lesson on a new area of content, and was a discussion lasting through the class period. The verbal behavior was categorized by a trained observer using Flanders' ten categories.

[2] Minnesota Student Attitude Inventory. RTH, editor.

This article by Elaine B. Chapline of Queens College was written expressly for this book and is published here for the first time. This article relates specifically to the article by Ned A. Flanders.

FIGURE 1

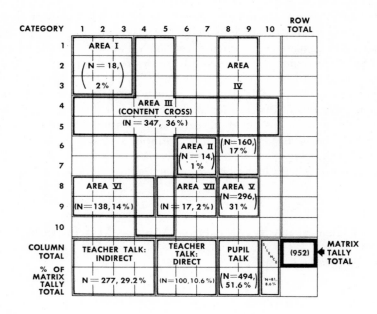

DESCRIPTION

Matrix interpretation initially involves developing an overview of the ways in which matrices can be descriptively summarized and of the nature of specified areas within the matrix. (see Figures 1 and 2).

Category totals, matrix tally total (i.e., total of sequential pairs entered on the matrix, N = 952) and the percentage of each of the ten categories are figured initially. Since the totals in columns and rows for each category should coincide, the accuracy with which the matrix has been produced can be checked. Next, percentage of teacher talk (i.e., categories $1 + 2 + 3 + 4 + 5 + 6 + 7$) and pupil talk (i.e., categories $8 + 9$) and of category 10 are calculated. The percentages of teacher talk which reflect indirect influence $(1 + 2 + 3 + 4)$ and direct influence $(5 + 6 + 7)$ are then spelled out separately. The I/D ratio (categories $1 + 2 + 3 + 4$ divided by categories $5 + 6 + 7$) provides a gross indication of the nature of a teacher's influence. The i/d ratio, as developed by Flanders, is calculated by dividing categories $1 + 2 + 3$ by $6 + 7$. It serves to focus on teacher influence without the presence of the categories which are most content laden (i.e., categories 4 and 5). Steady state cells occur on the diagonal across a matrix. These reflect the degree to which a specific verbal act was maintained for longer than three seconds. They

FIGURE 2

CATEGORY	1	2	3	4	5	6	7	8	9	10	ROW TOTAL	
1					1						1	
2		4	8	27	3	3		27	21	4	97	
3		1	5	16	14				7	1	44	
4		1	2	26	8	1		65	21	11	135	
5			5	18	27	2		3	14	9	78	
6			1	3	1	14		1		1	21	
7								1			1	
8		48	10	14	5		1	109	15	4	214	
9		40	11	15	10	1		2	170	31	280	
10	1	3	2	16	9			6	32	12	81	
COLUMN TOTAL	1	97	44	135	78	21	1	214	280	81	952	◄ MATRIX TALLY TOTAL
% OF MATRIX TALLY TOTAL	.1	10.2	4.6	14.3	8.3	2.2	.1	22.7	28.9	8.6	100.0	

29.2 Indirect					10.6 Direct			51.6	8.6		
Teacher Talk								Student Talk	Sil–ence		

I/D = 2.76
i/d = 6.43
I/D8,9 = 8.1

are cells 1-1 (i.e., row one, column one), 2-2, 3-3, etc. In the illustrative case, they account for 38% of the tally total.

The matrix areas which portray specific classroom behaviors are identified in Figure 1. Area 1 encompasses the tallies of categories 1–3 used in an extended, sustained fashion, that is, those which continue beyond three seconds. In the illustrative case, Area I accounts for two percent of the total tallies. Area II consists of the tallies of cells 6-6, 6-7, 7-6, and 7-7. These involve extended use of direct influence and account for one percent of the total. Area III has been labeled "content cross" by Flanders. In this case, 36% of the interaction is included in this area which incorporates all the tallies in categories 4 and 5.

Area IV consists of those cells in which student responses followed directly from teacher behaviors. For example, cell 4-8 indicates that a student response followed a teacher question, and cell 6-9 indicates that a student initiation followed a teacher direction. This area aids in understanding how the students entered into the lesson following teacher activity. Area V, 31% in the illustration, describes extended student talk.

The teacher's response to or use of student statements through indirect means is portrayed in Area VI, 14%, while teacher response through direct means is portrayed in Area VII, 2%.

INTERPRETATION

Inferences about the nature of a lesson may be drawn from matrix data through the formulation of hypotheses about what happened during the lesson. These hypotheses should be held tentatively or until they can be confirmed or refuted through the use of additional data.

In the illustrative lesson, information provided by the matrix in Figure 2 lists the tally total (952), percentage of teacher talk (39.8), pupil talk (51.6) and category 10 (8.6), I/D ratio (2.76), and i/d ratio (6.43). These items are helpful in establishing a general description of this lesson. Verbal participation was active and the pace of the lesson was fairly rapid as indicated by the tally total. That is, a large number of category transitions took place, obviously, within three second intervals during forty-five minutes.

Thus far on the basis of the information notes, this lesson may be described as one in which students spoke quite a bit and in which the teacher used a great deal of indirect influence. The nature of this indirect influence comes into focus in the i/d ratio, in which the frequent use of facilitating statements (categories 1-4) and minimal use of controlling statements (categories 5-7) is revealed. The $I/D_{8,9}$ ratio (i.e., categories 1-4 divided by categories 5-7 for rows 8 and 9 only) provides further evidence for this by pointing out the preponderance of the teacher's acceptance of and use of student ideas directly following student talk. Yet the steady state cells suggest that there were opportunities provided for the development and elaboration of ideas during the lesson.

In any matrix analysis, when dealing with the data in the multiple cells, a series of questions about how the lesson was carried out may be raised. For example, how may this lesson have started? What emerges as a frequent pattern of verbal interaction? From where did the ideas (or content) seem to come? How did the teacher seem to respond to student ideas? How did the students seem to respond to the teacher's ideas? What seemed to be the teacher's general role in this lesson?

The "classroom game" typically involves the teacher's taking initiative in starting a lesson. (See selections by Bellack and his associates.) A matrix cue about the beginning of interaction patterns may frequently be found in the teacher's use of categories 4, 5, or 6. The frequency of tallies in any cell in the matrix serves to call attention to the vitality of this particular verbal sequence in a lesson. In this matrix, the frequent use of brief, specific questions is suggested by the heavy loading in cell 4-8. Some questions which were probably broad and which sought responses involving the pupil's own ideas were also used. (see cell 4-9). Pupils also got into the interaction via their direct initiative while the teacher was talking (cell 5-9). These may have been questions raised by the pupils or reactions to what the teacher was saying. The frequent use of encouragement and/or praise (cells 2-8 and 8-2) suggests that the teacher may have been supporting continuation or expansion of pupil talk. This may have taken the form of a brief statement that served to encourage an individual pupil to continue or to elaborate on what he was saying.

The sequence of classroom events in this lesson is suggested by the nature of category 8. (Areas V, VI, VII). In a considerable number of instances, pupil talk continued longer than three seconds. That is, there were answers which involved some extension of ideas and which took longer than three seconds to speak (cell 8-8). There were some instances in which a pupils' answer led to elaborations which were not sought in the original question (cell 8-9).

The teacher's responses to the pupils' statements suggest that she was equally encouraging and accepting of ideas which were directly elicited by her questions and those which pupils initiated themselves. This may be seen by comparing the frequencies in cells 8-2 and 8-3 with 9-2 and 9-3. Also, she responded similarly to pupil responses and pupil initiations with questions and explanations, as seen by comparing cells 8-4 and 8-5 with cells 9-4 and 9-5. The almost complete absence of criticism or directions in response to pupil talk (cells 8-6, 8-7, 9-6, 9-7) suggests that the teacher found ways to use most of the ideas pupils expressed. If a student gave an incorrect response, for example, the teacher appears to have provided correction or clarification through statements other than criticisms. It seems plausible that some corrections could have been made through questioning (cells 8-4 and 9-4), clarification (cells 8-3 and 9-3), or explanation (cells 8-5 and 9-5).

The teacher's explanations and use of lecturing provide an interesting area for examination in this matrix (see column 5). During this lesson, the teacher frequently brought information into the discussion after a pupil's idea was expressed (cells 8-5, 9-5, 3-5). There appears to have been little straight lecturing by the teacher (cell 5-5), but rather a pattern in which the input of information and ideas was carried out by pupils and teacher.

The pupil's reaction seems to have been characterized by responsiveness which the teacher judged as appropriate. The sheer quantity of pupil talk suggests considerable participation in the lesson. The presence of pupil-to-pupil talk (cells 9-10 and 10-9). (These cells are used to denote pupil-to-pupil talk. This is to be distinguished from extended pupil talk which appears in cell 9-9) suggests that pupils were involved in the learning activity and interacting. This inference is based on the high quantity of acceptance and the lack of criticism (Areas VI and VII). Since the precise nature of the students' responsiveness is not identified on Interaction Analysis matrices, there is an alternative hypothesis regarding this teacher's reactions to the students. It may have been that the teacher did not respond with correction or criticism to the students' behavior even though these actions were not focused on the learning activity.

The quantity of category 10 (8.6%) and its meaning in this lesson is of specific interest. Some of the tallies indicate change of pupil speaker (cells 9-10 and 10-9), as noted above. There were instances, however, in which 10's follow questions and explanations. These may have been brief pauses in the sequence. They may also have reflected simultaneous speech in which one category could not be assigned by the observer. If this "bubbling over" of more than one speaker did occur, it was not viewed by the teacher as cause for exercise of control via directions or criticism as shown by the lack of any tallies in cells 10-6 and 10-7. The teacher's most frequent reactions to behavior classified as category 10 were questioning and explaining (10-4 and 10-5). One pattern which may have emerged is: question asked, brief pause, and questions restated or explained.

With the quantity of pupil talk as high as it was, it does not seem plausible that this was a lesson characterized by many silences or pauses. The likelihood seems greater that the 10's reflect some pauses, some transitions of speaker, and some simultaneous verbal activity which the teacher seems to have dealt with as a matter of course. She seems to have accepted the expressions (cells 10-1, 10-2 and 10-3) which were classified as 10's. She may have picked up one speaker's comments and have responded to those on several occasions.

The use of directions and/or the giving of assignments (category 6) was limited as shown by the low percentage of 2.2. About one-third of the directions appear to have grown out of some other verbal behavior, namely, teacher encouraging, questioning, and explaining, and pupil ideas.

SUMMARY

This illustrative lesson is characterized by considerable pupil talk and facilitation of pupil talk by the teacher. The teacher generally appears to have been serving as a question raiser, encourager and clarifier, and information giver. The matrix suggests that pupils were exercising considerable influence on the nature of the lesson. While there seems to have been a fairly rapid pace, there was time taken for expansion of ideas by both teacher and pupils.

The format used for interpreting this illustrative matrix may be applied generally. When skill in matrix interpretation has been developed, a marked feeling for probable specific ingredients of a lesson will result. Additional extra cues from the direct observer and information from the teacher on his objectives and purposes is necessary in order to select among plausible alternative hypotheses. In this way, it is possible to interpret a lesson quite accurately from a matrix.

23.   What Is Teaching? One Viewpoint

Marie M. Hughes

Psychologists, other researchers, and curriculum workers are in agreement that a most important variable in the classroom is that of the teacher.

The teacher behavior in the classroom that is most pervasive and continuous is, of course, the verbal action. The verbal and the nonverbal behavior of teachers is, according to Mary Aschner, "the language of responsible actions designed to influence the behavior of those under instruction" (1).

Indispensable data then for a description and analysis of teaching are verbatim records of what the teacher said and did and the response made by a child or group, including children's initiatory actions directed toward the teacher.

DATA OF THIS STUDY

The data of this study (2) were secured from 41 elementary teachers— 7 men and 34 women. These teachers had classrooms in 19 buildings in 8 school districts.

The representativeness of the group may be judged from the fact they received their training degrees in 22 different states. Their age range was 25 to 50 years; their teaching experience, 5 years to 30 years; with a bimodal distribution at the ninth and fifteenth years. They were career teachers and judged good by supervisory and consultant staff members.

Three 30-minute records were secured from each of the teachers by two observers working at one time in the classroom with the teacher's cooperation and knowledge of the exact time the observers would arrive to take the record. In general, the records were taken several days apart.

A brief episode from one 30-minute record may provide a more adequate picture of the data with which we worked:

Record #2620, page 2:

T.: Carl, do you remember the day you came to school and said you could play a tune on the piano? It was a tune we all knew and so we sang it with you. You found out you could play the same tune on the tone bells. I wonder if you'd play the same tune for us today.

T.: My! We liked to sing with you. Can we start our music time by your playing again and our singing with you? Why don't you play it on the tone bells?

Carl: I'd like to play it on the piano.

T.: Well, all right, you may play it on the piano if you'd rather. Do you want to play it all through once or shall we start right off together?

Carl: I'll play it through. (Played on piano "Mary Had a Little Lamb" with one hand.)

T.: That was very nice!

Carl: I think you could sing with me.

T.: All right, we'd be glad to. (Carl played and children sang.) Thank you, Carl.

Carl: You could even do all of it.

T.: You mean we could sing all of the verses?

Carl: I can even do "followed her to school one day . . . etc."

T.: I'm sure you can, Carl. Thank you very much.

What does the teacher do? It is obvious that there is a wide repertoire of behavior open to the teacher.

The teacher *tells* people what to do.

The teacher *sets* goals, the specifics of attention. "Today, we shall do the 25 problems on page 90."

The teacher *gives* directions. "Take your books out and open them to page 90." "Do not write your name."

The teacher *reprimands*. "Take your seat, Johnny."

The teacher *accuses*. "You didn't work very hard."

The teacher *admonishes*. This is, of course, before anything happens. "Don't forget to close the door." "Make sure you look up your words."

The teacher *supports* and *encourages*. "That's nice." "Good." "Fine." "O.K." "I knew you could do it."

The teacher *grants* or *denies* requests.

The teacher *clarifies* and *elaborates* on the problem or content under discussion.

The teacher *asks* questions.

The teacher *gives* cues.

There are many ways to categorize or organize the verbal behavior and nonverbal behavior of a teacher. It is the point of view of this investigator that the superior-subordinate relationship in the teacher-learner situation, with its culturally bestowed power position over the child, makes it impossible for the teacher to act in the classroom without performing a *function*[1] for some child group, or the entire class as recipients. It is the teacher who holds the power to give aid or withhold aid; to judge and to punish; to gratify or to deny; to accept or to ignore the response of a child.

Actually, children who are not participants in a given episode of interaction with the teacher do respond to his behavior (3, 4).

The presumptuousness of looking at teacher behavior from the standpoint of functions performed for the child is recognized. The 30-minute consecutive record often made it possible to follow actions and reactions through an episode and many times several episodes. In addition, for a four year period there had been consistent effort through interviews and paper and pencil tests to discover children's views of typical classroom situations. To date, responses have been secured from some 1400 fifth and sixth graders in three states (5, 6). Interviews have been held with younger children, and with junior high youths.

As expected, children react in an individual manner; however, there is a great range of intensity of reaction. In general, there is a high degree of emotionality, with children responding to elements in the situations that were not intended or foreseen by adults. Another tentative finding was that for any given teacher behavior, from 7 to 20 percent of those to whom it was directed appeared to make no response. They were not involved or they failed to identify with the situation when given the opportunity in interviews or paper and pencil test. The mode for this noninvolvement was 14 percent. Most of the teachers are, of course, aware of the phenomenon of one or more children seeming not to be "with it."

DESCRIPTION OF TEACHING

Figure 1 presents the mean distribution of teaching acts performed by the teachers during three 30-minute periods of teaching. It is immediately clear that the largest number of teaching acts falls within the category of controlling functions. Figures 2 and 3 present the mean distributions of teaching acts for teachers who are among the highest and those who are among the lowest in the exercise of control in the classroom. Since the present report is devoted largely to an exposition of Controlling Func-

[1] See the addendum to this article for an outline of the functions identified. RTH, editor.

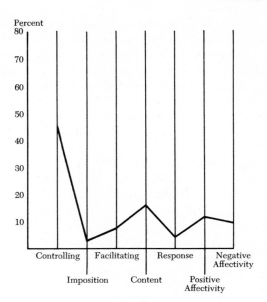

FIGURE 1

Mean Distribution of Teaching Acts for 90 Minutes Observation
for 35 Teachers

tions, and the Development of Content, a brief definition of the other
categories may be useful.

Teacher Imposition: These are acts where the teacher projects himself into
the situation. For example: In a few classrooms without routine procedures for
supplies, the teacher might say over and over again, "Keep your seat, I'll bring
it to you." Another is the expression of evaluation; e.g., on reading a story in a
foreign locale, "Their names are certainly queer." Moralizing is another act that
falls in this category. As may be noted in the figures, very few teaching acts
fall in this category.

Facilitating: These acts may be thought of as management functions that are
relatively neutral. All statements that designate time, change of schedule and
so forth. Those information seeking acts that are nonevaluative; that is, the
child is free to have or not have it, e.g.: "Who brought lunch money?" Rhetorical questions of "Wasn't that fun?" "Did you enjoy it?" "We're finished, aren't
we?" Such questions, if they evoke a response, secure a chorus of "yes" or "no"
as expected. More often than not the teacher does not wait for an answer.

These management functions differentiate least among teachers and
are the most stable with a teacher's series of records.

Personal Response includes meeting the individual requests of children,
listening to their personal interests and experiences unrelated to the content
under consideration.

These are all positive responses and most often are interactions between a teacher and a single child.

Positive and Negative Functions need little comment since they are the praise and reproof categories. It is realized that the use of positive and negative reinforcement controls behavior; however, by their very nature these teaching acts are, as a group, more affectively-laden. Therefore, it was deemed desirable to trace them out separately.

Although space does not permit an elaboration of these last three categories, it is hypothesized that they have much to do with the personal liking or not liking of the teacher. There is something in a personal response that conveys the idea, "You count—you are important enough for me to listen to you, and to do something just for you."

Approval and acceptance were expressed most often in a stereotyped manner: "Fine," "Yes," "O.K.," "Good," "All right." Such expressions without a definite referent served the purpose of allaying tension. It was one way of saying "All is well."

It is hypothesized that the acceptance of reprimands of any degree of intensity depends to a large extent on the teacher's use of *public criteria*. If he makes clear the elements in the situation that call for certain required behavior, children may protest, but they can accept the reprimand as just. Consistency of teacher behavior is another element in fairness.

In general, more acts of positive affectivity were recorded for teachers than of negative affectivity; however, Figure 2 depicting teachers high in control, shows two teachers who were more negative than positive in their teaching. The gross differences in distribution of teaching acts shown in Figures 2 and 3 suggest that the classroom is quite different for the children in attendance.

Controlling Functions

Our study showed that the teaching acts most frequently performed were those of control. By control, reference is not limited to discipline. Since these teachers were considered good teachers, their classes were well organized and generally attentive. By control is meant goal setting, directing the children to the precise thing to which they give attention. Not only is the content named for children, but they are held to a specific answer and processes of working. Such control is firm and pervasive. In many classrooms the control might be considered implacable. Sixty-eight percent of the teachers had one or more of their records with 50 percent or more of their teaching acts categorized as controlling. The teacher most often wanted only one answer and refused all others. For example, a third

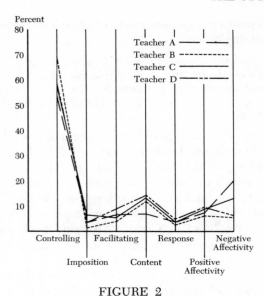

FIGURE 2

Distribution Patterns of Teaching Acts for 4 Teachers High in Controlling

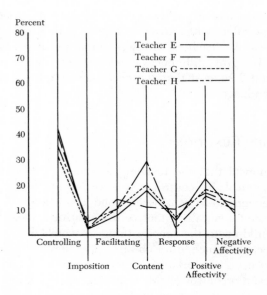

FIGURE 3

Distribution Patterns of Teaching Acts for 4 Teachers Low in Controlling

grade was reporting on books read, then classifying them according to theme. One little girl made a few remarks about her book and then said, "It's a fantasy." The teacher immediately replied, "You mean imaginative, don't you?" No reward for the use of a divergent word or a suggestion of any relationship or differentiation between the two.

The control of content is exercised by the teacher in the structure of the *what* to give attention to. In a third grade arithmetic class each child had a foot rule. The teacher structured the group by saying, "Today, we are going to study the middle line. What is it called?" Several children answered, "One-third," "a fourth," "a half." One boy was busy measuring some paper on his desk and said, "This is 6¼ inches." (Correct) The teacher replied, "Just the middle line today. We just talk about the half."

As long as the question or statement that structures the class or the individual requires but *one* answer, the teacher is in absolute control. Nothing more may properly occur until the next question is asked. Such structure of content appears to evoke memory but little more in mental activity.

When structure is open, more than one answer is possible. Indeed, there may not be an absolutely right answer. For example, "What might happen if the new highway went across the state by one route instead of another?" Closed structure of content resulted in question and answer between teacher and class—it was strictly recitation. Open structure, with more than one answer possible, resulted in participation of several pupils before re-entry of the teacher in the situation. In other words, more ideas were generated and more pupils became involved in the work.

CONTROL AS REGULATION OF WHO

Another phase of controlling behavior is that of regulating who will do what; answer questions, give the report, take lunch money to the office, etc. Such regulation can serve indirectly as punishment or as reward.

"Your work is finished, so you take the books to Mrs. Jones." At least a criterion of choice, "your work is done," is made public. In one episode the children were sharing their stories with one another and the teacher regulated after each story with, "Whom shall I choose, whom shall I ask to go next?" A child would then be named. As teacher choices followed one another, the excitement mounted over who was to be next and not over the content of the stories.

Other teachers set up some *neutral* manner of regulating. "Write your names on the board when you are ready and we shall take them in order." Another teacher had children put a slip on a spindle. Their stories were then read in order of completion. Some teachers made charts of committees who worked at the various housekeeping and management chores a week at a time.

We found in one sixth grade that the students considered the teacher unfair. He was perplexed, so we tried to find out why this perception. It turned out that Lou and Hazel always got to answer the telephone. They sat next to the office and could answer without moving about unduly. This fact had not been shared with the children; consequently, all they saw was unfairness.

The use of *Public Criteria* for the controlling actions of the teacher is suggestive. It ameliorates the power of the teacher. It gives the authority an impersonal embodiment.

CONTROL OVER MANY ACTIVITIES

The controls exercised are expressed in all kinds of activities. It was difficult to get hold of the criteria used by teachers in their expression of control.

A child was making cut-out paper pears to be placed in a cornucopia poster filled with fruits and vegetables. The teacher said, "Why don't you make them bigger?"

Child: I made them like they are on my grandfather's farm.
T.: Get the picture from my desk and make them big like that.

The teacher judged in cases of altercation or conflict of interest. Incidentally, the conflict of interest was frequently between teacher and child or group. To illustrate, a teacher said:

T.: Who do you wish to have help you with your reading?
Child: Madeline.
T.: How about Susan?
Child: Jane.
T.: Let's see. Mary would be a good one. Yes, go sit with Mary.

A junior high school teacher working with the English class putting out a paper said:

T.: Here are some interesting things about the Navy that we could put in the paper. Who wants to write it?
Agnes: I will. I read it and thought the boys might like it.
T.: No, you already have three things in. I'll write it myself.

We hypothesize that consistent use of *Public Criteria* might aid in reducing the conflicts with authority. *Public Criteria* are situationally placed:

T.: There is time for *one* story before noon.

T.: We had trouble with a certain kind of problem yesterday; therefore, we will work on similar problems today.

T.: The children using the saws are on the barn committee and must have them until they finish; therefore, you have to wait.

Public Criteria can also express the conventions and accepted ways of doing. "You have too many erasures on your paper to read it easily," instead of "I won't take a paper that looks like that."

PLACE OF CONTROLLING FUNCTIONS

This investigator believes that it is the business of the teacher to manage (control, if you prefer) the classroom so that learning for all the children present may proceed. Controlling functions will undoubtedly constitute between 30 and 40 percent of a teacher's behavior; however, the power component may be ameliorated through the use of:

Open-structure that permits some choice or requires more than one answer.

Increased Regulation (*who* is to respond) that is neutral or done with public criteria that expresses the reason for the choice.

Directions that are clear with limits so to reduce repetition of directions and lessen the number of reprimands.

Rules that are group developed, situationally oriented, and enforceable. They should make sense to children.

DEVELOPMENT OF CONTENT

There is a relationship between the development of content and the nature of the control exercised by structure. When the structure permits no exploration on the part of children it serves to delimit and restrict.

A primary class was reading about a baby elephant. They discussed its age and other things pertaining to the picture of the baby elephant. Finally Ben spoke up and said:

Ben: Look, here is an elephant with a tusk.

T.: Yes, that elephant is on the other page. Read this page and find out what Baby Elephant did when she got to the monkey cage.

It might have been profitable to raise the question why one elephant had tusks and the other did not. It can be hypothesized that the mental processes evoked by the different situations are likewise different.

In another class the teacher and class were looking at a large map of the two hemispheres, when one child asked where the local town was.

The teacher replied, "It is about here, but can't be seen on this map. I'll get you one and you can find it and other towns you know."

The teaching acts that develop content elaborate and add to the content or problem under consideration. Response is made to the data placed in the situation by the children. It is believed that children involved in content have something to say. They are encouraged in this by the teacher who respects their efforts. The teacher *stimulates* by offering several suggestions of ideas or of activities that might be done. The choice of doing, however, remains with the child. (It is, of course, proper to give a direction or an assignment, which then would be an act of control.)

Evaluation that keeps content as a referent is in this category. To illustrate, "You have used several kinds of sentence structure in your composition. Very good." The phrase, "That's good," spoken after a child has read the composition does not tell him whether he was good to have written it at all, or good to have read it, or just good to have gotten through the episode. In terms of compositions, he has received nothing definite that helps him move ahead with his writing. He has received teacher approval. With most of the evaluation made in the form of generalized approval or disapproval, such expressions foster dependence on teacher instead of judgment and interest in the content.

If children and youth are to become interested in subject matter for its own sake, do they not need to link their own experience and make their own personal inquiry in relationship to it? If children are not listened to, how can one know what concepts are developed or what interpretations are made?

An upper grade discussion had been going on concerning early California Indians.

T.: Incidentally, did the California Indians have a pretty easy life?
Arthur: No.
T.: Yes they did, Arthur. Don't you remember? Who can tell me about it?

What logic was Arthur using in his reply? Was it strictly subjective, "I wouldn't have liked it," or had he assessed the situation with some judgment?

When do children use a variety of mental processes such as making comparisons, explaining with some logic, noting relationships, generalizing from a series of data? What kind of questions and teacher responses evoke what mental activity (7)?

Perhaps teachers need to develop what might be called *creative use of interruptions.*

Not long ago a mother reported the disgust of her kindergarten son whose teacher allegedly told him that he couldn't talk about dinosaurs until third grade. The child had been to the Dinosaur Monument and Museum with his family. While there, the father had bought each boy a book which had been read at home.

One can conjecture all kinds of reasons why the teacher did not wish to get off on dinosaurs. However, the question remains, "In what situations do teachers act in ways that children can see them as people who *aid* in their personal quest for knowing? Since this child's dinosaurs were tied to Vernal, Utah, it might have been very stimulating to listen to his story and also mention the Berea Tar Pits within the city of Los Angeles, as another locale where bones had been found.

It is, of course, possible that the child wanted attention only. Even so, the school can meet such personal needs of children through the use of their explorations and inquiries in the development of content. It is suggested that children's questions and remarks be integrated with the lesson plan of the teacher.

The present study of teaching found that the most prevalent series of teaching acts were in question-answer test or recitation situations. Far too many such situations were spent in working for the specific answer wanted by the teacher.

Of the total group of 41, only 3 teachers had all of their records with 20 or more of their teaching acts in this category of development of content. Seventy-four percent of all records had 20 percent or less of teaching acts falling in this category of exploration, amplification, utilization of children's questions and remarks, evaluation and stimulation. This category has been described as working with the content or problem and called *development of content*.

Some relationships of one category to another may be of interest. Development of Content and Negative Affectivity correlate —.42 significant at the .001 level in social studies. This relationship is not unexpected, since teachers who use many acts of Negative Affectivity are not responsive to children's ideas and explorations even in subject matter.

Personal Response is correlated —.35 with Controlling and a —.38 with Negative Affectivity. Again, this is not unexpected and it holds for all records regardless of kind of work the classes were doing.

The point of view expressed in this report is that teaching may be described in terms of functions the teacher behavior, verbal and nonverbal, performs for the child, group or class to whom it is directed. It was found possible to categorize such teaching acts in seven categories: Controlling, Imposition, Facilitating, Development of Content, Personal Response, Positive Affectivity, and Negative Affectivity.

Control of the class was exercised in varied activities, but particularly in terms of *what* to give attention to and *who* was to do what; also, the how of doing was prescribed and enforced.

Management of the classroom for learning is the teacher's job; therefore control functions are necessary. It was suggested, however, that the power component the teacher holds may be reduced with changes in verbal behavior.

In dealing with subject matter, little attention was given to children's exploratory remarks or their questions. The questions teachers used for structure were usually closed; that is, asked for one *right* answer. It was suggested that one right answer evoked the use of recall as a mental process instead of stimulating a larger range of mental activity.

It was suggested that *responsiveness* on the part of the teacher to children's remarks, questions, personal experience (data they place in the situation), would lead them to greater involvement in content (subject matter) and stimulate use of higher mental processes.

Teachers demonstrated different patterns in teaching. Different patterns do affect the learning of children (8, 9).

REFERENCES

1. ASCHNER, MARY JANE. "The Language of Teaching." In: *Language and Concepts in Education,* Edited by O. Smith and R. Ennis. Chicago: Rand McNally Co., 1961. 124 p.
2. HUGHES, MARIE M. and Associates. *The Assessment of the Quality of Teaching: A Research Report.* U. S. Office of Education Cooperative Research Project No. 353. Salt Lake City: The University of Utah, 1959.
3. KOUNIN, J. and P. GUMP. "The Ripple Effect in Discipline." *The Elementary School Journal,* Fall 1958, p. 158-62.
4. KOUNIN, J., *et al.* "Explorations in Classroom Management." *Journal of Teacher Education,* June 1961, p. 235-46.
5. CARIN, ARTHUR. "Children's Perceptions of Selected Classroom Situations." Doctoral Dissertation, University of Utah. June 1959.
6. DE VANEY, ELENA. "Perceptions Among Teachers and Students of Varying Cultural Backgrounds." Doctoral Dissertation, University of Utah. October 1960.
7. ASCHNER, M. J. McCUE. "Asking Questions to Trigger Thinking." *NEA Journal,* September 1961, p. 44-46.
8. FLANDERS, NED. *Teacher Influence: An Interaction Analysis.* U. S. Office of Education Cooperative Research Project No. 397. Minneapolis: University of Minnesota, 1960.
9. SEARS, PAULINE. "What Happens to Pupils Within the Classroom of Elementary Schools." Paper read at American Educational Research Association meeting, Los Angeles, June 30, 1960.

ADDENDUM: THE UNIVERSITY OF UTAH REVISION OF THE
PROVO CODE FOR THE ANALYSIS OF TEACHING

All of the teaching functions that form the *Code for the Analysis of Teaching* have been identified from actual records of teaching. The *University Revision* added several functions to the original Provo Code and reorganized the larger categories to include the two categories of Imposition of Teacher and Functions of Personal Responsiveness.

The University Revision of the Provo Code for the Analysis of Teaching contains thirty-three functions that teachers perform in the classroom in interaction with children. These thirty-three functions have subscripts that describe the manner in which the functions are performed. We have retained this rather cumbersome but very useful Code so that the description of teaching might be as complete as possible. The Outline of the Code on the following pages includes the subscripts used.

These thirty-three functions are subsumed under seven large categories. . . .

Outline of The

UNIVERSITY OF UTAH REVISION OF THE PROVO CODE

For The Analysis of Teaching

CONTROLLING FUNCTIONS

Structure
  open
  closed
  intervention
  sequential
  orientation
  ongoing
    public criteria

Regulate
  open
  closed
  global
  routine
  neutral
  sequential
  direction
    public criteria

Standard Set
  recall
  teacher edict
  group developed
  universal

Judge
  direction
  punish
  turn back
  just

Reprinted with permission from *The Assessment of the Quality of Teaching in Elementary School: A Research Report* by Marie M. Hughes and Associates. U.S. Department of Health, Education, and Welfare, Office of Education, Cooperative Research Project No. 353. Salt Lake City, University of Utah, 1959.

IMPOSITION OF TEACHER

Regulate Self   Inform Appraisal
Moralize   Inform
Teacher Estimate of Need

FACILITATING FUNCTIONS

Checking   Demonstrate
  information   Clarify Procedure
  routine
  involvement

FUNCTIONS THAT DEVELOP CONTENT

Resource   Clarify
  routine   just
  child initiative   content
                                               generalize
Stimulate   summarize
  one   Evaluate
  three   just
Structure, turn back   negative
                                               positive
Content-Agree   with discrimination

FUNCTIONS THAT SERVE AS RESPONSE

Meets request   Interprets
  routine   situation
  makes arrangements   feelings
Clarify Personal   Acknowledges Teacher
  problem   Mistake
  experience

FUNCTIONS OF POSITIVE AFFECTIVITY

Support   Solicitous
  just
  stereotype   Encourage
  specific
                                             Does For Personal

FUNCTIONS OF NEGATIVE AFFECTIVITY

Admonish   Negative Response Personal
                                               public criteria
Reprimand
  public criteria   Verbal Futuristics
                                               public criteria
Accusative

Threat   Ignore

24. A Procedure for Assessing the Classroom Behavior of Students and Teachers[*]

Hugh V. Perkins

INTRODUCTION

The behavior of students and teachers in the classroom has been a focus of research for over two decades. A persistent methodological problem has been how to obtain reliable objective data on behavioral variables. The need for more refined instruments to measure these variables, the growing interest in pupil and teacher behavior in natural settings, and the specific requirements of a planned research project on under-achievement led to the development of the procedure reported here. . . .

The purpose of the present study was to develop a procedure based on reliable and valid instruments for measuring student-behavior, learning-activity, teacher-behavior, and teacher-role variables presumed to be related to differential achievement.

DEVELOPMENT OF INSTRUMENTS

Two instruments were developed: one entitled *Student Categories* and the other, *Teacher Categories*. The categories making up these instruments are listed and defined in Table 1.

The first nine student categories cover behavior and evolved as a refinement and an expansion of a set of six such categories reported by Kowatrakul (1959) and Sears (1963). The remaining six student categories cover learning activity.

The first ten teacher categories were based on the seven teacher-behavior categories used by Flanders (1960a) in analyzing classroom interaction. In research studies using the Bales-Gerbrands (1948) interaction recorder, Lamb (1962) and McKinstry (1962) identified nine teacher-role categories. These nine categories were combined and refined into the five teacher roles listed in Table 1.

Reprinted with permission from American Educational Research Journal, Volume 1, Number 4, pp. 249-260, November 1964.

[*] This research was supported by Public Health Grant MH 07344-01 and by the General Research Board and the Computer Science Center of the University of Maryland. The author gratefully acknowledges the contributions made to this study by Richard M. Brandt, Arianna Claypool, Angus McDonald, Jr., and Johanna C. Van Looy.

TABLE 1

Student Categories		Teacher Categories
LISWAT	Interested in ongoing work: listening and watching—passive.	1. Does not accept student's idea, corrects it: rejection or correction of student's response.
REWR	Reading or Writing; working in assigned area—active.	2. Praises or encourages student or behavior: enthusiastic acceptance of student's response.
HIAC	High activity or involvement: reciting or using large muscles—positive feeling.	2A. Listens to, helps, supports, nurtures student: accepting, helping response; also listening to recitation.
WOA	Intent on work in another curricular area: school activity not assigned to be done right then.	3. Accepts or uses student's answer or idea.
WNA	Intent on work of nonacademic type: preparing for work assignment, cleaning out desk, etc.	4. Asks questions about content (what? where? when?): wants to find out whether student knows and understands material.
SWP	Social, work-oriented—PEER: discussing some aspect of schoolwork with classmate.	4A. Asks questions that stimulate thinking (why? how?): encourages student to seek explanations, to reason, to solve problems.
SWT	Social, work-oriented—TEACHER: discussing some phase of work with teacher.	5. Lectures, gives facts or opinions about content: gives information in discussion, recitation, or committee meeting.
SF	Social, friendly: talking to peer on subject unrelated to schoolwork.	6. Gives directions, commands, or orders with which student is expected to comply.
WDL	Withdrawal: detached, out of contact with people, ideas, classroom situation; day-dreaming.	7. Criticizes or justifies authority: disapproves of conduct or work of student or group of students.
		10. Is not participating in class activities: is giving test or is out of room—class silent or in confusion.
DISC	Large-group discussion: entire class discusses an issue or evaluates an oral report.	LDR Leader-director—teacher initiative—active: conducts recitation or discussion, lectures, works with small groups.
REC	Class recitation: teacher questions, student answers —entire class or portion of it participating.	RES Resource person—student-centered, lesser role than leader: helps group or committee, brings material, suggests.
IND	Individual work or project: student is working alone on task that is not a common assignment.	SUPV Supervisor—teacher initia-

TABLE 1 (continued)

Student Categories		Teacher Categories
SEAT	Seat work, reading or writing, common assignment.	tive, passive, role during seatwork: circulates to observe and help.
GRP	Small-group or committee work: student is part of group or committee working on assignment.	SOC Socialization agent: points to and reinforces social expectancies and rules; criticizes behavior.
REP	Oral reports—individual or group: student is orally reporting on book, current events, or research.	EVL Evaluator: listens and gives mark for oral report individual or group; asks, "How many did you get right?"

COLLECTION OF DATA

Two-minute samples of the classroom behavior and learning activities of individual underachieving and achieving fifth-grade pupils were categorized during weekly observations in one or more of four academic subjects: language arts, arithmetic, social studies, and science. Efficient and objective categorization of 5 to 15 behaviors per minute was possible by using a Bales-Gerbrands (1948) recorder, an electrically powered machine that moves tape (paper on which categorizations are recorded) at a constant speed, thereby enabling the duration of each behavioral response to be accurately measured.

At the same time that pupil behavior was being observed and categorized, a second trained observer, using another Bales-Gerbrands recorder, was categorizing the teacher's behavior and role in successive two-minute samples. The 72 pupils in the sample and their teachers were observed by two-member observer teams in 2,410 two-minute samples totaling 80 hours extending over five months—January to June 1963.

RELIABILITY AND VALIDITY

The interobserver reliability of the four observers in the study was estimated by the following procedure. Each observer was paired successively with every other observer; each pair then participated in training sessions in which both members of the pair observed and categorized first a pupil's behavior and later the teacher's behavior and role. The number of seconds that one member of a pair recorded behavior (or activity or role) in a specific category was correlated with the number of seconds that the other member recorded in the same category while simultaneously observing the same pupil or teacher.

For the *Student Categories,* product-moment coefficients for the various pairings of observers ranged from .88 to .99 for five 2-minute samples, with a mean of .97 (obtained by means of Fisher's z transformation). For the *Teacher Categories,* the coefficients, again for five 2-minute samples, ranged from .83 to .98, with a mean of .94. . . .

FINDINGS

Since the total amount of observation time varied somewhat for different pupils and different teachers, the total amount of time for each category, pupil, teacher, and school subject was viewed as part of the whole and changed to percentages to achieve comparability. The behavior of underachievers and achievers in each of the 14 classrooms is reported in percentages by category and classroom in Table 3.

TABLE 3

PERCENTAGE OF TIME RECORDED IN EACH BEHAVIOR CATEGORY FOR UNDERACHIEVERS (U)
AND ACHIEVERS (A)*, BY CLASSROOMS; AND PERCENTAGE OF TIME SPENT IN
EACH LEARNING ACTIVITY FOR EACH CLASSROOM

Class-room		Student Behavior†									Learning Activity†					
		LSWAT	REWR	HIAC	WOA	WNA	SWP	SWT	SF	WDL	DSCN	REC	IND	SEAT	GRP	REP
A	U	20.0	32.4	14.0	2.3	9.5	6.7	5.1	1.1	8.9	0	33.6	22.4	32.2	5.7	6.4
	A	26.6	37.5	11.2	.8	9.3	7.1	2.0	1.8	3.7						
B	U	22.6	47.3	11.1	3.5	5.9	2.1	.5	1.0	6.0	0	35.8	6.9	53.5	.8	3.0
	A	19.2	46.4	12.4	6.8	4.9	.3	.6	.5	8.7						
C	U	27.6	34.2	9.2	5.9	5.1	2.6	1.1	4.5	9.8	4.2	23.8	9.9	58.2	4.0	0
	A	37.8	30.5	5.7	3.7	7.8	1.7	2.0	5.1	5.6						
D	U	32.5	18.3	6.3	19.0	7.2	.9	.7	3.6	11.7	13.5	36.2	1.4	28.6	1.9	18.3
	A	43.1	22.4	4.1	5.1	4.6	2.8	.7	3.9	13.3						
E	U	33.3	25.7	2.1	4.1	12.1	1.8	0	5.8	15.0	3.1	27.7	3.9	55.0	10.3	0
	A	33.4	33.2	3.1	3.9	6.4	2.3	1.4	5.0	11.6						
F	U	27.0	26.4	2.5	5.2	9.9	.9	.9	9.0	14.2	4.1	25.8	12.1	39.1	18.0	1.0
	A	27.1	24.9	4.2	12.3	4.0	8.8	2.0	6.9	9.7						
G	U	45.4	39.7	2.5	.2	3.3	1.5	.6	.4	6.4	0	46.0	0	49.4	4.6	0
	A	59.2	30.1	2.8	0	2.4	.6	.5	.4	4.0						
H	U	38.6	25.5	5.1	7.5	2.8	.7	5.3	5.3	9.1	17.5	43.1	14.0	17.2	8.1	0
	A	45.1	21.5	8.2	2.9	5.6	5.1	3.2	4.0	4.4						
I	U	17.3	33.4	5.2	10.8	7.2	1.3	1.3	5.1	18.4	0	62.1	0	28.8	.9	8.7
	A	26.9	34.5	6.8	4.0	5.1	4.5	.6	3.3	14.4						
J	U	29.6	25.7	12.0	5.6	5.8	4.8	1.6	4.4	10.3	8.6	13.8	.9	49.9	10.5	16.2
	A	26.6	22.8	13.0	2.7	4.3	9.7	3.7	6.3	10.9						
K	U	46.7	12.7	6.7	.6	3.9	5.7	3.0	10.4	10.5	24.7	41.4	4.1	22.5	5.5	1.7
	A	39.7	16.1	7.5	5.0	4.5	3.8	1.3	10.2	11.8						
L	U	35.1	32.0	8.0	.1	10.2	3.7	2.3	2.6	5.9	1.0	24.6	16.7	48.2	5.7	3.8
	A	28.6	41.0	6.6	.2	9.4	5.3	2.1	1.5	5.4						
M	U	31.8	31.9	8.8	.2	7.8	3.1	2.8	3.3	10.2	1.5	35.6	10.2	33.1	10.5	9.1
	A	32.0	35.2	6.7	3.1	6.4	6.2	1.4	2.6	6.3						
O	U	19.4	28.8	13.0	1.6	9.1	9.6	1.9	6.2	10.5	.3	22.1	10.0	57.6	8.8	1.2
	A	15.6	34.7	2.2	2.1	6.9	14.6	3.6	13.7	6.5						
X̄	U	30.5	29.6	7.6	4.8	6.8	3.9	1.9	4.5	10.5	5.5	33.7	8.0	40.9	6.8	5.0
	A	32.9	30.8	6.8	3.8	5.8	5.2	1.8	4.7	8.3						
S	U	9.1	8.5	4.0	5.2	2.8	3.1	1.6	2.9	3.5	7.8	12.2	6.8	13.9	4.7	6.1
	A	11.3	8.4	3.5	3.2	2.0	3.9	1.1	3.7	3.6						

* All pupils were in the fifth grade.
† See Table 1, left-hand column, for description of categories.

These data show that for approximately 75 per cent of the time the behavior of both underachievers and achievers was academic-work-oriented: listening and watching, reading or writing, high activity, or work with peers. A general pattern of pupil behavior in learning situations is discernible, but within this general pattern marked differences can be noted between and within classrooms. Mean differences between underachievers and achievers were significant for only two of the nine behavior categories: achievers engaged in significantly more social work with peers; and underachievers more frequently withdrew from the learning activity. . . .

The great variability of percentages for each category of learning activity in Table 3 and each category of teacher behavior and role in Table 4 shows clearly the uniqueness of each classroom as a learning environment. The extensive use of recitation and seat work (75 per cent of the time) and the infrequent use of discussion, individual work, group work, and oral reports are particularly evident in Table 3. In Table 4, the

TABLE 4

PERCENTAGE OF TIME RECORDED IN EACH BEHAVIOR AND
ROLE CATEGORY FOR 14 FIFTH-GRADE TEACHERS

Teacher	Behavior Category*										Role Category*				
	1	2	2A	3	4	4A	5	6	7	10	LDR	RES	SUPV	SOC	EVL
A	.7	.1	35.2	2.3	12.8	.7	14.1	12.4	1.5	20.2	45.1	0	43.3	.8	10.9
B	.3	.3	35.8	.9	15.3	0	6.8	10.4	.7	29.4	41.9	.6	54.2	.9	2.5
C	.6	.4	13.3	1.8	6.7	1.5	23.8	6.8	4.1	41.1	31.3	.4	57.7	3.3	7.2
D	.1	.5	46.5	5.4	7.4	.5	13.5	7.3	1.6	17.1	50.2	12.6	33.2	1.3	2.7
E	.1	6.5	29.0	5.0	6.4	1.0	14.9	3.7	2.4	30.9	57.5	0	38.4	1.6	2.4
F	.2	0	15.0	3.4	5.0	2.2	7.2	8.0	3.9	55.0	35.9	7.4	49.0	2.8	4.9
G	.6	.4	29.0	6.7	21.1	3.1	17.8	13.4	.8	7.3	64.5	0	33.9	.6	1.0
H	1.9	1.2	51.2	7.7	9.4	1.4	15.4	4.5	1.6	5.7	61.8	25.2	11.6	1.4	0
I	.4	0	19.5	1.9	16.4	.4	29.8	10.7	14.5	6.4	71.4	.2	16.0	12.3	.1
J	.2	.5	33.9	3.1	4.8	.4	17.9	4.2	1.3	33.9	42.2	6.4	48.4	1.0	1.9
K	.8	.5	28.4	6.6	14.0	3.2	20.1	8.6	3.1	14.6	66.2	.9	23.9	2.6	6.4
L	.4	1.3	52.4	3.1	16.5	.3	7.6	6.0	3.9	8.6	31.6	18.1	42.1	4.1	4.0
M	.3	1.0	57.2	4.8	9.9	.2	17.0	4.5	.8	4.3	63.0	9.6	21.5	.8	5.1
O	0	0	45.7	.7	7.5	.8	19.3	10.3	2.1	13.6	42.4	4.4	48.3	2.6	2.3
$\bar{X}$	.5	.9	35.2	3.8	10.9	1.1	16.1	2.9	3.0	20.6	50.4	6.1	37.3	2.6	3.7
S	.5	1.7	14.0	2.2	5.1	1.0	6.4	3.2	3.5	15.4	13.6	7.9	14.5	3.0	3.0

* See Table 1, right-hand column, for description of categories.

large percentages of listening-helping behavior shown for nearly all teachers would appear to be important in the facilitation of learning. In contrast, the low incidence of praise (1 per cent), asking 'thinking' questions (1 per cent), and using pupil's answer or idea (4 per cent) reveals that other important ways of assisting children to learn were rarely used. The almost exclusive use of the leader and the supervisor roles (88 per cent) by these teachers parallels the high incidence of recitation and seat work noted above. These findings raise the question whether greater variation and flexibility in types of learning activity and teacher role would stimulate learner curiosity and hence lead to increased learning.

The data in Tables 3 and 4 show that the instruments developed in this study do discriminate between underachieving and achieving pupils and between different kinds of teachers in terms of behavior, role, and learning situation and thus provide further evidence of the validity of the instruments.

DISCUSSION

How valid or representative is this picture of teacher behavior and classroom interaction as a picture of teachers, or teaching, in general? A partial answer may be found by comparing the results obtained by this set of *Teacher Categories* with those obtained by Hughes (1960) and Flanders (1960b). Although many of the categories of the three instruments are similar, differences in their definition or use by each research worker and dissimilarity among the teacher groups in the three studies clearly indicate that comparisons among the studies will not be wholly valid. The comparisons drawn are of necessity crude and speculative. They are limited to teacher-behavior and teacher-function categories and were made between mean percentages in each category for the total sample of teachers in each study.

Hughes's *Provo Code* (1959) was developed from an analysis of trained observers' written records of 41 elementary teachers' classroom behavior; it consists of seven teacher-function categories: (1) Controlling, (2) Imposition, (3) Facilitation, (4) Content Development, (5) Personal Response, (6) Positive Affectivity, and (7) Negative Affectivity. As stated earlier, Flanders (1960a) has seven teacher-behavior categories: (1) accepts feeling, (2) praises or encourages, (3) accepts or uses ideas of student, (4) asks question, (5) lectures, (6) gives directions, (7) criticizes or justifies authority; two categories of student behavior: (8) student talk—response, (9) student talk—initiation; and (10) silence or confusion. After data for categories 8 and 9 were eliminated, the percentages of total time that behavior was assigned to each of the seven teacher categories were computed for two groups of teachers studied by Flanders (1960b; App., pp. 34-35): 15 seventh-grade social-studies teachers and 16 eighth-grade mathematics teachers. Data from the present study used in these comparisons were the mean percentages (reported in Table 3) for seven of the teacher-behavior categories of 14 fifth-grade teachers.

The bar graph in Figure 1 shows mean percentages of various types of teacher behavior that may reasonably be compared. Although these comparisons may distort some of the categories or findings, it is interesting to note the high degree of similarity of classroom behavior among the

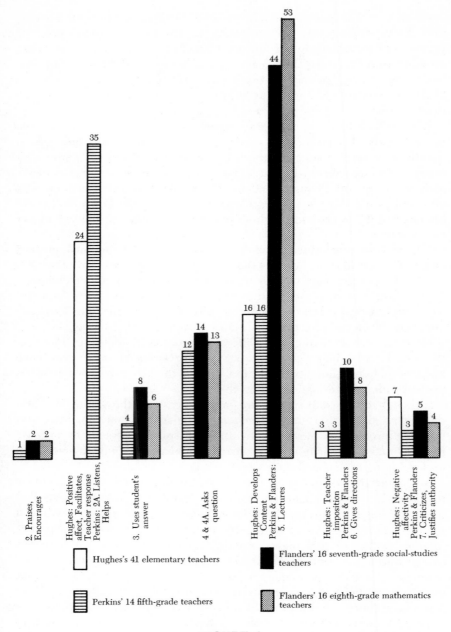

FIGURE 1

Mean Percentages of Teachers' Behavior in Four Studies of Classroom Interaction Grouped into Comparable Categories.

teachers in the three studies. The proportion of time spent by Perkins' fifth-grade teachers was fairly close to, or the same as, that spent by Hughes's elementary teachers in each of the following grouped functions: listening-helping (facilitating learning, etc.); lecturing (developing content); and giving directions (teacher imposition). On the other hand, Hughes's teachers spent twice as large a proportion of time criticizing or reprimanding their pupils.

With regard to those categories common to Flanders' study and the present study, the results were similar for praising or encouraging, asking questions, and criticizing or justifying authority. Flanders' junior-high teachers greatly exceeded Perkins' fifth-grade teachers in using student's idea, lecturing, and giving directions. The similarities between the results obtained by the *Teacher Categories* instrument of this study and those obtained by Flanders and Hughes are further evidence of the validity of this instrument.

Figure 1 reveals rather striking differences between junior-high and elementary teachers in the ways that each group structures and influences the learning experiences in their respective classrooms. Flanders' teachers appear to play a more active role, as evidenced by their more frequent use of the student's ideas, of lecturing, and of giving directions. Hughes's and Perkins' elementary teachers made greater use of listening, helping, supporting, and clarifying. This difference may not be real since Flanders did not have a helping-supporting category as such and may have assigned helping and supporting the student to such categories as using student's idea, lecturing, or giving directions.

Although these comparisons are only suggestive, the similarities and differences that exist among teachers in behavior, function, role, and teaching process, as measured by these instruments, seem to promise further breakthroughs in studying teacher influence and effectiveness and in developing a theory of instruction.

An important advantage of the procedure developed in this study is that it yields data on behavior, role, and learning activity in quantified form. Although certain qualitative and unique aspects may be sacrificed by the categorization process, the objective data that are obtained permit rigorous testing of hypotheses. Another advantage is that simultaneous categorizations of student and teacher behavior on the paper tape of recorders provide a permanent record of teacher-pupil interaction that may be subjected to pattern and sequence analysis.

A disadvantage of the procedure is the large amount of clerical time required to measure the length of each line (in seconds) on the tape and to record the duration of each behavioral response on a tally sheet. This disadvantage could be reduced by more elaborate instrumentation using calibrated tape or punched cards.

References

ANDERSON, HAROLD H.; BREWER, JOSEPH E.; and REED, MARY F. *Studies of Teachers' Classroom Personalities, III.* Applied Psychology Monograph No. 11. Stanford, Calif.: Stanford University Press, 1946. 156 pp.

BALES, ROBERT F., and GERBRANDS, HENRY. "The Interaction Recorder, an Apparatus and Check List for Sequential Content Analysis of Social Interaction." *Human Relations* 1: 456-63; November 1948.

COGAN, MORRIS L. "Research on the Behavior of Teachers: A New Phase." *Journal of Teacher Education* 14:238-43; September 1963.

FLANDERS, NED A. *Interaction Analysis in the Classroom: A Manual for Observers.* Minneapolis: College of Education, University of Minnesota, 1960a. 36 pp.

FLANDERS, NED A. *Teacher Influence, Pupil Attitudes, and Achievement.* Report of Cooperative Research Project No. 397. Washington, D.C.: U. S. Department of Health, Education, and Welfare, Office of Education, 1963. 263 pp. [Minneapolis: University of Minnesota, 1960b. 121+ pp. (Mimeo)]

GALLAGHER, JAMES J. *A System for Classifying Thought Process in the Content of Classroom Verbal Interaction.* Urbana, Ill.: Institute for Research on Exceptional Children, University of Illinois, 1962.

HUGHES, MARIE M. *Development of the Means for the Assessment of the Quality of Teaching in the Elementary Schools.* Report of Cooperative Research Project No. 353. Washington, D. C.: U. S. Department of Health, Education, and Welfare, Office of Education, 1960. 416 pp. [Salt Lake City: University of Utah, 1959. 313+ pp. (Mimeo)]

KOWATRAKUL, SURANG. "Some Behaviors of Elementary School Children Related to Classroom Activities and Subject Areas." *Journal of Educational Psychology* 50: 121-28; June 1959.

LAMB, HOWARD E. *Self and Role Concepts Related to Behavior, Intelligence, and Academic Achievement.* Doctor's thesis. College Park, Md.: University of Maryland, 1962. 166 pp. (Typewritten)

LEACOCK, ELEANOR. "Classroom Processes Study." *Theory and Research in Teaching.* (Edited by Arno A. Bellack.) New York: Bureau of Publications, Teachers College, Columbia University, 1963. pp. 112-17.

LEWIN, KURT; LIPPITT, RONALD; and WHITE, RALPH K. "Patterns of Aggressive Behavior in Experimentally Created 'Social Climates'." *Journal of Social Psychology* 10: 271-99; May 1939.

McKINSTRY, CLARENCE R. *The Behavior of Selected Fifth-Grade Students as Related to Subject Areas and Teacher Roles.* Doctor's thesis. College Park, Md. University of Maryland, 1962. 192 pp. (Typewritten)

MEDLEY, DONALD M. "Experiences With the OScAR Technique." *Journal of Teacher Education* 14: 267-73; September 1963.

SCHUELER, HERBERT; GOLD, MILTON J.; and MITZEL, HAROLD E. *The Use of Television for Improving Teacher Training and for Improving Measures of Student Teaching Performance.* Improvement of Student Teaching, Phase 1. New York: Hunter College, City University of New York, 1962. 127+ pp. (Mimeo)

SEARS, PAULINE S. *The Effect of Classroom Conditions on the Strength of*

Achievement Motive and Work Output of Elementary School Children. Report of Cooperative Research Project No. 873. Washington, D. C.: U. S. Department of Health, Education, and Welfare, Office of Education, 1963. 351 pp.

SPAULDING, ROBERT. "Affective Dimensions of the Creative Processes." Paper presented to the Association for Supervision and Curriculum Development, March 1963.

WITHALL, JOHN G. "The Development of a Technique for the Measurement of Social-Emotional Climate in Classrooms." *Journal of Experimental Education* 17: 347-61; March 1949.

SECTION FIVE

Games

OVERVIEW

IT would be difficult to deny, as we enter the last third of the twentieth century, that games are a significant aspect of American life. Sports captures the attention and devotion of a noteworthy segment of our population. This is best shown by the recent fantastic growth of professional football and basketball, as well as by greatly increased amateur participation in such sports as skiing, surfing, boating, bowling, and golf. Indeed, in some newspapers the sports section is as large as the news section or larger. Many men read the sports section of the newspaper first.

Furthermore, the language of games has become part of our daily vocabulary and thinking. Consider such statements as: "It's your turn to carry the ball." "He couldn't even get to first base." "That's a political football." "He struck out that time." "He's just a pawn in their plan." "He threw in the towel." A recent television detective series was entitled "Checkmate." There are many more such words and phrases, and we probably are not even aware of their origin in games.

It is no wonder, then, that educators have recently used this vantage point of games and sports and play to analyze teaching.[1] Since everyone knows about games, it is very easy to understand the

---

[1] Psychologists, too, have recently employed this perspective. See the works of Eric Berne and Thomas Szasz.

analogies used and educators have not had to be concerned about using an unfamiliar analogue. They have concentrated, instead, on identifying the similarities between teaching and games.

In the selections that follow, Phenix, Macdonald, and Hyman present three separate but overlapping sets of characteristics of games and play. They then apply these characteristics to teaching. These articles employ such concepts as rules, players, playing field, goals, and roles and use these concepts to study teaching. Although similar, the articles differ insofar as they abstract and outline different sets of characteristics. And these complement rather than oppose one another.

The articles also differ in their specific approaches. Macdonald identifies six *games in teaching* and then analyzes the factors he has previously borrowed from Leary within each game. He later shows the implications for educators of these concepts and games. Phenix takes Huizinga's elements of play and locates *play in teaching*. Phenix considers these elements central to teaching and further wishes to use them as standards for evaluating teaching. Smith, Bellack and his associates, and Hyman consider *teaching as a game*. Smith talks about the player, coach, and referee. Hyman expands the analogy by first classifying participants in the game into three categories and then considering scorekeeper, spectators, rules committee, and waterboy as well as player, coach, and referee.

Bellack and his associates present the rules of the classroom game as derived from the empirical study presented in the section devoted to the cognitive vantage point. The investigators conceptualized their data in terms of the rules of the game since their initial framework is derived from Wittgenstein's notion of a language game. This is itself a metaphor. Though these rules stem from their work with high school classes studying a unit in economics, evidence from other studies seems to show that they apply to a wide range of classes. The reader will notice this in the selections by Flanders, Hughes, Gallagher and Aschner, and Maccia, for example. In regard to rules, the reader should note that Hyman speaks about two types of rules, process and administrative. This distinction is made in order to focus on the critical aspects of teaching.

An interesting feature of these articles is the justifications they present for using the perspective of games. For Phenix, the justification lies in the necessary preparation for life in an age of growing leisure time. To prepare for life in the future, in which leisure, as opposed to work, will account for most of man's time, education (classroom teaching, as he uses the word) must be conducted in the spirit of play, the spirit of leisure. This requirement puts a tremendous burden on the teacher. It assumes, of course, that teaching has a powerful and long-lasting effect. Obviously, many readers will challenge both positions.

Macdonald draws on Western analytic philosophy and Eastern mystic philosophy to arrive at a playful way of talking about teaching that is quite serious in intent. For him, it is a way of combining the best of two schools of philosophy, each of which has significance for teaching. As noted earlier, Bellack, too, draws upon analytic philosophy by way of Wittgenstein, the father of this school of thought. For Smith, the justification is simply the easy fit of the analogy.

The chief pedagogical implication of this vantage point is that teachers and pupils play various games and roles. Therefore, as Macdonald notes, we may describe and evaluate teaching in terms of the games and roles being played. To say that a teacher is sometimes effective and sometimes not is inadequate. It is more meaningful to say that he is an effective teacher in the information-giving game but not effective in the inquiry game. This procedure, of course, requires standards for effectiveness in each game. The need is to establish them for as yet they do not exist. This approach also gives us a way of selecting and grouping teachers, for example, into teaching teams. We may wish to put a teacher who excels at the dialogue game or coaching role on a team with another teacher whose forte is the information-giving game or player role. The assumption is that, once we are aware of the various games and roles, teachers and pupils will be able to choose and play as they want. That is, people can determine their behavior and are responsible for it. It is here that we see one connection between the games vantage point and the psychological one proposed by Rogers and others.

There are other connections, too, as the reader will quickly see. For example, the referee resembles the teacher who evaluates the

pupil, as depicted by Flanders and Bellack. Yet there is a difference
in that a failure on the part of a pupil as player does not reflect upon
the referee; whereas a failure does reflect in some way on the
teacher, as conceived in other frameworks. The waterboy in this
perspective resembles the facilitating function of Hughes described
in the section on social climate. The reader should also note similarities between Phenix's concept of play and the concepts in the section
on aesthetics, especially in the articles by Hallman and Curran.

The previous paragraph hints at the issue of whether the games
analogy is an adequate one for teaching. Though these five selections
take the position that concepts from games can be successfully
applied to teaching, there remains some doubt. The significant
relationship of "when somebody wins, somebody must lose," which
is basic to games, seems to be absent in teaching. Where is the win/
lose idea in teaching? Also, by using the concept of games, how do
we account for homework? In short, the reader should consider
carefully the degree to which the games analogue is adequate for
teaching.

If we assume the adequacy of this framework, the question still
remains to be answered by future empirical work whether we can
reliably identify different games and roles in teaching. What exactly
do teachers do and say as they play the role of coach? What happens
in the interaction between teacher and pupils when we emphasize or
neglect the mastery game or referee role? How does teaching in the
spirit of play affect the social climate or psychological climate of the
classroom? The potential number of research projects growing out of
this perspective is great but appears to be virtually untapped. The
questions asked here are only a hint, as should be obvious to any
player or spectator.

25.   The Play Element in Education

Philip H. Phenix

It is commonly taken for granted that work is more important in human affairs than is play. It is said that work is at the center and play is on the periphery; that work determines success or failure, progress or decline, in individual life and in societies; that work is the *real* business of life, while play is a kind of accidental accompaniment of work arising from the fact that most human beings cannot or need not work all the time.

Correspondingly, it is customary to assume that education and work go together and that play has only a relatively minor role in teaching and learning. It is said that one studies in order to do one's job more efficiently or to secure advancement in rank or salary; that play is only justified to refresh one for more study leading to more success in work; and hence that play should have a small and subordinate place in any educational program; that not only does education prepare one to work, but work also educates, while play is essentially frivolous, teaching nothing significant and contributing virtually nothing to one's education.

Even if the view of play implicit in the foregoing assumptions is accepted, the reduction in the work-day due to modern technical advances is forcing a revision in our estimate of the importance of play in contemporary life and education. As machines release workers more and more from the necessities of labor, larger amounts of time and resources are opened to leisure-time pursuits, including play. Play absorbs an ever higher proportion of human interest and energy. In such circumstances, it becomes increasingly imperative that deliberate measures be taken to educate modern people to use their leisure time wisely. Thus, we are being forced to re-examine our educational institutions and their curricula to take account of the growing importance of play in the whole economy of life.

Any shift in educational provisions we may make in response to the new technology is doomed to failure as long as the conception of play as essentially a peripheral and insignificant type of activity is maintained. We moderns have to a large extent lost any sense of what play really is. We think of it as a form of activity which fills the hours between working times, as what people do in the evenings, on weekends, and on holidays, vacations, and after retirement, or what rich people, who do not have to

Reprinted with permission from *The Educational Forum*, 29: 297-306, March, 1965. Copyright © 1965 by Kappa Delta Pi, an Honor Society in Education, and reproduced by permission.

work and who are not socially conscientious, do to fill their time pleasantly. Given such ideas of play, it is difficult to generate much enthusiasm for educational programs to prepare people to play well.

One also recoils at the prospect of trying to fill the new leisure hours with enough new satisfactions. The tamer amusements soon pall, and to sustain interest stronger forms of entertainment are sought, including drugs, sexual adventures, actual or vicarious, intoxication, gambling, and displays of brutality. To combat these aberrations educators are urged to tighten up on discipline, increase the pressure of academic work, and give instruction in morality—all of which measures merely serve to compound the problem by intensifying rebellion and increasing the determination to escape from the oppression of labor and the boredom of self-indulgence.

The real need is for a complete transformation in our understanding of play. The classic study of this subject is found in a book by Johan Huizinga, called *Homo Ludens: A Study of the Play Element in Culture*.[1] From Huizinga's analysis it is clearly evident that play, far from being a trivial and peripheral human activity, has been one of the fundamental factors in the creation of culture. The impulse to play is deeply rooted in human nature, and from it have sprung the most varied flowerings of civilization—in language, law, philosophy, religion, science, and the arts. When the play spirit dies, the freshness, joy and spontaneity of life are quenched, and routine, compulsion, and mechanization supervene.

If play is essential to creative civilization, it is certainly an essential element in good education. Far from being incidental to the curriculum—a "fad and frill" introduced by soft-minded educationists—play may turn out to be the most important feature of the curriculum. From a deeper perspective, it can be shown that the play element in education should not primarily refer to physical education and recreation, or to recesses and "extra-curricular activities," but to the spirit in which all teaching and learning, in all studies whatsoever, ought to proceed.

In an extraordinarily perceptive essay by Joseph Pieper, entitled *Leisure, the Basis of Culture*, the close relation between play and culture demonstrated by Huizinga is further exhibited. Culture has its source in leisure, which is based on the contemplative rather than the manipulative attitude, and leisure is supremely exemplified in the activity of play. Pieper observes that "on one occasion St. Thomas speaks of contemplation and play in the same breath: 'because of the leisure that goes with contemplation' the divine wisdom itself, Holy Scripture says, is 'always at play, playing through the whole world' (Proverbs 8:30 f.)."[2] Furthermore, that this playful leisure belongs at the very heart of education is suggested by

[1] Boston: Beacon Press, 1955.
[2] Josef Pieper, *Leisure, the Basis of Culture* (New York: Pantheon Books, Inc., 1952), p. 41.

the fact that "leisure in Greek is *skole*, and in Latin *scola*, the English 'school.' The word used to designate the place where we educate and teach is derived from the word which means 'leisure.' 'School' does not, properly speaking, mean school, but leisure."[3] Pieper might have added that we need to transform our concept and conduct of schooling so as to bring it back to its proper center in leisure and play.

If such a transformation is to be effected, we need a clear understanding of what constitutes play. Huizinga suggests several characteristics which serve to distinguish play as an independent type of activity from other human undertakings, as follows:

First, play is *voluntary* and not subject to coercion or necessity. It is superfluous, not obligatory or indispensable in any given situation.

Second, play is not concerned with "real life," but with "*make believe*." It is not based on ordinary affairs, but is an occasion for something out-of-the-ordinary. There is in play an element of "ecstacy," in which the player is "beside himself" through participation in the extraordinary.

Third, play is *disinterested* rather than utilitarian. One does not play for profit, to satisfy any practical demand, or to solve urgent personal or social problems. He is so completely absorbed in the game that he takes no thought for himself. He is an "amateur" in the sense of one who by love of the game has lost concern for himself and his personal advantages in playing.

Fourth, all play has an element of *tension*. Play is contest. The players always strive to win. They "give their all" for the sake of the game. The struggle to achieve, the drive for prowess in the game, provide motive and zest to play.

Fifth, play is *limited* both spatially and temporally. It takes place within a specified field of action and occupies a definite segment of time. The game has boundaries and both a beginning and an end.

Sixth, play is always *ordered*. It is not haphazard or chaotic, but proceeds according to a definite pattern comprising the rules of the game. It is a formal type of activity, requiring careful discipline and high skill; it is not an amorphous and accidental sequence of events.

Seventh and finally, play is *social*. The rules of the game constitute an agreement by which the players are bound within a disciplined community. Furthermore, the play community tends to endure beyond the limits of a few games, becoming established as a permanent fellowship. Characteristically, the play community becomes an esoteric and somewhat exclusive society with its own secret rules known only to insiders. The prime purpose of this secrecy is to preserve the extraordinary quality of play life against the incursions of the commonplace which open publicity would invite.

It can be shown that these characteristics of play are exemplified in a

[3] *Ibid.*, p. 26.

number of different fields of human endeavor, and thus, that there is a close relation between play and cultural creation. Since education is concerned with the conservation, transmission, and (to some extent) the transmutation of culture, it is reasonable to expect the play element also to be central to teaching and learning. From this perspective, it is possible to evaluate the educational process in the light of the seven characteristics of play listed above, in order to judge the extent to which it succeeds or fails to embody the spirit of play.

What, then, can we say about the conduct of education, on the assumption that its excellence is to be measured by the criteria for play, which in turn is regarded as the source of vitality in cultural life? What would education be like in a society imbued with the spirit of play? Let us examine each of the seven characteristics in turn, as they would apply to education.

First, the activity of learning should be *voluntary*. Unquestionably, people do learn under conditions of compulsion. But this is not the ideal context for growth in knowledge and skill. It is hardly practicable to turn our backs at this date on universal compulsory education. We do not see fit to allow children to go to school or not, according to their own or their parents' inclination. Yet the fact must be squarely faced that obligatory instruction is likely to beget resistance to learning. The greatest goal of education is to kindle the *love of learning*, which stimulates a person to teach himself and to continue learning throughout life. If study is only done by compulsion and if sanctions are imposed for failure to get results, attitudes of resistance and resentment are generated which may permanently diminish a person's capacity to learn easily and well.

The mark of all good education is that it *liberates* the learner. In this sense all education ought to be liberal education. It is difficult to combine in one and the same process both compulsion and liberation. It seems more reasonable to suppose that the education of free persons begins with learning voluntarily undertaken. Even if we do require everyone to attend school until a certain age, it is possible to allow a certain amount of choice by the student as to what course of study he will pursue. It is hardly practicable to allow everyone within a given class to choose what he will study; that way lies chaos. Nonetheless, the student who has had an opportunity to elect the general line of study he will follow is justified in feeling that his activity is voluntary rather than coerced and thus worthy of his wholehearted commitment.

Possibly, the finest opportunities for fuller voluntary learning are to be found in the field of adult education. At this level the general compulsions of society are no longer in force, and a person seeks instruction solely because he wants to become wiser and more competent. The remarkable success of the Danish Folk High Schools in adult education seems to be due in no small measure to the fact that the people who attended them came eagerly and willingly, sometimes at considerable sacrifice, because they wanted to learn.

It is a general rule, then, in all education to capitalize upon the love of liberty. To be convinced of the powerful educational motivations inherent in freedom, one has only to contrast the rate of progress of a student who reluctantly grinds his way through a required course of study with that of a student who has "caught fire" intellectually in a field that he now regards as his own.

Freedom, then, is necessary to education in the spirit of play. But it is not sufficient. According to the second criterion for play, education should be an *extraordinary* kind of activity rather than an everyday one. By this standard, most contemporary education is unplayful. When everybody has to go to school, the experience readily loses its special charm. The "common school" becomes commonplace. The everyday easily lapses into the humdrum and the routine. In such an atmosphere learning becomes extremely difficult.

Unfortunately, the commonness of universal education, mainly carried on in public institutions, has been accentuated by the use of commonplace materials in the curriculum. Many curriculum specialists have argued that students learn best when they are taught by the use of familiar materials drawn from everyday life. The truth of the matter seems to be quite the opposite. The everyday and the familiar may not enlist the spontaneous interest of the learner nor excite his curiosity nearly as much as do unusual and extraordinary matters.

The clue to effective learning is the *stimulation of imagination*. The everyday is unimaginative. Imagination is kindled by what is unusual, out-of-the-ordinary. One of the most interesting examples of modern curricular revision is the "new" mathematics. In this subject students are now being taught relatively early to think in terms of sets, relations, functions, and axiomatic systems—matters which in the older mathematics were reserved for advanced study. These ideas are stimulating intellectually partly because they are unusual. Being general ideas of fundamental importance, they are in the long run far more significant educationally than would be concepts closer to everyday experience.

I am not arguing that what is taught should be so strange that it is unintelligible to the student. Just as the procedures of a game must be thoroughly intelligible to the player, so the subject matter of instruction should be clearly understandable to the student. Yet, neither a good game nor imaginative subject matter is ordinary, in the sense of being commonplace.

Closely linked to this second characteristic of play-inspired education is the third, namely, that learning should occur *disinterestedly*—in and for itself and not as a means to some further end. This is the essence of a truly *liberal* education. As John Henry Newman pointed out in *The Idea of a University,* the learning that befits a free man is that which is intrinsically valuable, and for which no justification on grounds of utility is sought. The liberal scholar is an amateur; he does not learn for money. He loses himself in the pursuit of understanding.

Most people today regard education unplayfully, as a means of gaining position and power. Education is, in fact, the chief instrument for upward social mobility in our highly fluid social and economic structure. Little wonder, then, that learning is so largely judged in relation to its cash value, that students are so often without motive for study unless they clearly see "what is in it" for them, and that a complex system of extrinsic rewards and punishments (especially in the form of ranks and grades) is required to make students work.

Many teachers, following one side of the pragmatist philosophy, have sought to base all instruction on problem-solving, on the mistaken conviction that learning occurs only, or in any case best, when the learner is faced with some difficulty in meeting a practical need. An understanding of the way in which creative energies are released in impractical play shows that the disinterested pursuit of an activity regarded as intrinsically valuable is more conducive to learning than are practical undertakings. It seems to be a general law of life that losing oneself in an absorbing activity is more practical in the end than direct prosecution of personal advantage. In education this means that students will learn more and better, if they are not distracted from learning by keeping their eye on the benefits which they intend their knowledge to secure for them.

Given our kind of society, organized so fully on a utility basis, it is definitely not possible for most educational agencies, which are expected to subserve and perpetuate the social system of which they are a part, to exemplify fully the spirit of disinterested play. Nevertheless, schools can to some extent act as countervailing forces; they need not wholly bend the knee to Baal. They can cherish ideals and to some degree realize these higher purposes in their programs. The first step in the reformation is for all who are concerned with education to understand the self-defeating nature of the pursuit of practicality and to encourage wherever possible the pursuit of studies in and for the joy of learning.

The fourth feature of education conducted after the manner of play is the presence of *tension.* Out of concern for the psychological well-being of students and for social harmony, many modern educators stress the need for "adjustment" and for insuring that every student feel "comfortable." The rigors of old-fashioned education are decried, and as far as possible competitive attitudes are eliminated in favor of cooperative ones. From the standpoint of play-analysis, these developments are partly mistaken. Human beings thrive on contest. They need to compete with one another in matches of prowess. They need the exhilaration of pitting their powers against the abilities of other contestants. Growth does not take place without challenge. To be comfortable and adjusted, in the usual sense of these terms, is to invite stagnation and degeneration.

Gordon Allport shows how essential "growth" motives are to the individual person. Such motives, in contrast with "deficit motives" maintain tension rather than diminishing it and stimulate one to strive toward cherished goals.[4] Tensions are not all good; they may cripple and destroy instead of energizing a person. The possibility of such destructive tensions is nevertheless no argument against the constructive drives toward excellence which belong in education modelled after the pattern of strenuous play.

What has been said of tension generally applies in particular to the stresses implicit in competition. From the play standpoint, education without competition would prove ineffectual. On the other hand, not all competition is profitable. Competition which is marked by hostility toward others is destructive to all concerned. In the desirable kind of competition, the competitors honor and respect one another. Each values his rival as an equal in a common enterprise. The participants strive for excellence in the mutual endeavor, finding stimulus for greater effort in each other's bid for supremacy, whether in games or in feats of knowledge and skill.

Teachers can use the "agonistic" element to great advantage in the organization of learning. Nothing so delights students as competitions in which they can put their growing powers to the test. The goal is not rivalry for extrinsic rewards, such as grades, in which one student achieves superiority over another in rank and at the other's expense, but opportunities to work competitively in the pursuit of excellence in speaking, composition, painting, calculation, or any other field of cultural activity.

The fifth characteristic of play, namely, *limitations* in space and time, is clearly a feature of good pedagogy. People learn best when they can clearly see the boundaries of their task. One can have a sense of accomplishment in dealing with discrete and manageable projects which have both a definite beginning and a definite ending. It is because of the need for limitation that the educational system is subdivided by clearly marked boundaries: in time, by class periods, sessions, courses, and grade and degree levels; in space, by classrooms, subjects, departments, divisions, schools and colleges. Whatever their drawbacks, these demarcations in time and space are necessary to the successful management of teaching and learning. No one can profitably set out to learn generally; everything needs to come in suitable parcels of duration and scope.

Anyone who directs students in their research projects can testify that

[4] *Becoming: Basic Considerations for a Psychology of Personality* (New Haven: Yale University Press, 1955), p. 68.

half the battle is won when the limits are clearly marked out. The unskilled investigator usually attempts far too much and fails to distinguish the essential from the non-essential in his selection of materials. Rigorous definition of what is to be argued and faithful adherence to the bounds thus set are essential to effective inquiry in any field of study.

Limitation is a corollary of the ideal of disinterestedness. A person cannot give himself unreservedly to the activity at hand and simultaneously have his mind on other objectives out beyond. Full concentration depends on having limits which focus energies within definite confines. A sovereign rule in learning as in play is to organize activity so as to secure single-minded absorption in each successive discrete unit of pupil endeavor.

The principle of limitation is particularly urgent in modern times because of the vast proliferation of opportunities and demands in our age of affluence and explosive expansion. Most people are paralyzed by the complexity of the world's problems and feel hopeless in the face of all there is to be learned and accomplished. To be freed from the oppression of overabundance, the practice of simplification through deliberate limitation is necessary. Only by doing as the good player does, in concentrating his whole being within the world of the playing field for the duration of the game, can today's richness of demand and opportunity be transformed from a paralyzing threat into a creative possibility.

The sixth feature of play-like education is *order*. Just as a game cannot be played without rules which define the admissible moves, so learning cannot proceed effectively without appropriate regularities. There is no topic in all pedagogy which is of greater interest to the average teacher than *discipline*. The teacher knows that nothing can be taught unless order prevails. The instructor's nightmare is that of a class out of control, his greatest threat the possibility of anarchy and rampant disorder.

But what kind of order, what means of discipline are admissable? Did we not affirm as the prime characteristic of learning that it should be undertaken in freedom? There must, then, be both freedom and order, or better, freedom *through* order. Anarchy is not freedom, for those who exist in such a state are slaves to their own impulses and to the impulses of others. There must be order for the effective organizing of conjoint activities, and likewise for the profitable channeling of individual creative energies. To be fully free, the order or discipline must not be one imposed from outside or handed down by superior authorities. It must be accepted by the participant himself as the law of his own chosen behavior.

In educational practice, the older idea of discipline as rigid control of students by force and threats violated the play ideal of freedom and as a result inhibited creative learning. On the other hand, the permissiveness of some modern schools violated the play ideal from the standpoint of order. Fortunately, the choice need not be made between these two extremes. Instead, we can have the disciplined freedom which is exemplified in play. There students understand and accept the rules of the learning game as their own principles of order, required for the successful prosecution of an undertaking freely chosen.

Seventh, education, conceived after the fashion of play would give rise to *enduring communities of learning*, tending toward exclusiveness in membership and distinctive esoteric types of activity. In its proper concern for equality and publicity, our democratic society has perhaps lost some of the positive values of social differentiation and privacy. No person really wants to be just like everybody else. He longs for uniqueness and distinction. He does not want to live wholly within the domain of the public gaze. He prizes privacy and special privilege. These demands can, of course, lead to all sorts of corruptions, including acts of cruelty and injustice. On the other hand, they stem from legitimate human values, for which provision should be made in the organization of social life.

One of the major impulses toward specialization is the longing for some *special* competence which not everyone can claim. The specialist identifies with his fellows in the same craft or profession and takes pride in his unusual competence. Moreover, every organized body of specialists tends to set a guard upon its house, carefully examining the credentials of those who seek entrance and excluding those who will not or cannot live according to the established rules. Each group also tends to create an aura of mystery about its activities, so as to intensify the impression that matters of unusual moment occur within the privileged circle of members.

In the domain of learning, the best analogues of enduring play fellowships are the organized academic, professional, and technical disciplines. Each of these specialty groups has its own official organizations, conditions of membership, codes, training requirements, and organs of publication. One of the best ways to induce interest in learning is to give students a sense that they are being offered a glimpse into the workings of an esoteric fellowship. For example, it makes history much more exciting if approached from the standpoint of "learning to think the way historians think" instead of learning history because "everybody has to know about the past." Again, if physics is taught as an initiation into the mysteries of the physicists' world, it gains immeasurably in imaginative appeal.

The seven characteristics of play thus provide a standard by which to judge the quality of education, on the assumption that the play element is a basic factor in all cultural creation. It is also reasonable to conclude, from this point of view, that education conceived within the framework of play will be increasingly necessary as a preparation for living in an age of growing leisure. If leisure is to be anything more than the absence of work—and what a dreary conception that is!—if it is to be a kind of activity in which genuinely humane qualities may grow and prosper, then there must be preparation for this creative sort of living through education conducted in the spirit of play. . . .

26.   Gamesmanship in the Classroom

James B. Macdonald

A Playful Way of Talking About Teaching

How shall we talk about teaching? If its intent is the development of rationality, then how do we talk about how teachers develop student powers of rational thought?

Here it seems we have at least two sources of contemporary insight for helping us develop a playful language. These two are the analytic philosophers and the modern psychological mystics, especially those persons presently involved in the examination of and experimentation with consciousness-enlarging drugs such as LSD.

The common thread in these diverse enterprises is the concept of the game. In the one case, from Ludwig Wittgenstein comes the idea of language games. In the other instance, after the eastern mystics, come the modern western psychological philosophers, such as Timothy Leary, Alan Watts, and Aldous Huxley, who expand this concept to the reality game.

Without attempting to be accurate or to be faithful to either development, the central concept of teaching as a potential series of communication games would appear to have unusual free-floating and playful possibilities. Further, it is without doubt a valid way of talking, although there is no way of knowing at present how useful it can be.

Arno Bellack, in a study of teaching, talked about it as a language game. Now what I'm going to do today is talk about teaching as *games*.

However, what here carries the concept of the game to a much more general level is best described by Timothy Leary as follows:

The use of the word "game" in this sweeping context is likely to be misunderstood. The listener may think I refer to "play" as opposed to stern, real-life serious activities of man. But as you shall see, I consider the latter as "game."

All behavior involves learned games. But only that rare Westerner we call "mystic" or who has had a visionary experience of some sort sees clearly the game structure of behavior. Most of the rest of us spend our time struggling with roles and rules and goals and concepts of games which are implicit and confusedly not seen as games, trying to apply the roles and rules and rituals of one game to other games.

A game is a learned cultural sequence characterized by six factors:

1. Roles: The game assigns roles to the human beings involved.
2. Rules: A game sets up a set of rules which hold only during the game sequence.
3. Goals: Every game has a goal or purpose. The goals of baseball are to score more runs than the opponents. The goals of the game of psychology are more complex and unimplicit but they exist.
4. Rituals: Each game has its conventional behavior pattern not related to the goals or rules but yet quite necessary to comfort and continuance.
5. Language: Each game has its jargon unrelated to the rules and goals and yet necessary to learn and use.
6. Values: Each game has its standard of excellence or goodness.

Teaching, then, can be considered a special kind of communication game or games, structured by our culture and learned by us. Each game has structure in the sense of Leary's six characteristics: roles, rules, goals, rituals, language and values.

This brings us to premise number three:[1] *Teaching is a set of communication games*. This paves the way for looking at common occurrences in classrooms from this perspective.

What follows, then, is the discussion of a number of teaching strategies as communication games, analyzed in terms of the six characteristics just discussed and their intent. The names of the "games" are drawn from experience and general knowledge of teaching and as such are purely suggestive of possibilities and labels.

GAMES TEACHERS PLAY

The Information-Giving Game. The most common communication game in our high schools may be called information-giving. This game is exactly what it suggests. The teacher has information which he forms and manages to send to the student receiver. The receivers are expected to take in this information without distorting it and signal the teacher that

---

[1] The first two premises in a section not included here are: There is no one reality in teaching; teaching is best characterized by its intent—the development of rationality. RTH, editor.

they have the information. The media by which messages may be sent are variable, but the intent of the process is relatively constant.

The roles assigned are clear. The teacher possesses the information, or knowledge of avenues of access to this information. His role is to present to, or put students in contact with, the ideas or facts in the most effective manner. The student role is also clear. He is to receive the information and be able to show the teacher that he has possession of it.

The rules of the game are less obvious, but derivable by analysis. Some of these are:

1. *The game should be played seriously*—all participants are expected to accept the worth and significance of the game and to cooperate and perform in a serious work-like atmosphere.
2. *The teacher directs the game*—students are expected to take their cues for responding from the teacher. The teacher of course is responsible for initiating and soliciting responses.
3. *Attention and cooperation are expected*—students are expected to be attentive and to cooperate with the teacher to achieve the goals of the game.

The goals of the game are also fairly obvious. Students are expected to be able to reproduce the information presented in whatever form the teacher calls for. Their reproductions are graded and become part of the competitive interpersonal data of our society. The goals of the game vary. Some are, for example, to please the teachers, beat fellow students, win access to social mobility, or simply to know something.

Rituals are also involved. Students are expected (usually) to raise their hands before responding. Teachers are expected to have the last word and "cap" any set of responses. People take turns and talk one at a time; and all follow the special procedures for handing in assignments, taking tests, coming and going, and relating to each other.

The language of the game is essentially framed in a question-answer, lecture, and discussion format. Outside the classroom the teacher talks about individual "IQ's," meeting the "needs" of students, "gifted," "culturally deprived," and a host of other things. Inside the classroom the special language relates to cueing the smooth wording of the process. "Who would like to tell us about Charlemagne?" might be interpreted to mean "All right, let's get started; who is first?" Each teacher has her use of "good," "o.k.," and other phrases that are a distinctive use of language in the communication process.

The values of the game are found in achievement. Excellence means knowing the subject, and excellent teaching means getting the information across. Most often the standard is a comparative one, sometimes an absolute one, and infrequently an individual one.

Mastery. A subvariety of information-giving is the mastery game. In general it follows the same kinds of prescriptions as information-giving. However, the special context of drill and practice provides variation for this game.

The goals, for example, might be thought of as "over-learning" or habitualizing rather than "just" knowing. Many skills fall in this area and the basic intent is to take them into cognition and make them so automatic that cognitive awareness of them is no longer necessary for behavior.

The Problem-Solving Game. The next most common appearance in high school is the problem-solving game. The teacher role is to present, get students in contact with, or evolve a problem with them. The teacher often knows *the* or *an* answer to this problem, but if not he has knowledge of how to solve it or faith that it can be solved. Oftentimes problem-solving takes place in a project or "activity" format.

The student role is more active than in information-giving. He is now expected to take some initiative, to think about what he is doing as well as what he is learning. The goal of the game is to come up with some satisfactory resolution of the problem, and standards of excellence are applied in terms of the teacher's judgment of the exhaustion of relevant sources of data in relation to the level of maturity of the students.

Rules of the game are built around the expectation that students will define or see a problem and set out systematically and thoughtfully to solve it. Contrary to information-giving, it is now taboo to expect the teachers to provide answers. Language usage now shifts to terms such as "resource materials," "critical thinking," and analysis of the process of reflective thinking with such concepts as inference, data, and evidence becoming part of the setting.

The Discovery or Inquiry Game. The discovery or inquiry game is a variant of problem-solving. The major difference rests in the goals of the game. Each begins with discrepancies to be resolved, but in inquiry the goal is shifted from the solution to the *process* of solving a problem.

The teacher role is to set the circumstances for discrepant awareness on the part of students. Students are expected to search, manipulate, experiment, and seek actively.

The rituals in this case may often become the modes of inquiry and be in essence the goals. Thus, when appropriate, a student must use the ritual of scientific method, or of formal logic, or of aesthetic criticism, or of moral and ethical evaluation.

The value of the game is in the playing, intelligently and with spirit. The outcomes of the game are seen primarily in terms of the process utilized, and excellence becomes awareness of the process of inquiry.

The Dialogue Game. Upon occasion the communication game can actually move to the level of dialogue. In a true dialogue game the roles of all present are the same—the attempt to move the discussion to the revelation of insights not present in *any* participant at the beginning of the interaction.

The rules of the game are:

1. One participates as a total person, not as a role player.
2. One is expected to be open, to reveal himself, and to receive from and listen to others.
3. One must be disciplined. One is expected to participate and one is expected to participate in the context of the contribution of others.
4. One must respond to others and therefore be responsible in relation to them.

No contributions are rejected, criticized, or judged per se. Participants, however, are expected to discipline themselves by the monitoring of behavior which reflects personal needs to talk, show off, play one-upmanship, defend themselves, or pull rank. The goal is to explore beyond the present member-awareness for insights and implications about the material which produces an aesthetic response or an insight (Aha!).

Further, the goal is to relate the forms of content or subject matters to the vitality which originally produced them; to bring the meanings that come out of a student's living into conjunction with the meanings inherent in the subject matter. Excellence is assured by the feeling of time well spent and the satisfaction of new awarenesses.

Ritual and language will be loosened and, although the spatial arrangements of facilities for dialogue may reflect circular rather than linear patterns, time may be used more flexibly; and the use of judgmental terms will be negated.

The Clarification Game. Attempts to relate students to meanings and values are often found in clarification procedures. The teacher, in other words, attempts to elicit personal responses, reactions, and meanings to life and subject matter. The teacher's role is to focus the student inward and the student's role is to express attitude feelings, aspirations, values, and impressions and to reflect upon them.

The rules of the game are very open. The teacher must never judge any student response; he must never ask questions for which he has a predetermined answer but only questions for which an individual student could possibly have the answer. Students, on the other hand, must freely express their real feelings, concerns and meanings.

The goal of clarification is the development of values and commitments in the form of personal meanings attached to content. Standards of excellence are difficult to express, but if the process is satisfying the worth is assumed.

The language involves such phrases as "tell me more about that" or "now I see what you're saying," or "you mean to say . . . ?" All language involves "I feel," "I think," and other first-person reference. Again, ritual is caught in the use of time and space of a personal and flexible nature.

POTENTIAL IMPLICATIONS OF THE COMMUNICATION IDEA

Six teacher strategies were described as communication games. The question may shift to, "What relevance or insights for teaching can we glean from this description?"

I should like to reflect briefly upon four kinds: those for students, those for teachers, those for principals, and those for researchers.

The Student. Students rarely have any insight into the nature of the teaching role. They accept what the teacher does as natural, although they seldom know why he does things. Further, they realize that teachers expect certain things from them, but they are not really in control of their own responses in a rational way. Thus, when asked why they violate expectations, many can truly answer, "I don't know."

A major aid to improving the classroom situation could be found by developing the student's awareness of the communication games teachers play. Reflect for a moment upon what it might mean to students to understand what is happening to them, as well as what is expected of them as outcomes. The awareness of varying roles, rules, shifting goals, standards of value and appropriate ritual could incalculably improve the student's ability to participate and utilize the communication context. The simple fact of knowing which game is being played at what time would be a real revolution in insight.

Beyond this, the concept of games could well be a tremendous liberalizing and perspective-giving insight for students. As students come to realize that all cultural activities are games and that the "real" world out there and in the lunchroom is as much a game as the teaching-learning process they might better come to know themselves and to be able to choose rationally those social games in which they wish to invest their time and effort. (And in the process be able to play them more expertly.)

The Teachers. If teachers came to understand the communication-game concept they might well realize the paucity of their use of potential learning contexts. One might be able to break down the dichotomous wall that exists in their minds today between teaching as information giving and "all that other impractical stuff." In its stead one could create a set of cognitive guiding-concepts known in terms of roles, rules, goals, rituals, language, and values—which could provide for teachers vehicles for self-insight and discovery, and which could be used as heuristic devices for developing a broader range of competencies.

At present, teachers do not possess a variety of models of styles or strategies to help them think rationally about teaching. Until we are able to provide models for them we cannot expect much change.

The Principals. Communication games provide tremendous possibilities for effective evaluation and improvement of teaching. The simple fact of rephrasing the question "How effective is a teacher?" to "How effectively is the teacher playing the communication game he has chosen?" "What is the teacher's repertoire of games?" and "Are chosen games appropriate to proposed outcomes?" could be a major step forward.

The value element would still be present in terms of valued games to play, but within that limitation the communication-game idea would appear to provide usable criteria for assessing teachers for the purpose of improvement.

Some of the criteria could be:

1. Does the teacher know what game is being played?
2. Do the students?
3. Is the game consistent? (i.e., within the rules, etc.)
4. Are the roles clearly delineated?
5. Are the rules clear?
6. Are the goals clear?
7. Is the language appropriate?
8. Are the rituals appropriate?
9. Are the standards known and clear?

The Researchers. In passing, a few comments for researchers seem relevant. One of the major problems with research in classrooms has been the failure to account for purposes of instruction within the research. To know that teachers are direct or indirect, for example, has little meaning outside the special communication context of the interaction (of which, hopefully, the development of rationality is the central intent).

Separating communication games by their various characteristics could provide clarity of conceptualization that is much needed and, in the process, could supply a list of variables that may be more productive. Just the simple matter of focusing some research on the variety of standards appropriate to different games would be a major improvement over the single-standard approach (achievement) now in vogue.

One final word of caution is in order. The position presented here is playful in mood though serious in intent. It is an attempt to build out of the particulars of teaching a framework which will, by its abstraction and generality, help bring new awareness of the particular, though perhaps not in specific terms of the abstraction itself. It would be well to heed T. S. Eliot's admonition:

> ... every attempt is a wholly new
> start, and a different kind of failure.

27.   The Name of the Game Is Teaching

Ronald T. Hyman

In all societies and cultures, everyone knows about games and their participants. Little girls and boys play London bridge, hide-and-seek, and Simple Simon. Older girls play hopscotch and jacks. Older boys play football, basketball, and other organized sports. Adults not only play games of their childhood but also learn new games, commercial games such as Scrabble and games in the public domain such as bridge and golf. Games are familiar to everyone—including teachers.

All games have certain common features:

1. Games have a goal or objective, e.g., to score the most runs in baseball, to score the most points in gin rummy, or to checkmate the king in chess.

2. Games are ordered by rules, and the goal is attained by playing according to the rules. If the rules are not obeyed, the game degenerates into chaos.

3. Games involve people who may be classified into three types: (a) Players—such as the fullback who actually scores the touchdowns in football; (b) Non-players—with a stake in the outcome of the game, such as coaches and managers, and (c) Non-players—without a stake in the outcome of the game, such as referees and scorekeepers.

4. Games involve a common playing area (a card table or a baseball diamond) and equipment with which to play the game.

These universally identifiable aspects of games can aid us in viewing teachers and pupils in action.

First, what is the goal of teaching? Learning! Teachers perform so that pupils can learn information, concepts, and skills. This is the primary but not exclusive goal of teaching. The primary goal is not good mental health or fun, though they do have a part in teaching.

Ideally, the teaching game is not competitive. The teacher and pupils are not opponents but have a common goal. In this way, the game of teaching differs from basketball and tennis in that what is gained (learned) by the pupil is not lost by the teacher. When the pupil improves, the teacher does not lose. On the contrary, only when the pupil improves, does the teacher win.

Second, the game called teaching operates on the basis of rules. Such rules as "The pupil may speak only when called upon," and "The pupils call the teacher *Mister* Jones while the teacher calls the pupils *John* and

Reprinted with permission from *Media and Methods,* Vol. 4, no. 8, April, 1968.

Jane," are in effect in virtually all classrooms. These rules may be labeled "administrative" rules. "Process" rules—those that govern the nature of the interaction between teacher and pupils—are the real focus of teaching. Process rules dictate, for example, that the teacher sets the topic to be discussed and decides on class activities such as lectures, films, and tests, that the pupil mainly responds to the teacher's questions, and that the teacher evaluates the pupil in his presence while the pupil evaluates the teacher with his classmates after the lesson is over. Unlike many of the administrative rules, these process rules are not written rules. Yet the process rules are strongly adhered to and, in effect, define the teaching game. They are as much in force as the written rules of tennis.

Third, who are the people involved in the teaching game? With few exceptions teaching involves two types of people, teacher and pupil. Usually there is one teacher and many pupils in any one teaching game. The teacher and pupils perform the roles of the three types of game participants noted before: players, non-players with a stake in the game, and non-players without a stake in the game. The game of football can be used to illustrate how the teacher and pupils take on these different roles.

The pupils are the halfbacks, fullbacks, and ends who score touchdowns, for it is they who are scoring (that is, learning) in the game. However, learning by the pupil does not preclude learning by the teacher, for teachers also learn during the game. The teacher may be likened to the quarterback whose primary function is to lead the other players in scoring points but who may, on occasion, score himself. Some pupil players run interference and block for the others, thus aiding them in their learning. They do so either at the request of the quarterback or at their own discretion. Hence, both teacher and pupil are players in the teaching game, the pupils mainly scoring the touchdowns.

The teacher is also the coach in the teaching game. He is the strategist who directs the play of his charges. As coach, the teacher determines when, how, and what the players will do. He plans schedules and instructs the pupils in the method of play which leads to learning. He teaches them how to listen, recite, gather information from reference books, take notes, prepare reports, and read the text. The teacher, like a coach who reviews the films of the previous week's game, goes over material previously learned and shows how the knowledge and skills gained may be applied in other situations. Perhaps most important of all the teacher as coach encourages his players while the game is in progress. As the pupils play, the teacher gives words of praise and urges them to continue learning. If the coach chastises his players, he does so only to bring about better performance.

The role of team manager (who ministers to the needs of all the players) also exists in the teaching game. The teacher and pupils share this role. They both erase the chalkboard, empty the pencil sharpener, distribute corrected homework assignments, and collect texts.

The role of referee is performed by the teacher in virtually all teaching games. The teacher as referee cites infractions of the rules and metes out appropriate penalties to the individual rule-breaker, or to the entire team. The teacher often says, "Remain after class a few minutes for doing that." It is rare that the pupil serves as referee although in some teaching games one or two pupils are in charge of noting minor infractions such as chewing gum or talking out of turn.

The role of scorekeeper also exists in the teaching game. The teacher usually performs this role. Only on occasion and only in certain teaching games do the pupils keep score. In such games the pupils suggest their score (grade, mark) to the official scorekeeper, the teacher.

From this analogy with football we see that the teacher and the pupils shift their roles during the teaching game, whereas in football different roles are performed by specifically designated people. The teacher and the pupils move from role to role. The teacher monopolizes a particular role or shares it with the pupils and vice-versa. Being alert to this shift in roles is crucial to understanding the teaching game. Unless one appreciates that the teacher performs many different roles during the game, he cannot comprehend the many acts performed. The game model demonstrates clearly and forcefully the multiplicity of roles performed by the teacher. Without the idea of teaching as a game before us, we would tend to forget this critical aspect of teaching, and this oversight leads many teachers to err in their judgment about what is going on in the classroom. That is, they fail to understand the nature of their roles.

It is also necessary to look at the role of rule-maker in games. The rule-maker may be an official committee, the creator of the game, some combination of these two, or even the players themselves. In the teaching game, some rules are made by people who are not participants in the game itself (such as the principal); however, most rules are established by the teacher and the pupils themselves. The degree of pupil participation in serving as rule-maker depends on the individual game situation. Generally, the teacher alone serves as rule-maker. It is he who makes explicit administrative rules (no gum chewing) and sets the stage for establishing the process rules (teacher talks three times as much as the pupils). Thus, it is interesting to note that the teacher not only makes the rules but, in addition, identifies infractions of the rules and metes out punishment as he performs the role of referee. It is interesting because in Western society the law-maker is generally not the judge. This unique aspect of the teaching game is often overlooked and often accounts for some of the statements about unfair behavior which pupils level at teachers. But this is the game as we know it.

Fourth, what are the playing field and equipment of the teaching game? Most games occur in a school classroom with desks and chairs. Today, teachers and pupils employ such equipment as films, film strips, recordings, slides, and broadcast media just as they do textbooks, paper, pencil, and chalkboard. The teaching game by its very nature necessitates equipment. What is more, the condition of the classroom and the equipment influence the game. A stuffy, undersized classroom with immovable desks and obsolete texts affects the teaching game just as a muddy field and a wet ball affect a football game.

Finally, we need to raise two questions regarding other aspects of the teaching game. First, players participate voluntarily in most games, and this largely accounts for the vitality and fun of the game. Does compulsory attendance in school affect the vitality of the teaching game?

Second, in most games players practice all week but score points only during the game. In the teaching game, students display their learning (that is, score points) not only during the actual game but during practice (homework) as well. Is the analogy therefore invalid?

To answer the first question, compulsory attendance does in some way detract from the spirit and fun of teaching in school. Teaching cannot always be exciting, but games are not always exciting either. To the second question, however, my answer is no. Though teaching and games are not identical, they are still similar enough to make the analogy helpful in understanding teaching in a special way.

If we as teachers wish to make teaching analogous to a game, then the key for doing it is our approach. The teacher establishes the tone of the situation. The environment he shapes not only affects how and what will be learned, but it contributes to the student's overall view of what teaching is all about and in what manner he will participate in it.

By keeping this model of teaching in mind the classroom teacher can create a more spirited and enthusiastic atmosphere. Perhaps the first and most important thing the teacher can do is to structure the situation so that he himself learns along with the pupils. The teacher can set up his game strategy so that the class inquires into areas which are open and which encourage all the players to score and win. For example, American history offers such areas as The Prevention of World War III and The Future of the Industrial City. Intellectual inquiry, rather than a re-hash of six or seven short homework study questions, can make the teaching game appealing.

In order to do this the teacher will need to sharpen up his coaching ability. The teacher as coach may need to teach his pupils new skills, e.g., to inquire intellectually into unsolved issues. This necessitates the continued observing and reviewing of the pupils' work. When the teacher criticizes a pupil's poor performance, he must do so according to intellectual standards and with a tone that will lead to subsequent improvement. This includes pointing out errors in logic, citing new references, and raising new questions. In this way, he need not feel guilty when he criticizes the student, and the pupil will learn how to play the game better. By concentrating on the roles of inquiring quarterback and coach, the teacher can profitably play down his role as scorekeeper.

One other procedure will help. The teacher can arrange for the pupils to play a variety of roles more often. As in baseball and football, the teacher as coach can call upon his better players to help him improve the play of others. Talented and expert players can give helpful hints and instruction to those who are in a slump. The pupils can serve as referees by judging debates and anonymously commenting on anonymous papers. Certainly players learn how to play any game, including the teaching game, from their teammates. This procedure will provide variety for the pupils and free the teacher from sole responsibility for specific roles. He will become more sensitive to the other roles he performs, especially the combination of rule maker and referee. By expanding the roles of the pupil, the teacher can infuse enthusiasm into the teaching game.

28. The Game of Thinking

B. Othanel Smith

When does one know the rules of a game, say, the game of checkers? Suppose he says, "No, you can't make that move" when someone moves a man backward, and he says this on any occasion when that move is made. Should we say that he knows one of the rules of the game, even though he cannot give a sophisticated statement of it? I think we should claim that he does know the rule. So it is with the rules of logic. To know that affirming the consequent is invalid is to recognize such affirmation when it occurs and to recognize thereby that the truth or falsity of the conclusion is still up in the air. The particular verbal form in which the rule is put is of no consequence in playing the game or in refereeing it.

The analogy between the game of checkers and thinking breaks down at least in one significant respect. A player in checkers is always called for infraction of the rules; learning to play the game entails learning the rules. But with thinking it is different. A player in this game, except among

"The Game of Thinking" by B. Othanel Smith is reprinted with permission from "Logic, Thinking, and Teaching," *Educational Theory*, 4: 225-233, October, 1957.

professionals, can take all sorts of liberties without anyone calling him for infraction of the rules and without the player himself even knowing that he is breaking them. In some cases, however, he will pick up certain logical rules in an *ad hoc* sense. Suppose a beginning high school student is given the following argument: If it rains, the streets are wet. The streets are wet. Therefore it rained. He will tell you quickly that the conclusion does not necessarily follow because the streets may be wet for some other reason. Perhaps the street sprinkler has come along. But when the content is unfamiliar and the argument complex, the student will seldom recognize the fallacy. He may fail to recognize the fallacy as such, if his reasoning is still at the level of concrete relations. Hence he could not go beyond cases of particular content. Nor could he recognize the fallacy in any general sense. Hence if the material relations in an argument go beyond his concrete knowledge, the student who has only an *ad hoc* command of the rules cannot detect logical mistakes. . . .

To continue a little longer in the metaphor, in the game of thinking the teacher is player, coach, and often referee. As a player, he engages students in thinking by asking questions and responding to their answers, by receiving questions and giving answers, and by many other devices and activities. In each of these there is a sort of give and take between teacher and students. But, having little knowledge of logic and being preoccupied with getting the student to understand facts and ideas, the teacher usually overlooks the logic of both his subject and of the class discussion. For instance, a history teacher discusses with his students the imperialism of a nation. He goes into the question of the extent and cause of the imperialism. But the concept of imperialism is not itself explicated, so that the students have varied notions of what is being talked about. The whole discussion is based on a vague and ambiguous term and thus thinking and learning are short-changed.

Now the teacher moves from the role of player to that of coach when he turns to the task of helping students work out a definition of imperialism. To handle this task, the teacher needs criteria by which to decide the adequacy of the definition worked out by himself and the students. As the teacher and students together analyze the concept of imperialism and give it the form of a definition, the teacher will help students from time to time to see what it means to define a term and to understand the kinds of rules by which the adequacy of a definition may be decided. He will show them, as appropriate occasions arise, that a definition lays down criteria for the use of a word, and that the definition we decide to give a word, or the usage we select, is related to the purpose we have in mind. He will show them that sometimes we define words by assigning whatever is named by the word to a class and then distinguishing it from other members of the class. On other occasions the teacher will show how to define words by pointing to instances, and in still other cases by reference to the operations we perform.

To reflect upon the work of the teacher is to see that there are many occasions when he could readily teach procedures of analysis and logical appraisal.

29. The Classroom Game

Arno A. Bellack, Joel R. Davitz, in collaboration with Herbert M. Kliebard and Ronald T. Hyman

One way of conceptualizing these results[1] is in terms of the language game of teaching and learning. Despite the fact that the rules of this game are not explicitly stated for any of the players, our sample of teachers and pupils obviously followed a set of implicit rules with few deviations. These rules define the teaching game. Although classes differ somewhat in details, for the purposes of an initial description of the classroom game, the results strongly support the assumption that common elements underlie much of the teaching game in that pupils and teachers follow a consistent pattern of language rules. It is as if the grammar of English had never been explicitly written, yet everyone generally spoke in essentially the same grammatical forms. It may be useful, therefore, to summarize these rules explicitly, *not as a prescriptive guide to future teacher behavior,* but rather, as a descriptive model of what actually occurs in classrooms like those in the present study.

The classroom game involves one person called a teacher and one or more persons called pupils. The object of the game is to carry on a linguistic discourse about subject matter, and the final payoff of the game is measured in terms of the amount of learning displayed by the pupils after a given period of play. In playing the game, each player must follow a specific set of rules. If one plays the role of teacher in this game, he will follow one set of rules; if one plays the role of pupil, he will follow a

Reprinted with permission from *The Language of the Classroom: Meanings Communicated in High School Teaching.* Arno A. Bellack and Joel R. Davitz in collaboration with Herbert M. Kliebard and Ronald T. Hyman. U.S. Department of Health, Education, and Welfare, Office of Education, Cooperative Research Project No. 1497. New York, Institute of Psychological Research, Teachers College, Columbia University, 1963.

[1] Results of the research reported in Section 2 on p. 82. RTH, editor.

somewhat different, though complementary, set of rules. One is permitted some deviations from these rules and the subsequent pattern will characterize one's individual style of play. These deviations, however, are infrequent and are relatively minor in comparison to the general system of expectations. In fact, the first rule, which might be called "the rule of rules," is that if one is to play the game at all, he will consistently follow the rules specified for his role. Otherwise, the game cannot be played.

Within the general set of rules defining the game, there are individual differences among teachers and classes in style of play. In one classroom, the teacher may specialize in one kind of move or sequence of moves, while in another class the teacher may specialize in a slightly different pattern of discourse. Notwithstanding these variations in style and differences in specialization of moves, the game is always played by a consistent set of general rules. These are rarely made explicit during the course of play; more often, they are defined implicitly by the sequence of moves that actually occurs. Regardless of whether they are explicit or implicit, both teachers and pupils are responsible for playing by the rules of the game.

These rules will be presented in the following order: (1) rules for the role of teacher; (2) rules for the role of pupil; and finally, (3) general rules for all players.

RULES FOR THE TEACHER

If one plays the role of teacher in this game, he will obey the following rules:

1. The teacher will be the most active single person playing the game. This means that he will make the most moves; he will speak most frequently and his speeches will usually be the longest. He is permitted some flexibility in the exact amount by which his activity exceeds the total activity of all other players, but in general, the ratio of his speech to the speech of all other players will be 3 to 1 in terms of amount spoken, and 3 to 2 in terms of the number of moves made. Moreover, these ratios will remain constant over several class sessions, unless he directs another player to assume his role temporarily.

2. The teacher is responsible for structuring the form and content of the game. He will specify the subject matter of the game, and the rules for the game. Within any particular setting, as in various baseball parks, there will be specific ground rules. The teacher is responsible for setting these ground rules and for making them explicit to the other players. In addition to setting up the initial structure of the game, the teacher is

responsible for launching new topics of discussion and for determining any changes that might occur in the form of play as the game proceeds.

3. The most frequent move of the teacher is called "soliciting." This is a directive move designed to elicit a specific response from the players called "pupils." Frequently, this move will be formulated in terms of a question, but may also be phrased in terms of a direct order, such as directing another player to speak, to open his book, or carry out any other action relevant to this game. If one plays the role of teacher, he is required to obey "the rule of proper questions"; that is, he must ask valid questions, stated in a logical form and concerned with substantive material so that some pupils in the game may be expected to answer. His intent must not be to trick the other players or pose impossible problems, but, rather, to formulate solicitations which will elicit from pupils legitimate responses that will move the game along.

4. After making a soliciting move, the teacher will normally expect a person playing the role of "pupil" to respond. It is then the teacher's responsibility to react to this response. Sometimes, he may react non-verbally, by nodding his head or perhaps by showing approval implicitly by moving to a new solicitation. In most instances, however, he is expected to react in an explicit fashion. Many of these reactions will be evaluative; that is, the teacher is expected either to approve or disapprove of the response made by the pupil player. In the majority of instances, his reaction will be at least somewhat positive. Frequently, he tells a pupil explicitly that he has made a "correct" or "good" response; in any case, he is expected at least to "admit" the pupil's statement, often by a short phrase such as "all right." When the teacher is forced, by the obviously incorrect nature of the pupil's response, to make a negative evaluation, usually he will not make this evaluation completely negative; that is, by reacting with such remarks as "No," or "You're wrong." Rather, he will offer some sort of qualifying evaluation, such as "Yes, but . . ," or he will point out that the pupil's preceding response was not entirely correct or to the point.

5. In addition to reacting to immediately preceding statements, the teacher is also responsible for occasional summaries of larger parts of the discourse. This may simply be a repetition of several preceding responses or some form of integration of the earlier discourse. In this respect, he is free to choose either the more repetitive or the more integrative style. When speaking the role of the teacher, one also has freedom to introduce, in summarizing reactive moves, additional logical and substantive meanings. Thus one may summarize by mere repetition, by more active integration, or by either repetition or integration plus additional meanings.

6. Although either the teacher or the pupil may express substantive and substantive-logical meanings, it is, primarily, the teacher who is

responsible for expressing meanings relevant to instructional processes. A large proportion of these "instructional moves" will be reactions which are metacommunicative: reactive statements about another player's preceding statements. This sort of metacommunication is almost entirely within the teacher's domain of play; unless requested to do so, pupils will rarely make this kind of statement. Because metacommunicative statements are made rather infrequently in linguistic games outside the classroom, the teacher must take particular care in making them. For example, if one speaks the role of the teacher in the classroom, he will undoubtedly be required to play other games outside of the classroom with principals, supervisors, superintendents, etc. When playing this outside game, in contrast to his classroom role, it is likely that the teacher will not normally make reactive metacomments to the principal: telling him that he is wrong, his statement is false, or his response is off the point. But in playing the classroom game, this is one of his primary responsibilities, aimed at shaping the responses made by other players so as to bring them more into line with his expectations.

Other kinds of instructional statements made by the teacher will concern classroom procedures to be followed in playing the game and assignments to be prepared by students. From an instructional-logical point of view, these will consist largely of stating facts or making straightforward directive statements telling the pupils what to do. Rarely will the teacher ever express an opinion about instructional meanings or justify any opinions he might state about them.

RULES FOR THE PUPIL

If one speaks the role of the pupil, his responsibilities in playing the game are much more restricted than those of the person playing the role of teacher. The pupil must remember that his eventual performance on some measure of learning determines the final payoff of the game both for him and for the teacher; therefore, it is assumed that he will learn. Regardless of whether one learns, if he speaks the role of the pupil, he will obey the following rules:

1. The pupil's primary task in the game is to respond to the teacher's solicitations. This usually involves answering specific questions posed by the teacher, but may also involve following direct orders given by the teacher, such as "Open your book," or "Get up and shut the window." Whenever the teacher makes a soliciting move, the pupil will, if at all possible, attempt some form of response. The response may be right or

wrong in terms of the teacher's expectations; it may be relevant or irrelevant to the ongoing game. In any case, the pupil is required to attempt some response to the teacher's solicitation. In extreme cases, the pupil may reply to a solicitation by saying, "I don't know" but this should be used rarely, if at all. The best policy for the pupil to follow in playing the game is "make a response whenever called upon."

2. The pupil does not structure the game; that is, he does not tell the teacher and other pupils what the game is to be about or how to play it. This is the task of the teacher. Occasionally, the pupil is called upon to give a report or to participate in a debate. This is a form of structuring, but pupils make such moves *only* when directed to do so by the teacher. Having fulfilled his assigned structuring obligation, the pupil will not structure again unless the teacher specifically directs him to do so.

3. In general, the pupil will keep his solicitations to a minimum. If he must solicit, he will restrict his questions to instructional matters. If absolutely necessary in order to continue playing the game, he may ask the teacher to clarify an assignment or explain some instructional procedure involved in the game. On the other hand, he does not solicit in regard to substantive matters, and certainly never makes a directive statement to the teacher such as "Speak" or "Get up and close the window." If the pupil makes such a solicitation, it is likely that he will be excluded from the field of play.

4. Even more important than the *don't* solicit rule is the *don't* react evaluatively rule. Under no condition is the pupil permitted to react evaluatively to a statement made by the teacher; that is, the pupil does not tell the teacher he is right or wrong, that he is doing well or doing badly. If the pupil has impulses in this direction, he must inhibit them, for they have no place in the classroom game. This applies both to positive and to negative evaluations of the teacher. Occasionally, the pupil may be asked to react evaluatively to another pupil's response. If asked to do so by the teacher, he may make this move; it should be brief and probably should not be too strong either in a positive or in a negative direction. Although not exactly achieving the status of a rule, the pupil should keep whatever evaluations he is asked to make as bland as possible.

5. A corollary of the "don't react evaluatively" rule is the general principle, "within the classroom, teachers speak The Truth." This principle holds by virtue of the teacher's role in the game and the rules guiding pupils' play. Except under extraordinary circumstances, pupils overtly accept the teacher's statements as the spoken truth.

On the other hand, pupils may or may not speak "The Truth." If one speaks the role of pupil, he must remember that merely uttering a statement does not guarantee that it will be accepted as true. In fact, an important part of the teacher's responsibility is to challenge, though mildly, pupils' statements which he believes to be invalid. In certain classes, pupils may even be challenged occasionally by other pupils.

6. In some classes, pupils are expected to make reactions that carry no explicit evaluative meaning. This will depend upon the ground rules established by the teacher. The only guide one can follow is the expectation of the teacher: does he or does he not expect the pupil to react to other pupils' statements?

7. Finally, a pupil player should remember that his primary task is to respond to the teacher's solicitations and to perform well on the final payoff test. If he fulfills both of these obligations and does not usurp the role of the teacher, then he will most likely play the game successfully.

SOME GENERAL RULES FOR ALL PLAYERS

In addition to the rules related to a specific role, there are some general rules that apply to all players. Regardless of the particular role one plays, he will obey the following rules:

1. The major part of the game will be played with the substantive meanings specified by the teacher's structuring of the game. From time to time, however, either player is permitted to wander from this central focus, sometimes to topics relevant to the substantive core of the game and occasionally to a topic which is thoroughly irrelevant to the principal subject matter. The teacher will usually initiate these off-target discussions, sometimes as a means of introducing or clarifying a substantive point. Occasionally a pupil player is permitted to introduce an irrelevancy, but this must not be done often in a single class session. The exact frequency depends upon the reactions of the person playing the role of teacher. In general, however, the discussion will take place within the substantive framework of the teacher's structuring.

2. From a substantive-logical or instructional-logical point of view, if the game is played within the substantive area of economics, or in any related subject area, the discourse will consist largely of empirical meanings. This means that for the most part, the moves will be statements either of fact or explanations; approximately 50 to 60 per cent of the speech will involve empirical meaning. Analytic meaning involving either definitions of terms of interpretations will be expressed much less frequently. The frequency of evaluative statements will also be relatively low in comparison to empirical statements. Thus, expressions of personal opinion about economic policies or attempts to justify opinions will appear relatively infrequently. Players will, however, be free to report opinions of others, such as public figures, or to report the arguments used by others

to justify their opinions. This does not mean that players are completely prohibited from expressing their own opinions and justifications, but that the general policy under which the game is played encourages the use of statements with empirical meaning.

3. As indicated in the preamble to this set of rules, one is permitted some deviations from the specified set of rules. In almost all instances, the range of these deviations depends upon the ground rules set by the teacher, which may be either explicit or implicit. In any event, one is responsible for learning and obeying these ground rules; for example, a teacher may vary his style of play so that he spends most of the game structuring, while the pupil's main task is simply to attend to the structuring and to respond whenever called upon to do so. A teacher may, on the other hand, choose to play the game principally as a question and answer exercise; if he so chooses, he is also responsible for reacting to pupil answers. The teacher may even choose a style of play characterized by a proportion of reactions larger than that usually seen in this game. If a pupil is indeed playing the game with such a teacher, his responsibility to react may be almost as compelling as his responsibility to respond. Thus, within the general rules of the game, the style of play may be modified in one way or another. Once the ground rules for a particular game have been set, however, it is wise neither for the teacher nor for the player to assume the other player's role. If one plays the role of teacher, part of his responsibility will be to set the ground rules and to see that these rules are obeyed in playing the game. In this sense, the teacher is expected to serve not only as coach and one of the players, but also as referee of the game. On the other hand, if one plays the role of pupil, he must learn the ground rules of the game even if the rules are not explicitly stated by the teacher.

4. In gauging wins and losses, players must remember that this is not a game in which one player, such as the teacher, wins while another player, such as one of the pupils, loses. Rather, there are relative degrees of winning and losing, and the teacher's winnings are a function of the pupils' performances. This is a peculiar, but important, characteristic of this game. While the teacher undeniably has the greater power and freedom in the course of play, he is ultimately dependent on his pupils for the degree of success he achieves in playing the game.

This feature of the game is a consequence of the criterion of success. The eventual aim of the game, the ostensible reason for the play, is the pupil's learning of substantive and substantive-logical meanings. Learning is usually measured by test performance; therefore, the teacher's success depends upon the pupil's test performance. If a pupil fails the test, implying that he has not learned, then the teacher, by implication, has not taught successfully. Thus, insofar as that pupil is concerned, the teacher has lost the game. A single teacher, of course, typically plays the game with many students, so that his wins and losses are scored over the total group of pupils, much as the team point system is used to score track meets. In calculating the results, several test failures may be offset by a number of brilliant test scores, although the precise formula depends upon the educational setting in which the game occurs. For some schools, success requires at least minimal performance by all pupils; in such schools, the teacher's overall score is considerably reduced for even one or two test failures, with proportionately less credit for high test scores. For other schools, a few exceedingly high scores overbalance a substantial number of low test results. In this latter setting, a few special pupil prizes, awarded by outside sources such as "Regents Scholarships" and "Merit Scholarships," may very well counterbalance many failures.

The general formula for computing a teacher's final score cannot be written because the weights assigned to various kinds of test scores depend upon other games played by other people. These outside players are called principals, superintendents, and school board members, and it would be wise for a person, when he begins to play the teaching role in a given setting, to determine the formula for success used by these outside players.

It is of historical interest to note that the general definition of success has changed over the years. Earlier forms of the teaching game were like other competitive games in which one person wins and another loses; the teacher was pitted against the pupil much like a baseball pitcher is pitted against the batter. But just as whist gradually evolved into bridge, the competitive type of the teaching game has changed to a more mutually dependent form of play.

In summary, it should be remembered that these are the rules of the game *as it is played, not necessarily as it should be played*. At this point, the concern is only with a description of the classroom game, and this description is summarized in the rules of the game. Depending upon one's opinion about what should occur in a classroom, the rules specified may or may not serve as prescriptions of teacher and pupil behavior. Regardless of any set of prescriptive guides that one might view as desirable, the rules thus far specified are based on a detailed analysis of what actually happened in the classrooms sampled.

SECTION SIX

Aesthetics

OVERVIEW

O F the vantage points considered in this book, the one of aesthetics is the most neglected. This neglect is evidenced by the paucity of material discussing teaching with the aid of such concepts as beauty, harmony, balance, rhythm, tempo, and form. Also, very few empirical studies have been conducted to describe what it is that constitutes artistry in teaching, or the art of teaching, or teaching as an art. Furthermore, programs for preparing teachers seldom devote attention to this perspective. The notion that teaching can fruitfully be viewed from an aesthetic vantage point comes as a pleasant surprise to many people already familiar with other perspectives.

The reasons for this neglect are not at all clear. There have been articles and books dealing with the role of art and music in the schools, and of the role in the schools of aesthetics in general. There have also been articles and books claiming that teaching is an art, meaning by that phrase that there are currently no "scientific" laws one can apply in his search for what and how to teach. But in spite of this literature there has been precious little analysis of the act of teaching from the aesthetic point of view.

Perhaps it is because of this lack that the authors represented in this section explicitly justify their investigations of teaching from an aesthetic vantage point. Swineford employs a double metaphor in the title of his article when calling artistic teaching the Cinderella of modern instruction. For him, the wicked stepmother is modern technology. Similarly, Huebner,[1] in an early unpublished paper, claims that approaching teaching as an art has value in our society, which is moving toward automation but crying out for individuality. This theme of meaning through art in a world of technology underlies Huebner's concern in his article included in this section and serves as the motivation for the analysis. For Curran also the impetus for making teaching an art is the desire to enrich lives that have become increasingly mechanistic. For Eisner, the aesthetic point of view is justified by its contribution to learning. To the extent that teaching lacks this qualitative aspect, learning is impeded or hindered.

Another reason why teaching is so seldom analyzed from the aesthetic point of view is that definitions of art differ widely. Philosophers have long differed on this topic, and one impact of the controversy may have been to discourage educators from entering the discussion. The few educators who have entered the discussion have not always agreed among themselves on what art is and what constitutes teaching as an art. Thus, the reader needs to scrutinize the overt and covert definitions used by the authors here. For example, Swineford's four criteria for artistic teaching are not the same as Curran's three steps for developing teaching into an art. Dewey's notion of what the teacher as artist does is not the same as Huebner's. Also, Huebner and Eisner disagree about symbolic meaning in art.

Yet the approaches of Curran and Huebner are similar in several ways. Curran's roots of the aesthetic experience revolve around many of the same concepts of Huebner's aesthetic valving, e.g., balance, unity and wholeness, order, and harmony. Also, both men speak of bringing meaning to teaching via an aesthetic attitude. They speak of removing the routine dullness and meaninglessness found too often in the classroom. They both consider art broadly, not narrowing it to painting, sculpturing, and writing. Huebner includes the scientist and the engineer as creative artists, and Curran goes so

[1] Dwayne Huebner. "The Art of Teaching." Unpublished manuscript, October, 1962.

far as to assert that there are no special subjects that have a high aesthetic potentiality. Note that Eisner similarly claims that qualitative intelligence is exercised in all walks of life.

There is strong agreement among the selections in this section that the aesthetic analysis of teaching must include concepts from both aspects of art. Art has its technical or craft side as well as its emotional side. For Curran, the technical side includes mastery in the use of textbooks, films, and other audio-visual aids. Conspicuously absent from his list is the chief tool of the teacher, language. It is primarily through language that the teacher expresses himself in the classroom and brings about the harmony out of conflict which is the essence of the aesthetic experience, according to Curran. Perhaps it is this lack of mastery of language, which is intangible, as opposed to the more easily achieved mastery of the audio-visual aids, which are tangible, that has brought about the dullness and routine deplored by Curran.

The second side of teaching as an art, the emotional aspect, deserves and gets the main thrust of each of the following articles. Mastery of the use of texts and other aids is necessary but hardly sufficient to yield artistic teaching. The emotional tone of the teacher is the main element. This Curran shows by his analogy of the short-story writer. Dewey, too, emphasizes this point in his brief selection. Indeed, to bring order from disorder, to tame chaos with intelligence, and to encourage self-initiation in the pupil requires more than the skill of a technician. It demands purpose, sensitivity, and acute awareness of life. It demands the infusion of rhythm, tempo, form, imagination, spontaneity, pacing, and harmony, to list but a few of the terms used by Curran, Eisner, Huebner, Hallman, Swineford, and Dewey.

It is interesting to note and consider the various types of people used in the analogies between teaching and art. Certainly Eisner's choice of the nightclub comedian is a bit unusual. Yet the parallels Eisner draws between the teacher and the comedian are apt. Would it be possible to use Eisner's concepts of timing and playing-it-by-ear as part of a formal instrument with which to observe teaching? Curran's short-story writer is also striking, as are his violin-maker and cook. But his sculptor molding clay is a familiar model for teaching. (Do teachers "mold" the minds, emotions, and spirits of their pupils?) Would it be possible to use Curran's three steps of building an art as the basis for observing classroom teaching?

Hallman's synthesizing article serves to focus our attention on the general topic of creativity. His four principles of creative teaching serve as a bridge between this section and the one on classroom emotional climate. He cites and draws upon Rogers, who is included in this book, Schachtel, and others for his principles of creative teaching. These same people also serve as a foundation for other articles, especially the one by Macdonald and Zaret. Hallman raises a significant point by connecting the self-actualizing person with an aesthetic need, an aesthetic drive. The interplay between aesthetics, creativity, and psychology is pertinent for the analysis of teaching. What role does the aesthetic drive, if there is one, play in teaching? How can we identify its manifestations during teaching?

Hallman further relates creativity to the cognitive vantage point (Maccia) by emphasizing the role of hypothetical thinking; to classroom social climate (Flanders) by discussing the role of freedom in creativity; and to communications (Packer and Packer) when dealing with the role of uncertainty. No doubt the reader will find other connections between this multi-faceted article and others in this book.

But in at least two ways Hallman differs from, rather than complements, other authors. His use of the word *manipulation* is not at all the same as Gerbner's in the section on communication. Nor is his definition of authoritarian behavior the same as Flanders' in the section on social climate. The reader is alerted to these differences as he himself interrelates the various perspectives and selections.

The article by Swineford serves as the lone selection directly based on empirical observation. Even though he would not get total agreement from other educators that his categories operationally define artistic teaching, the results of his study are consistent with points made by the other authors. The most significant one is "the paucity of artistic teaching in our schools." Swineford claims that this situation is a serious one for teaching and suggests that steps can and should be taken to alter it. Few would disagree with this point. The question is, what exactly should be done to encourage and promote artistic teaching? How can we do it?

The implications for further research are many, as stated by Hallman and Swineford. If, to use Huebner's term, this aesthetic perspective is to be fruitful, then much work lies ahead for educators. Is it possible to develop sensitive observational instruments based on such concepts as qualitative intelligence, psychical distance, wholeness and design, order and equilibrium, and aesthetic attitude? If so, would data from high schools, elementary schools, colleges, and nursery schools differ? Would we get significantly different results in economics, art, music, biology, mathematics, and English classes? What is it that artistic teachers do and say that makes them artistic? What relation, if any, is there between achievement and the aesthetic tone of the classroom as set by the teacher? How do we prepare teachers to teach artistically? These are but a few of the myriad of questions that need answering in this area, which more than any other lacks empirical research.

30. Artistry in Teaching

Clyde E. Curran

Most adults jog along submerged in routine. Tuning their lives to alarm clocks ringing, eating, catching trains, working and sleeping, they settle into a pattern of reoccurring events. The machinelike hum of their existence gives a deceptive impression of serenity. Instead of fulfillment that comes from a thoughtful use of energies, their strength ebbs under the repetitious tread of day-to-day living. Sensitivities encrusted, they develop immunities to any form of animation. Their home and work that can and should offer excitement become mildly endurable. When searching for the right word to describe their way of life, one immediately comes to mind—"dull." That thousands of people undergo a gradual draining of juice from their lives is tragic.

What can educators do to improve this condition? Teachers need to challenge youngsters so thoroughly, incite their interest in so many things, that when they leave school, routine cannot possibly dull them. This

"Artistry in Teaching" by Clyde E. Curran is reprinted with permission from *Educational Theory*, 3: 134-149, April, 1953.

implies that in addition to extending their interest along a wide horizon, students learn the necessary skills for furthering these interests and for penetrating deeply into a select few. If adults, through their contact in schools during their youth, become enthusiastic about doing a wide variety of interesting things, they will likely avoid boredom later. Not that specific games, or hobbies learned in school, should carry over into adulthood. This would do no more than provide a set of gadgets, infantile and adolescent toys. Something much more subtle than this occurs when students in school do worthwhile things that interest them. During the act of avidly pressing interest into broadening channels, changes take place in the personalities of the people involved. Their eyes take on a spark. They become vital. They build into their selves dynamic qualities that carry them through life with vigor. Personality facets charged with curiosity in youth, tend upon maturity to continue to reach out into expanding vistas. People who develop the habit of searching for and finding adventure in everyday things do not usually suffer from arrested development.

To state that stimulating interest gives the key to the situation solves nothing, for the question remains—how is this done?

How to arouse interest, even more important, how to promote worthwhile interest, is one of the major problems of teaching. Despite the amount of effort directed toward this problem, the results are meager. The fact that thousands of people are involved in work they relish suggests that teachers can improve their methods through watching these people to discover how they have developed this vital interest. Every craft, trade, and profession offers examples of people absorbed in their work—the gardener who keeps busy until dark because he likes what he does; the businessman motivated not by the jangle of the cash register, but by economic theory, the desire to improve his product, the challenge of advertising and marketing and the problems of interpersonal relations; scientists, writers, artists, and musicians, spending long hours in their studies and laboratories. Any job where people become involved in the act of creating which carries them on with enthusiasm serves as an example. Through observing busy people doing constructive work they enjoy, educators can find the clue for stemming lethargy. Through analyzing individuals creating, educators can discover ways for capturing and furthering the creative spirit.

TEACHING AS AN ART

Creative work that meets certain specifications is art. When it carries the creator on a wave of emotional exaltation to the point of completion, when the symmetry and balance of the finished job bring pleasure not only to the producer but to other people observing it, then the creation is art. Art, used in this sense not only pertains to pictures in galleries or music in concert halls, but applies to all affairs of men that take on fine proportions. Art brings about a union between moral-practical affairs and beauty. This does not mean that beautiful objects have an extraneous existence to the good and useful, but that people in satisfying the urgent demands of daily living can exercise affection and care so that the home, the world of commerce, and guiding rules of conduct become graceful.

Art breaks down into two components which originate from the same source and coexist in actual practice. One side concerns building, handling materials, tools, techniques, the union of mind, the senses and hands in the complex activity of constructing. On the other side are emotions—joy, delight, ectasy, the loving affections which show deep personal satisfaction. This latter division bears the name esthetic. A thing artistically done, and this can refer to almost any human endeavor, couples skill with emotion in such a way that the finished product is beautiful.

If educators, when searching for improved methods, take their inquiry into creative work, they soon become involved in the study of art. This does not mean just observing paintings and painters. They must watch people living finely balanced lives, creative people receiving pleasure from building and constructing. No trade or profession has a monopoly on this. All can require artistry, all can provide esthetic joy, despite the fact that few do, that thousands of people seldom have esthetic experiences.

This condition has become so common that symbolic esthetic representations (paintings and books) are scooped up for galleries and libraries. In addition to treasuring these because they perpetuate a rare quality that too seldom enters life, people have the mistaken notion that works of fine art generate the esthetic. Beauty comes from experience. Practically all existing esthetic theory has come from the hands of metaphysicians. Imaginative minds, longing for perfection, have probed the cosmos formulating poetic conceptions of absolute beauty, but in the light of human frailty, failing to tell how to obtain it. While searching in the realm of pure essence philosophers have overlooked how esthetic ideals relate to human struggle. Ideals of beauty receive their generative power and incubative warmth from people trying to understand and harness the forces that sustain them. People struggling, building, hating, and loving furnish the place of conception and fulfillment of esthetic ideals. The failure to recognize this is one of the tragedies of western civilization. While raking the heavens, while held spellbound by abstract visions of perfection, thinkers have overlooked where beauty exists. They have been too overwhelmed by grand ideas to look into something as humble as everyday living. They have built tremendous philosophic systems, in themselves works of art, into which they poured their own creative impulses, but have not brought grace into daily affairs. Generation after generation beholding these gigantic creations become awed, become incapacitated to see beauty in day-to-day existence, for did not sages tell them that the esthetic transcends experience?

It would seem absurd to suppose that teachers, practitioners of pedagogy, can accomplish something that the outstanding minds of our heritage have failed in, except for one thing. Teachers are steeped in human experience. This is their daily fare. True, philosophers and poets have had this advantage also, but for over two thousand years the very nature of their work takes them away from the dynamics of the home and market place. Although exemplifying artistry, their theories seldom explain in a way that can affect everyday living the process of creation. They become too enslaved to predecessors to break fresh trails. Teachers also follow tradition, but their work, their every move, brings them into direct contact with people. Soon the idea will grow that they have within their grasp a wonderful power. They can awaken themselves and those they contact. Through observing the all too few examples of individuals undergoing esthetic experience, they can pluck out techniques for furthering beauty. They can become artists, artists in human relations, purveyors of beauty in the difficult realm of the affairs of men.

The preceding suggests that teachers, through studying people engaged in creative work, can put procedures into schools that will forward the creative urge. When students become sufficiently enlivened through their contact with these new methods, they should develop personalities with sufficient vitality for overcoming the stultifying effects of routine. The foregoing also implies that a study of art (using the term in the broad sense developed above) will give educators insight into creative acts from which they can construct classroom technique. Through understanding more about how esthetic qualities enter people's lives and consciously perfecting methods that will extend the number of these experiences, educators enter the way to artistry in teaching.

Building teaching into an art takes three steps. First, teachers should become aware of how intense emotional satisfaction accompanies creative work. They should not neglect manipulation in art involving building and handling of materials, but once they can grasp and control the motivating force of emotions, they have mastered the most difficult part. This means educators should analyze the emotions of people engaged in creative work. Controlling classroom conditions so that students have opportunity for artistic expression is the second step in the act of teaching. The third step concerns the experiences teachers have while advancing the artistic possibilities of their work. Teachers as artists, among other things, strive for harmonious human relations. They lend themselves to a process in which groups of students work together. In this way they are like writers or painters who, in creating, become a part of the finished product. There is, however, a difference between the teacher and the painter. The painter works in isolation treating his material according to his personal taste. He, as the artist, has control of the entire process. Teachers, on the other hand, are but one of the hundreds of complex forces that bear upon students. They become engulfed in a complicated situation in which they control only a small part of their pupils' experience. Teaching-artists participate in, become vital elements of, the creative process. A painter does this only if his picture suddenly becomes alive and the parts of his personality that have gone into it spring into life. (Imaginatively this often happens.) Teachers function like catalysts within a gushing flow of human experience, speeding the learning process on its way. They differ from catalysts in that they have a concern about the outcome of their work, and as participants in the educative process, they as well as their pupils change. Considering how teachers' experiences can take on the excitement resulting from creating, is the third step in treating teaching as an art.

These three steps in developing teaching into an art closely follow three approaches to studying art. First, attention may focus upon the artist. Practising craftsmen offer examples of work methods that get results. While working, their experiences run from strain and frustration to intense satisfaction. Studying this behavior with its accompanying emotional responses to improve education constitutes a first step in making teaching artistic. Attention may also shift to the finished product—the painting or the literary composition. Conventional art forms differ from teaching. Observers in libraries and galleries can point out static objects, books and paintings, as the object of art, while in education the effective teaching process constitutes the finished product. In teaching, artistry exists within the complex pattern of moving human experiences. Art students may not only look at the worker or the finished product, but may take the role of consumers. Those who produce do this also. During every stage of their job, they taste what they have done, they sample appreciatively their efforts. Through adding here, taking away there, the final perfected composition emerges. Then they lean back and enjoy the satisfaction that comes when creative work reaches completion. Teachers do this too. The educator and the painter differ as they appreciatively view their work. Painters work with materials that come under their control with relative ease while teachers bound like corks on an ocean of seething experiences. Painters attach their signatures to finished compositions as an indication of completion like the period after the last sentence in a novel. Teachers reach no such state of cessation. The process of teaching and living are different dimensions of the same fabric. They both contain exalted moments followed by periods of quiescence, but no complete closure. They both flow, sometimes rapidly, sometimes slowly, sometimes tensely, sometimes smoothly, continuing on as the seasons do, one shading into another. Within this stream, teachers attain periods of fulfillment. These are their compositions, points where ideals become incorporated into the lives of their students. Boys and girls gaining sensitivity toward literature, young people growing in their understanding of themselves and their associates, and youths who can judge and think, constitute the color and form of teachers' completed creative work. Teachers turn to improvement in qualities of human experience for appreciative enjoyment.

Steps in Developing Teaching Artistry

The three steps in developing artistry in teaching are: (1) building teaching methods based on a psychological analysis of working artists, (2) instituting improvements in teaching activities through suggestions gained from observing objects of art, and (3) controlling this entire process from continually applying refined skills and sensitivities that grow from appreciatively observing the emerging creative teaching enterprise. Stated briefly, through studying the artist, the object of art, and those who appreciate art, then from this observation devising methods for classrooms, teachers may make their job more creative. How do they go about this? Answering the following questions suggests a way. What do artists do and feel as they create? What does the finished work contain? How do people react while enjoying art?

The large number of practical and fine arts offers educators limitless opportunity for this kind of study. Any craftsman who makes beautiful works which give people pleasure will serve as an object of study. While watching him as he creates, then viewing the finished job, then seeing how other people react to his work, educators can draw out a series of principles that will readily apply to classrooms. Studying the short story writer is suitable for this purpose. What does he experience as he writes? What, as a work of art, does the story contain? How do readers react?

What does a short story writer do and experience as he works? If a series of sensitive cameras would record every motion a writer takes as he composes, one phase of his job would immediately come to the front—technique. Writers, along with other craftsmen, handle tools. They master words, sentence structure, plot, characterization, and the refinements of composition that give their stories polish. Years of effort go into perfecting execution. They study two sources to refine technique. First they saturate themselves in the complex trappings of literary composition. They write, write, and write under the guidance of a competent critic who points out their strengths and weaknesses. Secondly, they become intensely aware of their environment, especially human conflict. Looking for and finding stories among familiar surroundings is also part of their skill.

Writers who go no further than mastering writing facility, however, will not produce art. All crafts require expert use of tools, but this alone does not create art. Musicians who play brilliantly but without feeling, painters who wield their brushes with machinelike precision but produce banal pictures, and writers who develop their work with clarity but leave their readers cold, illustrate this point. Technique does not contain the standard by which to measure the artistic merits of a job. In the preceding definition of art, two components were discussed—building and enjoying. Craftsmen must look to this latter quality for their norm. Artistic work must be esthetic, must be framed for enjoyment.

During every step of producing, the writer-artist takes the role of the perceiver, he anticipates the finished work experiencing a sense of fulfillment as each word fits into place. He handles his materials in a loving way, showing care for each sentence, each paragraph. As he works he undergoes the same delights that his work calculates to bring to the reader. Throughout the unfolding of his narrative he experiences an immediately felt joy. This vital, immediately sensed elation, this esthetic quality in writing, turns technical facility into artistry.

Writers must learn technique, but if they wish to produce art, they must bring esthetic quality to their work. Stories that have this quality say a great deal about the author. They say that he has deeply felt his surroundings, that these poetic experiences, this allowing ordinary events to conquer, to overwhelm him, has done something to his personality, for he has become a sensitive, alert, thoroughly alive individual. They say that he belongs to a brotherhood that includes sailors, hunters, explorers, laborers, businessmen, clergymen, scientists, lovers, children, all who have tasted adventure—physical adventure, adventure of ideas, and adventure of the spirit.

Esthetic experience elevates craftsmanship to art. An author who has not lived intensely, who does not infuse his work with the dynamics of his own vitality, may write well, but won't create art. What then accounts for the esthetic? What are the underlying conditions?

These questions have puzzled thinkers for hundreds of years. The discussion at hand requires only enough of this basic background for filling out the illustration of the writer as an artist. Traditionally philosophers sought esthetic fundamentals in metaphysics. (The limitations of this idea were pointed out earlier.) For centuries the idea possessed thinkers that a source of beauty existed, either divine or superempirical, from which esthetic experiences take on coloring. Philosophers envisaged essences from the fountainhead of beauty trickling into objects of art giving them grace. Theories of the esthetic became so ethereal that the realm of beauty was visualized as a shrine that everyday usage would contaminate. This heavenlike vision, however, did not show how daily events can become graceful. Ramifications of this approach have become so ingrained into our culture that an explanation of beauty which treats it as a way of experiencing seems crude. If instead of following the eyes of philosophers into the clouds, we undertake an analysis and description of beauty as it enters people's lives, a basis for understanding and extending esthetic experience can develop. An inquiry into the roots of esthetic experience, which conceives this as emanating from natural events, directs attention to biology and psychology. What biological and psychological attributes of men make it possible for them to undergo experiences of esthetic quality?

Roots of Esthetic Experience

Adjusting is the basic bio-psychological function of human beings. As they interact with their surroundings, as they live and experience, they continually become at odds with their environment. The process of living, daily and hourly, carries people into situations which call for adjustment. These conditions range from simple thirst to elaborate social circumstances, such as satisfying the need for shelter or putting congressmen in office. People continuously fall out with their environment. Rising states of anxiety or tension accompany unbalance.

People reach out into their environments for objects that will reinstate balance. Surroundings not only provide sustenance necessary for continuing life, but they also expose individuals to hazards. The world today abounds in dangers that range from disastrous physical conflict with automobiles to interpersonal relations. When people suffer a temporary displacement, they sense a feeling of frustration, a void enters their lives, they lack something. Acts of adjustment involve filling needs. Need denotes a temporary lack of balance. There is an urgency about needs. When people suffer from lacks, either the simple kind like not having enough food, or the more complex as failure to gain social recognition, they undergo an intense feeling of dissatisfaction. Needs held in suspense long enough result in physical harm, such as malnutrition or psychological damage, like permanent nervousness. With the attainment of balance come feelings of satisfaction, a release of tensions. Equilibrium brings a sense of contentment similar to the experience of a hungry man finishing a good meal.

Daily living continuously throws people out of adjustment, continuously demands that they reinstate harmony. This is fundamental to esthetic experiences. At the bottom of the esthetic as at the heart of living are flux and conflict balanced with order and equilibrium. An act of adjusting that reduces tensions completely, unifying disrupted energies so that a sense of harmony ensues, has esthetic quality. Pulsating patterns of life provide the foundations for such experience. Out of the oscillating flow of people living, comes disruption followed by order, tension by release, conflict by unity, unbalance by equilibrium, dynamic rhythm by quietude, and desire by satisfaction. These constitute the seeds of the esthetic, unity, harmony, order, and form generated from a background of disruption, conflict, rhythm, and desire.

Order does not automatically follow disruption. Life continues even though people carry unresolved tensions with them. The many unexplained fears and anxieties that practically everyone suffers testify to this fact. Sometimes only a partial fulfillment to need occurs leaving a residue of tensional states. Hundreds of accidental and unconscious adjustments happen that ease the pressure of mounting anxiety, but that fall outside the radius of control. Examples of these are the repairs to minor injuries that the body makes without medical aid or a fortunate arrangement of events that makes a job available to a man needing work. People may also passively adapt to the vicissitudes of life. They may endure chronic situations that not only fail to result in resolution of conflict but that actually cause physical and psychological regression. They may subsist but not grow, like plants placed in barren soil that continue to live but reach only a dwarfed semblance of what they could be. Individuals who fall into a meaningless and exhaustive routine suffer from this kind of malady. In the opening paragraph of this discussion they were referred to.

Although dynamic movement through conflict to harmony bears the germ of the esthetic, such resolution seldom happens spontaneously. Adjustment in contrast to passive adaptation or accidental restitution of balance, denotes that an ordering of environmental elements has taken place. To order in this sense means a conscious moving, a direct shaping of surroundings so that they more closely meet desired needs. Rather than leaving things to chance, people assert themselves to meet and modify conditions so they fit into their plans. Rather than allowing circumstances to impinge upon them in a way that leaves them mute, people who adjust dynamically exercise themselves in molding their environments. The direction of change, however, is not one way; it does not just move from the adjuster to the elements of the disturbing situation. People participating in acts of adjustment also change. Their personalities, what they are as people, become shaped. If the continuous falling out with surroundings serves as a stimulant for constructing ever-expanding areas of harmony, then adjusting individuals build habits and skills that enlarge their personalities. They become more keenly aware of the things around them. As they direct straining energies into ordered arrangements, events take on deeper significance. As they move out into the world making more unified bonds with their environment, through the adjusting process they add to a swelling reservoir of enriched meanings. Through expansive adjustment tastes grow, desires enlarge, and sensitivities expand. Although needs arise as they push on into situations that call for new adjustments, these serve as a catapult for extending the growth of their personalities.

No individual, regardless of how fortunate or how alert, saunters through life ever increasing the scope of his horizon, ever expanding the facets of his personality in unending placid sequences. All people continuously have experiences that call for adjustment, but despite effort expended do not reach a satisfying state of fulfillment. Even the most successful suffer almost daily from unfulfilled need. Life moves on but not unruffled. Accident and unresolved conflict take their toll of energy. All people at times flounder, often regressing rather than moving forward. They falter through many experiences that just happen, but do not have a beginning or ending. They stumble along missing street cars, stopping studies for lack of funds, roaming about because no job, no place gives satisfaction, loving but without fulfillment, marrying but without that consummation which draws people together with tightening bonds of affection, rolling along on a seemingly aimless drift. Out of what frequently seems hopeless confusion, lines of continuity can be traced. A pattern emerges giving a sense of balance. It is little wonder that people cherish order. At the moment when turbulence resolves into quietude, people experience satisfaction. When out of conflict, a restitution of harmony occurs. Particularly if the disturbance has been intense, people feel a sublime lift. Here is the essence of the esthetic. Within the stream of living with its faltering, its rushing on, its contrast, its accidents, and its fulfillment, resides the esthetic. It is an immediately felt quality that comes out of the flow from tensions to fulfillment. Without conflict resolving into harmony, without rhythm turning into form, without hazard as a prelude to peace, without need and fulfillment, there would be no esthetic.

TECHNIQUE AND CREATION

Just as technical facility alone will not create art, neither will isolated esthetic experience. It, like an electrical shock, comes and goes. When out of these immediately felt qualities men construct ideals of grace and beauty, giving them expression in concrete form, art develops. Out of the rising and falling waves of life, people have esthetic experiences that give them deep satisfaction. They yearn to cling to these. They wish to stop time and motion to dwell within these joyous moments. They cherish order, peace, graceful line, the quietude that comes with spiritual fulfill-ment. This craving converted into sculpture, painting, drama, philosophy, poetry, religion, and the daily affairs of men, is art.

Going back to the illustration of the short story writer, what gives his work an esthetic stamp? What converts writing facility into art? What the writer is as a person, the experiences he has had that shape his per-sonality—these make him into an artist. He has become aware of the yearning people have for order, peace, and beauty, because he has had this yearning too. He also has experienced need and frustration. He has had to adjust continuously as other people do, sometimes reaching an expansive balance, sometimes regressing, feeling defeated, knowing he has missed the mark. On occasions, like other people, he has undergone experiences in which from beginning to end there was a happy continuity. These experiences begin with expectation, mature into full ripeness, then culminate in satisfying fulfillment. Every moment of their duration gives him a sense of emotional elation, he anticipates the outcome at each stage of the development, and when they terminate, he feels a sense of joy. He has known, as all people do, these esthetic feelings. Unlike other people, he has a driving desire to tell about what he sees and feels. He has be-come acutely aware of these feelings and their source in human conflict. There are many ways to satisfy a longing for self-expression, to give esthetic experience a concrete setting, thus sustaining its ephemeral quali-ties. The writing artist has perfected a medium most suited to his talents —the story. As he writes, his own esthetic experiences go into the stories. The writing, as it unfolds under his skilled pen, touched with the excite-ment of recalled events, gives him esthetic pleasure. He, in this act of creating, finds fulfillment of a need to express himself.

What does the finished story contain? It is a segment of life; not raw life with its repetitions and monotonies, but a refinement. The author selects elements from his own experience that at one time excited him. He takes these and shakes them rigorously to remove excessive senti-mentality. Working from his desk, he treats them as though they had happened to someone else. Removed from the involvement of the actual happening, he can look back on it with an air of detachment. From this position, only the significant highlights stand out. Applying the perspec-tive of the skilled craftsman, he chooses among these vital events. With these distilled bits of experience, he creates an illusion, a dramatic illusion of life. These particles fit together giving a unified emotional impact. The whole structure takes on the author's character; not in the sense that he purposely injects his personality into the narration or explains events to the reader, but by the way the composition bears his style. A painting shows such marks of style as distinctive brush strokes or unique use of color. Writing also reflects the taste and technique of the author. In good writing as in good painting style and technique melt into the emotional tone of the composition. The author exists in the creation, but in an unobtrusive way. His mastery of technique consists in giving the reader direct contact with the story. Simple clear expression constitutes the achievement in style that writers strive for. They do not want flourishes of the pen to keep the reader from sensing that in the narration he also lives. When the reader loses himself, when he feels the emotional impact of the story, then the author has mastered style and technique. Short stories, when artistically done, grip the reader. It is as though he stands in the ocean waiting for a wave to hit him and while doing this he draws in his breath until finally when the wave does strike, there is a shock, a thrill, a relief that comes when the breath is released. The reader has been away. He now returns to the realities of his own life.

Clues for the Teacher

What can educators learn from the preceding discussion that will help make teaching more artistic? First, what did the writing artist reveal? He combined craftsmanship with the esthetic to create art. How can teachers bring these two attributes of art into their work? Take the first segment of art, craftsmanship; what have teachers done here? Years of successful work have gone into perfecting teaching techniques and materials. Due to this, educators have available to them scientifically designed textbooks, excellent testing materials, teaching methods based on an understanding of child development, elaborate visual aids ranging from improved blackboards to sound films and beautiful buildings constructed to give the maximum in efficiency and comfort. The work in improving teaching craftsmanship continues. Not all the new techniques are immediately put into school, but the lag between newly designed educational tools and practice is not too great. This is particularly true of textbooks, visual aids, tests and new buildings. Masterly facility alone, however, will not make teaching into an art. Artistic teaching, just like writing, requires that craftsmanship take on an esthetic stamp. Skill needs esthetic shaping before artistry results.

The wonders of technology can and should improve living conditions. Radios, automobiles, washing machines and television should give people more expansive lives. This generation has come to realize that despite the many material advantages of manufactured articles, the amount of work saved, and the entertainment they provide, they do not automatically give people richer, fuller lives. Artistic living takes more than labor-saving machines or devices for entertainment. This has become a commonplace observation. The same reasoning applies to education. Educators are in danger of improving techniques while failing in the fundamental task of developing teaching into an art. Writers know that better typewriters save time, but do not make them artists. Educators must also learn this. (Not that teaching facility can or has become too good.) If teachers want to develop into artists, concern for techniques alone won't do. They must bring esthetic quality into their work.

What events in classrooms provide teachers and pupils with esthetic experiences? How can and do these unite with technique to provide artistry? In the preceding treatment of the bio-psychological fundamentals of the esthetic, several elements were discussed. The immediate felt sense of joy people have when disturbances terminate was a focal point. This movement from unbalance to adjustment carries the seeds of the esthetic. As pointed out earlier, few experiences reach esthetic fulfillment. People living must continually adjust. As they do this, sometimes an expansive ordering of energies occurs; they reach a more unified balance; their personality grows. Sometimes the disturbances do not completely resolve and a hangover of irritated nerves carries on to dissipate energies. At other times, passive adaptation becomes such a characteristic way of meeting life's irregularities, that people become inert. They yield to life, but gain no satisfaction. They become mute acceptors of all that comes whether it bring tragedy or gladness. These last two ways of meeting life tend to rob people of experiences that have vital fulfillment. People who adjust this way, either go through life with a constant feeling of anxiety or sink into dullness. Here are the two conditions that rob people of esthetic experiences—the development of neuroses that use up energies and the listlessness that comes with meaningless routine. The humdrum and the erratic keep people from having experiences that give deep satisfaction.

This review of the roots of the esthetic, with the emphasis upon what stands in the way of these experiences, should give teachers an important clue. Working from the insight gained here teachers can take their first step in making teaching an art. They must alleviate the humdrum and the erratic from their classrooms. Doing this, although not promoting the positive side, does remove conditions that impair artistry in teaching.

First considering the humdrum, what is the basis for this in schools? Pupils doing things for which they see no purpose, for which they have neither the aptitude nor interest, constitute one class of activities that bore students. Much has been said about this during the last fifty years. Whether or not certain subjects should be included in the program just because they are good for students has been argued up and down. The fact still remains that regardless of how worthy educational experts may regard the school programs they have outlined, unless students have positive educational experiences in relation to them, they are valueless. Regardless of high-sounding teaching objectives and programs espoused by educators, when schools bore students, they need changing.

It should be said in passing that there are no special subjects that have a high esthetic potentiality. The clue to understanding the esthetic in teaching is how people relate to the subjects, the kinds of experiences they have, the joy they feel in the classroom. Not the subject, but the way it is presented and the suitability of the content in fulfilling teachers' and pupils' desires constitute the meanings it will have. Arguments for including one subject or excluding another take second place to making the classroom an alert place where pupils and teachers working together have exciting experiences, when teaching becomes an art.

What specifically are some of the things pupils do in school that have neither purpose nor interest? The hundreds and hundreds of assignments that teachers require when they or the students don't have the slightest notion what they expect to accomplish. Teachers may have a vague idea about the answers they want, but too often they have not thought whether or not the assignment provides the student with a positive experience. Many incidents in the average day at school illustrate this point. The working of arithmetic problems in a mechanical way when students and sometimes teachers don't understand the meaning of the symbols nor the significance, in terms of everyday living, of the answer. The tedious wading through volumes of literature while the teachers' own concern is that the students have read the book and can answer a few questions of fact. That the books bore both the teachers and students makes little difference. It doesn't seem to matter whether or not students grow in their enthusiasm for reading or develop refined taste. The endless memorizing of vocabulary and grammatical structure in modern and ancient language classes without treating language as a way to communicate. The hours and hours of sitting quietly, pretending to be busy, until both teachers and pupils reach a high tensional state which brings them to the brink of explosion.

Teachers need to be constantly alert. They must know whether the things they demand in class get the results they seek. This takes a day-to-day check on the personalities of their students to determine what changes occur and how the school has implemented these. They need to develop an awareness of purpose and to continually examine their techniques to see if they are successful in fulfilling objectives. They must strike out the meaningless, the mechanical, and routine activities that tend to slip into classrooms. No assignment or class activity should be organized that the teacher has not carefully considered in terms of purpose, in terms of the most likely way to carry it out and in terms of the effect it will have on the pupil. Every day in class must hold promise and give satisfaction both to pupils and teachers. Instead of just spending time in school, teachers and students must live exciting lives together.

IMPORTANCE OF SECURITY

Eliminating meaningless drudgery from classrooms constitutes one phase in promoting more artistic teaching. This, like medicine, keeps disease in check but does not provide positive health measures. Teachers can go far in removing the mundane from schools by keeping techniques sharpened through frequently weighing them against purposes on the one hand and measuring results in terms of student personality growth on the other. In addition to keeping meaningless activity from wasting time educators must take steps to remove the second blight that often stops pupils from having experiences of esthetic quality. They must provide a classroom atmosphere that will assure to both themselves and their students a feeling of security. Educators must make certain that the social and psychological composition of the schoolroom does not cause painful disturbances. Principles from clinical psychology applied to education through the mental hygiene movement have gained wide acclaim by educators. These hit directly at the problem of arranging the interpersonal contacts in the school so that each person feels a sense of security. When pushed far enough into the underlying theory, the psychology of personality dynamics becomes complex. Teachers, however, have available devices that rest on sound theory, but that do not require complicated psychological or medical analyses. Clinicians have stressed the importance of teachers establishing comfortable rapport with their students. This means students feel emotionally uncramped. It means further that they have opportunity to express themselves, to achieve success in their expression. This does not imply that they are pampered. It does mean that they come in contact with stimulating situations freed from harmful frustrations. Teachers learn from psychologists that a friendly, humorous, and at the same time businesslike classroom where the teacher appreciates student problems is emotionally conducive to learning.

Freeing students from tedious routine and providing emotionally serene classes, as important as these are, do not insure that students will have esthetic experiences. Pupils could go through schools where the smoothest of social climates prevail, where not an ounce of energy is wasted, where scientific planning has ironed out the distressing inefficiencies that exist in most schools; yet despite all this, not have one esthetic experience. In the preceding illustration of the writer at work, the movement from conflict to order was seen as fundamental to the esthetic. Taking steps to keep the humdrum and frustrating out of classrooms will not automatically secure esthetic fulfillment. Providing conditions under which teachers and pupils adjust in such a way that disrupted equilibrium serves as an opportunity to reach an ever-enlarging balance is the clue to bringing the esthetic into schools.

Importance of Understanding the Pupil

In purposely setting out to stimulate pupils so that they and teachers have experiences of esthetic quality, there are two places to focus attention: the student and the teachers. Looking at the pupils first as they live daily, they become at odds with their surroundings or suffer from temporary displacement followed by adjustments the same as the writer we talked about previously. They have needs. What they are as people, what environmental and genetic forces have done to shape them, provides them with desires. Imbalance with the environment activates these strong motivating forces. Situations in which they are at odds with surroundings arouse needs. For example, hunger stimulates a desire for food. Not all disturbing situations activate such simple desires. People at times crave affection, security, self-expression, and the opportunity to draw attention to themselves. These and hundreds more subtly shaded motivating forces ranging from desire for clothes to longing for order constitute the driving forces in people's lives. By the time youngsters reach school, their basic personality is developed to a high degree. They have sets of desires and attitudes that tend to activate them in fairly specific directions. This means that a six-year-old youngster upon entering school has sufficient personality development that certain situations tend to stimulate, to arouse his desires, to have meaning to him, while others don't. Teachers must know what these are and use them to develop students' personalities in desirable directions. They gain knowledge of their students' urges and drives by carefully studying them. They must know what influences have developed their pupils to date and what situations activate their interests and desires. Teachers' pupils become their material. Human experiences take shape under their hands as they develop into artists.

Drawing on an understanding of their students, teachers design situations that will pique their interests. They devise classroom organizations that will throw them out of equilibrium, that will create needs. Teachers know about the general pattern of students' desires from their broad experience with children and youth, their study of psychology, and the specific investigation that they make into the social-psychological backgrounds of each student. Building school work upon student-teacher interest, then giving pupils a chance to experience the joy of fulfillment, is the clue to bringing esthetic quality into teaching. No formula, no set of devices, no special selection of techniques, will accomplish this. The secret is in the teachers' thoroughly knowing their pupils, then in keeping with their personality development, organizing classroom situations which will challenge them. This they follow by pointing out ways students can see their needs through to satisfying fulfillment.

In becoming acquainted with pupils, teachers can use the excellent testing and observation instruments developed by psychologists, keeping in mind that the best psychological techniques are of little help unless these implement understanding. To classify students as superior, medium, or inferior, on the bases of test information tends to set up barriers between pupils and teachers. The teacher who approaches a group of students as if they were inept has little chance to do good work. Teaching-artists use testing materials to understand, not to judge. They should supplement these with person-to-person talks and observation of students as they work and play in school. Because of the prevalent use of scientific tools, these invaluable personal contacts are often overlooked.

After teachers know their pupils, they are ready to begin arranging stimulating classes. Here a question usually arises. How is it possible to stimulate youngsters? How can teachers be certain that interest is aroused? Only teachers so removed from their pupils that they do not know their personalities or the effectiveness of school experiences could ask these questions. Teachers who spend their time dispensing and hearing lessons without coming close to the desires of students have difficulty in knowing how to stimulate students or in knowing whether they have been successful in this enterprise. Every subject, every day in class offers opportunity to challenge students. For example, the senior class in high school literature, elected mostly by girls, is a place where teachers can take advantage of interest adolescents at this age have in the boy-girl relations by introducing them to the fine romantic stories, poems, dramas, and novels that have been written by famous authors. The idealistic way many notable writers have treated romantic love can serve as an almost unending topic of discussion for adolescents.

Teachers who gauge their work closely to the interests of their pupils do not find this a restricting disadvantage. Often educators decry the fact that youngsters don't take interest in the right things, that thus to shape learning from immature impulses would harness it to non-productive infantile interests. There are two things wrong with this argument. First, the majority of child and adolescent desires are not destructive, but can readily serve as springboards for reaching out into the culture. Boy and girl interests during childhood in dolls, active games, cowboys and Indians, and mechanical toys, when given direction can and do lead to constructive personality development. Adolescent concern for social status, for wholesome boy-girl friendships, for recognition by adults and for religious fulfillment in the hands of an artist-teacher can serve as a profound motivation to all varieties of learning.

Teachers harbor a second fallacy when they talk about the limitations imposed on them by working within students' interests. They assume that working within childhood interests confines their efforts to immature desires. They do not consider that children's interests can grow. Although classroom work may start with the present immature student interest, it doesn't stop there. A skilled teacher can easily feed and enlarge a childhood mechanical interest by showing the relationship between measuring, use of numbers, arithmetic, and the desire to construct mechanical toys. Through gradually relating immature interests to more extensive horizons, children grow. This process is at the heart of artistic teaching. Stimulating present interests, throwing youngsters out of balance as a prelude to helping them achieve a more expansive ordering of energies leads to growth. When youngsters go through this activity so they experience a joyous satisfaction as desires reach fulfillment, their experiences are esthetic. Where will teachers build if they don't start with the dynamic personal qualities pupils carry to school? This does not mean that all interests and desires students have are good or that all should reach fulfillment. The educative process involves judging among desires. When teachers so direct their work that students choose and act upon those desires that open up an expanding world, they have demonstrated artistry in teaching.

Teachers who thoroughly know their students find no difficulty in motivating them. They become adept in the many techniques suited to this purpose. They know when to praise, when to correct, particularly how to criticize in a way that will bring about improvement. They understand how youngsters working together will often tend to put out more effort than those working alone. They employ competition to stimulate, but keep in mind that it can have disastrous results. Winners can become falsely confident while losers suffer from chronic frustrations. They work with a student in a way that makes him feel he is part of an important enterprise, that what he does in forwarding or retarding this activity matters. They make certain that their students have a sense of direction, that they have both long term and short run day-to-day plans. The students know what they expect to do in school during the next few months and how they will go about this. As they mature, their plans take in a broader scope until they have well-defined objectives for life. When a student's course of action seems to take him away from his plans, he, with the help of more extensive experience of his teacher, can make corrections. Teachers who understand the importance of personal dynamics know that people don't expend energy unless they are involved in the purposes. This does not mean that students just play during class hours. It means that teachers through putting into practice sound knowledge about motivation can fill their classrooms with students actively working. People who do things they see sense in because these fit into their purposes and desires, who receive recognition and status for doing these things, who gain a sense of joy from fulfilling these desires, work hard.

TEACHER INVOLVEMENT IN ARTISTIC TEACHING

So far the discussion on bringing esthetic quality into schools has focused upon pupils. While talking about the way teachers organize classrooms, drawing upon extensive techniques, we should keep in mind that during this entire procedure teachers also have experiences. In addition to taking tedious meaningless acts out of pupils' hands, teachers must also be protected from monotony. Just as with students, the mental hygiene of teachers needs consideration. They must know what they do is worthwhile, that through their work they gain status.

A teacher who likes teaching, who is happy, who has mastered a variety of useful techniques and who goes through the conventional steps of classroom procedure with the usual decorum will not necessarily become an artist. It takes more than this. Going back to the illustration of the writing artist, we see him lending his own esthetic experiences to his work and at the same time receiving profound satisfaction from writing. He must write; a strong compulsion drives him to his desk. He handles his materials with care, moulding words, sentences, paragraphs and dramatic situations into stories. Everything associated with his work gives him pleasure. No one receives more enjoyment from the finished story than he. As he wrote it, he savored every moment. His anticipation of the perfected finished product drives him on with excitement, until he knows the satisfaction of holding the finished manuscript in his hands. Teachers who become artists have this loving affection for their work. Like authors who create, who put their own desires into their creation, teaching artists also live their work. When students triumph over confusion through acting upon wise judgments, they triumph also. When a paper comes to their attention that has provided a pupil with a sense of achievement, they also experience pleasure. They anticipate each day in the classroom for the adventure it can give, for here they express their cravings, the desire to stimulate youth, to point out all the exciting things in life, to extoll the pleasures of reading for they have known this pleasure, to rush down the path of science, for they have found wisdom here, to cultivate human understanding, for they have experienced the rewards in spiritual growth this provides, and to give their pupils a feeling for beauty and proportion in daily living because they also yearn to make living into an art. They give tests, correct papers, assign lessons, discuss problems with pupils and study the backgrounds of their students, but as artists they bring a passion to these endeavors. They sense the same tingle at the spine a seaman, hunter, or explorer has as he pushes into the known, for sharing their pupils' lives is a great adventure.

What does the finished work of teaching art contain? Take the story referred to previously—it too is life, not just the way we see it from day to day, but a refinement. Banalities have been removed. Irregularities that rob energy are cast out. Students live in designed social structures where they feel they belong, where they have friends, and where they can see their participation makes a contribution. Teachers and pupils live just as they do at home and in the community outside the school, but with a difference. In the home and out-of-school society, many uncontrolled events occur that needlessly disrupt, many desires arise that destroy, many frustrations mount until they lead to neuroses, and many urgent demands do not reach fulfillment. The classroom in the hands of the artist-teacher offers a controlled environment where with the aid of science many of these hazards have been eliminated. Where the out-of-school community moves at a faltering pace, too often set by accident, the classroom is intense. Here, as in the story, the kernel of life is given dramatic expression.

There is a similarity between artistic expressions in various media. All have rhythm resolving into order. Music, painting, and literary composition stand as models of orderly arrangements of sounds, colors, and words. This unity in objects of art is dynamic, constructed from pulsating rhythm beats. The art object needs but to contact a sensitive ear or eye to spring into life giving the observer a sense of joy similar to what the creator received while working out the line and form of the composition. Artistic teaching is like this too. The entire procedure follows lines that have graceful proportion. People moving from childhood through youth to adulthood set the sequential pattern for teachers. This process flows with rhythmical pulse oscillating from needs to fulfillment.

All artists handle their materials with affection. A violin-maker literally caresses a well-seasoned piece of maple suitable for the back of a violin. A cook arranges ingredients for a cake with care, visualizing each layer coming out of the oven as the flour, sugar, and butter are placed on the table. Sculptors actually fondle the stone they work with. Nowhere is this more true than in teaching, for here artists mold the minds, emotions, and spirits of people.

31.   Curricular Language and Classroom Meanings

Dwayne Huebner

AESTHETIC VALUES

The aesthetic valuing of educational activity is often completely ignored, perhaps because the educator is not sufficiently concerned with or knowledgeable about aesthetic values or perhaps because aesthetic activities are not highly prized today in society. Scientific and technical values are more highly prized consciously, and political values are more highly prized unconsciously or covertly. Valued aesthetically, educational activity would be viewed as having symbolic and aesthetic meanings. At least three dimensions of this value category may be identified.

First is what Bullough calls the element of psychical distance.[9] The aesthetic object, in this case educational activity, is removed from the world of use. It is a conditioned object which does not partake of the conditioned world; that is, it has no use, no functional or instrumental significance, and consequently may partake of or be symbolic of the unconditional. It is possibility realized, ordinarily impossible in the functional world. It is spontaneity captured, normally lost in the ongoing world. Because of aesthetic distance, the art object, in this case educational activity, is the possibility of life, captured and heightened and standing apart from the world of production, consumption and intent. The art object has beauty. Educational activity can have beauty.

The second dimension of the aesthetic category is that of wholeness and design. Because the aesthetic object stands outside of the functional world it has a totality and unity which can be judged or criticized. The art critic speaks of balance, of harmony, of composition, of design, of integration and of closure. The art object may be a source of contentment and peace, of a unity to be found only in the realm of perfection, the land of dreaming innocence. Educational activity may thus be valued in terms of its sense of wholeness, of balance, of design and of integrity, and its sense of peace or contentment.

[9] Edward Bullough. "Psychical Distance as a Factor in Art and an Esthetic Principle." In: *A Modern Book of Aesthetics*. Melvin Rader, editor. New York: Henry Holt and Company, 1952.

The third dimension of aesthetic value is that of symbolic meaning. Any aesthetic object is symbolic of man's meanings. It reflects the meanings of the artist as an individual; it also reflects the meaning existing in and emerging from man as a life form. The aesthetic object, indeed educational activity, may be valued for the meanings that it reveals, and may be valued for its truth. Educational activity is symbolic of the meanings of the educator, as an individual and as a spokesman for man. The teaching of educators who are spiteful, unrealized human beings reflects these inner meanings. The meaninglessness and routine of much educational activity today reflects the meaninglessness and routine of a mechanistic world order. In the rare classroom is the possible vitality and significance of life symbolized by the excitement, fervor and community of educational activity. Educational activity can symbolize the meanings felt and lived by educators. . . .

AESTHETIC RATIONALITY

When classroom activity is viewed from the point of view of an aesthetic rationality, quite different categories of meaning are derived. As with the ethical, a variety of aesthetic viewpoints is possible, but Paul Valery's[11] view will be used here. The general scheme is that the teacher creates an aesthetic object to which the students respond. Their responses may also be considered aesthetic objects to which the teacher responds as a critic. The intent throughout classroom activity is not a search for preconceived ends but a search for beauty, for integrity and form and the peace which accompanies them, and for truth as life is unveiled through the acting and speaking of the participants.

Valery defines the execution of a work of art as a "transition from disorder to order, from the formless to form, or from impurity to purity, accident to necessity, confusion to clarity."[12] André Maurois expands this by stating that aesthetic "order must dominate an actual disorder . . . the violent universe of the passions, the chaos of color and sound, dominated by a human intelligence. . . . In great music, the torrent of sound seems always on the point of turning into hurricane and chaos, and always the composer, . . . soars over the tempest, reins in the chaos. But it is because the chaos has overwhelmed us that we are moved when it is checked."[13]

The teacher, then, in classroom activity can tame the incipient chaos and dominate it with human intelligence. Classroom activity can seem

[11] Paul Valery. *Aesthetics*. Translated by Ralph Mannheim. New York: Bollingen Foundation, 1964.
[12] *Ibid.*, p. 158.
[13] *Ibid.*, p. 163.

ready to disintegrate but for the aesthetic order imposed by the teacher. The influence of this ordered disorder upon the student, if it is an object or event of beauty, is to make him mute.[14] But the response is not dead silence, nor a response of admiration, but of "sustained attention."[15] The artist's intent is "to conjure up developments that arouse perpetual desire,"[16] "to exact of his audience an effort of the same quality as his own,"[17] and "to provoke infinite developments in someone."[18]

The students, awed by the teacher's art, can be moved, then, "to the enchanted forest of language . . . with the express purpose of getting lost; far gone in bewilderment, they seek crossroads of meaning, unexpected echoes, strange encounters; they fear neither detours, surprises, nor darkness; but the huntsman who ventures into this forest in hot pursuit of the 'truth,' who sticks to a single continuous path, from which he cannot deviate for a moment on pain of losing the scent or imperiling the progress he has already made, runs the risk of capturing nothing but his shadow."[19] So the student seeks to dominate his newfound chaos by his own intelligence, and as a critic the teacher responds with critical concern but sympathetic intent. Classroom activity unfolds in a rhythmic series of events, which symbolizes the meanings of man's temporal existence.

Here, then, are concepts which could serve in an aesthetic rationality of educational activity: the continual caging of chaos, psychical distance or non-instrumentality, beauty or harmony and form, truth as unveiled meaning, and criticism. How can these concepts be used to explore the meanings of classroom activity? It would be possible to use these notions to discuss the dynamics of teacher-student interaction. Yet more fruitful in this day of knowledge and intellectual concerns is to hint at the place of knowledge in educational activity from the point of view of aesthetic rationality.

First, knowledge can be viewed as the ordering of particular bits of chaos. The irrational or unconditioned constantly creeps out of all forms of knowledge. As Jaspers states:

We become aware of the fact that in cognition we have moved in categories which, even in their totality, are like a fine filigree with which we grasp what at the same time we conceal with it . . . pushing ahead restlessly into the ocean of Being, we find ourselves always again and again at the beach of categorically secure, definite, particular knowledge.[20]

[14] *Ibid.*, p. 58.
[15] *Ibid.*, p. 161.
[16] *Ibid.*, p. 193.
[17] *Ibid.*, p. 161.
[18] *Ibid.*, p. 151.
[19] *Ibid.*, p. 48-49.
[20] Karl Jaspers. *Truth and Symbol.* Translated by Jean T. Wilde, William Kluback and William Kimmel. New York: Twayne Publishers, 1959. p. 38 and 79.

In science it creeps out through the continual destruction and construction of existing concepts and theories through the methodologies of science. In social ideologies it creeps out through the onslaught of circumstance. Thus in teaching, educational activity must order, but the unbridled chaos should not be hidden from the student. To do so is to deprive him of the element which calls forth the mute response, the "sustained attention" and the "perpetual desire."

The psychical distance or non-instrumentality of valued educational activity means that the playful involvement with the tools and products of knowledge need not be subjugated to the demands of social or biological necessity. The teacher and the students can be freed from the demands of utilitarianism, and the classroom can become a place where the purity and beauty of knowledge may be enjoyed for itself. The student can be freed to use knowledge to heighten his own significance, to enlarge his own sensitivities to the world, and to realize what he could be. The near infinite possibilities of knowledge and knowing can be hinted at, and the mysteries of the world can be pointed to without the need to reduce them to problems to be solved.

Aesthetically valued, knowledge has more than power; it has beauty. As a man-made form its balance and harmony, its composition, its integrity and wholeness, point to the peaceful possibilities inherent in human existence. The scientist, the engineer, as well as the artist, are creative artists who engage in the creative evolution of new forms and who bring harmony to a discordant world. Participating in the making of his own knowledge, the student can recognize his inherent potential to add to, and conversely to subtract from, the possibility of man-made beauty. Intellectual disciplines as well as aesthetic crafts are vehicles for this continuing creation.

As an aesthetic form, knowledge in educational activity becomes symbolic of man's meanings and of his discovered truths. Knowledge as an aesthetic form is a token of man's responsiveness to his own feelings and inner life and to his being a part of its world. Scientific forms of knowledge point to man's willingness to listen to and observe the world around him and to be conditioned by the unknown world. Technical forms of knowledge are symbolic of man's power over the world, and of his desire to shape the world into his own image. Knowledge treated as having an existence beyond the individual or separated from man may be symbolic of man's unwillingness to assume responsibility for his own condition. Knowledge being made and remade in educational activity may symbolize that the educator recognizes that his knowledge is but one of the flowers of his life, which blooms and dies, and yet is the seed of new life.

Finally, the act of criticism becomes a part of the aesthetic process. All aesthetic events and forms must be able to withstand the criticism of knowledgeable and responsible critics. The utterances and acts of teacher and student are proper targets of sympathetic but critical concern. Scientific criteria of empirical validity, parsimony, and logical structure are instruments for the criticism of scientific knowledge. Pragmatic considerations can be a form of criticism of social ideologies. Teacher and students, through their conversations, engage in the mutual criticism of each other's orderings, and thus contribute to the continued transcendence of form over chaos.

In conclusion, present curricular language is much too limited to come to grips with the problems, or rather the mysteries, of language and meaning of the classroom. The educator must free himself from his self-confining schemas, in order that he may listen anew to the world pounding against his intellectual barriers. The present methodologies which govern curricular thought must eventually give away.

Identifying and proposing a solution to the twofold problem of describing and valuing educational activity identified in this paper is but one attempt, among many that should be made, to reformulate aspects of curricular language. With it other meanings of classroom activity might be identified. As Conant points out, the significance of scientific theory is not its validity, but its fruitfulness. The scientific value of these roughly sketched ideas will be their fruitfulness. Their technical and political value are of no significance. Their ethical and aesthetic meanings may be pondered.

32.   The Teacher as an Artist

John Dewey

That teaching is an art and the true teacher an artist is a familiar saying. Now the teacher's own claim to rank as an artist is measured by his ability to foster the attitude of the artist in those who study with him, whether they be youth or little children. Some succeed in arousing enthusiasm, in communicating large ideas, in evoking energy. So far, well; but the final test is whether the stimulus thus given to wider aims succeeds in transforming itself into power; that is to say, into the attention to detail

From *How We Think,* John Dewey, © 1933. Reprinted by permission of D. C. Heath and Company.

that ensures mastery over means of execution. If not, the zeal flags, the interest dies out, the ideal becomes a clouded memory. Other teachers succeed in training facility, skill, mastery of the technique of subjects. Again it is well—so far. But unless enlargement of mental vision, power of increased discrimination of final values, a sense for ideas, for principles, accompanies this training, forms of skill ready to be put indifferently to any end may be the result. Such modes of technical skill may display themselves, according to circumstances, as cleverness in serving self-interest, as docility in carrying out the purposes of others, or as unimaginative plodding in ruts. To nurture inspiring aim and executive means into harmony with each other is at once the difficulty and the reward of the teacher.

33. Qualitative Intelligence and the Act of Teaching

Elliot W. Eisner

In this paper I would like to discuss a special variety of intelligence that is exercised in most teaching acts and to indicate how this type of intelligence contributes to the successful execution of those acts.

The need to develop fresh conceptions with which to analyze teaching becomes apparent to anyone who reviews the research on teacher effectiveness. While new developments in instructional practice are not scarce —note the advent of team teaching, programmed instruction, closed circuit and airborne television—research findings provide little evidence that the new teaching practices are leading to more efficient learning. Somehow research studies designed to assess the differential effects of various types of instructional procedures usually terminate as members of the not-so-exclusive club of "no significant differences."

New developments in theory are also plentiful. B. F. Skinner has operationalized his conceptions of learning through the teaching machine; Jerome Bruner has formulated a set of technologies through which thinking occurs; and J. P. Guilford has developed a theoretical structure of the intellect which identifies some of the components that constitute human thought.

"Qualitative Intelligence and the Act of Teaching," by Elliot W. Eisner, is reprinted from *The Elementary School Journal*, 63: 299-307, March, 1963, by permission of The University of Chicago Press. Copyright © 1963 by The University of Chicago Press.

Although the theoretical positions of Skinner and Bruner differ in many ways, they both share the view that the process through which something is taught significantly affects the efficiency and the usefulness of the learning. In Skinner's view, efficiency is achieved if the learner can proceed through a program that consists of very small units of information so constructed that the student moves through them with minimum error. The student obtains immediate feedback to each response he makes and since ideally his responses to these programmed units are correct, he obtains positive reinforcement.

Bruner's approach to the problem of teaching and learning is quite different from Skinner's. Bruner has developed a conception of three technologies through which children and adults learn. These technologies are called the enactive, the ikonic, and the symbolic. Each provides the individual with a means of storing and retrieving data.

In a lecture on "The Nature of Intellectual Growth" given at the University of Chicago in November, 1962, Bruner said, "By enactive representation I mean a mode of representing past events through appropriate motor response. . . . Ikonic representation summarizes events by percepts and images, by the spatial, temporal, and qualitative structures of the perceptual field and their transformed images." The symbolic, which is employed when the individual acquires discursive language, is held to be the most economic and most flexible storage and retrieval system. It enables the individual to cope successfully with problems that might not be handled so well by the enactive and ikonic technologies.

Bruner believes that if teachers can identify the generic coding systems or structures that constitute the disciplines and if they can identify the dimensions of the conceptual unit that children can handle successfully, it will be possible to teach almost anything to almost anyone.

Although Skinner and Bruner differ with respect to the most efficient process through which learning takes place, they both hold that with the appropriate method, children would be capable of learning much that we now consider beyond their capacities.

J. P. Guilford has taken still another tack in his research, one that could lead to conclusions almost polar to those of Skinner and Bruner. Guilford has used factor analytic methods to formulate a structure of the intellect.

The building blocks of the structure are relatively specific abilities that fall into several major dimensions, among them the conceptual, the figural, and the structural. In each dimension, divergent or convergent thought processes may be used. By using the battery of tests that Guilford has constructed to measure these conceptualized unitary abilities, it is possible to obtain a psychometric profile of the trait abilities of different individuals. From such a profile one could conclude that the problem in formulating an educational program for a student is primarily a task of determining the kind of trait abilities he possesses and then designing an educational program appropriate for those abilities.

From such a conception one could also conclude that the likelihood of being able to teach almost anything to almost anyone is small and that it would be much more realistic to differentiate the educational diet for students having different patterns of trait abilities. Differences in education would not be merely a matter of using different methods, but one of differentiating the content of instruction.

Yet even with these new developments in educational practice and research, the problem of identifying the components of effective teaching still persists. This problem is so great and so central to education that competent observers like Guba and Getzels, reporting in the *Journal of Educational Psychology* (October, 1955) have concluded, "Despite a large number of investigations, relatively little more is known than was known [about teacher effectiveness] in 1900."

Perhaps recognition of ignorance is a form of knowledge, but with the vast sums spent on research (Herbert S. Conrad, director of Research and Statistical Service, U.S. Office of Education, reports that the U.S. Office of Education alone spends in excess of ten million dollars annually in support of educational research) and literally hundreds of research studies published each year, one may wonder why knowledge in this area is so scant. Why is it that after eighty years of psychological study in education the number of hard facts that can be passed on to teachers regarding the way teaching may be most effectively pursued is exceedingly small?

Plenty of hypotheses are available. One may claim that educational inquiry is much more complex than other types of inquiry and hence it will take more time to develop more effective methods of teaching. One may claim that the level of research competence of those working in educational research is too low. One might also postulate that educational research is dependent on research in other disciplines and cannot proceed any faster than research in those fields. Finally one may claim that educational research has for too long been concerned with descriptive studies and too little effort has been spent understanding how educational change may be most effectively engendered.

I am sure you can add more explanations to the list. Explanations are plentiful, and there is probably some truth in all of them. But perhaps educational research has found it difficult to produce significant findings on the conditions that make for effective teaching because it has neglected at least one very important component inherent in every teaching act— the teacher's use and control of the qualitative, an activity made possible through the use of what may be called *qualitative intelligence*.

I would like to develop this notion by looking at some of the assumptions that are employed in the education of prospective teachers. One of these assumptions is related to a kind of Platonism which holds that the most useful tool for good teaching is good theory. We implement this assumption by asking the teacher in training to take courses in educational psychology, in philosophy of education, in curriculum, and in methods of teaching various subject matters.

Student teaching is generally held off until the latter part of the student's program. This practice reflects the belief that if the student is to understand what he is to observe in the classroom, he needs some theoretical and conceptual tools. High-level comprehension of theory in learning, child development, and curriculum is supposed to provide the student, when he has completed student teaching, with the most useful tools for teaching. Indeed, these courses are considered so important that in most states an individual cannot be certified to teach unless he has taken and passed a specified number of them. Yet if one asks teachers how useful the theories provided in these courses are in teaching, one should not be surprised to find a lack of enthusiasm.

Now it may be that teachers underestimate the practical value of theory. But perhaps they do not. Perhaps much of what is most useful in teaching does not rest on theoretical considerations at all. Perhaps one reason why we have found it so difficult to identify the conditions that make for effective teaching is that we have neglected to consider the qualitative aspects of teaching and the qualitative intelligence of teachers.

What is qualitative intelligence and what contribution does it make to the successful execution of the teaching act? Qualitative intelligence can be considered, in part, as the ability to formulate qualitative ends and to employ qualitative means in the efficient acquisition of those ends. In the relationship between such means and ends, qualitative thought is employed. After this rather abstract statement, I would like to describe some situations where qualitative intelligence is exercised.

Perhaps the most obvious examples are found in the activities of the musician and the visual artist, those most concerned with the qualitative. One of the primary tasks of the visual artist is the conception, control, and organization of qualities. A quality may be conceived of as the experience of anything sensible, provided that symbolic meaning of the sensible is disregarded. Such sensibles may be a product of the imagination as, for example, the experience you have when I suggest that you envision a brilliant arrangement of yellow and orange. Your experience in visualizing these colors is essentially qualitative.

Qualitative experience is also produced by the perception of physically real sensibles. Such sensibles may be experienced as either dominantly qualitative or symbolic. For example, the color red may be experienced qualitatively when it is experienced exclusively as color; symbolically, when it is conceived of as standing for *stop*.

Qualitative experience, therefore, is the sense of life one undergoes when conceiving or perceiving sensibles devoid of symbolic meaning. Qualitative intelligence is displayed in the degree to which qualitative ends are conceived and efficiently attained. The visual artist often conceives of a qualitative end, a particular mood or rhythm he wants to create, and controls qualities (color, line, shape, form, composition) so that this end is achieved. Qualitative concerns are expressed and qualitative intelligence is exercised in all walks of life by practically everyone.

You may be wondering what this has to do with teaching and with research that attempts to understand the conditions that contribute to effectiveness in teaching. The relationship between qualitative intelligence and teaching may become clearer if we examine one other domain in which qualitative intelligence is exercised, namely, acting.

Specifically, let us look at the night-club comedian, particularly the one who is able to change the form and content of his act as it unfolds. I have chosen a night-club comedian as an example because there are certain important parallels between his actions and those of a teacher and because the good ones display a very high degree of qualitative intelligence.

Here we see an individual whose task is to achieve a certain qualitative response in his audience. He conceives of qualitative ends—certain kinds of qualities that we call laughter, joy, happiness—and engages in activities designed to elicit qualities that constitute those ends. In these activities he must pay attention not only to the symbolic meaning of his language but also to the rhythm, tempo, pace, and timing of his speech and actions.

He must listen with a qualitative ear to the qualities the audience generates, for a line late but a second is dead. He is able to perceive the qualitative flow of events and is able to control his actions—pace, tempo, timing, emphasis—accordingly, always relating his actions to the data (in this case, qualities) provided by the audience and the ends he wants to achieve. He literally knows how to play it by ear, to carry on a qualitative dialectic between the audience and himself.

There are several parallels between such actions and the actions of teaching. For one, the teacher, like the actor, is concerned with the control and guidance of a group of people. Whatever a teacher may wish to achieve in the classroom, the necessity of organizing and guiding human interests and actions is always present.

Further, teachers, like actors, attempt to communicate to groups of people in an audience-like situation, and while the ends of comedy and instruction differ markedly, both the actor and the teacher employ qualities to enhance communication; both must come through to the people with whom they work.

In addition, both the actor and the teacher must be able to control their actions in such a way as to capture the attention and interest of those to whom their message is directed. Knowing something and wanting to communicate it are hardly sufficient for achieving communication. The qualitative tone of a discussion or lecture is, as everyone knows, extremely important in determining not only the content of the message but the way it is considered after it is received.

Finally, much that the teacher tries to attain in the classroom is dominantly qualitative rather than dominantly symbolic or theoretical. This is especially true in subjects like poetry, history, art, music, and literature. In these subjects especially, the desired end of teaching is not limited to giving students a mere knowledge of a poem, a period, a painting, a symphony, or a plot, but also includes helping the students experience the qualities built into the work.

For example, a student whose experience of a symphony is limited to knowledge about its formal structure would miss experiencing whatever aesthetic quality it possessed. In history, a student who could not experience the qualitative *Zeitgeist* of the great events, people, and periods of the past, would have a limited historical experience indeed. Some subjects seem to be more concerned with symbolic or theoretical ends than others. While many might consider mathematics to be one such subject, it is well to remember that many of the greatest mathematicians considered the study of mathematics an aesthetic activity and looked upon the discovery or creation of new mathematical relations as comparable in aesthetic quality to any experience that can be derived from the arts. This suggests that purely conceptual or symbolic inquiries can have a qualitative character. This aspect of qualitative experience, however, will not be discussed here.

What I am suggesting is that the acts of teaching and acting have important and significant parallels and that teaching, while concerned with some ends that are not relevant to acting, is concerned with many other ends that are. Intelligent control of qualitative elements necessary in acting is also necessary in teaching insofar as teaching is partly a task of acting and achieving communication between teacher and individual and group. The qualitative controls that teachers employ can enhance teaching and can be instrumental to theoretical ends embodied in certain subjects and can also be used to achieve qualitative ends incorporated in other subjects. Teachers who are able to control qualities intelligently are probably better able to produce the kind of classroom atmosphere that will facilitate the type of learning that they value.

Visits to a few classrooms will provide ample evidence of the fact that diverse qualities pervade different classrooms. In some classrooms the atmosphere possesses qualities that may be described as energetic, active, and enthusiastic; others might be described as languid, placid, and quiet; still others as monotonous, anxious, and rigid. Such atmospheres are a function of the classroom's qualitative components. Such components are the individual qualities generated by the students as they respond to and act upon the symbolic meanings and qualitative characteristics produced by others. Collectively, they produce what we commonly call *classroom atmosphere*.

I am not suggesting that classrooms can or ought to be kept at one qualitative level at all times. I am suggesting that the teacher, to the extent that he has qualitative control, can be effective in creating the type of classroom environment that is appropriate for different types of learning.

Primary-grade teachers are perhaps most likely to exercise such concerns and controls. These concerns and controls tend to diminish as one moves upward through the grades, so that by the time the student reaches college, the amount of variability in teaching strategies and in qualitative techniques is quite small compared with those in the primary grades.

Qualitative intelligence also makes possible the perception of the qualitative. I should point out that it is my view that intelligence is exercised in increasing degrees as man discriminates between more and more complex and subtle qualities. Discrimination between black and white, for example, is a simple task. Perception of discrimination of the subtle qualities in a Gauguin or in the counterpoint of Stravinsky is quite another matter. Sensitivity or appreciation of such qualities is a product of qualitative intelligence. Thus, I follow Dewey's lead that appreciation is a creative or intelligent act. The control of qualities can be achieved only when the actor is able to perceive the qualities that emerge from his ongoing activities. To be able to play it by ear means that one's decision-making is going to be made on the spot and that one will use, as those decisions, the qualitative and theoretical responses of the class or the audience.

We have long considered the preplanning of curriculum and the construction of lesson plans essential activities for effective construction. Yet relatively little attention has been paid to the type of immediate decision-making that all teachers engage in in the act of teaching.

We have also considered theoretical thought the most important and perhaps the only useful tool for making teaching decisions. I believe most of us who teach would admit, if pressed, that the majority of our teaching decisions in the classroom are not made on the basis of theoretical considerations at all. Part of this is probably due to the limitations of theory in the behavioral sciences at the immediate decision-making level in the classroom. Human interactions are too rich to be adequately described by behavioral-science theory at its present state of development. As theory grows and as it becomes more complete, we may reach a point at which it may be more useful, but the likelihood of ever obtaining a network of theory adequate for directing all or most human action in the classroom seems to me to be small.

Aristotle was quite aware of the limitations of theory in practical realms. In his *Metaphysics* he distinguishes between three types of knowledge: the theoretical, which has as its end knowledge "of what is of necessity"; the practical-practical, knowledge whose end is action; and the practical-productive, knowledge whose end is making. Aristotle held that by their very nature the actions of men could not be understood with the certainty that was possible in the three theoretical sciences: theology, mathematics, and physics. And in the *Nicomachean Ethics* he says:

> Our discussion will be adequate if it has as much clearness as the subject matter admits of, for precision is not to be sought for in all discussions any more than in all the products of the crafts . . . for it is the mark of an educated man to look for precision in each class of things just so far as the nature of the subject admits; it is evidently equally foolish to accept probable reasoning from a mathematician and to demand from a rhetorician scientific proof.

Here Aristotle tells us that the practical sciences cannot be known as well as the theoretical and also that the way in which they come to be known differs. Practical knowledge is acquired through experience in action; theoretical knowledge, through study. If we translate this view into expectations for theory and practice in preparing teachers, certain implications follow.

First, Aristotle's distinctions among the sciences suggest that theoretical knowledge is unlikely to be sufficient for guiding the teaching act, since by its nature teaching is a practical rather than a theoretical science. The great number of unique transactions occurring among individuals in the classroom is likely to make theoretical knowledge useful in only a suggestive way. Its application always needs to be tempered with art.

Second, Aristotle's distinction between the practical and the theoretical implies that some things can be learned only through practical experience. The value that teachers generally place on practice teaching may be evidence of the fact that what they learn as classroom teachers, even in the role of the student teacher, could not be and was not learned in the university seminar. Some things, it seems, one may learn only through action.

Third, Aristotle's distinction between the practical and the theoretical suggests that if theoretical knowledge is to be of any use it needs to be learned in conjunction with or after practical experience in the classroom. Theoretical concepts are likely to have little meaning if the teacher in training is unable to link them to the practical matters of teaching. Current practices in teacher education proceed in just the opposite fashion: first the student learns theory, and only afterward does he try his hand at teaching.

Fourth, it suggests that if useful theory for teaching is developed, it will have to take into account what is appropriate for the particular teacher as well as for the class, since knowing depends as much on the

nature of the knower as it does on that to be known. There is an idiosyncratic dimension to teaching that is unlikely to be defined by any single
principle.

There are, I believe, certain relationships between Aristotle's conceptions of knowing and the type of knowing that Dewey discusses in *Art as
Experience*. Each of these conceptions speaks to the question I raised in
the earlier part of this paper, namely, why has research found it so difficult to identify the conditions that make for effective teaching. Dewey
suggests in *Art as Experience* that the kind of knowledge and intelligence
employed in the production of art is different in character from the kind
of knowledge and intelligence employed in scientific inquiries. The
artist, for Dewey, "knows" the rightness of a particular color or shape on
canvas by its "feel"; the comedian knows he is pacing his dialogue correctly by the laughter of the audience; the teacher knows he is getting
through to students by the qualities displayed in their behavior, qualities
that often speak much louder than words. Dewey was aware of this way
of knowing, and teachers with experience are aware of it as well. Perhaps
if researchers were able to measure the extent to which individuals are
aware of and able to control qualities and if institutions engaged in
teacher-training could develop ways of fostering such intelligence, some
of the conditions that contribute to effective teaching could be better
understood and better developed.

It has been suggested that the type of intelligence that I am describing
cannot be developed: we cannot teach students to be sensitive and, to
use a term often used, intuitive to the qualitative happenings in a class.
It is often held that either you have this talent or you do not; either you
are sensitive and responsive to such qualities or you are not. It seems to
me that this point of view is based on a highly questionable conception
of talent.

Such a view conceives of talent as a dichotomously distributed ability,
a matter of all or nothing. But even sex, the geneticists tell us, is not a
matter of all-or-nothing. One has merely to look at the kinds of qualitative intelligence that art, music, and acting schools develop to become
convinced that almost anyone can increase his ability to cope intelligently
with qualities. Not everyone can become a Rouault or a Barrymore, but
almost everyone can become better able to conceive of and control
qualities.

If intelligent control of the qualitative components of teaching is important in teaching, and I believe it is, then it might be well to try to
help students who are preparing to teach to acquire such control and to
consider it when we attempt to understand effective teaching. Perhaps
recognition of this dimension of teaching is inherent when we say, as we
have so often said, that teaching is both a science and an art. We imply

that the scientific aspect of teaching relates to practice based on theoretical principles, the artistic, on those aspects of teaching governed by qualitative considerations. Perhaps it would not be too bizarre to propose that a good teacher of acting be on the staff of schools of education.

In developing the notion of the role of qualitative intelligence in teaching, I have risked overstating my case. I do not for a moment disregard the importance of subject-matter competence, personality disposition, or knowledge of useful theory in the behavioral sciences.

There is no single variable that is likely to define the effective teacher. There are probably many types of effectiveness in teaching, and perhaps the question that should ultimately be raised is "What teacher of what subject matter is effective with what students?" It seems likely that there is a high degree of specificity to effective teaching. Yet even with such specificity, one of the major components of teaching is acting, whether the teaching takes place in a lecture, in a large discussion group, or in a small seminar. The qualitative dimension of acting is always present and always important. To the extent that this aspect of teaching is disregarded or carried out unintelligently, to that extent is learning impeded. If greater understanding of the components of effective teaching is to be acquired and if skill in teaching is to be furthered, it would seem wise for teachers and researchers to take into account the qualitative components inherent in the teaching act.

34.   Principles of Creative Teaching

Ralph J. Hallman

I. The Problem

It has been established that creative potentials exist commonly in all normal children [1] and also that there are theoretical grounds for believing that creativity can be taught.[2] But the teaching methods which can best elicit creative responses from pupils have not yet been clearly identified.

"Principles of Creative Teaching" by Ralph J. Hallman is reprinted with permission from *Educational Theory*, 15: 306-316, October, 1965.
[1] Ralph J. Hallman, "The Commonness of Creativity," *Educational Theory*, XIII, 2 (April, 1963), 132-136.
[2] Ralph J. Hallman, "Can Creativity Be Taught?" *Educational Theory*, XIV, 1 (Jan., 1964), 15-23.

This delay probably stems from the ambiguities which characterize both creative and teaching processes.

For example, the creative act cannot be deliberately planned. Creative teaching cannot be prescribed nor written into lesson plans. Consisting as it does of immediate encounters with specific problems and persons, it remains individualized. It can neither be fully explained nor accurately communicated in formal concepts. Rather, the teacher must himself invent creative techniques in the course of his day-by-day activities, and these techniques will appear as having been unforeseeable. Being unpredictable, they confer freedom, for they encourage the teacher to react spontaneously to his concrete situation, to the cues which come directly from students, from the subject matter, and from the uniqueness of the problem at hand. They consist in the connecting of meanings which unforeseeably arise.

This paper makes the claim that certain principles can be identified which will assist the teacher in discovering these creative procedures.

II. The Principle of Suggestion

The principle of suggestion identifies the teaching *methods* which can most effectively promote creative tendencies in pupils. It defends indirect rather than direct methods of instruction as being appropriate to creativity.

This principle derives from three central features of the creative process: it is autonomous, spontaneous, and metaphoric. Its autonomy places the creative act outside the control of the deliberative faculties. Its spontaneity means that creativeness cannot be forced. It cannot be taught authoritatively. It can only be encouraged. Teaching becomes the art of suggesting, the art of supplying cues, indicating possibilities, associating apparent irrelevancies. It is itself a creative act. This is the third meaning: suggestion is metaphoric in nature. It stimulates associative tendencies, sets into motion connotative operations, and encourages combinatorial activity.

This process therefore calls for teaching techniques which are suggestive, flexible, experimental, imaginative, and manipulative. It is thwarted by methods which are authoritative and geared to the communication of predetermined truths. Suggestion emphasizes the importance of the unsaid, the seemingly unrelated, the apparently irrelevant. It produces quantities of ideas, concepts, imagery. It permits these to remain in a state of flux. It creates gaps in evidence, registers them, extends them, transplants them. It encourages the students' own metaphoric activity to fill in the gaps.

This principle can be clarified by reference to the methodology of John Dewey, who describes the process of learning as the clarification of uncertainties in our experience. Uncertainty brings out intelligence, and the intellect in turn functions to dispel uncertainty. It does so by identifying means and by charting directions toward which the given data point. These pointings are suggestions. For Dewey, they are tentative plans of action, or hypotheses. But they appear first as suggestions, for they reach beyond the immediately given. The process of entertaining suggestions is thinking, and thinking proceeds as a search for connections among consequences and antecedents. Consequently, every thought is creative. Every thinking act is an "incursion into the novel."

Creative teaching methods are also experimental. Again, Dewey's argument that the scientific method is the only means for bringing intelligence to bear upon human difficulties supports this position. Thinking, he says, begins in experience, and it ought to end in experience. It is the means for increasing efficiency in our living, and hence can never be separated from decision-making and from action. Experimentation deals with concrete troublesome situations; suggestions become instruments for clearing up the trouble.

Flexibility is the third characteristic of creative teaching. This quality belongs to the personal aspects of methodology. Individuals vary with respect to natural endowments, interests, and social histories. Managing these idiosyncratic factors such that they contribute to the creative process demands a maximum of flexibility. This means that classroom techniques will include not only the relatively stable procedures connected with all inquiry but also the improvisations necessary for handling unique events. Creative teaching methods will be directed by intelligence, but they will be continuously modified by the imaginative insights growing out of on-going states of affairs.

Imaginativeness is the fourth characteristic of the suggestive method. As the only device for avoiding mechanical responses, an alert imagination becomes the heart of the creative act and the key to creative teaching. The very manner in which the imagination functions causes it to be creative. Though directed toward concrete, on-going experiences, it also reaches far back into experiences of the individual, and even of the race, and brings forward materials which combine with the immediately present data in exciting new ways. It adds meaning to experience.

Finally, the principle of suggestion calls for teaching methods which encourage the skillful manipulation of objective materials as well as of ideas. This emphasis on manipulative skill implies that creating is never complete unless some aspect of the environment has been changed. In the creative process, and in creative teaching and learning, acting and thinking are inseparably linked. The act of handling materials facilitates a sensing of the meaning of what is occurring in a given educational encounter.

The research literature which supports a methodology of suggestion comes invariably from those educators who are deeply concerned with problems of creativity. For example, Harold Rugg's last book, *Imagination*,[3] explores the connections between suggestion and hypnosis, between suggestion and the techniques of the Zen masters and the principles of Yoga and of Taoism. These studies convince Mr. Rugg that the techniques of suggestions as employed by mystics, poets, and intuitive philosophers in the West will eventually influence educational practices in the direction of creativity.[4]

III. THE PRINCIPLE OF ENCOUNTER

The principle of encounter identifies the kind of *curriculum* which facilitates creative teaching and creative learning.

Specifically, it asserts that the experimental situation, here defined as encounter, constitutes the basic unit in the educational process. It further describes this unit as a complex but integral whole involving the teacher, the pupil, and a particular subject matter. As used in this paper, the concept carries the meanings assigned to it by such therapists and educators as May,[5] Barron,[6] Schachtel,[7] and Dewey.[8] It is existential, problematic, purposive, open, unitary.

To define the curriculum as existential means that the one real datum which makes up the educative process is the existing pupils and the existing teacher who confront each other in a concrete, problematic situation. This confrontation has immediate import for their separate existences for the very reason that it is mediated by a real life problem. Each person in the encounter learns to participate in the inner experiences of the other because of the common circumstance which binds them together. These inner experiences are dynamic; they are movements—toward increased understandings, toward greater self-realization, toward creative development. Such encounters comprise the content of education. Out of them will come whatever learnings are available, whatever changes can be

---

[3] Harold Rugg, *Imagination* (New York: Harper & Row, 1963), Chapters 8-12.
[4] *Ibid.*, p. 210.
[5] Rollo May (ed.), *Existential Psychology* (New York: Random House, 1961), p. 75. See also Rollo May, "The Nature of Creativity," *Creativity and Its Cultivation*, ed. H. H. Anderson (New York: Harper and Brothers, 1959), p. 58.
[6] Frank Barron, *Creativity and Psychological Health* (Princeton, N.J.: D. Van Nostrand Co., 1963), Chapter 7.
[7] Ernest G. Schachtel, *Metamorphosis* (New York: Basic Books, 1959), p. 240.
[8] John Dewey, *Democracy and Education*, Chapter 11.

effected in both teacher and pupils, whatever expansion of consciousness may occur.

Barron refers to this existential quality of encounter as a "vitalizing transaction," which may be "as frail as love or blessedness." It is a live and growing thing, a personal relationship; and it becomes the purpose of psychotherapy, as well as of education, to nourish this relationship in constructive, self-initiating directions, to expand the range of choices among the participants and hence to provide for experiences of increased freedom.

To define encounter in terms of the problematic means that the engagement occurs in the first place because of the individual's basic need to establish productive relations with other people, and because he discovers in his experiences unsettled factors which inhibit these relationships. The encounter begins as indeterminate probings, as exploratory and experimental thrusts, as tensional and disturbing but wholly curious surveys and scannings.

Again, Dewey's view of the curriculum throws light upon this idea. He explains that the thoughtful modes of behavior are generated by the confrontation of unaccustomed elements, that these elements make the encounter a personal one. They bring to experience the qualities of immediacy and commitment. Active participation in the encounter dissolves away uncertainty, connects up meanings, overcomes cultural discontinuities, and consequently contributes to the achievement of inner freedom. Personal involvement brings the individual's own past to bear upon the problem at hand, and it evokes the cumulative culture of mankind. The past in all of its dimensions has its say, presents its constancies, and stands ready to be transformed into new expressions.

The function of the curriculum therefore is to strengthen the learner's relation to his world, which means to aid in the achievement of freedom, of responsiveness, and of responsibility—these ends are achieved as the student experiences purposiveness among elements of the encounter. Thus, the curriculum has not completed its work until its informational components have entered into the free play of imagination, until the learner has discovered within this information the connections which will carry his experiences forward, until he has imposed something of his own vision upon it. In short, the purpose of the curriculum is to stimulate the free play of imagination, to activate the student into creative ventures, and to provide for the added freedom which this kind of activity generates. Of the various characteristics of encounter, openness is probably the most important. It facilitates creativeness, permits freedom, and softens rigidity.

According to Rogers, openness means that the individual is able to perceive his world directly rather than through predetermined categories; it means that he is aware of the existential moment as it actually is. Open-

ness is that condition within the individual which is most closely associated with creative potentiality; it is the opposite of psychological defensiveness and of rigidity; it is the permeability of boundaries among beliefs.

Discovered in therapy, openness becomes for Rogers a powerful educational weapon. It encourages individuals to become adaptive, to make
responsible choices, to become more aware, self-expressive, and free to
change.[9] It maintains the freshness of experience. In short, it makes the
encounter creative. In Schachtel's words, it provides for an enlargement
of personal experience.[10] According to Fromm, openness characterizes
teaching at its best, as teaching is conducted, for example, by the Zen
masters.[11] The only thing that the Zen master can teach, the only curriculum he can follow, the only content which he can convey to the pupil
is the pupil's own immediate existence.

The fifth characteristic of encounter refers to its integrated nature. It
is a unitary act of perceiving, feeling, reflecting, willing. The whole person
is involved. No boundary lines arise between the pupil and the subject
matter, between the pupil and his tools, nor between the pupil and the
teacher. More particularly there are no boundary lines between the categorized subject matters. Subject matter loses its logical orientation under
manipulative, playful attitudes.

This aspect of encounter has far-reaching implications for the traditional curriculum. It suggests, for example, that when defined in terms
of the hard core subjects the curriculum will not easily promote creativity.
Since creativeness is the same wherever it occurs—the same in the arts,
sciences, business affairs, and daily living—a curriculum which promotes
creativity will find its organizing principle within the creative experience
itself rather than in a systematized hierarchy of discrete subjects. For
this reason it also rejects as incompatible the concept of general education, the theory that a well-rounded person can be developed by exposing
him to a certain spread of courses, and the notion that enrichment counter-
balances overspecialization.

Personality formation does not result from an exposure to a specified
list of subjects. Growth toward selfhood is not necessarily nourished by
general education courses, nor need it be thwarted by specialization.
Variation in subject matter neither prevents nor cures overspecialization,
alienation, or uncreativeness. The liberal arts may not serve as an antidote
to the increasing particularization of knowledge; for the arts, no less than
specialized courses, may produce only technically qualified individuals.
The problem is not whether we should teach specialized courses, or gen-

---

[9] Carl R. Rogers, "Learning to Be Free," *Conflict and Creativity*, p. 277.
[10] Ernest G. Schachtel, *Metamorphosis*, p. 240.
[11] Erich Fromm, "Psychoanalysis and Zen Buddhism," *Zen Buddhism and Psychoanalysis* (New York: Harper & Brothers, 1960), p. 116.

eral courses, or a scattering of subjects. The problem is to teach whatever we have at hand in a creative manner. When we teach creatively, any subject matter, however specialized or however general, will promote integration of the self.

Thus, traditional methods and curriculums tend to make technicians out of students. If the subject matter is literature, then pupils become literary technicians; if it is electronics, then they become electronic technicians. To be sure, technical knowledge and technicians are necessary in scientific, industrialized societies. This is not the argument. We must also have some assurance that literary and electronic technicians shall have also learned to function creatively and to appreciate creative products.

IV. THE PRINCIPLE OF THERAPY

The principle of therapy serves as the criterion for selecting educational *aims*. Applying this principle isolates creativity as a major goal, and it suggests the corollary aims of freedom, self-initiative, and responsibility. The achievement of these aims constitutes therapy just as it defines the educative process.

These concepts—creativity, freedom, initiative, responsibility—are logically related. The creative imagination functions as an instrument for achieving freedom. It provides the individual with a wide range of adaptive responses and consequently extends the area of choice. But freedom implies the capacity to initiate one's own inquiries and to make one's own discoveries. And freedom, together with self-directing capacities, imposes the requirement that an individual accept an increasingly larger share of responsibility for choices and actions. Thus, when therapy or education is successful, the individual approaches the world creatively. He initiates his own encounters, and he takes responsibility for what he does.

This view has wide support among psychologists. Perhaps Carl Rogers has been most insistent in urging that education regard itself as therapy and that it pursue therapeutic goals. He argues that the aim of education is to assist students to take self-initiated action, to be responsible for such action, to become self-directive, to adapt flexibly to new situations, to cooperate effectively with others.[12]

The most important implication which psychotherapy has for the classroom teacher is its non-authoritarian attitude. Both Fromm and Rogers emphasize this requirement. Fromm again refers to the Zen masters, who seek no power of any kind over their pupils; who reject all authority ex-

[12] Carl R. Rogers, *Client-Centered Therapy* (Boston: Houghton Mifflin, 1951), p. 388.

cept perhaps for their own particular specialties.[13] Rogers argues that the exercise of authority over pupils destroys creativeness and self-initiative. He explains that the teacher should never set lesson plans, lecture, evaluate, criticize, assign grades, or give examinations. He must only arrange opportunities for students to learn to become responsibly free.[14]

Few teachers are willing to reduce their authority so drastically, and Rogers agrees that the initial stages of this kind of education produce considerable chaos. But it is the only education which can help an individual to learn to be free. But what exactly does the teacher do to help pupils discover within themselves the grounds for directing their own affairs? Four things, Rogers believes.

First, he can demonstrate his non-authoritarianism by placing complete trust in the pupil to choose his own way in learning and to discover his own information. It is because we distrust the student that we lecture him, assign tasks which *we* have selected, transmit to him *our* information, insist upon his following *our* directions. Second, the teacher can stand as a real person without sham or deceit. He serves as a model, provides resources, suggests. He shares the inner experiences of the learner, and in this encounter he begins to clarify his own feelings and to expand his own consciousness. He begins to understand the student just as the student begins to understand him. He effects changes in the student by expanding his own awareness.

Third, he can become effectively non-authoritarian by learning to prize the student. Accepting the individual as inherently worthy permits him to enter into experiences of pupils in ways which can release creative tendencies. Encouraging the pupil to affirm the worth of his own existence also encourages him to accept others without defensiveness. Valuing self and valuing others characterize creative individuals.

Fourth, the teacher displays non-authoritarianism by his ability to understand the student's reactions from the inside, to be empathetically aware of the way the process of learning appears to the student.[15] Recognizing that this capacity is largely limited to trained therapists, Rogers nevertheless believes that it is also a condition of creative teaching. It is an act of encounter, an act of being fully engaged, fully open and responsible.

Non-authoritarianism thus becomes a major application of therapeutic principles to education. This attitude develops as the teacher builds into his own behavioral responses the traits of trust, honesty, acceptance, and empathy.

A second application of psychotherapy involves the counterpart to this

[13] Erich Fromm, *Zen Buddhism and Psychoanalysis*, p. 124.
[14] Carl R. Rogers, *Conflict and Creativity*, p. 282.
[15] Carl R. Rogers, *Conflict and Creativity*, p. 281.

attitude, namely, the achievement of self-direction on the part of the student. The principle of self-activity is of course time-honored in the history of educational philosophy. As used in this essay, it is not intended to express any new or unusual meanings. But it does require a new setting and a new emphasis. The new setting is its function in therapy; the new emphasis is its role in creativity.

Referring again to Zen, Fromm notes the importance of the Buddhist doctrine that no person can save another, that each man must save himself. Education likewise must remain a process of self-education; no one can teach another directly. The Zen master joins such other notables as Socrates in the emphasis on teaching as midwifery. The teacher can only provide his presence, his responsiveness, and the condition of openness. The kind of growth which involves personality formation occurs only as a result of what the pupil does to himself and for himself.

The therapists who have recently identified themselves as existentialists [16] agree in making the achievement of self-direction the most important new dimension in their system of therapy.

Rollo May, a leading spokesman for this group, observes that there are in therapy, and in teaching, certain built-in tendencies which take away the student's decision making opportunities.[17] These pose a continual threat to his own growth. Every direct act which the teacher performs promotes the tendency on the part of the pupil to rely upon those activities, rather than his own, for his growth or for his failures. Yet it becomes precisely the aim of therapy, and of teaching, to support him in making decisions and in initiating behavior.

The existential therapists associate man's neurotic condition with his failure to learn to make decisions and to act upon them, and they therefore equate these learnings with therapy. May, for example, argues that the core of modern man's neurosis is "the undermining of his experience of himself as responsible, the sapping of his willing and deciding."[18] Therapy consists in encouraging man to accept responsibility; it consists in learning to be free.

Learning to become self-active and self-responsible becomes a central task in education. These learnings confer upon man his essential humanness. Says May, "Decision and responsibility are the distinctive forms of

[16] The following therapists contributed to the book, *Existential Psychology:* Rollo May, Gordon Allport, Herman Feifel, Abraham Maslow, and Carl Rogers. The existentialist movement now has its own publication, the *Review of Existential Psychology and Psychiatry,* which is edited by Adrian van Kaam. It lists twenty-one members on the editorial board, twelve of whom are doctors of medicine, indicating a strong emphasis on therapy.

[17] Rollo May, *Existential Psychology,* p. 43.

[18] Rollo May, "Will, Decision, and Responsibility: Summary Remarks," *Review of Existential Psychology and Psychiatry,* Vol. I, No. 3 (November, 1961), 250.

consciousness in the human being who is moving toward self-realization, integration, maturity."[19] Tillich also argues that these outcomes do not merely refer to what might be more or less preferable in human life; rather, they are the conditions of man's very existence. Says Tillich, "The power of deciding makes men human."[20]

Learning to become self-active and self-responsible are creative learnings. In the sense that the creative person is the self-actualizing person, the individual creates himself as he organizes his energies into patterns of living which are responsive to other persons. And the organization of his energies itself is an act of decision. Decision and action become essential to the creative life.

V. The Principle of Deferment

The principle of deferment describes the part which *evaluation* plays in the creative and educative processes.

Since this essay concerns itself primarily with the teaching side of education, the concept of deferment has been chosen to indicate the teacher's role in assigning value. It applies particularly to the judgments which are continually made in the daily operation of the classroom—making assignments, summarizing material, structuring class discussions, choosing goals, assigning grades. Deferment of the teacher's final judgments in these activities has one major purpose: it encourages self-initiative and promotes self-evaluation. The concepts which link up the attitude of deferment on the part of the teacher with self-evaluative tendencies on the part of the student form the meaning of this principle.

These concepts can be briefly summarized: the deferment of final solutions and choices stimulates the exploratory tendencies of students; such probings move beyond what is given to what is possible; the testing and choosing of possibilities characterize the creative process; the criteria for making these choices are personal and aesthetic; therefore, self-evaluation becomes the only basis for making choices which will carry forward the creative process. And finally, the capacity for self-evaluation calls for an independence of spirit and a feeling of self-worth.

The first of these ideas refers to the teacher's capacity to delay closure, to postpone the final settlement of a question which is under discussion, to entertain tentative conclusions. This does not mean that the student is left without direction or that his education deals with loose ends of information. But it does mean that the teacher refrains from imposing his own formal systems upon classroom activities in order to bring them to

[19] *Ibid.*, p. 256.
[20] Paul Tillich, "Existentialism and Psychotherapy," *Review of Existential Psychology and Psychiatry*, Vol. I, No. 1.

some predetermined end. The creative teacher avoids finalities. He continually shifts the limits of openness and closure as his emphasis moves from subject matter to pupil and back to his own concerns; balance between deferment and closure remains a precariously shifting one, as is the teacher's own involvement.

Hypothesizing is a second concept which enters into the meaning of deferment. Defined as the capacity to go beyond what is given, it serves as the logical connection between deferment and creativity. Deferment facilitates hypothesizing; hypotheses in turn reach beyond the data at hand; and going beyond the immediately given characterizes creative activity. To hypothesize means that the pupil freely engages in speculating, guessing, associating—in dealing with what is not yet present. And the environment which can best initiate and sustain this speculative venture is the condition of deferment.

The search for possibilities requires the acceptance of self as the source of judgment in making choices. Thus, self-evaluation becomes the third ingredient in the principle under discussion. At least three factors converge to make self-evaluation a necessary ingredient in creative education. First, creativity flourishes under conditions of conflict, ambiguity, and even chaos. Second, the creative individual functions as a self-assertive, independent person. Third, the grounds for judging original productions are personal, aesthetic ones.

Ample evidence has accumulated to support the view that creativity flourishes under conditions of conflict, that creative individuals prefer qualities of complexity, imbalance, and ambiguity and show an aversion to the settled, the symmetrical, and the ordered.[21] Tension forms part of the motivational drive of the creative person. Disorder arouses inventive tendencies and presents challenges to create new orders and more aesthetically satisfying structures. Hence, it is preferred by the gifted person.

This preference explains the creative person's predisposition to reject the conventional and to break up the orderly. For example, Barron finds that creativeness always involves an act of rejection preceding an act of construction;[22] and Golovin argues that every creative act both transcends prior experience and contains a revolt against it.[23] The very fact that creating entails abandonment of the status quo isolates the creative person and induces feelings of anxieties.

Thus, creative living and teaching inescapably incur certain risks, and

[21] Frank Barron, "The Disposition Toward Originality," *Scientific Creativity*, eds., C. W. Taylor and Frank Barron (New York: John Wiley, 1963), p. 146. See also Frank Barron, "Creative Vision and Expression in Writing and Painting," *The Creative Person*, The Institute of Personality Assessment and Research, University of California (Berkeley: Mimeographed, 1961), pp. II-1-19.

[22] Frank Barron, *The Creative Person*, p. II-10.

[23] N. E. Golovin, "The Creative Person in Science," *Scientific Creativity*, p. 16.

this is why principles of creative teaching must emphasize the qualities of self-worth, self-reliance and self-responsibility.

The element of risk involved in creative acts, including creative teaching, has several dimensions. For example, the mere fact that creativity seeks out possibilities and rejects actualities poses a threat to the established order. Creativity is essentially revisionistic; in searching for novelty it rejects conformity. Risk arises in connection with any innovation. It consists in the fact that the individual must judge changes as occurring in the direction of improvement and of social cohesiveness. It consists in creating objects which may have no significance for culture and therefore which may disrupt communication among people. It consists in the possibility that his inner sense of values may err in the direction of eccentricity, that his choice of goals is spurious, that his impulse to be unique will remain an end in itself rather than a condition for further fulfillment, that his nonconformity is only a neurotic symptom rather than a source of courage. The risk consists in the possibility that symbolic freedom and rebellion will extend into overt aggression. Perhaps the real risk is that a sense of social sympathy will not grow to match his courageous strivings for self-hood.

But if creativity involves risk, it also holds out the possibility for deeply rewarding social relationships. Maslow discusses these possibilities.[24] There is, he argues, a necessary connection between self-fulfillment and social sympathy. The individual who expresses in his living those values which he himself has created must of necessity express them in the form of social feelings. Thus, the two poles of individuality and conformity are complementary, not opposed. The more fully one actualizes himself, the more socially responsible he becomes.

An independence of judgment can easily run into self-assertiveness, into anti-social feelings of rebelliousness of exhibitionism; but these nevertheless belong in the creative environment, and it behooves the creative teacher to accommodate them in his classroom. These are not desirable forms of behavior, and they make teaching difficult. They add to the burden, as well as to the challenge, of creative teaching. How does the teacher channel such attitudes into productive activity?

For one thing, he can exploit an inherent dynamic of the creative drive itself, namely, its aesthetic component.[25] The creative individual accepts chaotic materials without threat because his own confidence assures him that he can impose an orderliness upon them which will be both aesthetic and accurate. He is strongly motivated by this need for aesthetic elegance.

---

[24] A. H. Maslow, *Toward a Psychology of Being*, Chapter 6.

[25] The nature and importance of the aesthetic drive in creativity is discussed in my article, "Aesthetic Motivation in the Creative Arts" which was published in the Summer 1965 issue of the *Journal of Aesthetics and Art Criticism*.

Physicists often argue that a theory is right because it is elegant. Maslow finds that this aesthetic need is invariably present in the behavior of self-actualizing people. Because these individuals make use of their unconscious urges without fearing them and accept their impulses without defending against them, they can release their creative energies into formal patterns of enjoyment.

Thus, the aesthetic drive which motivates the creative pupil places a powerful weapon into the hands of the teacher. As an internal force in the pupil, it is the counterpart of the creative teacher's own efforts. The teacher becomes a partner to the pupil. His deferring attitude joins the aesthetic tendency in the pupil to produce an autonomous functioning of the pupil's personality. It merges with the student's predispositions for self-discipline in the creative conduct of his life.

VI. CONCLUSION

The problem of how to educate for creativity remains among the most important of the unsettled questions in contemporary culture. It is an urgent question and merits the attention of our best minds. At stake is the possibility of a richer life for mankind generally, and at the same time the hope of discovering a therapeutic process which will cure souls.

35.   Artistic Teaching—The Cinderella of Modern Instruction

Edwin J. Swineford

What has happened to artistic teaching? Little artistic teaching is expected from the student teacher or the intern, and the conclusions to this brief study indicate that, in fact, only one in ten experienced teachers demonstrate superior artistic teaching behavior. Moreover, the chances are that this one superior-rated, artistic-teaching instructor was rated average or below in artistic teaching as a student teacher. Six out of ten experienced teachers studied failed to demonstrate any artistic teaching behavior. A superficial observation, based on the limited data of this

"Artistic Teaching—The Cinderella of Modern Instruction" by Edwin J. Swineford is reprinted with permission from *The Journal of Teacher Education*, 15: 281-286, September, 1964.

study, would be that, after the first two years, the degree of artistic teaching is in inverse proportion to the years of field experience.

The current emphasis on teaching machines has tended to mitigate the importance of the art of teaching, or what some British writers call craftsmanship in teaching, or the art of tuition. The science of teaching has played the role of the wicked stepmother and relegated the art of teaching, the neglected Cinderella of modern instruction, to the dustbin. The purpose of this investigation was to put the spotlight on artistic teaching in order to see what this Cinderella looked like in selected public school classrooms.

PROBLEM, DEFINITION, AND PROCEDURE OF THE STUDY

The *problem* of the study was to determine what artistic teaching behavior was demonstrated by thirty-three junior high school teachers who had been teaching from one to five years. The study also attempted to establish the relationship between length of teaching experience and artistic teaching and the relationship between superior-rated student teachers and artistic teaching behavior in the field.

Artistic teaching, as used in this study, refers to the skills and knowledges demonstrated by classroom teachers who meet any one or all of the following criteria: [1] (1) Indicate that the teacher has a clearly conceived ideal, goal, or vision which he seeks to achieve. (2) Reflect an emotional purpose and energy to achieve this ideal. (3) Employ refined skill, ingenuity, or style in the execution. (4) Recognize professional and social responsibilities.

Artistic teaching, then, is not just experienced teachers in action. It represents high-grade action which stems from a worthy ideal, pursued with feeling and purpose, employing refined means for its accomplishment. It is teaching that is scientific in its formulation, philosophical in its conceptualization, and refined and polished in its execution.

The *procedure* of the study involved a follow-up study of thirty-three student teachers who were in the investigator's procedures class and under his supervision in student teaching and who have now been teaching in the public schools of California from one to five years.

Extensive data on the preservice teaching behavior of the thirty-three participants were available from the rating sheets, anecdotal reports, and eight classroom observation reports of each participant. Data on the field classroom teaching behavior were obtained by visiting each teacher on

[1] Adapted from Valentine, P. F. *The Art of the Teacher.* New York: D. Appleton and Co., 1931.

the job for two separate observations with subsequent interviews.[2] The criteria postulated for artistic teaching were utilized in the analysis and classification of individual teaching behavior. Incidents of artistic teaching under each category of the definition are given in List 1.

The relationship of teaching experience to artistic teaching was determined by comparing, for each year of the five-year experience period, the incidents of artistic teaching grouped under the four criteria of the definition of artistic teaching (Table 1).

The relationship between the preservice rating of the participants and their artistic teaching behavior in the field was determined in the final phase of the study, which concludes with comments on the implications of the study.

FINDINGS OF THE STUDY

1. Incidents of artistic teaching behavior of thirty-three teachers, with from one to five years' professional experience, are described in the statements of List 1. The degree to which each of the participants demonstrated artistic teaching behavior was determined by the investigator on a six-point scale as he made the classroom observations and recorded the incidents of artistic teaching. Over half (60 per cent) failed to demonstrate artistic teaching in the observations; only one out of ten was rated "superior" in artistic teaching; a rating of "good" was assigned to nine, or 27 per cent, of the teachers; "some" artistic teaching was demonstrated by 13 per cent of the remainder. An attempt was made to make these ratings objective by basing them on the factual data of the classroom observation and other data accumulated by the investigator from his continuous relationship with the student in professional classes and in the field.

The incidents of artistic teaching demonstrated by all the teachers in the study were classified under the four criteria of artistic teaching as follows: Criterion 1 (Envisages an Ideal or Goal), 10 per cent; Criterion 2 (Reflects Emotionalized Purpose), 27 per cent; Criterion 3 (Employs Refined Skill), 58 per cent; Criterion 4 (Recognizes Professional and Social Responsibilities), 5 per cent.

The incidents are classified in List 1 under the appropriate criterion of the definition of artistic teaching. This classification was based on a knowledgeable decision of the investigator who was guided by supportive evidence from the modified case studies of each participant.

[2] Iota, Instrument for Observation of Teaching Activities, Kinney, Bradley, Kaltenbach, Owen, and Washington, was used.

2. The relationship between teaching experience and artistic teaching was difficult to establish since the incidents of artistic teaching represented the behavior of different teachers with varying lengths of professional experience. On the basis of volume of incidents of artistic teaching, the data showed that the teachers with three years of experience ranked highest in artistic teaching. The incidents of artistic teaching fell off after the first year, went up in the third, and dropped in the fourth and fifth years. The decline in volume of incidents in the fifth year was noteworthy. The number after each statement in List 1 indicates the year of field experience in which the incident was observed.

Insight into the changing nature of artistic teaching in relationship to experience was provided by an analysis of the incidents of artistic teaching for each year. The teachers in their first year of field experience seemed to lean heavily on their student-teaching experience, refining previously learned procedures or adding a creative touch to them. Generally the first-year teachers stayed within the circle of the traditional or previously learned teacher role. Adjusting to their initial solo responsibility as a teacher and studying the students in this new relationship seemed to characterize the teaching behavior of the first-year teachers. Criterion 1 (Envisages an Ideal) contained only 4 per cent of the total incidents of artistic teaching of first-year teachers. In contrast, 15 per cent of the incidents of artistic teaching of teachers in the third and fourth years of experience were classified under Criterion 1. Criterion 3 (Employs Refined Skill) contained 64 per cent of the total incidents of artistic teaching for the first-year teachers, a percentage which was slightly higher than that of any other year.

The teachers who were in their second year of field experience seemed to draw in and do little experimenting, focusing more attention on the basic aspects of teaching. They demonstrated more mature and professional relationships with students than the first-year teachers, using the tools of their profession with more craftsmanship. An increase over the first-year teachers in the volume of incidents of artistic teaching under Criterion 2 (Reflects Emotionalized Purpose) was noted.

Teachers in the third year of field experience turned to new methods and procedures, employing them to meet the needs of students in their classes. In terms of the total volume of incidents of artistic teaching, the teachers in the third year demonstrated the highest volume of the whole five-year period. The teacher personality seemed to come to life in this third year, developing new approaches as it worked through a deeper subject matter knowledge.

Teachers in the fourth and fifth years of field experience moved to specialization or depth in limited areas. They tended to rely on one style or approach which they had developed out of their own experience. They demonstrated insight and knowledge of their own capabilities, along with an understanding of the scope or framework of their professional responsibilities. There was an increase in incidents of artistic teaching under Criterion 1 (Envisages an Ideal) and a decrease under Criterion 3 (Refined Procedures). Incidents of artistic teaching under Criterion 4 (Recognizes Professional and Social Responsibilities) dropped off from the first years of teaching. The emphasis in artistic teaching in the third and fourth years was a clarification of and decision on what was to be done, combined with an emotionalized purpose or drive to achieve the goals with a minimum of emphasis on the means or procedures. The teacher now appeared secure and professional, with fewer but more effective techniques. Artistic teaching in the fourth and fifth years seemed to be related more to the teacher's personality, image, drive, planning, and decision making. Table 1 shows the distribution of incidents of artistic teaching under each Criterion.[3]

3. The third problem of the study was the relationship between the general rating of the student teacher in training and his rating as an artistic teacher in the field. Twelve student teachers of the thirty-three in

TABLE 1

DISTRIBUTION OF INCIDENTS OF ARTISTIC TEACHING BY YEAR AND CRITERIA

Field Experience by Years	No. of Teachers Studied	Frequency of Incidents of Artistic Teaching Classified by Criteria							
		Criterion 1		Criterion 2		Criterion 3		Criterion 4	
		No.	Per cent	No.	Per cent	No.	Per cent	No.	Per cent
1	7	5	4	25	24	70	65	8	7
2	6	9	11	22	33	35	51	4	5
3	9	11	7	46	31	85	58	6	4
4	5	8	15	17	33	27	51	1	2
5	6	4	14	9	33	14	50	1	3

the study were given a composite rating of superior, a rating based largely on the Iota Instrument for Observation of Teaching Activities; eight of the twelve were rated superior in artistic teaching in the field. Additional information on the relationship of student-teaching composite ratings to artistic teaching was obtained by selecting the teachers in the field with the highest artistic teaching rating and comparing it with their composite rating as a student teacher. Fourteen teachers earned a top rating in artistic teaching in the field. Of this group it was found that eight had a

---

[3] Due to editing and compressing some incidents for clarity, the figures in Table 1 and List 1 vary in their totals.

composite student teacher rating of superior. It appears, then, that two out of three of the student teachers who were rated superior on a composite rating later were rated superior in artistic teaching in the field. Half of the experienced teachers who were rated superior in artistic teaching came up from the pool of former student teachers who had been rated good, or lower, as student teachers.

IMPLICATIONS OF THE STUDY

(1) The findings suggest the need for a more comprehensive follow-up study of teachers in the field.

(2) The paucity of artistic teaching in our schools is so serious that administrators and teachers should undertake a systematic study of this problem.

(3) The nature of artistic teaching is such that it is usually not caught in the net of traditional observation instruments or ratings.

(4) Some of the aspects or details of artistic teaching behavior can be taught directly to student teachers or interns.

(5) The low frequency of incidents of artistic teaching under "Envisages an Ideal" and "Recognizes Professional and Social Responsibilities" needs further investigation. Modifications in content and procedures in preservice professional courses may be needed.

(6) Traditional student-teaching practices may not provide a suitable environment for the development of artistic teaching.

(7) The relationship between artistic teaching and tenure needs closer study.

Artistic teaching, the Cinderella of modern instruction, has been spotlighted in this study; an attempt was made to measure and analyze it. The investigator leaves this study with the nagging fear that piecemeal decomposition of artistic teaching may destroy it completely!

Demonstration of Artistic Teaching by Experienced Teachers

Incidents are listed under the four criteria postulated in the definition of artistic teaching. The number (1-5) after each statement refers to the years of field experience of the teacher.

Criterion 1—Envisages an Ideal

1. Analyzes own strengths and weaknesses in subject matter knowledge (1).
2. Critically examines the purposes of the school and philosophy of the administration (2).
3. Treats the class or group as older and more intelligent than they really are as individuals (2).
4. Demands more high-level learning outcomes (generalizations, understandings, appreciations, etc.) (2).

5. Appraises class situations expertly and exercises mature judgment in decisions (2).
6. Is alert to new possibilities and opportunities to achieve learning goals (2).
7. May shift lesson to take advantage of a surprise resource (3).
8. Can extend the discussion or consideration of an issue without losing the main thread (3).
9. Teaches with an individual style which reflects his unique personality (3).
10. Demonstrates confidence and professional pride in his work (3).
11. Can look at himself objectively and critically as he goes through the teaching act (3).
12. Extends teaching experiences into new subjects or different grade levels (4).
13. Looks upon himself as a teacher of youth instead of a subject teacher in a particular grade or school (4).
14. Accepts multiple responsibilities in the school without feeling exploited or overworked (4).
15. Turns frequently to the teaching of ethical or moral precepts (4).
16. Teaches without sham or pretense (4).
17. Plans and develops his own teaching materials and visual resources (4).
18. Possesses a clear conception of his professional responsibilities and acts within this framework (5).
19. Motivates and guides by basic or long-range goals (5).
20. Identifies himself as an authority in a particular subject or area and receives school recognition for this expertness (5).

Criterion 2—Reflects Emotionalized Purpose

1. Becomes increasingly sensitive to the value of time and its profitable use (1).
2. Exudes a drive or force which is felt by the students (1).
3. Keeps the direction and movement of the total lesson in the teacher's hands (1).
4. In explanations has all the facts at fingertips (1).
5. Solves many problems or issues on the spot (1).
6. Is cognizant of student needs and searches for solutions to individual student problems (1).
7. Develops a sense of humor appropriate for the particular class or age level (1).
8. Demonstrates love of youth by actions or decisions in working with them (1).
9. Builds his teaching around his own strengths (2).
10. Maintains open and direct communication with all members of the class (2).
11. Heads straight for the teaching-learning goal without deviation (2).
12. May extend teaching beyond the four walls of the classroom (2).
13. Knows how to talk to youth on informal occasions (2).
14. Suggests understanding and sincerity in tone of voice (2).
15. Relates to youth by participating with them in class activities (2).
16. Considers student growth more important than his own ego gratification (2).
17. Pieces parts of lesson into a unified whole (2).
18. Moves deliberately and confidently with students and faculty (3).
19. Works toward professional goals without regard to popularity with students (3).
20. Maintains poise and purpose regardless of distractions in class (3).

21. Utilizes more interrogative than declarative sentences in class discussions (3).
22. Can make quick, accurate, and penetrating analysis in front of the class (3).
23. Acts unhurried and organized in teaching activities (3).
24. Extends teaching skills and knowledges by summer and extension classes (3).
25. Prepares students ahead of time for later learning (3).
26. Can improvise, adopt, and adapt when leading class discussions (3).
27. Appraises climate for learning; may change the lesson in midstream (3).
28. Fills room with a variety of long- and short-range activities and projects for individuals and groups (3).
29. Has the ability to reach the students with words (3).
30. Modifies program as the result of insight or new facts and not because of student or parental pressure (3).
31. Accepts teacher responsibility in class, in the school, and in the community (3).
32. Watches for changes in students (3).
33. Takes each step one at a time without leaving gaps in instruction (3).
34. Challenges the class by academically stretching each student to his limit (4).
35. Engages in many informal communications with students before and after class (4).
36. Anticipates the possible range of student resistance to learning and takes steps to overcome it (4).
37. Increases number of individual communications with students by personal comments on written papers (4).
38. Appreciates and profits from administrative supervision (4).
39. Has skill in planning and presenting lessons that fit perfectly into the fifty-minute class period (4).
40. Lives up to the teacher image he has developed in the school and community (5).
41. Blends into the social and economic level of the class, but remains aloof and removed from them academically (5).
42. Has good physical and mental health; appears vital and sensitive (5).

Criterion 3—Employs Refined Skill

1. Maintains and paces the lessons to match student abilities (1).
2. Moves more deeply and thoroughly into phases of subject matter being taught; teaching reflects a satisfaction from this depth (1).
3. Gives short, direct, and complete explanations (1).
4. Uses new materials and taps additional resources (1).
5. Faces problems of control quickly and directly (1).
6. Isolates and puts sharply into focus selected major learnings (1).
7. Stimulates critical thinking with cues, hints, or guidelines (1).
8. Engages in selected, critical review that is fresh and original in approach (1).
9. Plans lessons which may involve some mental anguish on the part of students (1).
10. Assigns homework which evolves from and reinforces the lesson (1).
11. Carries students back through the steps by which the lesson was developed (1).

12. Draws all students into class discussions and activities (1).
13. Spends extra time motivating and establishing readiness (1).
14. Provides for creativity on part of students (1).
15. Maintains a simple, direct relationship with individual students in the class (1).
16. Profits from the experiences and skills of other teachers (1).
17. Plans activities with minimum amount of teacher work and maximum amount of student production (1).
18. Defines class standards clearly and objectively (1).
19. Takes definite steps to build strong class morale (2).
20. Encourages students to question issues and be critical of thinking processes (2).
21. Organizes blocks of subject matter or daily lessons around a meaningful problem or core (2).
22. Enriches presentations with teacher-created materials (2).
23. Dignifies individual students by accepting or recognizing their contributions to the class (2).
24. Holds individual students responsible regardless of what total class may do (2).
25. Possesses skill and knowledge to handle student's emotional reactions (2).
26. Gives students time to think at their own pace (2).
27. Makes complicated explanations or processes appear clear and simple (3).
28. Is brisk in pace to class as a group but patient and slower with special students who need support (3).
29. Employs a variety of devices which require students to discriminate or sift through a mass of facts for the exact response (3).
30. Reinforces profusely (3).
31. Regards the students as individuals and accepts their differences (3).
32. Reacts to problems by use of intellect, not emotions (3).
33. Puts mystery into the teaching of routine subject matter (3).
34. Relates subject matter content to the meaningful world of the adolescent (3).
35. Builds new subject matter on learnings he helped them acquire in other classes or in lower grades in school (3).
36. Sow seeds of knowledge which will not come to bear until later (3).
37. Operates within the framework of fair play accepted and understood by the students (3).
38. Utilizes grades to help and guide the students in their total development (3).
39. Organizes lesson so as to eliminate gaps or dead spots (3).
40. Experiences support and understanding from the class in times of personal or professional crisis (3).
41. May successfully deviate from traditional routines or procedures followed by a majority of the teachers (3).
42. Learns about himself by studying student reaction to his teaching (3).
43. Strikes when class is keyed up to learn and receptive to a particular kind of learning outcome (3).
44. Moves along with the times and comes up with fresh ideas to spark sharp lessons (3).
45. Occasionally employs for emphasis the colorful speech idioms currently used by youth (3).

46. May sit back and let the students' ideas and verbalizations temporarily dominate the class (4).
47. Teaches with an individual style or flair which is deliberately conceived and employed (4).
48. Acts as a team member with the students as they all work toward learning outcomes (4).
49. Discriminates among goals and concentrates on critical ones for a specific class (4).
50. Is apt in getting students' attention (4).
51. Moves on a high intellectual level and may overlook occasional childish behavior (4).
52. Utilizes the knowledge and leadership of star students (4).
53. Makes the class as a group look better academically than would be expected from an analysis of the individuals in the class (4).
54. May concentrate on or specialize in the use of selected audiovisual resources which give the teacher extra power (4).
55. Spends time in class teaching students how to live and learn together (4).
56. Reduces volume of student responses; requires definite answers of high quality (5).
57. Checks errors or misconceptions in students' thinking and clears them up as he goes along (5).
58. Fills the bulletin and chalk board with solid subject matter content and materials relative to the lesson (5).
59. Puts the spotlight on errors or mistakes which may be common to the class (5).
60. Accepts students as being less than perfect and expects them to accept him in the same way (5).

Criterion 4—Recognizes Professional and Social Responsibilities

1. Shows sensitivity to parental reactions (1).
2. Subordinates popularity with students to respect from co-workers (1).
3. Compares class achievement with that of other classes (1).
4. Looks critically for learning that is taking place (1).
5. Thinks of himself as a member of a school team (1).
6. Knows the goals of the school and reflects this knowledge in teaching behavior (1).
7. Overtly shows pride in self and school (1).
8. Seeks ideas from co-workers (2).
9. May draw on community experience to enrich classwork (2).
10. Enjoys a superior teaching image in the school and community (3).
11. Has the support and understanding of the school administration (3).
12. Experiences support and enthusiasm for himself as a teacher from a majority of the students (4).

Strategies

OVERVIEW

Tʜɪs section is different from the others. In the preceding six sections it is fairly easy to abstract concepts shared by the authors. In the section on aesthetics, for example, such concepts as beauty, form, balance, and conflict unify the various articles; and in the section on communications, the concepts of input, output, channel, message, and feedback are held in common by the authors. But in this section it would be difficult to find a unifying set of terms for the seven selections. This section serves as a culmination of the others, for a strategy is a deliberate pattern of actions aimed at achieving a specific goal. A strategy comes after we determine the goal and understand fully the nature of the activities to be performed. Thus, we need a strategy, or strategies, to achieve certain cognitive behavior or to bring about a particular emotional climate in the classroom. In these two senses, at least, this section stands apart from the others.

Moreover, the articles in this section do not concentrate on describing or analyzing the nature of strategy but rather present strategies for teaching. Socrates presents a strategy to show that there is no such thing as teaching but only recollection; Coombs presents some moves that can be combined to create a strategy for teaching concepts; Oliver and Shaver present two teaching styles, or strategies, for presenting public issues; Taba and her associates present an analysis of teacher-pupil interaction aimed at getting pupils to perform on various levels of three cognitive tasks; Berry presents a strategy derived from computer programming; Suchman presents a strategy for teaching the pupil an inquiry strategy in science; and Schwab and Klinckmann present a strategy for teaching the new biology that consists of three stages of discussion.

The concept of strategy is used in situations where the attainment of one's goal is blocked by someone or something. To overcome the conflict posed by the opposition, whatever it is, a strategist maps out his plan of attack according to the strengths of his forces and his opponent. He carefully interrelates the order and timing of his actions. He even plans for possible retreating and regrouping actions. He takes into account his opponent's possible behavior. His strategy, in short, is a plan for the most efficient and quickest victory in light of his opponent's position and the prevailing general conditions.

It is no wonder, then, that strategy is first and foremost a concept used by the military. In war we have the prime example of someone deliberately and forcefully countering the actions performed against him. Strategy is also employed in such games as chess, tennis, and basketball, in which one person or team matches ability with another person or team with the intention of overcoming competition. Strategy is used in other situations, too, where there is conflict, e.g., political race for office, world diplomacy, labor-management relations, and race relations.

As always, we must ask whether the concept of strategy and its accompanying concepts of attack, retreat, force, enemy or opponent, and timing can be meaningfully applied to teaching. Are there sufficient similarities with war and chess, for example, to warrant the use of the concept of strategy in teaching? Many would strongly argue that there are, that strategy applies closely to teaching. It applies because there are specified goals to be attained in the classroom and a variety of means can be used to attain them. Furthermore, teachers and pupils often see each other as opponents, not only for leadership control of classroom activities, but also in a battle of wits related to the topic at hand.

Some would argue that strategy applies to teaching just as it applies to any situation where goals are to be attained. That is, strategy in teaching is a plan for achieving the goal of learning, but that goal in no way implies a victory for the teacher and a defeat for the pupil. The teacher and pupil are to be viewed as cooperating in a plan that benefits both of them but primarily the pupil. In the sense that a teaching strategy is a plan to attain certain goals and to guard against undesirable results, the concept of strategy is meaningful for teaching.

Obviously, the authors in this section feel that strategy does apply to teaching, whether they say so explicitly or by implication. According to Taba and Elzey, "the chief task of teaching . . . is to determine the order of learning tasks and to pace each step appropriately. This is a crucial point in the formulation of teaching strategies, and one against which current teaching methods commit the greatest errors." Perhaps the most famous teaching strategy is the one named after Socrates. The famous selection from the Meno illustrating the Socratic style is a demonstration to Meno of how to conduct inquiry. Socrates employs his particular strategy, while at the same time commenting about it, so that Meno will understand it. Also, he talks about geometry, as opposed to such concepts as virtue and piety. A careful reading and analysis of this selection from Plato will reveal the elements of Socrates' strategy. The reader is asked to consider which points are crucial to this style of teaching. (I use the term "teaching" in spite of Socrates' objection.) For example, is it possible to employ the Socratic strategy if we do not accept the fact that man acquires his knowledge not in this life but at some other time? Is it possible to use this strategy with areas of mathematics other than geometry? Can we use it with history? With economics? With literature? With biology? With physics? With art? With music? If this strategy cannot be used with a particular subject, then we must consider in what ways this subject differs from geometry.

A further clue about the Socratic strategy appears in the article by Oliver and Shaver. In their research on teaching social studies within a framework of public issues, these researchers set forth several dimensions for describing the act of teaching. Then, within these dimensions, they describe two styles, one of which is the Socratic analytic strategy. It will be helpful to the reader to use their specification of the Socratic style as a means of examining the selection from Plato.

Schwab and Klinckmann assert that discussion is the best teaching method for getting pupils to understand biological processes. But they are interested in much more than cognitive understanding. They choose the discussion method because it provides the "energy of wanting" needed for intellectual understanding and because it leads to a positive emotional climate in the classroom. It is a way of establishing a warm interpersonal relationship with the pupils. To do all this the teacher needs to work through the three stages of discussion outlined. That is, the teacher must work according to a strategy which requires him to change his behavior as the discussion advances.

Taba, too, speaks of strategies for teaching thought processes. By analyzing classroom discourse along three dimensions—designation, function, and levels of thought—Taba and her associates are able to describe the flow of classroom talk and the effect of various strategies on the thought processes performed verbally. This is similar to Oliver and Shaver's attempt to study the effect of the recitation and Socratic styles on learning outcomes and teaching behavior.

Coombs is interested in strategies for the teaching of concepts to pupils. But since he and his team (he worked under B. O. Smith and cites that team's study in his article) have not come up with a complete description of teaching strategies, he here limits his discussion to verbal moves which may then be combined into strategies for the teaching of concepts. The reader may wish to compare his "moves" with those of Bellack and his associates in another chapter.

Suchman and Berry differ from the others in that their strategies are, in essence, to get the pupils to develop a strategy. Suchman is interested in having the pupils inquire productively and therefore his approach is to teach the pupils a strategy. Part of the teacher's strategy is to present a concrete problem and then to require the pupils to solve that problem by asking only questions that can be answered yes or no. Though Suchman concentrates on the three stages for pupil inquiry, the reader will easily be able to extract the components and justification of the teacher's strategy. Berry, too.

wants to instill the sense of strategy in his pupils' minds by having the pupils behave according to a strategy. He borrows his strategy from the computer and requires the pupil to give instructions to the teacher-computer as a means of teaching pupils to be explicit when giving instructions. Berry, like Socrates, uses mathematics in his demonstration and suggests that this strategy can be used with other subject fields.

Three studies in this section deal with the analysis of teacher-pupil verbal behavior. Taba and her associates, Oliver and Shaver, and Coombs (representing the B. O. Smith team) analyze classroom discourse. The reader may wish to compare their three sets of categories. Furthermore, since these are all involved in content analysis regarding thinking strategies, it would be worthwhile to compare them to the studies in the section on the cognitive vantage point. A word about the units of analysis used in these three investigations is appropriate. Taba and her associates, and Oliver and Shaver both use the unit of thought, though they define it differently. In its full report the Smith team defines venture as "a segment of discourse consisting of a set of utterances dealing with a single topic and having a single overarching content objective."[1] The team identifies nine types of ventures according to their objectives, one of which is the conceptual venture. The moves within this conceptual venture unit are described by Coombs in the article included in this section. It is important to note that none of the three units of analysis is a time unit. The reason for this is most accurately presented by the Smith team. "It is unlikely . . . that strategies would be found in time-sample units. . . . A strategy is a pattern which occurs in the verbal behavior of the classroom, and units in which strategies are found will occur as part of the organization of the discourse. To divide the discourse into time periods, or number-of-occurrence segments, is to risk fragmenting whatever strategies may occur in it."[2]

As already pointed out, this section relates to all the other six chapters. Most directly it relates to the cognitive vantage point, as the titles of the articles alone suggest, and to the classroom emo-

---

[1] B. Othanel Smith, Milton Meux, Jerrold Coombs, and Graham Nuthall. *A Tentative Report on the Strategies of Teaching*. Urbana, Bureau of Educational Research, College of Education, University of Illinois, 1964. p. 5.

[2] *Ibid.*, p. 4.

tional climate suggested by Schwab's application of Rogers' ideas. Schwab also reminds one of Galloway (communications) when he suggests that, by using his eye, the teacher can nonverbally communicate his interest in each individual pupil. The concept of strategy is readily found in the section on games in the Smith and Macdonald articles. Finally, Oliver and Shaver point out that the attempts of the Socratic style to teach the pupil to think on two levels at the same time is reminiscent of Jensen (classroom social climate) and of Dewey, as noted earlier.

Further research on the topic of teaching strategies is clearly needed. We need to be able to describe the elements of the strategies many teachers do in fact use and to measure the effect of these strategies upon students and teachers. The six problems for research suggested by Oliver and Shaver are sufficient to suggest the direction of future thought and work. If strategies are as important to teaching as Taba and Elzey claim, the task facing educators will be challenging and enormous.

36.   The Meno

Plato

Soc: . . . In that confiding, I will gladly inquire with you into the nature of virtue.

Meno: Yes, Socrates; but what do you mean by saying that we do not learn, and that what we call learning is only a process of recollection? Can you teach me how this is?

Soc: I told you, Meno, just now that you were a rogue, and now you ask whether I can teach you, when I am saying that there is no teaching, but only recollection; and thus you imagine that you will expose me in a contradiction.

Meno: Indeed, Socrates, I protest that I had no such intention. I only

The Dialogues of Plato: The Meno, translated by Benjamin Jowett, is reprinted by permission of The Clarendon Press: Oxford, 4th Edition (Vol. I) 1953. (Diagrams do not appear in the original Greek text. I have modified the diagram which appears in this 1953 edition, added others, and inserted markings in the dialogue to aid the reader. RTH, editor.)

asked the question from habit; but if you can prove to me that what you say is true, I wish that you would.

Soc: It will be no easy matter, but I am willing to do my best for you. Suppose that you call one of your numerous attendants, whichever you like, that I may demonstrate on him.

Meno: Certainly. Come hither, boy.

Soc: He is Greek, and speaks Greek, does he not?

Meno: Yes, indeed; he was born in the house.

Soc: Attend now, and observe whether he learns of me or only remembers.

Meno: I will.

Soc: Tell me, boy, do you know that a figure like this is a square?

Boy: I do.

Soc: And you know that a square figure has these four lines equal?

Boy: Certainly.

Soc: And these lines which I have drawn through the middle of the square are also equal?

Boy: Yes.

Soc: A square may be of any size?

Boy: Certainly.

Soc: And if one side of the figure be two feet long (AB) and the other side two feet (AD), how much will the whole be? Let me explain: if in one direction the space was two feet long, and in the other direction one foot, the whole space would be two feet taken once?

Boy: Yes.

Soc: But since this side is also two feet, there are twice two feet?

Boy: There are.

Soc: Then the square is twice two feet?

Boy: Yes.

Soc: And how many are twice two feet? count and tell me.

Boy: Four, Socrates.

Soc: And might there not be another figure twice as large as this, but of the same kind, and having like this all the lines equal?

Boy: Yes.

Soc: And how many feet will that be?

Boy: Eight feet.

Soc: And now try and tell me the length of the line which forms the side of that double square: this is two feet—what will that be?

Boy: Clearly, Socrates, it will be double.

Soc: Do you observe, Meno, that I am not teaching the boy anything, but only asking him questions; and now he fancies that he knows how long a line is necessary in order to produce a figure of eight square feet; does he not?

Meno: Yes.

Soc: And does he really know?

Meno: Certainly not.

Soc: He fancies that because the square is double, the line is double?

Meno: True.

Soc: Now see him being brought step by step to recollect in regular order. (*To the boy.*) Tell me, boy, do you assert that a double space comes from a double line? Remember that I am not speaking of an oblong, but of a figure equal every way, and twice the size of this—that is to say of eight feet; and I want to know whether you still say that a double square comes from a double line?

Boy: Yes.

Soc: But does not this line become doubled if we add another such line here? (add BE to AB; BE = AB)

Boy: Certainly.

Soc: And four such lines, you say, will make a space containing eight feet?

Boy: Yes.

Soc: Let us describe such a figure: Would you not say that this is the figure of eight feet?

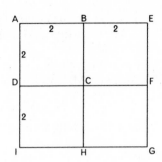

Boy: Yes.

Soc: And are there not these four divisions in the figure, each of which is equal to the figure of four feet?

Boy: True.

Soc: And is not that four times four?

Boy: Certainly.

Soc: And four times is not double?

Boy: No, indeed.

Soc: But how much?

Boy: Four times as much.

Soc: Therefore the double line, boy, has given a space, not twice, but four times as much.

Boy: True.

Soc: Four times four are sixteen—are they not?

Boy: Yes.

Soc: What line would give you a space of eight feet—for that gives a fourfold space, of sixteen feet, does it not? (AE yields a square of 16 feet)

Boy: Yes.

Soc: And the space of four feet is made from this half line? (AB yields a square of 4 feet)

Boy: Yes.

Soc: Good; and is not a space of eight feet twice the size of this (ABCD), and half the size of the other (AEGI)?

Boy: Certainly.

Soc: Such a space, then, will be made out of a line greater than this one (AB), and less than that one (AE)?

Boy: Yes; I think so.

Soc: Very good; I like to hear you say what you think. And now tell me, is not this a line of two feet (AB) and that (AE) of four?

Boy: Yes.

Soc: Then the line which forms the side of the eight foot space ought to be more than this line of two feet (AB) and less than the other of four feet (AE)?

Boy: It ought.

Soc: Try and see if you can tell me how much it will be.

Boy: Three feet.

Soc: Then if we add a half to this line of two, that will be the line of three. Here are two (AB) and there is one (BJ); and on the other side, here are two also (AD) and there is one (DL) and that makes the figure of which you speak?

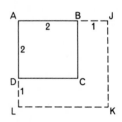

Boy: Yes.

Soc: But if there are three feet this way (AJ) and three feet that way (AL), the whole space will be three times three feet?

Boy: That is evident.

Soc: And how much are three times three feet?

Boy: Nine.

Soc: And what was to be the number of feet in the doubled square?

Boy: Eight.

Soc: Then the eight foot space is not made out of a line of three feet?

Boy: No.

Soc: But from what line?—tell me exactly; and if you would rather not reckon, try and show me the line.

Boy: Indeed, Socrates, I do not know.

Soc: Do you see, Meno, what advances he has made in his power of recollection? He did not know at first, and he does not know now, what is the side of a figure of eight: but then he thought that he knew, and answered confidently as if he knew, and felt no difficulty; now he feels a difficulty, and neither knows nor fancies that he knows.

Meno: True.

Soc: Is he not better off in knowing his ignorance?

Meno: I think that he is.

Soc: If we have made him doubt, and given him the 'torpedo's shock', have we done him any harm?

Meno: I think not.

Soc: We have certainly, as would seem, assisted him in some degree to the discovery of the truth; and now he will wish to remedy his ignorance, but then he would have been ready to tell all the world again and again that the double space should have a double side.

Meno: True.

Soc: But do you suppose that he would ever have started to inquire into or to learn what he fancied that he knew, though he was really ignorant of it, until he had fallen into perplexity under the idea that he did not know, and had desired to know?

Meno: I think not, Socrates.

Soc: Then he was the better for the torpedo's touch?

Meno: I think so.

Soc: Mark now the further development. I shall only ask him, and not teach him, and he shall share the inquiry with me: and do you watch and see if you find me telling or explaining anything to him, instead of eliciting his opinion. Tell me, boy, is not this a square of four feet which I have drawn?

Boy: Yes.

Soc: And now I add another square equal to the former one?

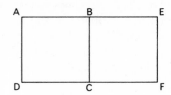

Boy: Yes.
Soc: And a third, which is equal to either of them?

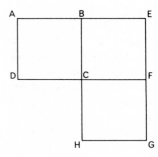

Boy: Yes.
Soc: Suppose that we fill up the vacant corner?

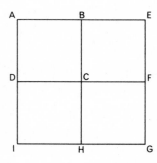

Boy: Very good.

Soc: Here, then, there are four equal spaces?

Boy: Yes.

Soc: And how many times larger is this space (AEGI) than this other (ABCD)?

Boy: Four times.

Soc: But we wanted one only twice as large, as you will remember.

Boy: True.

Soc: Now, does not this line, reaching from corner to corner, bisect each of these spaces (DB, BF, FH, HD)?

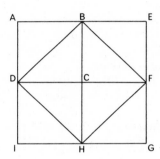

Boy: Yes.

Soc: And are there not here four equal lines which contain this space? (DB = BF = FH = HD; they contain space DBFH).

Boy: There are.

Soc: Look and see how much this space is.

Boy: I do not understand.

Soc: Has not each interior [line] cut off half of the four spaces?

Boy: Yes.

Soc: And how many such spaces are there in this section (DBFH)?

Boy: Four.

Soc: And how many in this (ABCD)?

Boy: Two.

Soc: And four is how many times two?

Boy: Twice (that is, DBFH is twice as big as ABCD).

Soc: So that this space (DBFH) is of how many feet?

Boy: Of eight feet.

Soc: And from what line do you get this figure?

Boy: From this (DB).

Soc: That is, from the line which extends from corner to corner of the figure of four feet?

Boy: Yes.

Soc: And that is the line which the learned call the diagonal. And if this is the proper name, then you, Meno's slave, are prepared to affirm that the double space is the square of the diagonal?

Boy: Certainly, Socrates.

Soc: What do you say of him, Meno? Were not all these answers given out of his own head?

Meno: Yes, they were all his own.

Soc: And yet, as we were just now saying, he did not know?

Meno: True.

Soc: But still he had in him those notions of his—had he not?

Meno: Yes.

Soc: Then he who does not know may still have true notions of that which he does not know?

Soc: And at present these notions have just been stirred up in him, as in a dream; but if he were frequently asked the same questions, in different forms, he would know as accurately as anyone at last?

Meno: I dare say.

Soc: Without anyone teaching him he will recover his knowledge for himself, if he is merely asked questions?

Meno: Yes.

Soc: And this spontaneous recovery of knowledge in him is recollection?

Meno: True.

Soc: And this knowledge which he now has must he not either have acquired at some time, or else possessed always?

Meno: Yes.

Soc: But if he always possessed this knowledge he would always have known; or if he has acquired the knowledge he could not have acquired it in this life, unless he has been taught geometry. And he may be made to do the same with all geometry and every other branch of knowledge; has anyone ever taught him all this? You must know about him, if, as you say, he was born and bred in your house.

Meno: And I am certain that no one ever did teach him.

Soc: And yet he has these notions?

Meno: The fact, Socrates, is undeniable.

Soc: But if he did not acquire them in this life, then he must have had and learned them at some other time?

Meno: Clearly he must.

Soc: Which must have been the time when he was not a man?

Meno: Yes.

Soc: And if there are always to be true notions in him, both while he is and while he is not a man, which only need to be awakened into knowledge by putting questions to him, his soul must remain always possessed of this knowledge; for he must always either be or not be a man.

Meno: Obviously.

Soc: And if the truth of all things always exists in the soul, then the soul is immortal. Wherefore be of good cheer, and try to discover by recollection what you do not now know, or rather what you do not remember.

Meno: I feel, somehow, that I like what you are saying.

Soc: And I too like what I am saying. Some things I have said of which I am not altogether confident. But that we shall be better and braver and less helpless if we think that we ought to inquire, then we should have been if we thought that there was no knowing and no duty to seek to know what we do not know;—that is a belief for which I am ready to fight, in word and deed, to the utmost of my power.

Meno: There again, Socrates, your words seem to me excellent.

Soc: Then, as we are agreed that a man should inquire about that which he does not know, shall you and I make an effort to inquire together into the nature of virtue? . . .

37. Teacher Style and the Analysis of the Student-Teacher Dialogue

Donald W. Oliver and James P. Shaver

A BROADER VIEW OF DISCUSSION STYLE

Although we can dissect the dialogue into any number of appropriate dimensions, and identify teaching behavior along these dimensions, we recognize, at least intuitively, that there may well be certain *general* styles of teaching which are commonly observed. In dealing with the problem of describing these general styles, an important question arises: Which of the various dimensions set forth should be considered central, and which should be considered secondary in the definition of such styles? In determining the effect of a general style of teaching on learning outcomes, for example, is it more important that teachers be alike in the posture used, in the intellectual operations performed, in the amount and direction of affectivity shown, or in all three areas? Experimentally, there are at least two strategies one might use in answering this question. One might obtain a large sample of teachers, give them the same materials to teach, ask them to direct the class's attention toward the analysis and clarification of controversial political issues, observe the range and profiles of behavior that follow and relate these to learning outcomes. Or, one might define two or more particular styles of teaching along those dimensions of behavior that one felt were critical, train teachers to play the styles, observe to what extent the dimensions of teaching not included in the definition were also affected by the different styles, and again determine the relationship of behavioral dimensions to student learning. In the long run, we are saying that our ability to identify and differentiate teaching styles is justified by the kinds of predictions we can make about learning outcomes. No matter how different two teaching styles may appear to an observer, with or without the tools of systematic observation, they are "significantly different" from an educational standpoint only if they lead to different learning outcomes.

In our own work we have chosen the latter course: To define styles according to certain conceptual dimensions, train teachers to play these styles, and observe what differences occur, if any, in behavior as well as differences in the learning outcomes of students. We might illustrate this

Reprinted with permission from Chapter 12 of *The Analysis of Public Controversy: A Study in Citizenship Education.* U.S. Department of Health, Education, and Welfare, Office of Education, Cooperative Research Project No. 8145. Cambridge, Harvard Graduate School of Education, Harvard University, 1962.

approach by describing two style models we have investigated experimentally. We have called these styles "recitation" and "Socratic" teaching.

Recitation teaching. Probably the basic characteristic of recitation teaching is the teacher's attitude toward and control of knowledge. He provides through reading assignments—usually a text—and through his role in class discussions the correct information which the students are to know. The teacher expects the student to respond when called upon to fill in the sequence of information which the teacher wishes to develop in class. This involves mainly relating personal experiences or repeating or paraphrasing what the teacher or a text has said, although it may require the use of some independent thought, such as reorganizing previously read material or applying it to a new situation. In essence, then, evidence of learning is contingent upon the extent to which the student can respond to questions regarding information given him by the teacher, either in class or through texts and other media.

Socratic teaching. Socratic teaching, as we have conceived it, is clearly adversarial. When the center of discussion is a controversial political topic—as in our work—Socratic teaching requires that the student do more than describe the controversy in the terms in which the teacher, or assigned materials, have presented it. Rather, the Socratic teacher requires the student to take a position on the issue, state that position, and defend it. Here the emphasis is not only on knowledge provided by the teacher, as background for the discussion, but on the process by which the student arrives finally at a decision about the topic under consideration, on the careful consideration of alternative decisions, and on the utilization of analytic concepts and strategies, regardless of the position which is finally reached.

Describing General Styles Dimensionally

While these brief descriptions of the two styles suggest that we "know" what are, in fact, the differences between Socratic and recitation teaching, when one begins to perform as a teacher, the general descriptions very quickly prove themselves inadequate. It is this fact that has led us to the more microscopic dimensional analysis. We found we needed a more precise and reliable way of describing the teaching performance than casual recall based on anecdotal records. It should be clear, however, that the microscopic analysis does not replace the general style description. Theoretically, it will simply provide us with a more precise way of defining "natural" teaching styles.

To illustrate how these two levels of description are related, below we have defined some of the similarities and differences between Socratic and recitation teaching according to the dimensional analysis given previously [in this report and outlined here].

Statement posture. Recitation teaching is characterized by a high frequency of "stating" and "question asking," with less emphasis on "questioning" or "expressions of self-doubt." With its adversarial nature, Socratic teaching shows a much higher frequency in "questioning" responses.

Discussion posture. Recitation teaching tends to be descriptive; it is assumed that the truth of the situation is available and that one has only to present and clarify information or an analytic structure by which information can be organized. The attempt to push the student toward a personal decision in which values are at stake is inappropriate for this style. The Socratic style is clearly dialectical. It assumes that the problem can be clarified only in an adversarial context in which various points of view can be presented and defended.

Both recitation and Socratic teaching may emphasize either substantive or analytic responses. The recitation teacher, however, will be concerned with the substance of the issue only insofar as he is interested in clarifying it and presenting the correct position. In the process of clarifying, he may well be analytic, asking that his students explain, "What are the possible ways one might look at this problem?" The concepts which the students apply to this analysis will be those given them by the teacher as correct. The recitation teacher will often avoid giving an answer to the substantive issue, feeling that here knowledge is not certain so he should only attempt to present his students with the knowledge and concepts which they should use in resolving the problem *outside* of the school. In using the Socratic style, on the other hand, the teacher focuses directly on the substantive issue and possible answers to it. From time to time, however, the Socratic teacher may depart from the dialectical posture and treat the problem analytically in order to facilitate conceptualization of the problem. The structure used for such an analysis by the Socratic teacher may have been taught in a descriptive manner, or if the teacher maintains a "pure" style throughout, will likely have evolved from a dialectical discussion of the proper framework for viewing controversial political issues.

Statement types. Recitation teaching involves mainly factual claims. The teacher tends to deal with descriptions of reality, rather than with the truth or goodness of these descriptions. The recitation teacher in maintaining the sequence of his lesson—to the extent that it is successfully programmed—tends to proceed by gradual, well-related steps, using a great many summarizing, repeating, and focusing statements. The socratic teacher, on the other hand, in dealing with political controversy, tends to ask for value judgments and to challenge them.

Factual claims will deal mainly with the background to the issue and as support for value statements. There is also a sequential factor involved in socratic teaching. It is likely to involve an emphasis on factual statements and questions as the discussion gets under way with the emphasis on value issues coming later. Recitation teaching, as far as we have been able to ascertain, does not reflect any sequential pattern.

Intellectual operations. Except for the fact that the socratic teacher is engaged in an adversarial role, there is no reason to expect that socratic teaching will evidence any different patterns of critical thought than will recitation teaching. The recitation teacher may question relevance, ask for or give evidence, or ask his students to qualify statements. However, our experience is that the socratic teacher does use more of these operations dealing with political controversy. It is also likely that because the teacher and students are engaging in controversy rather than talking about it, the intellectual episodes are more complex than in recitation teaching.

The procedural dimension. Procedurally, we have considered the teacher as the channelizer of a dialogue between him and the students, regardless of which of the two styles he is using. This, perhaps, points up our cognitive bias. It seems to us, however, that it is more fruitful to investigate procedural style differences within a limited context of general classroom procedures. If, for example, the teacher ordinarily withdraws to the back of the room to let students run the discussion, this is less a matter of style than general pedagogical methodology. The concept of style for us assumes a common curriculum, common objectives, and a common procedural context. Variations that occur with this much held constant, then, we would denote "style." The number of times a teacher is required to act procedurally to control deviance, for example, would be a matter of style.

The affective dimension. Theoretically, one may not link high or low affectivity with any particular style. In practice, the socratic discussion tends to be highly charged with negative affect because of the open controversy on the cognitive level, which spills over into the affective domain.

UTILITY OF A DIMENSIONAL ANALYSIS OF TEACHER OR DISCUSSION STYLE

We are suggesting here, as indicated by our previous discussion, that a dimensional analysis of teacher style might be useful in a number of ways. First, it allows us to define general teacher style more precisely. Instead of beginning with polar constructs such as student-centered—

teacher-centered or democratic-autocratic, for example, and developing categories to differentiate the poles, we define a number of dimensions of teaching, and then proceed to identify the characteristics of a teacher whom one would judge to be "student-centered," "democratic," "truth-seeking," or "Socratic." Thus, we are not trapped with a conceptualization of teacher behavior that works with only limited types of teaching.

Second, it allows us to describe variations in teaching styles which may or may not significantly affect learning outcomes. Instead of setting up styles in terms of single dichotomies and defining these operationally with "good" and "bad" categories, we can attempt to identify commonly observed styles of teaching, and determine which elements in the style, when varied, will or will not affect learning outcomes. Thus we can develop an empirical approach to the evaluation of teacher style. In the socratic style, for example, we can ask whether the affective overflow which occurs when the student feels a personal threat to his ideas is a necessary part of the style, or is a low affect socratic just as effective? In other words, is it the logical performance of the teacher which makes the learning more or less effective (if it is), or is it the logical performance plus the affective charge injected into the discourse.

From a research point of view this methodological approach allows us to investigate a number of interesting problems:

1. Is it possible for individual teachers to manipulate their behavior and play more than one style, or must we identify teachers who have natural styles we wish to investigate and compare?

2. If it is possible for teachers to manipulate their style, and play more than one style, what are the variations that occur within a single style, and are there overlapping areas in which one style cannot be differentiated from another?

3. Assuming that students were subjected to two quite different teaching styles on a systematic basis over a sustained period of time, under what conditions would this difference result in any different learning outcomes?

4. What is the relative importance of the intellectual or other personal characteristics of students, the style of teaching, and the personality of the individual teacher in effecting learning outcomes?

5. Is it possible to develop an observational instrument to describe not only the general style factors of the teacher, but also sufficiently complex intellectual processes that occur in the classroom, so that it can be used to assess learning outcomes?

6. How difficult is it to train teachers to operate consistently from a particular teaching style, and are there personality factors which make certain teachers incapable of learning some styles of teaching?

In our own work we have focused mainly on the first five questions, and have simply sidestepped the last question by selecting teachers for our research who were sufficiently flexible to teach in a variety of ways. It should be noted, however, that most of the people who have taught for our experimental program could handle socratic teaching with ease, and had more difficulty avoiding challenging the student's value position and initiating an adversarial dialogue. The problem of teacher training, therefore, would seem to be not only whether or not the teacher is sufficiently quickwitted and flexible to perform in a dialectical context, (the major problem of beginning teachers), but also whether or not he can tolerate giving doses of "truth" when they are called for. And the problem here may stem from basic temperamental differences among people, something professional educational programs can probably do little about. (Analogously, there may be temperamental as well as intellectual characteristics which cause some physicians to specialize in surgery and others to specialize in internal medicine.)

The Two Styles Investigated

In the course of our work we have focused mainly on the analysis, conceptual differentiation, and quantification of two complex teacher styles. We have called them the Recitation-Analytic Style (RA) and the Socratic-Analytic Style (SA). Since we have already described the distinctions between recitation and socratic teaching, the following brief operational definitions of the two styles should be adequate.

RECITATION-ANALYSIS

Recitation-Analysis (RA) as we define it involves the following steps:

1. A controversial case is read aloud.
2. The students are first asked to describe what took place in the case in their own words. This step is called *descriptive recitation.*
3. Students are then asked to tell why the situation in the case might be considered either good or bad. Students are not to give a personal evaluative reaction. They are to begin the analysis of the case by using the thought process concepts. This involves:
   (a) Describing the conflict in the case according to general social and political values;
   (b) Telling what important factual assumptions relate to the conflict;
   (c) Telling what analogies one might give to put the values in this particular case in perspective;

(d) Telling what consequences one might anticipate if any of the possible decisions suggested in the case were made;

(e) Telling whether any words in the cases might create special definitional problems;

(f) Telling how one goes about dealing with these definitional problems;

(g) If there are questionable factual assumptions in the case, telling what evidence the students might gather to support a particular claim, and what evidence already in the case supports any particular claim; and,

(h) Telling whether there are any rhetorical devices, such as the use of loaded words, which might influence one's judgment.

4. Students then summarize what particular alternative decisions are available in this particular case, and what important considerations one might take into account in arriving at an intelligent qualified decision.

In the initial stages of RA teaching much of the analysis and application is simply explained to the students by the teacher. As the treatment proceeds, however, the students carry out more of the analysis without the teacher's help, and they are simply told whether or not the analytic concepts are correctly applied.

SOCRATIC-ANALYSIS

Socratic-Analysis (SA) involves the following steps.

1. A controversial case is read aloud to the students. (Same as RA).
2. The teacher first asks students to recite events in the case to assure himself that the major points are understood.
3. The students are then asked what their personal feelings are about the situation described.
4. After several students have given an evaluative reaction, and a description of their position justifying the reaction, the teacher begins a period of intensive questioning, concentrating on one student at a time.

(a) If a student simply says, "This situation is bad," the teacher then asks him to explain what is so bad about it. The student then usually repeats his position.

(b) The teacher appears enlightened and then verbalizes for the student, if he has not done so for himself, a general social value which supports his position, or the violation of which disturbs him. The teacher then attempts to persuade the whole class to agree with the student's position. Usually most students will agree, since controversial cases tend to be loaded in one direction.

(c) The teacher then presents a second situation (telling it as an informal story) which illustrates the same values in conflict as those described in the case, except that the value loadings are reversed. For example, if a Negro sit-in case is presented which stresses equal opportunity as good and ignores the value of property rights, an analogy might be used to present the confiscation of American property in Cuba by Castro, which would make the importance of property rights more salient.

4. Usually students are unable to resolve the inconsistency between their feelings about the case and the analogy. They know that both involve the same value conflict, but they are sympathetic to equality in one and property in another. When the students have reached some degree of agitation, the teacher suspends the intensive questioning and asks the student to deal with the contradiction analytically. He shows the student how to qualify his position, how to question the factual assumptions the teacher commonly makes, and how to deal with the definitional licenses the teacher takes. This step is much the same as step three in RA teaching.

SA teaching is an attempt to teach the student to think on two levels simultaneously while he is discussing a case. The student must deal with the problem of persuading the teacher that he is taking a reasonable position with respect to the problem presented in the case. This is the argumentative level. At the same time, he must see that this can be done more effectively by using the political values and critical thinking concepts taught earlier. This is the analytic level. Initially, even after the students are taught the analytic concepts, few see their relevance to the controversial discussion. They tend to argue "blindly" in the sense that they have no conscious framework by which to analyze the nature of the problem. The teacher can argue more forcefully, because he can anticipate how to maneuver the student into unavoidable inconsistencies. We attempted to teach this two level consciousness by bringing the argument to a halt after a period of frustration, and asking the student to apply the concepts to this particular argument. If the student is unable to do this, the teacher "explains" the argument in terms of the analytic concepts. ("I am attacking your value by the use of this analogy. You can counter this analogy with one of your own, qualify your position and make the analogy less relevant, or you can find some important difference between the situation in the analogy and the situation in the case, which also makes the analogy less relevant.")

After some analysis the argument may or may not resume. This depends on the timing and the enthusiasm of the class. While initially, the class is a patchwork of two phases: Socratic questioning———→ analysis and application of concepts———→ Socratic questioning, the teacher works in the direction of less and less analysis as the students become more proficient in using the concepts to guide their arguments. The tone of the class theoretically should move from a strictly adversarial one to one of a mutual search between teacher and students for an intelligent position in the case.

In comparing the *socratic* element of SA teaching with RA teaching, there are two striking differences. First, Socratic teaching demands relatively long interchanges between student and teacher. The student cannot be led into an evaluative or definitional inconsistency in one or two statements. The teacher must first establish what the student's position is, suggest exceptions through analogies or counter cases or through contradictory evidence, and counter the student's defense. RA teaching, on the other hand, deals with the problem presented in the case only from an abstract position, never from the point of view of the student's personal commitment. The teacher would ask, for example, "What are some of the ways we might deal with the problem presented in this case?" Several different students can then summarize alternative positions in a sentence or two. The teacher might then ask, "What is the relative importance of the two conflicting values in this case when we consider this particular position. . . . ?" Although one position may be given sustained analysis in RA teaching, no person is asked to defend the position, and thus, no person becomes involved in a protracted dialogue with the teacher.

Second, as we have already noted, the level of affect in socratic teaching tends to be high. In RA teaching the student is asked only to apply a set of analytic concepts to a particular case. The student has no commitment to the analytic content other than its existence as something that the teacher has taught him. Nor is he asked to state a commitment to a position in the case. Misapplication of a concept requires an immediate corrective response from the teacher. In a socratic discussion, however, the teacher has no immediate responsibility for the inconsistencies or "holes" in the student's position in the argument. The student has autonomy to accept any position he chooses as long as he can withstand the teacher's probing. The student becomes excited and often agitated because he sees that two values, which he himself holds and is committed to in the argument contradict one another. It is this dissonance in his own position which usually provokes his affective responses, rather than his particular commitment to one position or another, or the disagreement between himself and teacher, although the impact of the latter cannot be discounted. . . .

RESEARCH IN TEACHING STYLE

Our first systematic experiment in teaching style was set up to test some initial ideas about distinctions in the teaching styles which we planned on using as a basis for more extensive experimental teaching. In this experiment we asked two major questions:

1. Is it possible for individual teachers to manipulate their behavior and play either a socratic or recitation role when called upon to do so, or must we identify teachers who have natural socratic and recitation styles?
2. If it is possible for teachers to manipulate their general style of teaching, what variations occur within a single style, and are there overlapping areas in which one style cannot be differentiated from another?

The instrument developed primarily to differentiate recitation from socratic teaching was used in an attempt to answer these questions. A brief description[28] of it is called for before discussing the experimental results.

Teaching Style Content-Analysis System: Form A. The central problem in developing an observational system for the quantified description of teacher behavior such as that in which we are interested, is to develop a set of categories which will have meaning in terms of the specific teaching styles to which it is to be applied. The instrument, i.e., Form A, which we are discussing here actually is composed of two sets of categories. Categories 1 through 6 (as shown in Table 12.1) are affective categories; categories 7 through 12 are cognitive categories; and categories 13 and 14 are procedural. In scoring, then, the observer must infer the cognitive significance of verbal behaviors, as well as their affective implications. Each scorable act is categorized in a cognitive category *and* in an affective category—including the categories which indicate that either a cognitive or affective message was not discernable. For scoring purposes, the cognitive and procedural categories are grouped together so that no double scoring takes place between them (or it would be a triple scoring scheme). . . .

The primary function of the cognitive categories is to answer questions about differences between the cognitive messages expressed in discussions led by teachers using the two teacher styles. Central to the description of

[28] For a more extensive and detailed treatment of the thought immediately behind this instrument and of the instrument itself, the reader is referred to James P. Shaver, "A Study of Teaching Style." Doctoral Thesis, Harvard Graduate School of Education, 1961. (Footnote numbering is retained, as it appeared in the original article.)

the two styles is the extent to which teachers using each deal with *descriptions* of the controversial case at either the specific or analytic levels as opposed to dealing with the evaluation of events presented in the cases. Categories 8 and 9 are set up specifically to identify differences of this kind. Category 7 (suggests inconsistency) is meant to identify the attempt by the teacher to arouse personal value conflicts on the part of the student by suggesting that he is making contradictory decisions in similar situations (the case and an analogy). Category 12 (analogy) thus has obvious significance. Categories 10 and 11 were employed to make the cognitive subsystem exhaustive.

The procedural categories provide a meaningful exhaustive category system which allows us to gather data about possible procedural problems incidental to the styles. They may also be useful at some later point when and if we compare teaching styles which differ mainly in the procedural area. It should also be pointed out that although we may *think* the behavior of teachers who are role playing recitation-analytic and socratic-analytic teaching differ significantly, we will not know this until the assumption has been tested by some such scheme as we are here describing.

TABLE 12.1

BRIEF DEFINITIONS OF THE CATEGORIES IN A PRELIMINARY OBSERVATIONAL
SYSTEM FOR THE DESCRIPTION OF TEACHER STYLE

Affective or Socio-emotional Categories

1. SOLIDARITY—Status raising language or tone of voice; strong approval or acceptance or another person. Often indicated by enthusiastic acceptance of another's ideas.
2. LOW POSITIVE AFFECT—Signs of mild approval or acceptance of another person, or of his ideas.
3. TENSION RELEASE—Action interpreted as tension reducing or attempting tension reduction, e.g., laughing or telling a joke.
4. TENSION—Behavior indicative of a state of tension, such as stuttering or becoming tongue-tied.
5. LOW NEGATIVE AFFECT—Statements or acts indicating mild disapproval or rejection of another person, e.g., disbelief of, skepticism about, a statement by the other person.
6. ANTAGONISM—Deflating, derogatory, or highly negative statements or actions.
   NEUTRAL—Acts or statements with no affective message discriminable by the observer.

Cognitive Categories

7. SUGGESTS INCONSISTENCY—An attempt to lead another person to see inconsistencies in his values, claims, or definitions.

8. DESCRIPTIVE—Statements which describe events, i.e., make claims about what reality is like, was like, or will be like.
9. EVALUATIVE—Statements which evaluate events, i.e., statements of like or dislike, right or wrong, good or bad.
10. REPEATS, SUMMARIES, FOCUSES—Statements that restate what has happened during the discussion, or bring attention to what is happening or going to happen.
11. CLARIFICATION—Statements that attempt to clarify the content of the discussion, i.e., clear up the meanings of statements or specific words.
12. ANALOGY—Statements wetting up for consideration a situation similar to the one under discussion. The situation set up may be hypothetical or one which it is claimed existed, exists, or will exist.
    NON-COGNITIVE—Acts with no cognitive—including procedural—message discriminable by the observer.

Procedural Categories

13. DIRECTS TASK-ORIENTED BEHAVIOR—Statements directed at controlling behavior which is in line with the task of the group, or at delineating what that behavior will be.
14. CONTROLS DEVIANT BEHAVIOR—Statements directed at controlling behavior which detracts from the accomplishment of the group task.

It should also be mentioned that unitization, i.e., the breaking of behavior into bits to be categorized, was based on the "single item of thought." In general, the unit to be categorized was the simple sentence, with complex sentences usually scored as individual units, but with compound sentences broken into their component parts.

RELIABILITY ATTAINED

Bale's adaptation of Chi-Square was used to estimate reliability for the study presented below. . . . All of the Chi-Square values are well below the maximum allowable to meet the criteria we adopted—a probability of .50.

Discussions for Experiment One. Using, then, the observational instrument which has been described, an experiment was carried out to determine whether the same teachers could use two styles as different as the Recitation-Analytic and the Socratic-Analytic.

First the basic concepts to be used in the analysis of societal issues were presented to the seventh grade students. Then a series of 14 cases was used to begin the teaching of the process by which the analytic concepts were to be applied to concrete problems. Each case was to serve as the basis for a one-period discussion and was not embedded within a total unit framework—except that each case had in common a problem in civil rights as its focus. It was during this period that the Project teachers first attempted a sustained treatment according to the two different teaching styles.

The ten class periods were spent in the discussion of cases based upon U. S. Supreme Court cases presenting instances in which decisions had to be made in regard to the application of basic principles of American government—freedom of speech, religious freedom, due process, etc. Each case presented a specific situation involving a conflict between at least two principles. The cases were very brief, two to four double-spaced pages, and were designed as a simple vehicle by which the student could be introduced to the application of the concepts and operations of critical thought to situations of societal conflict.

The teachers were instructed to use at least the first twenty to twenty-five minutes of each class period leading a discussion using the style assigned to that particular group. These first twenty to twenty-five minutes were tape recorded for later scoring with the Form A instrument. In line with the objectives of the Project, this initial discussion was to lead into an analysis of the cases in an attempt to get the students to apply critical thinking skills to the problem under discussion. The teachers were thoroughly familiar with the teaching objectives and the conceptual framework, and all had practiced both teaching roles. In addition, some time had been spent in discussions among the teachers trying to anticipate particular stylistic problems which might arise. In this particular experiment, we were interested only in measuring the initial socratic phase of the Socratic-Analytic style as compared with Recitation-Analytic.

Style confirmation. In scoring the tape recordings, we were first interested in determining whether or not there were over-all differences in behavior—that is, differences that held up when all categories were compared at once—when the teachers were using the two styles. For each of the four experimental teachers, we sampled six discussions in which the teacher was trying to use each of the two styles. This was a total of twelve discussions for each teacher. (Because of varying rates of interaction, and some variation in length of scoring time, the frequencies of interests in each category were converted to proportions so as to provide a common base for comparison.)

The basic question at this point, then, is: How are style differences as interpreted and played by the teachers reflected in the over-all quantitative description of the teachers' behavior obtained with the observational instrument? Did the teachers in fact succeed in playing the two different styles (at the abstract level of our categories)? . . . The ratio testing the interaction between style and category is significant beyond the .001 level.

Therefore, with the conclusion that the teachers were able to effect great over-all differences in style, a second question becomes pertinent:

Which of the individual categories contribute to these global differences? The following generally stated hypotheses, in conjunction with Table 12.5, suggest the categories in which we would expect to find stylistic differences particularly reflected.

1. In the area of affect we would anticipate that while recitation teaching is going to require more low positive affect in carrying out its general program of reinforcement of correct responses, there is no reason to expect more highly loaded positive affect, or solidarity. Moreover, the highly argumentative socratic situation should reflect a greater amount of both low negative affect and antagonism than the recitation. And we expected the teachers to use more tension release—telling of jokes and laughing—with the socratic style in order to keep tension under control. The affect-laden socratic situation also would lead to a prediction of fewer affectively neutral acts.

2. Because of the differing focuses of discussion with the two styles, the teachers should make more descriptive statements with the recitation style, and ask for more evaluations with the socratic style. It is presumed that socratic teaching will emphasize consideration of inconsistencies in the student's position, and therefore the teachers will suggest more evaluative inconsistencies with this style while avoiding a statement of their own positions. While the argumentative situation might have indicated such a result, we did not anticipate that socratic teaching would necessitate any greater amount of disagreement with descriptive statements made by students.

3. Two categories seem rather directly related to the different nature of lesson organization for the two teaching styles. While socratic teaching involves an intensive and lengthy intercourse with individual students centered around the values expressed by the student, recitation teaching requires planning organized around the teacher's conception of the adequate treatment of the problem. It is necessary, as recitation moves from one student to another and as each responds to the teacher's queries, that this organizational structure be maintained. We therefore would expect that the recitation teaching would result in a greater proportion of acts in the repeats, summarizes, and focuses category. This same factor might well have a similar effect in the clarification category.

4. It is obvious from our stylistic models that socratic teaching should result in many more analogies than would be the case with recitation teaching.

5. A high frequency behavior categorized in the category of direct task-oriented behavior is calling on students. Because of the difference in duration of periods of student-teacher interaction, we can expect a

TABLE 12.5

PREDICTED DIFFERENCES IN CATEGORIZATIONS OF BEHAVIOR
FOR TEACHERS ATTEMPTING TO USE THE TWO STYLES

Category*	Style for Which Greater Proportion Predicted	Fate of Hypothesis
Solidarity	No Difference	Rejected
Low Positive	Recitation	Accepted
Tension Release	Socratic	Rejected
Low Negative	Socratic	Accepted
Antagonism	Socratic	Accepted
Neutral	Recitation	Accepted
Evaluative, Gives	No Difference	Rejected
Evaluative, Asks For	Socratic	Accepted
Suggests Inconsistency, Evaluative	Socratic	Accepted
Descriptive	Recitation	Accepted
Disagreement with Description	No Difference	Rejected
Repeat, Summarize, Focus	Recitation	Accepted
Clarification	Recitation	Rejected
Analogy	Socratic	Accepted
Directs Task-Oriented Behavior	Recitation	Accepted

* Categories are not included in which there were insufficient frequencies for analysis or which were not considered central to the styles.

greater proportion of categorizations in this category when the recitation style is to be in use.

A brief comment is in order on those which were rejected. While the teachers did use more behavior categorized as solidarity when using the recitation style, this seems to be a reflection of the reinforcing function. But this result raises the question of the appropriateness of timing of that solidarity and tension release evidenced during socratic teaching. The greater proportion of evaluative statements during socratic teaching probably reflects two factors: the difficulty of talking about value issues without expressing one's own commitments; and, the expression of one's own values in order to draw out value statements on the part of students. It should be noted that the difference is between about one percent on the one hand and two and one-half on the other. That the teachers disagreed with more descriptive student statements while using the socratic style is probably a function of the argumentative nature of socratic discussions, as well as a reflection of the success of recitational programming—i.e., setting up a series of questions based on assigned material and sequenced so that student errors in response are avoided. The lack of difference in clarification simply indicates that the discussion needs to be clarified at certain points with either style.

Results of the Comparison Between Recitation and Socratic Groups

The most obvious fact about the [test] results of the differential treatment experiment is that groups taught by the two treatments turn out to behave in an astonishingly similar way on all measures of learning outcomes administered. This result is consistent with general findings in "methods" research. Few experiments, however, have operated under such carefully controlled curricula, or have actually demonstrated marked differences in teaching style quantitatively, as we have. Regarding the general finding we might make the following comments.

1. The instruction was probably generally very effective across styles. All teachers were selected not only because of their ability to play to style roles well, but also because of their general excellence as teachers. The materials were especially prepared to teach a particular analytic framework. The teachers were involved in the development of the materials, the preparation of lessons based on the materials, as well as the actual teaching. With this combination of resources, it is reasonable to assume that a powerful instructional situation resulted, regardless of the particular style employed by the teacher.
2. All measures except SIAT* No. 4 (the Socratic Discussion Test) assessed the student's use of analytic concepts either implicitly in the substance of an argument or explicitly in a non-stress situation. It is therefore surprising, actually, that the recitation groups did not perform consistently better on all measures other than SIAT No. 4. Since the analytic framework was learned as well by the socratic groups, one might assume a tremendous redundancy of treatment, so that despite much less explicit discussion of the framework in the socratic groups, they grasped certain basic elements of the system as well as did the recitation groups. It is very difficult to explain, however, why the socratic groups did not do better on SIAT No. 4. Two of the most plausible explanations might be explored. First, there may be something deficient in the test. The most obvious deficiency, we think, is in the amount of behavior sampled (actually only 15 minutes). While this gives us a great deal of behavior when compared with pencil-and-paper tests (some 225 acts), it constitutes a very brief discussion. It also makes the assumption that there is homogeneity across topics which may be used as the basis of such a discussion. This assumption requires further exploration. Second,

---

* SIAT is an acronym for Social Issues Analysis Test. RTH, editor.

there may be something deficient in the instructional situation: the students may have been too young to gain substantial benefit from use of the analytic concepts in a persuasive situation; or the treatment may have been too brief to have made a significant impact. It is our impression that both of these situations may, to some extent, be true. We would say that *most* of the students had difficulty translating the analytical framework into a usable tool when engaged in a dialectical discussion. Whether this difficulty is related to intellectual maturity, or whether it is a general phenomenon is difficult to say.

It is very possible that there is an interaction between individual personality characteristics and the student's ability to benefit from one style or the other. In other words, some students may learn from one style and be inhibited by the other style, and *vice versa*.

38.   The Logic of Teaching

Jerrold R. Coombs

The phrase 'the logic of teaching' at present has no settled usage. Here we will use the phrase to refer to a particular aspect or dimension of classroom teaching activity. Teaching has many dimensions. One dimension has to do with the interaction between the teachers and his students. This interaction is described by such terms as 'lecturing,' 'discussing,' 'rewarding,' 'permissive,' 'acceptive,' 'authoritarian,' 'democratic,' etc. Contrasted with this is the dimension having to do with what the teacher does or has the student do with the subject matter being taught. The interaction of teacher and student with subject matter is described by terms such as defining, explaining, comparing and classifying. This latter dimension is what we call the logic of teaching. There are several ways in which activities in the logical dimension of teaching can be analysed and described.[1] In this paper we will be concerned with only one way of looking at the logic of teaching.

"The Logic of Teaching" by Jerrold R. Coombs is reprinted with permission by The University of North Carolina Press, from *The High School Journal*, 50: 22-29, October, 1966.

[1] For an analysis of the logic of teaching from a different but compatible point of view see B. Othanel Smith, Milton Meux, et al., *A Study of the Logic of Teaching*, Bureau of Educational Research, University of Illinois, 1962.

Teachers spend a considerable amount of their classroom time attempting to get students to learn the concepts, procedures, generalizations, etc. which comprise the content of subjects such as physics, history, English, and mathematics. In history classes, for example, teachers teach such things as the concept of imperialism and the causes of the American Revolution. In physics they attempt to get students to learn, among other things, the laws of motion and the concept of mass. Teachers of mathematics instruct their students in the formula for calculating the area of a rectangle and the procedure for finding the square root of a number. For lack of a better name these concepts, procedures, etc. will be called 'content items.' Of course, the teacher's aim in teaching a content item is not merely to have students remember a description of the concept or a statement of the generalization. It is rather to have them understand the concept or generalization and be able to use it to interpret experience, solve problems, and the like.

In teaching one of these items of content, say a generalization, the teacher introduces to the class or has the students introduce, information relevant to making clear what the generalization is and what evidence there is to support it. While information is sometimes introduced by means of concrete operations, for the most part it is introduced verbally. There are many different types of information relevant to making clear what is involved in a generalization and giving evidence in support of it. The same is true of any item of content. For example, the teacher may subsume the generalization under a more general statement. He may give facts which are instances of it. He may compare it to or differentiate it from other generalizations.

For the sake of brevity we will call a verbal activity which introduces one particular bit of information a 'move.' Activities which introduce different types of information constitute different types of moves. A move may be made by the teacher, by a student or by the teacher and one or more students together. Quite often the teacher initiates a move by asking a question and a student completes it by giving the desired information.

Regardless of what one considers the aims of education to be, it is certain that teaching the content of various subjects is an important part of the teacher's job. Moreover, it seems reasonable to assume that the types of moves used in teaching an item of content, the quality of these moves, and the patterns in which they are used are important factors in determining how well the content item is learned. If this assumption is reasonable, then educational theorists concerned with the logic of teaching will be interested in determining what types of moves and what patterns of moves are most effective in teaching each type of content item.

Educational theorists have been interested in this question for many years, nor have they been hesitant in saying what sort of pattern of moves is best. Francis Bacon urged teachers to use what we would now call inductive techniques in their teaching.[2] Among other attributes this technique has the feature of recommending a pattern of moves such that a generalization is introduced only after particular factual instances of it are introduced. Textbooks on teaching methods have for many years described inductive, deductive and inductive-deductive teaching methods.[3] In the deductive method a generalization is introduced first and then particular instances of it are introduced. The inductive-deductive method refers to a pattern in which particular instances are introduced first, then the generalization, then more particular instances.

Despite our long acquaintance with these methods no clear superiority of any one of them over the others have been demonstrated. An analysis of what goes on in the classroom suggests two possible reasons for this state of affairs. First, inductive and deductive methods, as usually explicated, are relevant only to the teaching of concepts and generalizations, whereas a number of items of content other than concepts and generalizations are taught in the classroom. Second, a great many different types of moves are used in teaching concepts and generalizations that are not represented in descriptions of inductive and deductive methods. Thus it is possible that two specimens of inductive teaching may differ more significantly than inductive method differs from deductive. Further, the various types of moves relevant to teaching any given content item occur in a great variety of patterns, most of which cannot be assimilated to inductive, deductive or inductive-deductive patterns.

There is a need, then, to gain a more adequate conception of the kinds of content items that are taught and of the types of moves relevant to each kind of content item. This is a prerequisite to developing sound knowledge concerning the types of moves and the patterns of moves a teacher must use if he is to be maximally effective in getting students to learn an item of content. The remainder of this paper will present a way of describing items of content and moves that was developed from an analysis of verbal activities carried out in actual class sessions.

As mentioned earlier, observation of classroom practices reveals that teachers, and students, explore a number of different kinds of content items. Some of the more important of these are: cause-effect relationships, rules, procedures, evaluations, and concepts. A full explanation of these types of content items cannot be given here but a few examples of each

[2] Francis Bacon, *The Advancement of Learning.* (Oxford: The Clarendon Press, 1900), p. 171.

[3] For an early but lucid exposition of these patterns see Charles De Garmo, *Principles of Secondary Education,* Vol. II: *Process of Instruction* (New York: The Macmillan Company, 1908), pp. 75-149.

will perhaps give some indication of what they involve.[4] When a teacher teaches such things as the conditions which brought about the reformation, or the results of putting metalic sodium in water, he is teaching cause-effect relationships. Rules which might be taught in the classroom include such things as rules of grammar, laws of the state or the country, rules of games, and geometry theorems. When we teach the steps to follow in solving problems, making cakes, doing long division and constructing graphs, we are teaching procedures. To teach an evaluation is to teach that some action, event, etc. is to be assigned a particular value rating. We teach evaluations when we teach that democracy is good, that tardiness is bad, or that cramming is inefficient.

The kinds of moves relevant to teaching one sort of content item are not usually relevant to teaching another. The moves relevant to teaching all the various types of content items cannot be described here. Thus we will confine our attention to the kinds of moves relevant to teaching one sort of content item, namely concepts. When one teaches a concept he teaches a set of criteria or conditions which define a class of things. Thus if one teaches the concept of even numbers, he teaches a set of criteria by which one can tell what things are and what things are not even numbers. These criteria may also be viewed as criteria governing the use of the term or phrase that names the concept.

The types of moves that may be used in teaching concepts are described and illustrated below.

1. *Criterion description.* In this type of move some characteristic or feature of the concept is described or pointed out. In teaching the concept of a triangle, for example, the teacher may state that a triangle has three sides. This states a characteristic of the concept of triangle and so constitutes a criterion description move. The terms 'characteristic' and 'feature' must be understood here in a very broad sense. They include a function of the concept, the characteristic use of the concept, a disposition of the concept, a capacity of the concept, a condition necessary to produce the concept and the emotional import of the concept.

2. *Classification.* Identifying the concept as a sub-class of some more inclusive class of things constitutes a classification move. The classification move below occurred in a discussion of the concept of nerve impulse.

S: They're (nerve impulses) all a sort of electrical charge, isn't it? Here nerve impulse is categorized as being included in the class of electrical charges.

3. *Analysis.* This type of move is one in which a set of parts which

---

[4] For a full description of the various types of content items taught in the classroom see B. Othanel Smith, Milton Meux, Jerrold Coombs, and Graham Nuthall, *A Tentative Report on the Strategies of Teaching,* Bureau of Educational Research, University of Illinois, 1964.

together make up the concept are noted or described. In a discussion of the concept of the brain stem a description of the brain stem as being made up of the medulla, the mid-brain, and the pons would constitute an analysis move.

4. *Analogy.* This type of move likens the concept to some other concept or states the ways in which the concept is like some other concept. The following example of an analogy move occurred in a discussion of the concept of the nervous system.

> T: What would it (nervous system) correspond to in a building?
> S: A telephone system of wiring—set up of electrical wiring?
> T: Yes, more of an electrical set-up. That is, it would be subject to carry, communicate or transport. It would correspond to your— carrying something—messages from place to place and—something tells you something and the answer being given, and then there is the answer brought *back* and being carried out.

While this move is somewhat vague with respect to saying how the nervous system is like the wiring system of a building, it does seem to be trying to establish that they function in much the same way, i.e., they both carry incoming and outgoing messages.

5. *Differentiation.* This type of move states that the concept is different from some other concept or notes the ways in which it is different from the other concept. The following differentiation move was initiated by the teacher in teaching the concept of probation.

> T: What's the difference between probation and parole?
> S: Well—parole, you're free, you don't have to report to your probation officer.
> T: Are you sure?
> S: No.
> T: Elizabeth?
> S: Parole—you have to serve part of a prison sentence. Probation— you don't, but you still have to report practically every week.
> T: Do you agree with this?
> S: In this parole—you still have to get out on good behavior or something. You have to get in there first, then you get out.
> T: 'Parole' refers to your good behavior in *prison* and your release to some probation officer—then that way he is, of course, free as long as he is doing what he is supposed to. As long as he does not violate the terms of his parole.

Discussion in this move is directed toward differentiating probation from parole. The difference noted is that a person has to have served time in prison to be on parole, whereas this is not true of probation.

6. *Positive instance*. To effect this type of move the teacher or student points out or describes something and notes that it is an instance or sub-class of the concept. The following positive instance move was made by a teacher teaching the concept of a simple reflex.

> T: Swallowing when the food reaches the back of the tongue is a simple reflex.

7. *Negative instance*. In this type of move something very similiar to a positive instance of the concept is pointed out or described, and it is noted that this thing is not an instance of the concept. In the example below the teacher is attempting to teach the concept of thinking, and a student suggests what turns out to be a negative instance.

> S: We still think when we sleep. We dream.
> T: No. Not when we dream.

8. *Instance substantiation*. This is a move in which a positive or nega-tive instance is pointed out, named, or described, and the reasons or evi-dence for concluding that it is a positive or negative instance are dis-cussed. The following move occurred in a discussion of the concept of romantic poetry.

> S: I said it was romantic because I think the—poet (inaudible) the better man, and a romantic poem does that.
> T: All right, that's one of them—point in favor of it being a ro-mantic poem. Shirley?
> S: Well, the romantics realized how—that life was what it *was* and they didn't try to shield it, and this definitely is the way it is. Society does make the better-than-average man conform or it tries to—so that's it. (The poem being discussed makes the point that society makes the better-than-average man conform.)
> T: All right. A characteristic of romantic poems is that they show *man* not necessarily in harmony with society but in harmony with nature and therefore in conflict with society. This, then, is the way that the romantics see the individual, very often, and in this sense the poem is romantic, wouldn't you say?

In this move a poem is pointed out and reasons for saying it is a romantic poem are discussed.

9. *Instance production*. Discussion of the way in which an instance of the concept may develop or be produced constitutes an instance produc-tion move. In teaching the concept of a salt the teacher could initiate an instance production move by asking the students how one could make a salt.

10. *Enumeration*. In this type of move a set of sub-classes of the con-

cept are named or described and it is indicated that every instance of the concept fits into one of these sub-classes. The following move occurs in a discussion of the concept of alkali family.

> S: The members of the alkali family are lithium, sodium, potassium, rubidium, cesium, and francium.

Implicit in this statement is the indication that every instance of the concept of alkali family is a member of one of these sub-classes.

11. *Meta-distinction.* This type of move notes the different kinds of meaning a concept name can have, the different kinds of definition a term can have or the different types of criteria a concept can have. In the following example the teacher initiates a meta-distinction move in teaching the concept of propaganda.

> T: Now, what can we call that kind of a definition of a word as opposed to the effect that a word has on us emotionally? Linda?
> S: The intellectual approach and the emotional approach.
> T: All right. Now, what is the emotional side of a word called?
> S: Well, it's the reaction that refers to the word which is not necessarily the definition.
> T: All right. Does anybody remember how we distinguish between the real definition of a word and the emotional effect that the word has on us? Mary?
> T: Didn't we have words that could—all depend what experience the person had with the word which determines the emotional meaning of it for the person. Then there's one in the dictionary —it would have—the meaning—more at—simplified definition, not as you (inaudible).

In this move the emotional effect of a word is distinguished from its descriptive content, i.e., the meaning of the word set forth in a "real" definition of it.

Several additional kinds of moves have been omitted from this account because they are rarely used or because they are relevant to only a very narrow range of concepts. A number of different sorts of concepts are discussed in the classroom, and not all of the moves are relevant to every type of concept. Some concepts, such as the concept of lung, have observable instances; others, such as the concept of density, do not. The concept of atom may be analyzed into parts, whereas the concept of trust may not. Thus a positive instance move can be used to teach the concept of lung, but not the concept of density. An analysis move may be used in discussing the concept of atom but not the concept of trust.

Knowledge of the kinds of content items taught and the moves used in teaching them is valuable not only to the educational researcher, but to

the teacher as well. Teachers are often not quite clear about what they
are trying to do in discussing content. Thus their discussions sometimes
wander aimlessly. A clear idea of the content item he is attempting to
teach gives the teacher a criterion in terms of which he can determine
what is and what is not relevant to the discussion.

Knowledge of moves enables the teacher to be more critically conscious
of the progress of the discussion. He knows what kinds of information
have been introduced, and can better determine what further information
might be useful. Also if teachers become consciously aware of the moves
they use, they can try out various types and patterns of moves, note the
results and communicate their experiences to their fellow teachers. It
might be said, then, that knowledge of content items and moves gives
teachers a vocabulary in terms of which they can understand and talk
about teaching activity and thus gain more control over it.

39.   Pretending to Have (or to Be) a Computer as a Strategy in Teaching[1]

Paul C. Berry

The flurry of interest in curriculum development, with its new math and
new science and its projects in reading, social studies, and English, has
brought together three sorts of people far more often than ever before.
One of these three is the teacher. The second is the scholar, who now
periodically deserts his laboratory or study to try to explain to teachers
and thence to children what he feels are the exciting and the fundamental
ideas of his discipline in the modern age. The third is the psychologist
(with or without the prefix "educational"), who is charged both with
suggesting how the new ideas are to be conveyed to children and with
testing afterwards whether they have been learned.

At the heart of most of the new curriculum efforts is an attempt to instill

"Pretending to Have (or to be) a Computer as a Strategy in Teaching," by Paul C.
Berry is reprinted with permission from *The Harvard Educational Review*, 34: 3
(Summer 1964), 383-401. Copyright © 1964 by President and Fellows of Harvard
College. As reprinted here, this selection from Paul C. Berry has been abridged to
include only pages 383-385 and pages 397-401.
[1] Work reported here was conducted as part of the program of the School Mathematics and Science Center of the University of Minnesota, supported by Grant GE-3
from the National Science Foundation.

in children a way of thinking, both a general approach to a subject and the detailed steps of the various operations involved in mastery of that subject. The psychologist is constantly insisting to the teacher and the scholar, "You specify the behavior, and I'll tell you how to produce it or test for it." For the scholar, intent upon getting children really to understand some portion of his thinking or technique, specifying the precise component mental operations turns out to be surprisingly difficult. He finds that he can not clearly explicate the processes of his own thinking, nor can he recall how his present style of thinking was built up. Similarly, the psychologist, while more confident that complex thinking must be achieved through the integration of many smaller component mental operations, is also very remote from a detailed understanding of the human thinking mechanism.

Therefore, faced with the practical problem of educating children to new mental operations, we are still searching for ways to break down the global descriptions of the activities of each curriculum into smaller components that make more manageable elements in a program of instruction. There is one group of people to whom the problem of breaking up complex acts into smaller components, or of assembling some set of simple acts into one much more complex act, is very familiar. These are the persons who write the sequences of instructions, called programs, for electronic computers. (This meaning of "program" is independent of the word as it is used in "programmed instruction.") I believe that some of the techniques of the computer programmer can be borrowed by the educator as a means for making much more explicit what component skills go into a complex act and how the components are linked together. This suggestion does not assume that children's brains resemble electronic machines but merely that mental tasks are information-processing operations and share that characteristic with operations that are programmed for computers.

For the inexperienced, writing the program that gets a computer to carry out even a simple operation can be a chastening experience. Computers, being intolerant of ambiguity and devoid of common sense, go ahead and do just what they are told. The resulting absurdities frequently reveal the shortcomings of badly stated instructions. Like programmed instruction, computer programming requires explicit statement of all of the steps involved in a complex behavior. However, computer programming goes beyond explicit statement of the details and provides a precise and testable model for assembling all of the component operations into a total more complex behavior. This permits verification not only that the various steps are clearly stated, but also that they are all present and accounted for and are effectively connected together. For this reason, writing a computer program is a very instructive way to start thinking about teaching. Fortunately, it is writing the program that is the most useful part of the procedure, so that you can do it even when you can't afford a real computer on which to run the program or even if you refer to operations which are impractical with existing computers.

When the teacher tries to produce a computer program (or at least the flow diagram of a program) as a way of specifying the details of an activity that is to be taught, he is pretending to *have* a computer on which the program might eventually be run. It is also possible to involve children in the task of programming; if the children themselves construct the program, they may share some of the benefits of increased awareness of what goes on in complex activities that they otherwise take for granted. Since children can't be expected to handle a real computer, this has to be arranged otherwise. The teacher can get children to give their instructions to him, and he can then carry them out in very literal fashion, thus pretending to *be* a computer.

We can distinguish three possible ways in which it is useful to imagine a computer program for a mental operation that we want to teach:

1. The teacher pretends to have a computer for which he writes a program that provides the operations of whatever task he is interested in, in whatever way seems simplest or most logical. This is useful in making clear the logical structure of the task.

2. The teacher pretends to have a computer for which he prepares a program which as far as possible represents the actual skills, errors, weaknesses, and virtues of human (or child) performance. Such a program in some sense is a description of the child's performance. Comparing the program for what children seem to do with what is logically required to do the work well then offers a way of identifying needs for training.

3. The teacher pretends to be the computer, letting children build up their own programs by successive approximation. They may thus obtain much greater insight into the activity they are programming and (hopefully) greater ability to modify their own operations to make them appropriate to the task at hand. Even if they don't reap this benefit, the teacher may see to what extent the children have explicit control over the operations and what implicit assumptions may limit their performance. . . .

GETTING CHILDREN TO DO THE PROGRAMMING

It is difficult to get small children to draw up a complex plan in advance. But the advantages we have enjoyed by pretending to program may also be obtained by the child (at least to an extent) by jumping right into a procedure in which his instruction statements alone guide the action. The child gives the instructions, and the experimenter carries them out as literally as he can. Or he may deliberately misinterpret ambiguous instructions in order to make the ambiguity apparent.

The experimenter explains the procedure to the child as follows: "Now we will play at a special way of doing counting. I'm going to pretend that I don't know anything at all about how to count. I'll have some things in front of me, and I am supposed to count them. You have to tell me what to do. I am pretending to be very stupid and my memory is very bad, so you have to tell me each little thing to do, one at a time, and then I will do whatever you say."

Fourth example. Experimenter had a tray of about 30 beans scattered more or less randomly. The child was a six year old first grader.

> Child: Pick a bean.
> (Experimenter singles out a bean to look at but does not touch it.)
> Child: Say the first number. That is "one."
> E: One.
> Child: Remember that.
> E: You want me to remember it? I have a very bad memory. If you want me to remember it, I'd better write it down.
> Child: OK, write down 1. (E writes down 1).
> Child: Pick another bean.
> E: I don't understand.
> Child: Pick out a bean. The way you did before.
> E: OK. I've got a bean.
> Child: Write down the next number.
> E: Where?
> Child: Write it where you wrote that other one. Cross out the first one and write this instead.
> (E crosses out the 1.)
> E: What am I supposed to write now?
> Child: Write the next number.
> E: I don't know the next number.
> Child: The next number is 2. Write 2. Now go back and do it again.
> (This continues until 7 beans have been counted.)
> Child: What bean are you counting?
> (E points to it.)
> Child: Is that the same one you counted before?
> E: I don't know.
> Child: You don't know! You're supposed to keep track of them.
> E: You didn't say that.
> Child: Well, it's no good if you don't keep track of them.
> E: What should I do now?
> Child: We'll just have to start over. Pick out a bean.
> E: OK.
> Child: No, really pick it up. (E picks it up.) Write down 1. Pick out a bean.
> E: What am I supposed to do with this bean in my hand?
> Child: Just keep holding it. Pick out a bean.
> (E holds out the bean already in his hand.)
> Child: No, not that one, pick out a bean *that's on the tray.*

(E picks out a bean from the tray, adding it to the first one in his hand.)
Child: Write down the next number, which is 2.
(This continues until all are counted.)

In this example the child was probably never in any doubt about how to proceed, but his instructions were initially too elliptical to be useful in guiding the experimenter. He made check-off much more explicit than it was before.

Fifth example. The experimenter placed on the table a large gear-wheel with about 20 teeth. The child was the same six-year-old.

Child: Pick out one of those teeth.
E: OK, I've got one.
Child: No, put your finger on it. (E complies.)
Child: Write down 1. No, use your other hand. Put the other hand on the gear so you can write with the other hand. Now move your finger to the next gear. Put down 2 where you had 1. Now move your finger to the next gear. Put down 3. Now move your finger to the next gear. (E moves to adjacent tooth but backs up, returning to the one counted before.) No, no, you can only go forward. Move to the next one forward from where you were. (E complies.)
(This procedure continues until the count is at 24.)
Child: Something's wrong. You've gone too far. You're going around again.
E: What's wrong with that? You didn't say anything about that.
Child: No, you aren't supposed to go around again. Just do them all once.
E: Well, what should I do now?
Child: Where did you start?
E: I don't know.
Child: We'll just have to start over. Now this time make a mark where you start.
(E makes a pencil mark on the gear.)
Child: Now write down 1. Move forward to the next gear thing.
(After a while.)
Child: Have you come to the mark yet?
E: I didn't notice.
Child: Well, it doesn't matter, but keep looking for the mark. When you get to it, we have finished.

The child made explicit the need for a stop-decision and the role of marking as a signal that all are counted. This routine took advantage of the natural array of the teeth around the gear wheel.

Sixth example. In programming the computer we made explicit the need for a list of integers. The following fragment shows that the child was forced into much the same procedure.

Child: Write down the next number.
E: I don't know what that is.
Child: Well, what number have you got now?
E: I've got 6 written here.
Child: Well, 7 comes after that. Write down 7.

E: You'll have to tell me what to write down every time.

Child: All right.

E: Why don't you tell me how you get the next number to write down, and I'll be able to do it myself.

Child: Well, 7 comes after 6.

E: Yes, but how do you know that?

Child: You just know it, that's all.

E: How can I get to know it too?

Child: You'll just have to learn it.

E: But I can't remember things.

Child: Well, I'll tell you all the numbers right now, and you write them down. Then you will know all of them.

E: OK.

Child: 1, 2, 3, 4, 5, 6, 7, 8, 9, 10, 11, 12, 13, 14, 15, 16, 17, 18, 19, 20, 21, 22, 23, 24, 25, 26, 27, 28, 29, 30, 31 . . . that's really enough, you won't need more than that.

(At the next instance.)

Child: Write down the next number.

E: What is it?

Child: Look on your list.

E: What should I look for?

Child: Look for the next number.

E: How can I? I don't know what it is.

Child: What was the last number you had?

E: 7.

Child: Look for that, then.

E: I've found it.

Child: Write down what comes after it; that's right, 8.

Thus the child, under the pressure of the inadequacy of his own instructions, invented the same list procedure as we used in the program, except that his depended upon the order in the array of numbers in the list.

EXTENDING THE METHOD

It would be possible to make the task more difficult and the program more general if the child were unable to see the task on which the experimenter was working. This would certainly force explicit consideration of the selection of a routine. It would also be possible to record the instructions generated during one such session and attempt to use them in another session. In this fashion the child could build up a more general and more explicit program, just as is done by the machine programmer. It is possible to imagine the separate instructions stored in discrete places, the locations connected together by a sort of map. Such a map would represent the flow diagram used in programming computers and yet would be a familiar concept to children who often play games that involve following a route across a board according to the throw of a die.

In the examples presented here, detailed specification is provided for quite fine steps of a small task. There is no reason that the steps could not be either finer still, or much larger. One could write a program for a much more complex task (e.g. marketing, or inventory) in which counting was treated as a simple operation which could be called without further explanation of its details. Nor is it necessary that the task involve mathematics. Specifying the operations and providing the map that links them together in an operating sequence could be done for tasks that involve no mathematical procedure whatever, provided (and this is the important point) that a clear way to state the directions is possible.

Summary

The explicit statement of procedures required for programming a computer is suggested as a model:

1. To specify components of a task,

2. To compare the features of children's performance with what is logically required for the task, and

3. To show the child how to make his own instructions explicit by doing the programming himself and seeing its consequences.

Elementary counting among first graders is presented as a miniature example of these procedures, but it is believed that they are far more generally applicable.

References

Feigenbaum, E. A. and Feldman, J. (eds.) *Computers and thought.* New York: McGraw-Hill, 1963.

Garvin, P. L. (ed.) *Natural language and the computer.* New York: McGraw-Hill, 1963.

Greenberg, J. (ed.) *Universals of language.* Cambridge: M.I.T. Press, 1963.

Lovell, K. *The growth of basic mathematical and scientific concepts in children.* New York: Philosophical Library, 1961.

Newell, A., Shaw, J. C., and Simon, H. A. Elements of a theory of human problem solving. *Psychol.* Rev. 1958, *65,* 151-166.

Piaget, J. *La genèse du nombre chez l'enfant.* Geneva, 1941, Translated as: *The child's conception of number.* London: Routledge and Kegan Paul, 1952.

Tomkins, S. S. and Messick, S. (eds.) *Computer simulation of personality.* New York: Wiley, 1963.

40.   Inquiry Training in the Elementary School

J. Richard Suchman

Skills of scientific inquiry are being taught to elementary school children at the University of Illinois through the use of motion pictures and
verbal "experimentation." For the past three years, a research project
known as the Illinois Studies in Inquiry Training [1] has been experimenting with the teaching of strategies and tactics of scientific inquiry to children who learn to apply them in question-and-answer investigations.
Short films of physics demonstrations pose problems of cause and effect.
The children learn to attack these problems with questions by which they
gather data and perform imaginary experiments. The teacher provides
the answers to the questions.

A portion of a typical session would go something like this: (The children have been shown a film of the "Ball and Ring" demonstration.) [2]

Pupil: Were the ball and ring at room temperature to begin with?
Teacher: Yes.
Pupil: And the ball would go through the ring at first?
Teacher: Yes.
Pupil: After the ball was held over the fire it did *not* go through the ring,
right?
Teacher: Yes.
Pupil: If the ring had been heated instead of the ball, would the results have
been the same?
Teacher: No.
Pupil: If both had been heated would the ball have gone through then?
Teacher: That all depends.
Pupil: If they had both been heated to the same temperature would the ball
have gone through?
Teacher: Yes.
Pupil: Would the ball be the same size after it was heated as it was before?
Teacher: No.
Pupil: Could the same experiment have been done if the ball and ring were
made out of some other metal?
Teacher: Yes.

Such questioning continues for about thirty minutes as the children
gather data, identify variables and determine their relevancy to the prob-

Reprinted with permission from *The Science Teacher*, 27:42-47, November, 1960.
[1] This project is supported by a grant from the U.S. Office of Education, Department of Health, Education, and Welfare and by The Research Board of the University
of Illinois.
[2] A brass ball just fits through a brass ring. The ball is then heated and placed on
the opening of the ring which is held in a horizontal position. It does not slip through
at once but is held in place by the ring. After some time has passed the ball drops
through.

lem, and formulate hypotheses of cause and effect which they test experimentally. No data are given that the children do not obtain through observation or from the teacher's "yes" or "no" answers to their highly structured questions.

To these children and others who are inquiring into the causes of physical phenomena, science is the discovery of new relationships. Children sometimes discover by accident; and sometimes "discovery" is carefully contrived by a skillful teacher. Whichever way it occurs, children are typically thrilled by the sudden new insights, and the learning that results has deep roots. But if we are going to teach the child how to discover meaningful patterns independently and consistently in a highly complex environment, we must teach him how to probe aggressively, systematically, and objectively, and how to reason productively with the obtained data. In other words, we must teach him the skills of inquiry.

OBJECTIVES

Inquiry training is designed to supplement the ordinary science classroom activities. It gives the child a plan of operation that will help him to discover causal factors of physical change through his own initiative and control, and not to depend on the explanations and interpretations of teachers or other knowledgeable adults. He learns to formulate hypotheses, to test them through a verbal form of controlled experimentation, and to interpret the results. In a nutshell, the program is aimed at making pupils more *independent, systematic, empirical,* and *inductive* in their approach to problems of science.

THE STRATEGY OF INQUIRY

The children are given a general three-stage plan to guide them in their investigations and help them develop a logical, systematic approach. Each stage has its own goal and a set of tactics helpful in attaining it.

STAGE I. EPISODE ANALYSIS.

Goal: The identification, verification, and measurement of the parameters of the problem.

In order to perform the operations of this stage, the child must learn to use a set of categories to describe and analyze each episode. Taken together, these categories form a logical system in which each element has an established relationship to the others. The episode-analysis categories are as follows:

1. *Objects:* Objects are the easiest elements for the children to recognize. Familiar objects that are clearly visible pose no problems. The chief difficulty is identifying *all* the objects, whether or not they are visible, familiar, or seemingly unimportant. Included in this category are *systems,* two or more objects combined to form a functional unit. As such they have certain properties that the objects do not possess separately. Water is an object; a beaker is an object. A beaker of water may be regarded as a system.
2. *Properties:* Properties relate to both objects and systems. A property of an object is its predisposition to behave a certain way under a given set of conditions. Properties may be identified through experimentation. By placing an object under varying conditions and observing the resulting changes, a person can determine as many of its properties as he may desire. The identification of objects by their properties is generally more useful than identification by name.
3. *Conditions:* Conditions pertain to the state of objects or systems. While the identity of an object remains constant, its conditions may change. Conditions are identified by observation or measurement.
4. *Events:* Events are defined as changes in the conditions of objects or systems. If an object moves, evaporates, expands, or merely gets hotter, an event has taken place. Events are the consequences of changing the conditions of objects or systems. The type or amount of change that is necessary to produce a given event is a function of the properties of the objects and systems involved.

Using a question-asking strategy to obtain the kinds of information defined by this system of descriptive categories, the child can collect and organize data which provide grist for the mill of inductive investigations.

Episode analysis involves a number of tactical operations. Careful observation must be supplemented by instrumentation and measurement. Many parameters or condition changes are not directly observable, yet may be critical factors in the causation of an event. If the child confines his attention to those variables which are striking or obvious, he is bound to overlook many highly significant dimensions. A thorough and orderly assessment of the objects, conditions, and events of an episode increases the probability of gathering all of the significant data.

One problem is that people tend to perceive new events and situations as total patterns (Gestalts) unless they have a specific set to analyze and a system of categories on which to base an analysis. Total perceptions may be superficial and misleading, causing children to make false analogies to similar total patterns. It is typical, for example, for children to conclude that a bimetallic strip is melting when it is held in a horizontal position over a flame so that it bends downward. The total pattern of this episode is identical to others in which a heated object melts. Yet a careful analysis would reveal the fact that the melting point of the metals is never even approached when the bending occurs.

STAGE II. DETERMINATION OF RELEVANCE.

Goal: The identification of the conditions that are necessary and sufficient to produce the events of the episode.

Not all the parameters identified in Stage I are critical. Often many can be changed without altering the events of the episode. The process of determining criticalness is accomplished through experimentation. Various conditions and objects are changed, one at a time, through a series of controlled verbal experiments. The effects of these changes on the events of the episode are noted. Obviously, only when critical conditions are changed, will events change. Thus, experimentally, the child can determine the relevant variables. This is strictly an empirical solution to the problem of causation. It brings the child halfway to the ultimate goal of understanding the causation of events. More complete comprehension includes the recognition of the events as necessary consequences of universal principles that make a certain set of conditions necessary and sufficient. Stage III is devoted to the search for these principles.

STAGE III. EDUCTION OF RELATIONS.

Goal: The formulation and testing of theoretical constructs or rules that express the relationships among the variables of the observed physical event.

During this phase, experimentation is still the principal tool of inquiry, but each experiment is designed as a critical test of some hypothetical construct. Obviously, the scope of operations must extend well beyond the domain of the original event. This stage demands a higher degree of conceptual sophistication, flexibility, and imagination than the others. The problem of designing an unequivocal test for an hypothesis can be as taxing as formulating the hypothesis itself. The child sees his objective as the discovery of rules that express the relationship between variables. He learns that the value of any rule he constructs is a function of (1) its validity within a specified realm of applicability and (2) the scope of this realm.

THE METHOD OF INQUIRY TRAINING

During the past three years the inquiry-training program has evolved into a somewhat structured pedagogical procedure. At the fifth-grade level, ten seems to be the optimum group size. With classes of thirty or more, the remaining children serve as nonparticipating observers who have an important evaluative role. Rotation permits all children to participate in turn. The training sessions are about one hour long and thus far have been held at weekly intervals, although we now believe that more frequent intervals and shorter sessions would be desirable.

Practice, corrective feedback, and exposition are incorporated into each training session. While they are generally applied in a regular sequence, a degree of flexibility in their use is maintained. A typical training session is organized in the following way.

PRESENTING THE PROBLEM

A silent motion picture of a physics demonstration provides the problem episode. Typical of the demonstrations used is the "Collapsing Varnish Can."[3] As any teacher of science knows, children who do not have well-developed, operative concepts of atmospheric pressure and condensation are exceedingly perplexed by this demonstration. In producing the current series of stimulus films—40 demonstrations in all—we tried to capitalize on this perplexity to provide an intrinsic motivation for inquiry. Our technique is predicated on the belief that the drive to "find out why" can surpass in sustained motivational power almost any other classroom incentive.

In addition to their motivational function, the films pose cause-and-effect problems in very specific terms. They make available some parameters and suggest areas where important additional parameters might be sampled. In short, the films provide a portion of empirical experience which the child must then relate to his conceptual systems. To the extent that these systems are not sufficiently developed to accommodate the experience, he must expand and strengthen them through inquiry until he is capable of explaining the episode.

THE PRACTICE SESSION

Immediately upon seeing the film, the children begin the inquiry process. All probes are verbal, originate from the children, and must be so phrased as to be answerable by "yes" or "no." Keeping the inquiry at the verbal level permits the teacher and the rest of the group to keep track of most of the information the children are obtaining. The questions must originate from the children because the selection and design of questions are as much a part of inquiry as the interpretation one makes of the answers. The questions must be answerable by "yes" or "no" because in this

---

[3] The condensation of water vapor inside a corked varnish can reduces the inside pressure and permits the can to be crushed by the atmospheric pressure.

way only can the child be discouraged from transferring control of the process to the teacher. "Yes" or "no" questions are hypotheses. The teacher in answering merely establishes the tenability of the hypothesis. If the children were permitted to ask, "Why did the can collapse?" the responsibility for selecting the kind of information to be supplied next would be on the shoulders of the teacher. The children would thus be relinquishing their roles as inquirers by returning to the traditional dependent role of obedient listeners and memorizers. This would inhibit the occurrence of inquiry behavior.

The children have two types of questions available to them as information-gathering tools. In identifying parameters in Stage I they may simply ask questions of verification. Since the film provides stimuli that are one step removed from firsthand experience, the children have recourse to verification questions to confirm or test their hunches as to the identity of objects and their conditions at any given time during the episode. They may also need to check the specifics of the observed events, e.g., what happened when. As indicated previously, adequate verification and identification of parameters is an essential first step.

The second type of probe is the experimental question. The child states a set of conditions and postulates a resulting event. The question is answered by the teacher in terms of whether the postulated event will or will not be the result. If the conditions of the experiment are not complete or clear enough to permit the teacher to give an unequivocal answer, he may say, "That all depends" or "Tell me more." Either of these answers tells the child that his experiment has not been sufficiently controlled. Presumably every experimental question is a test or part of a test of an unstated hypothesis. If the child suspects that the cork in the varnish can was a necessary condition for the collapse of the can, he might ask, "If the cork had not been placed in the mouth of the can before the can was cooled, would the same result have occurred?" The teacher's answer of "no" supports the hypothesis that the corking of the can is a necessary condition and tends also to lend support to an hypothesis that the can must be kept airtight while it is being cooled. *But the child must make these inferences himself from the empirical data he obtains.* He cannot test his hypotheses *directly*, even if such questions are phrased as "yes"-"no" questions. If the child had asked, "Does the cork have anything to do with the collapsing of the can?" the teacher does not answer the question. Such a query tends to tap the *teacher's* understanding of the relationships involved. The child is asking the teacher to make certain inferences *for him* and in so doing is relinquishing some of his own responsibility in the inquiry process. Such questions are frequently asked by children, even after they have been trained for several months. The standard response by the teacher is, "What could you do to find that out for yourself?" This retort, without the slightest note of admonition, puts the responsibility right back where it belongs.

THE CRITIQUE

Generally the inquiry session is terminated by either the achievement of the objectives, the inability of the children to proceed without further conceptual development, or the expiration of time. The latter is usually the case. Following the inquiry session is the "critique," a period in which the strategy and tactics of the group are reviewed and evaluated by the teacher, the nonparticipating members of the class, and the members of the participating group itself. It has been our practice to tape record each inquiry session and utilize the tapes as a point of departure. But we now feel that this is not entirely necessary, particularly if the critique immediately follows the inquiry session. Immediate "feedback" has long been recognized by psychologists as an important condition for effective reinforcement. Some comments and suggestions by the teacher are best made during the course of the inquiry session itself. If this practice is followed to excess, however, the children may be distracted too often from the physics problem at hand. This may impair their efficiency in this work.

The principal function of the critique is to correct weaknesses in the inquiry of the children and to build up a repertoire of tactics that will increase their accuracy and productivity. At times, the critique becomes something like a lecture-discussion in which the teacher may be trying to help the group conceptualize the general design of inquiry strategy. Sometimes special recordings of model inquiry sessions are played. These provide clear examples of the strategies and tactics that the teacher wants the children to utilize.

The critique is indispensable; when it is eliminated morale slips and inquiry becomes progressively worse.

CONCLUSIONS

Preliminary analysis of the results of three pilot studies suggests the following conclusions about inquiry training.

The inquiry skills of fifth-grade children can be improved over a fifteen-week period as a result of the methods described herein. Most of the children who receive training become more productive in their design and use of verification and experimentation. They develop a fairly consistent strategy which they can transfer to new problem situations. They make fewer untested assumptions; they formulate and test more hypotheses; and they perform more controlled vs. uncontrolled experiments in the course of their inquiry.

The children have little apparent desire to improve their inquiry skills per se. The chief motivating force is the desire to comprehend the causation of the observed episodes. An explanation by the teacher might satisfy this desire, but in the absence of such explanations the children accept inquiry as a means to their goal. Whenever inquiry is not directly related to the satisfaction of their need to "find out why," they show little interest in the strategies and tactics being discussed. Thus methods for constant improvement are desirable.

Our final conclusion for the present is that inquiry skills cannot be successfully taught to this age group as an isolated content area. The major focus in elementary science education should remain the *content* rather than the *methods* of science. Inquiry training and abundant opportunities to attain new concepts *through* inquiry, however, seem to produce increments in the understanding of content as well as an important new grasp of the scientific method and proficiency in its use.

41.   Teaching Strategies and Thought Processes

Hilda Taba and Freeman F. Elzey

The development of critical thinking has figured as an important objective of education for a long time. Yet, the implementation of this objective in curriculum construction and teaching has been sporadic and ineffective for a variety of reasons.

First, thinking has been treated as a global process. Consequently, the problem of defining thinking is still before us, as is the need to identify its specific elements, especially in terms which are helpful to planning effective teaching strategies. In a jungle of definitions, thinking has meant anything that goes on in the head, from daydreaming to creating a concept of relativity. Neither has knowledge of the development of thinking been too adequate. While Piaget has spent his lifetime in studying the development of thinking and has produced a quantity of reports, until recently, his work received scant attention in the United States.

Reprinted with permission from *Teachers College Record*, 65: 524-534, March, 1964.

Implementation of thinking as an educational objective has also been handicapped by several questionable assumptions. One rather widely accepted assumption is that reflective thinking cannot take place until a sufficient body of factual information is accumulated. Teaching which follows this assumption stresses factual coverage and burdens the memory with unorganized and, therefore, rather perishable information.

An opposite, but equally unproductive, assumption is that thought is an automatic by-product of studying certain subjects and of assimilating the end-products of disciplined thought. Some subjects are assumed to have this power independently of how they are taught or learned. Inherently, memorizing mathematical formulae or the steps in mathematical processes is assumed to be better training than memorizing cake recipes, even though both may be learned in the same manner and call for the same mental process—rote memory.

The combination of these factors has prevented the focusing of attention on the development of teaching strategies designed to stimulate productive and creative thought. The curriculum is seldom organized to focus on active discovery and the use of abstract ideas. Classroom learning experiences are not usually designed to provide a cumulative sequence in the maturation of thought which is at once psychologically sound and logically valid.

All this has contributed to considerable underachievement in the mastery of autonomous and disciplined thought processes. Hence, a rather frequent criticism of current teaching-learning procedures is that they tend to cultivate passive mastery instead of an active discovery of ideas— a tendency to follow "recipes" in solving problems instead of analyzing them and searching for generalizations with which to organize the needed facts and to plan an attack on them (1, 3).

Cognition Revisited

Recently, there has been a renewed interest in the study of cognitive processes in general and thinking in particular. For example, Bartlett (1) and Rokeach (15) have been concerned with open and closed thought. Getzels and Jackson's study (8) of creativity and Gallagher's study (7) of productive thinking employed the classification of divergent and convergent styles of thought. Sigel (16) has been interested in the relationship of the styles of organizing and labelling to personality dynamics.

The difficulty with such studies is that the findings about general cognitive styles fail to shed light on the processes by which these styles are acquired. Consequently, the data cannot be translated into guidelines for more effective teaching.

The study of thinking in elementary school children, on which this paper is based, set out to examine the processes of thought in the classroom in terms which are capable of shedding a light on the learning and teaching of certain cognitive skills in the school setting. The fundamental assumption was that thought consists of specific, describable processes which are subject to training, not in some category of powers which are inherent in the individual. Therefore, the study sought to create categories for analyzing thought which described learnable, and therefore also teachable, processes of thought. Specific processes in three cognitive tasks were identified: (1) concept formation, (2) the making of inferences and the induction of generalizations from interpretations of specific data, and (3) the application of generalizations to explain new phenomena and to predict the consequences of certain events and conditions. Critical thinking *per se* was excluded because the curriculum offered meager opportunities for its development.

The study was also conducted under conditions which presumably offered optimal conditions for the training of thought processes. First, the 20 elementary classrooms involved followed a social studies curriculum which centered on a series of basic ideas and was organized for an inductive discovery and development of these ideas. In addition, the curriculum outline also included a planned sequence of learning experiences designed to enhance the development of generalizations and their application to solving problems (4).

Finally, the design for the study provided for special training of the teachers in the analysis of thought processes and in devising effective teaching strategies for their development. In other words, the study proposed to explore thinking under conditions which included the twin impact of the curriculum and of specified teaching methods.

The Theoretical Framework

The study, as well as the curriculum which provided the context for it, and the training of teachers were based on several concepts regarding the nature of thought and its development. First among these was the idea that the maturation of thought follows an evolutionary sequence in which the simpler mental operations form a basis for the creation of the increasingly more complex and abstract mental structures. For example, the learning experiences in the curriculum outlines were arranged so that each preceding step developed skills and cognitive operations which constituted a prerequisite for the next more complex or more abstract mental operations. The cycle of these operations usually began with the analysis of a concrete instance of the general idea on which the unit was centered and ended with the formulation of the idea and its application to new problems and situations (*4, 18*).

The exploration of the logical structure of the three cognitive tasks with which the study was concerned revealed another, more specific series of hierarchically ordered sequences of thought processes.

1. For example, the sequence in concept formation begins with enumeration of concrete items, such as listing the differences one would expect to encounter when traveling in Latin America. The next step is that of grouping these items on some conscious basis, such as deciding the basis on which to group together "climate," "weather," and "altitude." The process ends with labeling of classifications, such as deciding to subsume a group of items under "standards of living." These steps constitute a necessary sequence in the sense that each preceding step is a prerequisite for mastering the next one. Underlying the steps are still other cognitive processes, such as differentiation of certain properties of phenomena or events with some degree of precision and an ability to abstract common elements and to determine the basis on which to group and label them.

2. In a similar manner, the logic of interpreting information and making inferences involves the assimilation of specific points of information, followed by relating several points to each other and making inferences or generalizations which go beyond that which is explicitly given.

3. The process involved in applying known facts and principles is a bit more complex, involving as it does divergent lines of prediction as well as the hierarchies of leaps in each according to the distance, ranging from the most immediate consequences to the most remote—such as predicting that water will bring grass, in comparison to predicting that the presence of water will cause nomads to cease to be nomads and turn to building cities.

The logic of the sequential steps in this process is not entirely clear. This unclarity is reflected in the rating scheme used. Obviously, the individual must draw upon his memory for the relevant information to form any predictions at all. But he must also relate this information to the requirements of the situation and to construct the parameters of conditions necessary for the predicted consequences to occur. This process entails both the construction of chains of consequences, such as water → growing crops → settling down → building cities, and the perception of the logical relationships between the conditions and consequences.

The chief point about the sequences in the development of thinking is that a deficiency in mastering the first step, such as the analysis of concrete instances, leads to incapacity to function on the level of the final step, such as the formulation of generalizations. The chief task of teaching, then, is to determine the order of learning tasks and to pace each step appropriately. This is a crucial point in the formulation of teaching strategies, and one against which current teaching methods commit the greatest errors.

Cognitive Commerce

The concept that the cognitive operations are an active transaction between the individual and his environment or the material was another idea which influenced the design both of the curriculum and of the study. Children inevitably build mental schemes with which to organize the information they encounter. The quality of the learning experiences determines the degree of productivity of these schemes. All learning experiences teach what Harlow (10) calls "sets to learn." Depending on the teaching strategies employed, children may learn to look for the structure of the problems set by the learning tasks or for arbitrary procedures. They may acquire a disposition to search for relationships and patterns among ideas and facts, or to look for single "right answers."

When the teaching strategies pay little attention to creating models for thinking, children tend to acquire faulty or unproductive conceptual schemes with which to organize information or to solve problems. For example, procedures such as asking students to name the important cities in the Balkans, without revealing the criterion for importance or without developing such a criterion with the class, leave students no alternative but to guess what the teacher wants or to recollect what the book said about the matter. Repeated experiences of this sort cause students to adopt irrational, unproductive, and arbitrary models of thinking and a dependence on memory rather than on judgment or inference.

Burton (2) cites an extreme example of an irrational or mechanical model or schema. He describes an elementary school child who made good grades in arithmetic because she "came up" with the right answers. When asked how she decided when to use which process, she explained her method as follows: "I know what to do by looking at the examples. If there are only two numbers I subtract. If there are lots of numbers, I add. If there are just two numbers and one is smaller than the other, then it is a hard problem. I divide to see if it comes out even, but if it doesn't, I multiply." Evidently this child had built a scheme to fit the manner of presentation of problems in the arithmetic book. By applying the scheme, she was also learning an unproductive model of thinking or a "set" which excluded understanding the structure of the problems.

The idea of thought as an active organization of mental processes underscores the importance of addressing teaching strategies to the development of autonomy and productivity. Effective teaching is seen as consisting primarily of what we get out of the children instead of what we put into them (16). In other words, helping students to develop a basis for and a method by which to judge the importance of cities may be of greater value than their simply knowing which cities are important.

Of special relevance is the idea that thought matures through a progressive and active organization and reorganization of conceptual structures. The individual fits the information he receives at any moment into the conceptual scheme he already possesses. When the requirements of the situation do not fit his current scheme, however, the individual is forced to alter it or to extend it to accommodate new information. Piaget (14) calls this fitting process "assimilation" and the process of alteration "accommodation."

This process suggests a teaching strategy which includes a rotation of learning tasks, calling for the assimilation of new information into the existing conceptual scheme with information that requires an extension and reorganization of the scheme (12). Prolonged assimilation of facts without a corresponding reshaping of the conceptual schemes with which to organize them is bound to retard the maturation of thought. On the other hand, a premature leap into a more complex or a higher level of thought is likely to immobilize mental activity and cause reversion to rote learning or, at any rate, to a lower level of thought. Students need a sufficient amount of assimilation to have the "stuff" to think with. But they need equally a challenge to stretch their modes of thinking and their conceptual schemes. An appropriate transition from one to the other demands a proper match between the current level and that which is required. Determining the proper match is perhaps one of the most difficult tasks in teaching and constitutes, in effect, a new concept of readiness and pacing. This task is complicated by the fact that the mastery of abstract communications, such as language and number, often masks the actual level of thinking. Verbalization may deceive the teacher and lead him to assume that thinking is more advanced than it is and, hence, to pushing the child's verbal habits of learning beyond his level of thinking (13).

REASONABLE HOPES

It seems reasonable to assume that, given an adequate analysis of the learning processes involved in certain important cognitive tasks, and teaching strategies which effectively implemented the principles of sequence, of active mental organization, and of adequate rotation of assimilation and accommodation, it should be possible for all students to achieve higher levels of cognitive operation than seems possible under current teaching. Furthermore, it is not beyond possibility that by far the most important individual differences may be found in the amount of concrete thinking an individual needs before formal thought can emerge. This difference may distinguish the slow but capable learner from one who is incapable of abstract thought. It is not beyond possibility, therefore, that many slow learners can achieve a high level of abstract thought, provided that they have the opportunity to examine a greater number of concrete instances than the teaching process typically allows. The employment of teaching strategies which are scientifically designed for the development of cognitive skills may make it possible to develop cognitive processes at a much higher level and in a greater number of students.

This rationale set certain requirements for the methodology of studying the development of thought processes in the classroom. It required, first, securing records of classroom transactions. Second, it required a multi-dimensional analysis of these transactions in terms of what the teacher does, of what the responses of the students are, and of the product of the interaction.

Four discussions were taped in each of the 20 classrooms. Because the curriculum outline projected learning activities, it was possible to place each taping at a point in a sequence at which a specified cognitive task of concern to the study occurred. The first taping was made during the very first class session in which enumeration, grouping, and classification was the chief task. The next two tapings recorded discussions involving interpreting data and formulating inferences from them: one an interpretation of a film, and another at a point at which students reported information from preceding research, compared and contrasted their data, and attempted to express their findings in generalizations. These tapings were taken at the midyear. The final taping, at the end of the year, was of discussions involving application of previously learned knowledge to predicting consequences from described hypothetical conditions.

UNITS AND SCORES

One problem in analyzing classroom transactions for the purpose of describing thought processes is to decide on units of analysis which are at once capable of being scored accurately and which express sensible units of thought. In this study, the time sampling was discarded in favor of a "thought unit." "Thought unit" was defined as a remark or series of remarks expressing a more or less complete idea, serving a specified function, and classifiable according to a level of thought. It is, therefore, possible for one word or an entire paragraph to be designated as a "thought unit." For example, the word "cement," when it occurs in the process of enumerating materials for building houses, is considered a thought unit. So is a paragraph, such as "The people in the other country do not have electric saws and things that the men in this country use to build houses. The children help chop the wood and can do a lot of things to help build the houses. But the children over here cannot do very many things because of the danger."

In order to describe simultaneously the teaching acts and the levels of thinking of students, the verbal transactions were "scored" by three different "ratings." The first is that of *designation*. It describes the source of the thought unit—whether it emanated from the teacher or from the student and whether the person is giving or seeking information. The code symbols for designation are *child gives* (CG), *child seeks* (CS), *teacher gives* (TG), and *teacher seeks* (TS).

The rating of *function* describes how a thought unit functions in the context of discussion. When applied to remarks or questions by teachers, these ratings may be used to describe teaching strategies which affect the subsequent thought of children.

Two large groups of function ratings may be distinguished: (1) questions or statements made by the teacher or the students which are psychological or managerial in their function and unrelated to the logic of the content. Statements of this type include those that express agreement (A), approval (AP), disagreement (D), disapproval (Dp), management (M), and reiteration (R). (2) The second group includes teacher or student statements which function to give direction to discussions, but which at the same time can be rated according to the logic of content. Such ratings include focusing (F), refocusing (F2), change of focus (FC), deviating from focus (Fd), controlling thought (C), extending thought on the same level (X), and lifting called to a higher level (L).

The third rating, called *levels of thought,* describes both the student's and the teacher's verbal behavior by specifying the logical quality and the level of thought expressed. A separate rating scheme was developed for each of the three cognitive tasks. For each of these tasks, categories were established which represent the hierarchical levels of thought, according to their level of abstraction and complexity. These categories refer to the specific thought processes which need to be mastered in a sequential order, because performing on the preceding level is a prerequisite to being able to perform on the next. Thus, the rating scheme represents the developmental sequence for each cognitive task. In addition, within each category, distinctions were made between the irrelevant, the disconnected, and the related information or content.

The rating scheme used for designating the levels of thought for each of the cognitive tasks is as follows:

Cognitive task: Grouping and labeling [1] (giving or seeking)

10 specific or general information outside of focus
11 specific or general information within focus
12 specific or general information with qualifications
30 grouping information without basis
31 grouping information with implicit basis
32 grouping information with explicit basis
40 categorizing information without basis
41 categorizing information with implicit relationships between items
42 categorizing information with explicit relatonships between items

Cognitive task: interpreting information and making inferences:
                              (giving or seeking)

10 specific or general information outside of focus
11 specific or general information within focus
12 specific or general information with qualifications and relationships
50 specific reason or explanation that does not relate to the information
51 specific reason or explanation that relates or organizes the information
52 specific reason or explanation that states how it relates or organizes the information
60 irrelevant or incorrect inference which is derived from information
61 relevant inference which is derived from information
62 relevant inference which is derived from information and expresses a cause and effect relationship, explanation, consequence, or contrast
70 relationship between information which implies an irrelevant or incorrect principle or generalization
71 relationship between information which implies a principle or generalization
72 principle or generalization which is derived from information

Cognitive task: predicting consequences (giving or seeking)

90 correcting the cause or condition
Establishing parameter information
100 relevant information
101 relevant information for establishing the total parameter (if-then) or for a particular hypothesis or prediction
102 relevant information for the total parameter or any particular prediction with appropriate explanation
Establishing parameters of conditions
110 irrelevant or untenable condition for the total parameter or for the particular prediction or hypothesis
111 relevant condition without connecting it with relevant information
112 relevant condition and information and establishing logical connection between them
Prediction: Level one, immediate consequences
               Level two, remote consequences
120-220 incorrect or out of focus prediction
121- 221 prediction with no elaboration

---

[1] Categories in the 20 series were originally reserved for "general information" but were later combined with the 10 series.

122-222 prediction accompanied by explanation, qualification, differentiation, comparison, or contrast
123-223 prediction accompanied by a stated or implied principle

In determining the level at which to rate a particular thought unit, it was necessary to consider the context in which the thought unit occurs. For example, the statement, "a hammer, because you can drive large nails with it," may be rated as "specific information with qualifying statement" if it is offered in response to the task of naming tools used in building a house; it merely gives additional information about the hammer and does not constitute a reason for naming "hammer." If the focus is on identification of tools most useful to primitive people, however, the same response would be rated as "relevant inference derived from information," because the phrase is an explicit reason for naming "hammer."

FUNCTION AND LEVEL

In describing the effect of teaching strategy on thought levels, four groups of function rating are especially important: focusing (F), extending the thought on the same level (X), lifting thought to a higher level (L), and controlling thought (C). Focusing establishes both the topic and the particular angle for its treatment. It sets the cognitive task. For example, the statement by the teacher, "If the desert had all the water it needed, what would happen?" establishes the central focus for discussion and calls for prediction of consequences.

The coding system also specifies the shifts in subject matter (change of focus), the degree to which the teacher finds it necessary to bring the discussion back to the original topic (refocus), and the number of times that the discussion wanders from the subject (deviation from focus).

A statement of the teacher or a child is coded as extension of thought (X) when it gives or seeks additional information or provides elaboration and clarification on an already established level. The following example illustrates a series of extensions on the level of providing specific information:

(1) C Malobi took the money home with her	CG 11
(2) T What did Malobi do with the money?	TS 11
(3) C She saved it.	CG 11X
(4) C She put it underground.	CG 11X
(5) C She put sticks and tin over it.	CG 11X
(6) C Before she did that, she put it in a little pot.	CG 11X

A thought unit is functioning to lift the level of thought whenever the teacher or child seeks or gives information that shifts thought to a higher level than had previously been established. In the following example, the teacher attempts to lift the level of thought from giving information to explanation:

(1) C They carried things in baskets on their heads.	CG 11
(2) T Explain why.	TS 61L
(3) C I suppose they can carry more things that way.	CG 61L

A question may function to extend the thought in one context and to lift it in another, as illustrated in the following example:

(1) C They were working fast on the house.	CG 11
(2) T Why?	TS 51L
(3) C They wanted to get the house done before the rain came.	CG 51L
(4) T Why?	TS 51X
(5) C Because unless it is finished, the rain will destroy it.	CG 52X

The inquiry on line two is rated as teacher seeking to lift the level of thought from the established level of giving specific information to the level of inference. The child's response provides the reason on the level sought by the teacher. The same inquiry on line four and the child's response on line five function to extend the thought because the level at which the question is asked has already been established.

Controlling of thought occurs when the teacher performs a cognitive task that students should be induced to do. This is the case when the teacher gives a category for classification, an inference in interpretation, or a prediction in the task of applying principles.

Strategic Patterns

As elements of teaching strategy, the frequencies of these functions may represent either effective or ineffective teaching strategies. For example, frequent shifts in focus may be needed at some points in the discussion to introduce sufficient information to form a basis for comparison and generalization. Other tasks may require that the discussion remain on one focus long enough to provide full treatment of the subject before proceeding to another, higher level of thought process. Frequent refocusing may indicate a faulty handling of the sequence in thought processes, which results in the necessity for constantly having to bring the children back to the focus. This multiple coding scheme makes it possible to depict the flow of the classroom discussion by charting the sequences of transactions between the teacher and the children, the changes in the level of thought during the discussion, and the effect of these strategies upon the level and the direction of thought. The flow of thought can be reconstructed even though the specific content of the discussion is not given.[2] For example, an empirical sequence of thought may, when trans-

---

[2] Charts based on empirical observation will be published later as a part of the report to the US Office of Education of a study of "Thinking in Elementary School Children" (Project No. 1574).

lated from the code, be read as *child gives specific information, teacher seeks an extension of that information, child provides the requested extension, teacher seeks to lift the level of thought from the "information" level to the "reason" level, child provides a reason as requested by the teacher,* and *teacher gives approval to the child.* In a similar manner, any sequence of ratings can be reconstructed from the observationally developed flow charts.*

When the flow charts identify individual children, then one can describe the characteristic modes and levels of thought of particular pupils, such as a tendency to operate only on the level of concrete information or on the level of inference and generalization, the tendency to remain focused or to stray from the focus, to give relevant or irrelevant information, etc. It also permits the accounting of the frequencies of the various thought patterns which prevail in the classroom group and the discrepancies between what the teacher seeks and how the children respond.

Data of this sort depict the various strategies which teachers may employ and their consequences. For example, when the teacher attempts to raise the level of thought very early in the discussion, this typically results in the children's returning to a lower level and in their inability to sustain discussion at the higher levels of thought. On the other hand, a strategy representing an effective pacing of shifting the thought onto higher levels seems to follow a characteristic course. The level of seeking information is sustained for a considerable time during the first portion of the discussion. Grouping is requested only after a large amount of information has been accumulated. The result is that in a fairly brief period, children transcend from grouping to labeling and then to providing reasons for labeling and to inferences.

Other strategic patterns that have been empirically identified include the teacher's repeated attempts to steer discussion to the inferential level without permitting the development of a body of needed information; in such a case, the children repeatedly return to the information level. Or when there is a constant change of focus, the children's thought alternates between several levels, is not sustained at the higher level, and gradually stabilizes on the most primitive one.

Some Implications

This multidimensional analysis of classroom transactions has several advantages. First, by combining the description of the teacher's acts in terms of their explicit functions with the assessment of the logical quality

[* See the addendum to this article for two such charts selected from the full report. RTH, editor]

of student responses, it is possible to evaluate the impact of the teacher's behavior in terms of its productivity. This addition of the dimension of the logical quality of the content of thought carries the analysis of classroom transactions a step beyond what has been available to date. Most current studies of classroom transactions concentrate more or less exclusively on the analysis of the psychological functions of teaching acts (5, 11). This emphasis has evoked the criticism that teaching is explained and controlled exclusively in terms of psychological principles and that the logic of teaching and of its product in learning is overlooked (17).

A further advantage lies in the fact that, in addition to describing the impact of teaching exclusively in terms of the frequencies of specific acts, this scheme permits studying the cumulative impact of certain patterns or combinations of acts, including their pacing. It is at this point that a transfer is made from the study of teaching acts to the study of teaching strategies. Flanders (6) has taken a step in this direction by describing the points of shift in the nature of teaching acts.

Finally, the scheme permits the examination of the effect of teaching strategies in terms of a measurable change in a specified outcome—levels of thinking in this case—and thus frees the study of teaching from the necessity of inferring the effect from the assumed consequences of the frequencies of certain types of teacher behavior.

A preliminary analysis of the typescripts of classroom discussion reveals an enormous influence of teacher behavior on the thinking of students. This impact is exercised in a variety of ways: by the nature of the questions asked, what the teacher gives to the students or seeks from them, the timing of these acts in the total sequence, which ideas are picked up for elaboration and which are passed over, points at which approval and disapproval are given, etc. For example, the focus which the teacher sets determines which points students can explore and establishes the models for thought they can practice. Of great importance is the sequence of mental operations called for and the appropriateness of this sequence to developing productive thought models.

It seems clear, further, that the level of thinking attained is influenced not only by the nature of the single act by a teacher just preceding a given response. The level of thought attained seems to be determined by the whole pattern of transactions: the particular combination of focusing, extending, and lifting; the timing of these acts; the length of time spent on a particular focus, such as exploring specific descriptive information before examining causes or attempting explanation; the distance between the mental operations of the students at the moment from the level required by the teacher, and the points at which the teacher seeks information from students and gives it. These combinations, not merely the frequencies alone, constitute a teaching strategy.

Only a casual identification of these strategies is available at the moment of writing this article. The variations in the patterns are too numerous to permit analysis by ordinary means. The staff, in cooperation with experts in computer programing, has developed a high-speed computer program designed to aid in accounting for these patterns. Such a computer program should permit the identification of the elements and the cumulative patterns of strategies associated with high and low performance.[3]

The findings so far suggest that if the acquisition of skills in autonomous thinking is to be a realistic objective, a much more thorough study of and experimentation with the appropriate teaching strategies and their impact on the development of thinking is called for. As Flanders (6) suggests, any step in the direction of specifying productive teaching strategies should lead to a more adequate understanding of the connection between teachers' behavior and student response. A scientific mapping of such strategies should also add considerably to the developing theory of instruction, and especially to our understanding of the conditions which maximize the development of higher mental processes on the part of all students, not only the intellectual elite.

References

1. BARTLETT, F. E. *Thinking: an experimental and social study.* New York: Basic Books, 1958.
2. BURTON, W. N. *The guidance of learning activities.* New York: Appleton-Century, 1952.
3. BUSWELL, G. T., & HERSCH, B. Y. *Patterns of solving problems.* Berkeley, California: Univer. California Press, 1956.
4. *Contra Costa County Social Studies Units, Grades 1-6.* Pleasant Hill, California: Contra Costa County Schools, 1959.
5. FLANDERS, N. A. *Teacher influence, pupil attitudes, and achievement.* Prepublication manuscript of a proposed research monograph for the U. S. Office of Education, Cooperative Research Branch, Washington, DC, 1960.
6. FLANDERS, N. A. Some relationships between teacher influence, pupil attitudes, and achievement. Ditto *MS* of a chapter submitted to the AASA, the NTBA, and the NEA Classroom Teachers Division. No date.
7. GALLAGHER, J. J., ASCHNER, MARY JANE, PERRY, JOYCE M., & AFAAR, S. S. A system for classifying thought processes in the content of classroom verbal interaction. Ditto MS. Urbana, Ill.: Institute for Research on Exceptional Children, Univer. Illinois, 1961.
8. GETZELS, J. W., & JACKSON, P. *Creativity and intelligence.* New York: Wiley, 1962.
9. GUILFORD, J. P. Basic conceptual problems in the psychology of thinking. *Annals NY Acad. Sci.,* 1961, *91,* 9-19.

[3] Such a computer program has been devised by P. J. Stone and M. S. Smith as a general sequence analyzer, planned to identify recurrent patterns in a list of events.

10. Harlow, H. F. The formation of learning sets. *Psychol. Rev.*, 1949, *56*, 51-60.
11. Hughes, Marie, *et al. Development of the means for the assessment of the quality of teaching in elementary school.* (Mimeo.) Salt Lake City: Univer. Utah, 1959.
12. Hunt, J. McV. *Experience and Intelligence.* New York: Ronald Press, 1961.
13. Peel, E. A. *The pupil's thinking.* London: Oldbourne, 1960.
14. Piaget, J. *The psychology of intelligence.* London: Routledge, Kegan Paul, 1947.
15. Rokeach, M. *The open and closed mind.* New York: Basic Books, 1960.
16. Sigel, I. Cognitive style and personality dynamics. Interim report, Merrill-Palmer Institute, 1961.
17. Smith, B. O. Concept of teaching. *Teach. Coll. Rec.*, 1950, *61*, 229-241.
18. Taba, Hilda. *Curriculum development: theory and practice.* New York: Harcourt, Brace & World, 1962.

Addendum: The Patterns of Classroom Interaction

Figure 1 presents the first 40 thought units in a third grade tapescript. In this flow chart, the thought units are represented by equal intervals on the horizontal axis and their level on the vertical axis. Thus, the systematic progression of the thought units and the relative levels of thought can be presented diagrammatically. The thought units of the teacher are indicated by "T" along the horizontal axis. The horizontal arrows, such as appear for thought units 7 and 13, represent the teacher's request for an extension of the thought expressed just prior to these units. The vertical arrows shown for thought units 9, 15, 28, and 36 depict the teacher's attempts to lift the thought to a higher level. Thought unit 10 (L), indicates that the child complied with the teacher's request for a lift in level and produced a thought unit at the 41 level. The other letters represent other function codings such as reiteration, approval, agreement, etc.

By examining the chart, the flow of thought can be reconstructed even though the specific content of the discussion is not given. For example, the sequence of thought presented in thought units 12 through 17 may be read as: child gives specific information (unit 12); teacher seeks an extension of that information (unit 13); child provides the requested extension (unit 14); teacher seeks to lift the level of thought from the "information" level to the "reason" level (unit 15); child provides a reason as requested by the teacher (unit 16); teacher gives approval to the child (unit 17).

Reprinted with permission from *Thinking in Elementary School Children* by Hilda Taba, Samuel Levine, and Freeman F. Elzey. U.S. Department of Health, Education, and Welfare, Office of Education, Cooperative Research Project No. 1574. San Francisco, San Francisco State College, 1964.

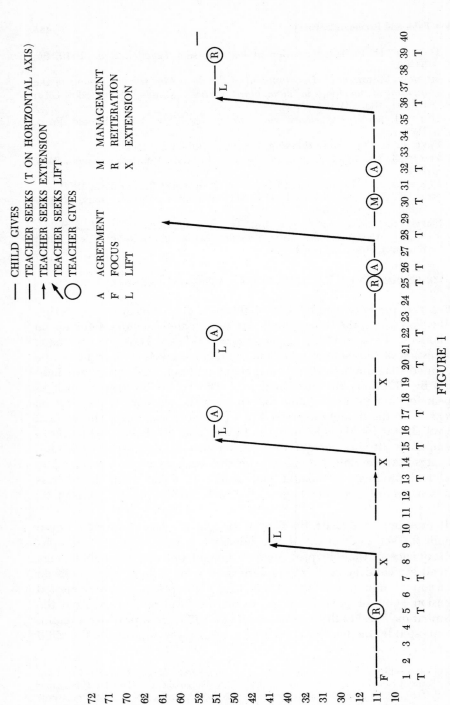

FIGURE 1

Flowchart of Classroom Interaction

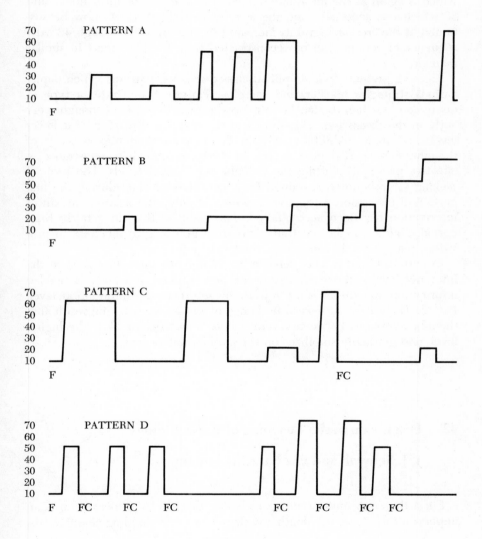

FIGURE 2

Class Discussion Patterns

Other patterns can be depicted by this method. For instance, the child gave an unsolicited lift at unit 21 which was approved by the teacher at unit 22. The discussion then dropped back to the information level at unit 23 where it stayed until the teacher attempted to lift the thought at unit 28. This was unsuccessful as indicated by the child's response at unit 29 which is again at the information level. The teacher sought a lift at unit 36 which was successful and the level of thought seems to now be sustained at the "reason" level as indicated by the units 37 through 42. Any sequence of codings can be reconstructed from the flow chart in similar manner.

Figure 2 presents four simplified class discussion patterns which depict various strategies teachers may employ. Pattern A illustrates a type of discussion in which the teacher attempts to raise the level of thought very early in the discussion. This results in the children returning to a lower level, and their inability to sustain discussion at the higher levels of thought. Pattern B depicts a type of discussion which demonstrates an effective pacing of shifting the thought onto higher levels. The level of seeking information is sustained for a considerable time during the first portion of discussion. Grouping is requested only after a large amount of information has been accumulated. The result is that, in a fairly brief period, children make the transitions from grouping to labeling, to providing reasons for labeling, and, finally, to inferences.

In pattern C the teacher repeatedly attempts to steer discussion to the inference level without permitting the development of a body of needed information and the children repeatedly return to the information level. Pattern D illustrates a constant change of the focus, with the result that thought alternates between several levels, is not sustained at the higher level, and gradually stabilizes on the most primitive one.

42.   Discussion in the Teaching of BSCS Biology

J. J. Schwab and Evelyn Klinckmann

For a thorough understanding of bodies of knowledge discussion is an important tool. A greater depth and degree of understanding characterizes

Reprinted with permission from *Biology Teachers' Handbook*, Joseph J. Schwab, Supervisor. Biological Science Curriculum Study of the American Institute of Biological Sciences. New York, John Wiley and Sons, 1963. Adapted from *Eros and education*, by J. J. Schwab and Evelyn Klinckmann. Copyright 1958 by the authors. Permission granted to the BSCS for publication.

knowledge gained in this way. Further, discussion of a certain sort is indispensable for the development of the intellectual arts and skills required to traverse a pathway of understanding. This is true because discussion itself can be an engagement in and practice of the activities of thought and communication involved in those intellectual arts and skills.

There is another reason why discussion of a certain kind can be a valuable means to developing an understanding of the processes of biological science. It is that discussion can utilize the "energy of wanting" in the pursuit of educational goals.

Appetite, or wanting, leads us to action. This energy of wanting is as much the energy source in the pursuit of truth as in the pursuit of other contemporary values—pleasure, power, fame, friendship, or security. Therefore, a means of education that utilizes this energy source is an effective means—although, of course, other criteria also must be used in selecting the best educational means.

Discussion is especially appropriate as a means of utilizing the energy of wanting because it can tap motivating forces. It provides something in its initial phases to which the energy of the student can attach. This is true because the students' desire to like and be liked can be directed toward the teacher if the initial phase of discussion is conducted properly. In later phases of discussion this energy, originally attached to the teacher as a person, can be transferred, by appropriate discussion techniques, to the desire to want and to practice the qualities which the teacher as an educated person exemplifies.

Discussion of the type that is a means of understanding processes of biological science and can tap motivating forces in the student is a situation composed of four factors. The central factor in this situation is a certain kind of face-to-face relation between teacher and student. The other three factors are enabling or supporting factors. These are the administrative organization of the school, the physical conditions of the classroom, and the curriculum materials. These supporting factors are important as they aid in establishing the kind of face-to-face relation which is central as a beginning to constructive discussion; they also are important because they can facilitate the channeling of the effects of this relation toward desired outcomes of the curriculum.

The first and central factor in discussion is a certain kind of face-to-face relation between teacher and student. This must be established from the first day, but its characteristics should continue to be apparent throughout the school year. The desired relation is based on a direct interpersonal relation between teacher and student. By this is meant that teacher and student meet as individual person to individual person. The key to this kind of interpersonal relation can be called "reciprocity of evocation and response." Let us try to illustrate this by describing what might occur on the first day of a class—what, in fact, should occur on the first day.

Some students will be curious about, have an interest in, the teacher as a person; that is, the teacher "evokes" interest in some students. As the teacher presents his introduction to the course work, he will glance from student and note responses in certain students which indicate this interest. As he notices it, the teacher can, in turn, respond by momentarily halting the movement of his eyes and for a brief period directing his remarks to each student who shows an interested response. By doing this the teacher shows that the student has evoked his interest and he is responding by recognition of this student as an individual person. We should notice that reciprocity of evocation and response requires recognition of and liking for students as *individuals;* it also requires recognition of and liking for individual *qualities* of persons.

This kind of interpersonal relation cannot be established the first day with all the students. In fact it is not desirable to do so, since it is only over a period of time that different students will show an interested response. In addition, over a period of time different qualities of students will become apparent to the teacher, and he can respond to them in different ways. Students are quite aware of their differences; if a teacher treats all alike, a lack of respect for the teacher can ensue. Thus by recognition of only a few students the first day, and by recognizing others because of different qualities on subsequent days, respect as well as liking for the teacher can begin to be established.

Let us describe one concrete example of recognition of different qualities of students. A student has shown little interest in either the teacher or what has been going on in class. The topics of classwork have been primarily related to biochemistry. The teacher suspects that the disinterested student is mainly interested in outdoor activities—in camping, hunting, and fishing. One day the classwork deals with the problems of field research in ecology. The teacher directs more questions than in previous class periods to the disinterested student and finds by his response that the hunch about the student's interest is correct: He shows an interest in this topic he had never shown in biochemistry. One of the culminating points of the classwork on the problems of field research is the fact that certain biological problems cannot be dealt with in the laboratory because this changes factors which are key variables in the field situation. The student shows even greater interest in this because it is the first time he has realized that science is not always conducted by white-coated men in laboratories. A whole new aspect of biology has been opened for him, and from then on he shows greater interest in all the classwork.[1]

Let us return to the question of the teacher showing a liking for stu-

[1] This, like the other illustrations presented, has been slightly fictionalized, but it is based on the actual experience of a teacher and student.

dents and responding to being liked by students. This has sometimes been criticized as indicative of a weakness on the part of the teacher. It may be—if the teacher *needs* these indications of liking for his self-assurance. But the mature teacher who does not need them can still welcome them. Moreover, the teacher is not manifesting indiscriminate liking, which would include what is infantile in the student. He manifests a liking for what is a central characteristic of growing up—the students' potential maturity of intelligence and of *wanting to know*. This is a prime and eternal characteristic of the young which teachers *should* like—but which we too often ignore or even destroy, so that often the youth of high school age has the last remnant with which teachers can work.

It is difficult to describe accurately the quality of the initial establishment of a genuine interpersonal relation involving reciprocal evocation and response, but to describe the extremes which are the two pitfalls of such an attempt will help to define the limits of the desirable relation. One pitfall is an over-anxiety on the part of the teacher to be liked. This is perhaps most often a fault of the beginning teacher. An over-anxious teacher will overstate his wish to respond to or to like the student. Then respect is lost. The other pitfall is coldness on the part of the teacher. This may be a simple coldness or may take the form of impatience or of being preoccupied with other matters. In each case, the teacher is likely to reject the curiosity and interest of the student, which may lead to the loss of some liking, since the student once rejected is less likely to try again.

We can review the characteristics of this first phase of discussion by making a check list of these characteristics clarified by examples of behavior typical of them. Notice that some of the items listed are positive descriptions of our discussion characteristics, some are negative.

TEACHER-STUDENT INTERACTION IN EARLY PHASES OF DISCUSSION

A. Recriprocity of evocation and response

1.(+) Teacher shows signs of recognizing students as individual persons. (Looks directly at individuals to whom speaking; lets gaze move to one student after another while speaking, momentarily stopping gaze at each one. This indication of genuine awareness should not be confused with the "gimmicky" version typical of some television masters of ceremony.)

2.(−) Teacher shows signs of relating to class as an amorphous mass. (Few or no direct glances at individuals; eyes do not move from one student to another; looks at back of room, out of window, or apparently at students but with glassy stare indicating no real recognition.)

3.(+) Teacher shows signs of recognizing individual qualities of students. (Speaks and relates to different individuals in different ways. On subsequent days, this might be shown by the teacher's remembering comments of individual students from one day to the next and referring to them where pertinent. This might also be shown by directing questions to students with certain interests when they relate to the topic and when these students have not previously participated actively.)

4.(—) Teacher shows coldness toward students. (Lack of spontaneity, of naturalness as a person; impatience; preoccupation.)

5.(—) Teacher shows over-anxiety to be liked. (Is gratified by obvious and insincere flattery; lets students "walk all over him"; does not invoke his authority when necessary for fear of being disliked.)

As described, the establishment of a genuine interpersonal relation leads to a mutual liking between teacher and students. But a second stage in teacher-student interaction usually occurs and is essential if the necessary respect for the teacher is to be established. This is the stage of provocative testing of the teacher's judgment. This phase is essential since the adult-youth difference is not a sufficient basis for respect as it may be in the parent-child relation. In the teacher-student relation, the student justly demands the right to admit the adult to the role of teacher. [This is a just demand because the adolescent student does not admit to an inevitable and necessary childishness. Since a child (as against an adolescent) does admit this, the adult-youth difference is sufficient in a parent-child relation: with this admission, the adult status is a solace to the child.]

The provocative testing of the teacher's judgment can occur in a multitude of ways, but all have essentially the same characteristic of being an inappropriate contribution to the business at hand. This may take the form of pretended eagerness; contributing an esoteric application or source; presenting irrelevant opinions or facts, manufactured questions, irrelevant skills, or irrelevant bits of knowledge. An example of presentation of an esoteric application or source is the exceptionally brilliant student who brings up for discussion a matter which may be related to the topic in hand but which is far beyond the current understanding of the other members of the class. If the teacher succumbs to the temptation to discuss what to him may be more challenging and interesting, even though the class as a whole will not benefit from it, he has failed in his judgment. Very occasionally such a discussion, if brief, may be beneficial to the class as a whole in that it may provide glimmerings of possibilities which the average students have not yet suspected. Such a discussion extended or indulged in too often is, however, a failure on the part of the teacher.

An example of presenting irrelevant skills is the student with unusual ability in painting who discovers his biology teacher is interested in this form of art. The student then uses every opportunity to interject his special skill into the discussion to attract the attention of the teacher. If the teacher responds by providing the attention, without appropriate indication to the student that his contribution is irrelevant, the teacher has failed in his judgment.

The purpose of these various offerings is to test the teacher's judgment —even though the students, as a rule, are not consciously aware of this. Thus the proper response to these provocations is an immediate, clear communication to the student of the teacher's awareness of the questionable nature of the proffered contribution. Along with this, however, the teacher must be careful not to reject the student along with the offer. For example, if the contribution is esoteric, the teacher may suggest that the student ask after class; he may wait patiently while a contribution is presented, then merely continue with the business at hand, but without revealing by facial expression, posture, or gesture either contempt, impatience, or a patronizing patience. Another possible response is to indicate the connection of the contribution with another aspect of the material without blaming the student for not seeing this connection. Or the teacher may even postpone consideration of the contribution, with the permission of the student, on the grounds of the prevailing interest of the group or of personal privilege.

A somewhat different way of handling provocative testing is to compliment a student occasionally when he makes a particularly relevant contribution or expresses himself especially well. In this way students become aware of good examples of relevance and use of language and may be encouraged to improve their own contributions accordingly. Such occasional compliments also indicate that the teacher can distinguish between the relevant and the irrelevant, the poorly expressed and the well expressed, and thus may eliminate to some degree the students' need to test the teacher's judgment.

If such provocative testing is successfully handled by the teacher, such success will be evident by the subsequent behavior of the students. This behavior will entail a continued participation, but with fitting contributions; it will also entail the students' ignoring opportunities of reopening tangential points or questions. With partial success, the students will continue to participate with fitting contributions but will immediately remind the teacher of his promise to deal with the earlier, inappropriate contribution. ("Last week you said we could talk about . . .") Lack of success will be indicated by the continuing provocative behavior of the students. Occasionally the latter may continue to occur with particular students. This may not be as much a failure on the part of the teacher as an inability on the part of the student to establish a working relation with any person who to him is an authority-figure. Continued patient handling, as suggested, may lead the student to discover the profit and pleasure in a relation with an adult. In other cases, only professional aid which is outside the teacher's task and for which, as a teacher, he is not responsible, may be the answer.

A third phase in teacher-student interaction involves another kind of testing on the part of students. This is the testing of the psychological space—the degree and kind of tolerance the student may expect from the teacher—of the class. This very often takes the form of students' showing eagerness to talk and attract attention, to contribute to the early class discussions by offering at least superficially appropriate contributions. These contributions may reveal awkwardness or error or may be a misapplication of intelligence or judgment. In this case the student needs to be reassured that his attempts will be accepted as attempts, not as definitive measures of his powers or limitations. Such acceptance makes possible future growth.

The appropriate response of the teacher to this form of testing is to be measuredly and discriminatingly kind while providing correction and assistance. To withhold correction and assistance is to reveal an indiscriminate permissiveness inconsistent with the role of teacher; the student wants to be taught, he wants to be accepted as a *learner*—not just accepted. A lack of kindness or actual destructiveness is revealed by demanding inappropriately adult standards, by expecting the student to show adult responsibility toward words, choices, and decisions. The students are not adult; one of the things they must be helped to learn is adult standards.

Let us present an example. The students are asked for a common language word that can be used for the statements technically known as *hypotheses*. One student says *idea* and is rejected out of hand by the teacher. This is demanding inappropriately adult standards pertaining to meanings of words. The way the teacher should work with the proffered contribution is to assist the student to see that "idea" is too broad in its meaning, but that by properly qualifying "idea" he would have a term that meets the requirements of the original question—for example, "a *possible* idea."

These two ways of handling contributions—demand of inappropriately adult standards and indiscriminate permissiveness—are the two pitfalls that set the bounds of appropriate response by the teacher to the contributions which test the psychological space of the class.

We can review the characteristics of teacher-student interaction in the later phases of discussion, in which the two types of "testing" behavior occur, by making a check list of these characteristics.

Teacher-Student Interaction in Later Phases of Discussion

B. *Provocative testing of teacher's judgment*

1. Students test judgment by inappropriate contributions. (Pretended eagerness, esoteric application or source, irrelevant opinion or fact, fake interest, manufactured questions, display of irrelevant skills, irrelevant bits of knowledge.)

2. (+) Teacher responds to such tests by indicating awareness of questionable usefulness of proffered contribution. (Suggests student ask after class if contribution is esoteric; waits patiently, then continues; indicates connection of contribution with other aspect of problem; postpones contribution on ground of prevailing interests of group or of personal privilege.)

3. (+) Teacher does not reject student with offer. (When responding as illustrated under 2, the teacher does not reveal contempt, impatience, or patronizing patience by expression or posture; does not blame student for not seeing lack of relevance to matter under discussion; does not peremptorily postpone consideration without permission of student.)

4. (+) Students participate with fitting (appropriate) contributions.

C. *Testing of psychological space of class* (*psychological space: degree and kind of tolerance student may expect from teacher*)

1. (+) Students show eagerness to talk and attract attention by at least superficially appropriate contributions.

2. (+) Teacher responds by being measuredly and discriminatingly kind. (Does not reject student; does not "make fun of him" or "ride" him because contribution is not precisely appropriate.)

3. (+) Teacher responds by correction and assistance. (Continues to work with the student who has made the contribution until the student has moved at least slightly toward a better understanding that he had; does not shift question immediately to another student if contribution is not exactly what teacher had in mind.)

4. (−) Teacher shows inappropriately adult standards. (Expects students to show adult responsibility toward meanings of words, choices, decisions.)

5. (−) Teacher shows indiscriminate permissiveness. (Does not correct and assist students.)

6. (+) Students show responsibility toward words, choices, decisions.

If the three preceding stages—the establishment of a genuine interpersonal relation, the successful handling of provocative behavior and of behavior testing tolerance and acceptance—have been successfully traversed with a class, the teacher has in his hands a potent instrument. . . .